BOB BROEG

Memories
of a
Hall of Fame Sportswriter

ﻬ

SAGAMORE PUBLISHING
Champaign, Illinois

Editor: Lawrence Hamilton Miller
Production Manager: Susan M. McKinney
Dustjacket design: Michelle R. Dressen
Proofreader: Phyllis L. Bannon

Cover photo by: David Stradal
Interior photos courtesy of the *St. Louis Post-Dispatch,*
Alfred Fleishman, and author's collection.

ISBN: 1-57167-010-6
Library of Congress Catalog Card Number: 95-67285

Printed in the United States.

Dedicated to

Lovely Lynne, the last of the fair ladies in my life, women who have aided and comforted me, and who don't receive all deserved praise and credit in this book.

Thanks to men honored and mentioned in these pages and, also, to video visionary Lawrence Hamilton Miller. His work would have delighted Joseph Pulitzer, Jr., if the publisher were still living, because Larry proved you *can* stuff eight big tomatoes into one literary can.

_____

୬

1

For years, the story of my first inhale was kept from me like a military secret. When I was born, the doctor said that if I lived, I'd be crazy. Now that's a helluva intro, isn't it!

Dear Mom had a tough time with the birth of her first child, me, back in 1918, a year when a diphtheria epidemic and WW I ended the lives of many infants and many young men.

Primly, Mom was attended by a female doctor. Not a midwife, but an M.D. On my actual birth day, the medical lady was in a hurry, eager to host a dinner.

So in the afternoon in the kitchen at Virginia and Pulaski in south St. Louis, Madame Mal Practice used her forceps like ice tongs, grabbing me fore and aft, rather than left and right. One tong scarred my left eye, permanently blurring my vision. No corneal transplants back then. The other tong dug into the back of my cranium.

So, yeah, I had a hole in my head from day one.

The doctor discarded me on the kitchen table, turned to my distressed Aunt Maggie and Aunt Millie, and told them she had better bind Mrs. Broeg's breasts. No mother's milk for me, she insisted, because if I lived, I'd be crazy.

The "other" Bob Broeg, my father, arriving home after 15 hours of bread wagon driving, burst into the house at that instant, just in time to hear my death sentence pronounced. Pop was a short, stocky man, my lifetime hero, and a local amateur light-weight boxing champion in his youth. But he didn't lay a glove on Mrs. Mal Practice. Instead, he ran her straight and immediately out of our home. And then he ran himself three blocks north to the office of an old friend, Dr. Willard Hans.

Dr. Hans, a big, unruffled, leisurely man, was convinced by Pop that now was a good time to hurry. Arriving at our upstairs three-room flat, he took command.

"He's going to be all right," tut-tutted the Doc as he stopped the bleeding and patched up the helpless critter. But the vision in my left eye has remained totally blurred. If my right eye were in similar shape, I would need a tin cup and, if able to write my name, never could have read it.

My aunts and Mom told me that when I was still an infant, my great-uncle Louie Broeg saw me for the first time, juggled me for a bit, ran his fingers through my thin blond locks and pronounced, "He's going to be a writer!" If I told you other instances in which my Mom and aunts told weird tales about Uncle Louie's ESP perspicacity, you, too, would wish to have known the man. I wish I had known him better.

I did show an early interest in writing, which my parents encouraged by buying the four St. Louis daily newspapers then published, for two cents each. I gravitated early to the sports pages, particularly baseball.

When I was eight years old, the 1926 Cardinals brought home St. Louis' first pennant winner since 1888, when Pop had been a toddler. The Cards won that '26 Series against the Yankees and St. Louis erupted in a rousing celebration. Neighborhood whistles blew, horns tooted, fireworks exploded and Model-T cars careened. What excitement! Pop and the three neighbors in our four-family flat celebrated with a backyard party.

When the 1926 World Series was safely won, someone produced a bottle of whiskey, which was illegal (ahem!) except for medicinal purposes. The medicine proved worse than the disease and dear Pop became gastronomically upset. I remember him upchucking into the alley ashpit. Talk about a sign of the times!

Pop had many reasons to be upset with me, as I proved to be a precocious child. Going three or four times a week to dime-admission movies playing in two neighborhood theaters, I was fascinated by my silent-cinema heroes—the amazing German shepherd, Rin-Tin-Tin; the master of horror movies, Lon Chaney Sr.; the swashbuckling Douglas Fairbanks, Sr.; and my shoot-'em-up favorite, Tom Mix, with his "wonder" horse, Tony, a black horse with white blaze and ankle cuffs.

I'd been sad when the march of progress took Pop off his horse-drawn bakery truck. In my occasional visits to the bakery, he'd let me meet his horses, "Jim" and "Jack," one white, the other black. But now he drove a top-heavy electric truck with a 30-mile limit as a speed governor. And one noon as Pop stopped by close to our neighborhood—we were in his delivery route—I hurried up to surprise him at a nearby grocery store.

Some surprise. Climbing aboard in the driver's seat, I accidentally kicked the pronged electric key and, to my youthful horror, the truck lurched forward along the curb. Across the street loomed a thick, formidable telephone pole.

Turning the corner sharply, I looked ahead and, lo!, the truck was purring as it moved relentlessly toward the backside of a parked car that belonged to the grocer's neighbor, a baker. I lost my cool, turned the truck onto the sidewalk, and crashed through a brand new lattice-style wooden fence.

After I turned the fence into kindling, the double curb caught the back wheels of the truck and ended my adventure. Alerted by the grocer, Pop rushed his beefy body out the door and leaped onto the truck, gruffly commanding me to go home.

Why he let it go with only an angry order, rather than a swat or kick into my tiny heinie, I'll never know. I do know I raced home and slunk into the house. When Pop came home for "dinner," as they called his heaviest mid-day meal, he pushed aside Mom's appealing plate, lowered his head and cried.

Mom was startled until Pop told her how I might have been killed. He'd urged the grocer, a good ol' Dutchman named Otto Ummelman, to get the fence fixed and not to report the mishap to the big bread bakery. The cost would be about 25 bucks, not exactly salt-and-peanuts then.

My days as a budding Barney Oldfield were ended, but my interest in baseball would never end. Wouldn't someone take dear little "Robert" to the ball game?

Sure, someone would. Uncle Will Wiley, Mom's oldest brother of nine children, most of whom had been shortlived, stepped up to the plate. Uncle Will was a foundry worker with limited income, so Mom ponied up the 75 cents for a bleacher seat in the right-field pavilion.

The date is unforgettable for me: May 30, 1927. Decoration Day, then; Memorial Day now. The anatomy of my first day at a major league ball park:

First, the sound leading the sight . . . the musical note of bat meeting ball in hitting practice. Second, the beguiling aroma of popping corn and the dusty scent of peanuts. Third, and particularly appealing, the odor of grilled hot dogs buried in sweet buns still smelling of the bakery.

Never did the green of grass seem greener or the white of uniforms and balls whiter than to a nine year old who had learned baseball on grimy brick streets, city sidewalks, and dirt alleys or on fields patched with clumps of weedy grass. And our uniforms? Almost as dirty as the scuffed covers of our tired, taped baseballs.

Honestly, I don't remember too much about the double victories scored by two Redbird standbys that magical day. Righthander Jesse Haines, whom they later labelled "Pop," and a small southpaw named Bill Sherdel, were the winners. "Wee Willie's" change-up pitch was called a "slow ball" then.

I remember well a dumpy right-fielder who roamed the outfield closest to we pavilion patrons. He wore a singular uniform, a kind the Cardinals never wore again. Adorned across the left breast of the white flannel shirt, immaculate because it had been dry-cleaned, was a single red bird. Atop it in black letters was the word: "World." Beneath the bird, again in black, was another word: "Champions."

I was fascinated by the logo and also by the solemn-looking, round-faced outfielder. This was his last regular major-league season. But I would meet him again and again, years later. His name was Billy Southworth, eventually the manager of three St. Louis pennant winners (1942-43-44) and one at Boston (1948).

Oddly, I don't have much recollection of that dazzling first double dip of the stocky second baseman located yards ahead of Southworth, but he would grow on me—and fast. His name was Frank Frisch.

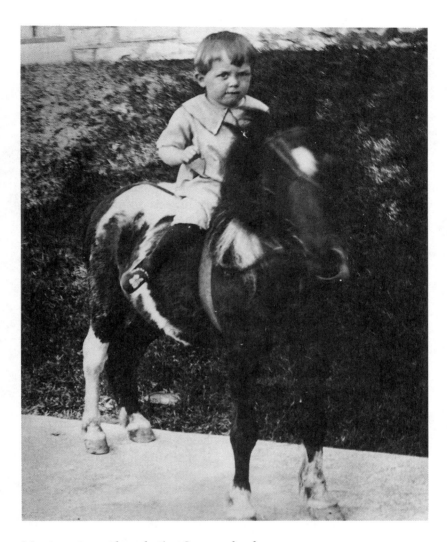

Me at age two—the only time I ever rode a horse.

2

 è.

During the span of my childhood, in terms of general public affection, baseball was first and boxing was second. When I was only six, however, Red Grange's dazzling six-touchdown performance for Illinois against Michigan helped glamourize college football.

Grange also was fundamental in the NFL's emergence. The Galloping Ghost's pro debut with the Chicago Bears on Thanksgiving Day, 1925, drew a sell-out crowd. Still, pro football wouldn't become a money-making game until the advent of television.

High school basketball was popular in many states, notably Indiana, Kentucky, and Illinois. The college game was so obscure, that in the mid-'30s sportswriter Ned Irish joined forces with Madison Square Garden and created the National Invitation Tournament, which quickly eclipsed the colleges' own infant NCAA tournament.

When you finished playing basketball in college, you probably were at the end of the line. For years, only rough-tough nightly barnstorming encounters between white Original Celtics and black Renaissance teams made money.

But boxing, like baseball, offered more bucks, if also more bangs and gave participants a shot at a sizable payday. Like the match that changed Henry Armstrong from a road runner into a perpetual-motion pugilist.

Armstrong, a.k.a. Jackson, was a gandy dancer working on railroad tracks in south St. Louis when a fluttering page from my favorite publication, the *St. Louis Post-Dispatch*, blew into his face. Henry peeled the sports page off his schnozz and read the story of Cuban featherweight Kid Chocolate winning $10,000 for a fight the night before.

That did it. Henry, always on a dog-trot, ran home faster than usual that night and told his Grandma he planned to box for a living. By 1938, he had won and held three world boxing championships at the same time—featherweight, welter, and light—and barely missed a fourth.

Prior to a fight with middleweight champion Ceferino Garcia, whom he'd once decisioned, Armstrong was offered $75,000 to take a dive. He told the bad guys to stuff their offer. Ruminating years later, Henry would sigh, "They must have got to the referee instead. He gave me only a draw in my (1940) fight with Garcia."

Henry Armstrong

Although my interest in boxing wavered over the years, it did not wane. I saw boxing as a socially desirable stepping stone upward and out of the ghetto. The list of champions reflected the triumphs of Germans, Jews, Irish, Italians, Blacks, and Hispanics.

One of the heroes of my youth was a former hobo named William Harrison (Jack) Dempsey. He won the heavyweight championship the year after I was born. Dempsey, the "Manassa Mauler" (I do love those descriptive old nicknames) had by 1919 become a full-fledged friend of my first *Post-Dispatch* boss, Ed Wray, who'd helped him with a few bucks when Dempsey was bumming his way east.

Over the years, if I needed quick service at Dempsey's restaurant on Broadway , all I had to do was mention "Ed Wray of the *Post-Dispatch*." And if Jack didn't immediately break off from a good-natured greeting he was giving elsewhere, my seat and service preceded him. I had a hard time picking up the tab, but I always insisted. Because that's the way Mr. Wray and the *Post-Dispatch* wanted it: Pay your own way!

Although Dempsey was Mr. Wray's favorite—everybody on the staff called John Edward Wray "Mr. Wray"— he maintained that the best champion he had ever seen was James J. Jeffries. Jeff had retired unbeaten in 1904 before his repugnant and unsuccessful "white-hope" comeback bid against Jack Johnson six years later.

Dempsey was a tiger in tights, chestnut-bronzed, dark-whiskered, he was my Pop's favorite. And mine.

When I was five—at a time when my mental picture of my father is dominated by winter long johns or summer short-sleeved cotton knits—Pop's work day ran 3 a.m. to 3 p.m., so he slept hard and fast.

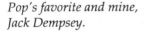

Pop's favorite and mine, Jack Dempsey.

One night in 1923 Pop asked Mom and me to listen to the punch-by-punch of the Dempsey-Firpo fight on the headpieces of a rudimentary crystal-set radio broadcasting sporadically and faintly from a sideboard table in the kitchen.

When the fight ended quickly, I hurried into the bedroom, tugged at my father's shoulder, and said, "Pop, Pop, Dempsey knocked him out in two." Without opening an eye, the weary bread winner sighed a relieved thank you and fell back asleep.

Next afternoon Pop returned from work, a newspaper in hand as usual, and teased me. I'd certainly short-snorted him with a fight description, giving only the outcome and ignoring the most amazing five minutes of fighting. Dempsey knocked Firpo down nine times. Firpo, Argentina's fierce, proud Wild Bull of the Pampas, decked Dempsey twice, once knocking the champion into the self-protecting hands of ringside reporters. A close encounter of the brief kind. Classic.

Because they were rare, the charm of heavyweight championship fights were enhanced in those days. By 1926, married to screen actress Estelle Taylor, Dempsey had fought only exhibitions. He was ring rusty.

That was the same year my mother took my brother Freddie and me on our first day-long train trip. We visited Mom's older brother, Rob Wiley, a foundry worker at Batavia, a suburb due west of Chicago on the Fox River.

During our week-long stay at Batavia, Uncle Rob's wife, Helen—"Aunt Ella" to us—took the Broegs into downtown Chicago for a look-see and movies. I was thrilled during the trip when the commuter train elevated.

On State Street, I saw bright-colored, football-style pennants draped around a combination vaudeville-movie house. Posters trumpeted a four-round exhibition between Jeffries and his old-time rival, Tom Sharkey. Even though Jeffries was old for boxing (51), I shilled for our party to go to the fight, but Mom and Aunt Ella preferred a movie across the street and off we went.

The accompanying vaudeville show included the only "quick-change " artist I have ever seen. One person performed a skit, buzzing back and forth behind a screen to change clothes and characters.

At week's end, Pop drove our first car up the ribbon highway from St. Louis —a 1927 four-door black Chevrolet with a red-trimmed curlicue side ornament. He asked me about our visit. I mentioned the quick change actor and the excitement we had experienced as we'd left the downtown theater.

Newsboys had scurried along the street, shouting: "Valentino's dead . . . Rudolph Valentino." Their words had brought gasps from Mom and Aunt Ella.

Handsome Rudolph Valentino was much too gushy for my eight-year-old tastes. He was the "Sheik of Araby," the national silent-film heart throb. Some women emerging from the theater simply fainted, I told Pop.

Then I mentioned I'd wished we'd gone across the street to watch the other movie and the vaudeville and Jim Jeffries and ... Pop interrupted and turned to Mom. Indignantly, he asked, "You mean to tell me, Alice, you had a chance to let this boy see James J. Jeffries box!" He made her walk home.

Just kidding.

From then on, Pop brought home weekly the pink-covered *Police Gazette*, a slick-paper publication featuring fighters and (ahem!) voluptuous women. He also brought home *Fight Stories*, a monthly pulp-magazine fiction and *Ring Magazine*, published by a New York man, Nat Fleischer, who was to boxing with his monthly ratings what St. Louis's J.G. Taylor Spink's *The Sporting News* was to baseball. Pop also brought me *The Idol of Fistiana*, a book by Fleischer about Dempsey.

Dempsey finally fought in September, 1926, meeting ex-Marine Gene Tunney at Philadelphia's Sesquicentennial Stadium (now JFK Stadium). The night of the Dempsey-Tunney fight, neighbor Louie Sika had arranged for us to hear the bout at the home of a barber customer with enough wherewithal to own a good, cabinet-elevated radio. Tunney, son of a New York tenement-area grocer who'd grown up above his father's store, won the championship handily from a creaky Dempsey.

Pop took it hard, silently. I held up until we stopped at our neighborhood filling station, where Art Meyer, who cleverly had installed a radio in the transom of his front door, expressed his regret. My boyhood disappointment expressed itself with tears. I cried again the next day when I read Dempsey's response to his wife's question about what happened. Endearing himself forever, the old champ said gallantly, "I forgot to duck, honey."

Boxing rang my bell, but baseball was first. That's why I felt much better in a few hours when the Cardinals clinched their first pennant. Many of the players had watched the fight the night before in Philadelphia and had arrived late and rain soaked in New York for their game with the Giants.

All in all, 1926 was a great year. But 1927 was better. Despite a troublesome appendectomy, '27 was one of the brightest years for me, despite the fact that I was barely old enough to comb my own hair. In May, along with our neighborhood and the world, I listened in fascination to radio bulletins about the "Lone Eagle," slim-jim Charles A. Lindbergh, who was seeking glory and a $25,000 prize if he could make the first transatlantic flight.

The night he flew toward France, ring-announcer Joe Humphries of Madison Square Garden delayed the fight between Jack Sharkey and Jimmy Maloney. He used the timer's clanging bell to call the crowd to silence in prayer for "Lindy." In my home area, folks gathered outside Art Meyer's filling station through the night as the radio boomed out messages describing the plucky pilot's flight.

Fewer than 34 hours later, fighting sleep and having only eaten a sandwich and a half, "we" landed in LeBourget Field near Paris. "We," of course, was the modest flyer's reference to himself and to his silver monoplane, the "Spirit of St. Louis."

President Calvin Coolidge wouldn't let the two-legged national treasure fly back to America, but when Lindbergh and his plane came back via a U.S. cruiser, the cities of New York and Washington had huge ticker-tape parades. A gala reception was also planned in St. Louis, which felt the greatest sense of pride. Happily, the city had an opportunity to add a special touch.

Cardinals owner Sam Breadon had decided to delay the Redbirds' first world championship rings presentation until the Giants came to town. Breadon had been blistered for trading Rogers Hornsby to the Giants for Frank Frisch following the 1926 season. The Cards owner wanted to make sure Hornsby could participate.

The serendipity of Lindbergh's post-flight availability resulted in the aviator presenting the rings. I have a framed photo of the delightful occasion when the 26-year-old blond pilot made the presentation to the 40-year-old Series hero Grover Cleveland Alexander. The grinning joy of bow-tied plate umpire Charley Moran is great.

A year later, Lindbergh flew his plane back from a goodwill trip to South America. St. Louis was his last stop before delivering his doughty plan to the Smithsonian in Washington. Here, all schoolchildren were excused and transported by streetcar and bus to the riverfront.

*Lucky Lindy
presents the
Cardinals with
their first World
Series champion-
ship rings.*

We lined the levee for miles. Lindy flew his "Spirit" up the Mississippi, dramatically demonstrating his stunt and mail-pilot skills. He virtually skimmed the water before flying his plane *under* Eads Bridge. If I didn't wet my pants, I certainly wanted to.

In late September, while I stood at a window in my south side Mt. Pleasant school and watched a pitch-dark late afternoon rain, a horrific tornado devastated the city's northeast side. The savage twister killed 86, injured 500 and inflicted $10 million in damages. It tore the right field roof off the Sportsman's Park pavilion and dumped twisted wood and steel into Grand Avenue. The center field flagpole was blown down. Girders were bent.

Although my ball park appearances were few in 1927, I saw something that never left my memory. Pitching for the Redbirds, righthander Vic Keen rendered Pittsburgh shortstop Glenn Wright unconscious with a pitch that accidentally hit Wright in the head. The horror of the felled ball player was compounded by the sight of an hysterical Keen running around the mound like a chicken with its head cut off.

At 31, Keen was completely unnerved and positively through with baseball. He quit the game and went back to Baltimore, where he achieved a meaningful career, raising—if you will—chickens.

When players from the Cardinals' first championship ballclub came to town for a reunion a half-century later in 1976, I couldn't resist asking Keen about the frightful occasion and its impact. Past 80, Vic nodded and remembered. "Wright was great about it," he recalled, "but I simply lost my nerve. Besides, it worked out well. I've had a good life."

Life was good for me, too, in 1927, especially after my emergency appendectomy saved my life, prompted a growth spurt, and gave me a newly prodigious appetite.

Often, at home, with the grocery store across the street offering four heaping scoops of ice cream for a dime, we'd mix the frozen treat with flavored bottle soda. These concoctions made great hot weather treats, but I learned to like sundaes better and Cokes, although they were harder to get. But thanks to a trip to Memphis, iced tea became a staple at home. Pop's brother-in-law, Fred Isele, a Swiss name pronounced "Eye-zeel-ee," took his wife, my Aunt Millie; their young son, Fred; and me on a motor trip to Memphis.

Uncle Fred's uncle Martin Isele helped construct the Peabody Hotel, which was big stuff to me. After all, the Peabody had ducks in a lobby fountain pool. The Iseles had their own small hotel located near the produce markets of Memphis. They also had fabulous meals created by their black staff. It was the first time I got to know black people personally.

Pop's chubby sister had a great knack of getting along with people of a different color. I believe I inherited some of that from her, too. Thanks, Aunt Millie. She also bequeathed me an impressive profane vocabulary.

The blacks in the Isele restaurant kitchen treated me to the first southern-fried chicken I'd ever tasted and, also, to my first iced tea, laced then with sugar and lemon. But years later, when the docs benched me from the booze, straight iced tea became my satisfying substitute.

The cooks had a passion for the baseball exploits of the Southern Association Memphis Chickasaws and the Negro National League's Memphis Red Sox. The Chicks played nearby. One morning I found my way to Russwood Park, a framed Double-A structure. I peaked in and noted a close left field with grass sloping to the fence. My blood was stirred. I had to see a game. And after repeated hints to my aunt and uncle, I did.

So in 1927, I saw my first professional ball games, major and minor, cemented a love affair with the Cardinals, and began a childhood hero "romance" with Frank Frisch, who wouldn't know me from a cold "Bud-weis-ah," (his New York accent) for nearly another 20 years.

3

With his chorus girl ankles, Babe Ruth seemed top heavy. Of course, so do many chorus girls. When I first learned about this most amazing athletic animal (my Babe . . . Ruth, that is), I began to understand that ball players who accomplished big feats didn't need big feet.

On a day in the Roaring Twenties razzmatazz era of short skirts and speakeasies—I was too young to admire one or partake of either—Pop came home from work with an amusing tale for Mom's ears only.

As a bread salesman, Pop nightly rode the "owl" streetcar to work; it ran hourly from midnight to dawn. In the still of the night, Pop arrived in midtown on a Grand Avenue streetcar, facing a long walk to the bakery, located on Forest Park Boulevard at Vandeventer.

Unaware my rabbit ears twitched with boyhood reportorial curiosity, Pop whispered a gossipy secret to Mom.

The silence of his walk had been broken by a loud, booming laugh. A half-block away was a high-rent brothel run by a madam using the name of May Traynor. She was no relation to baseball's Pie. Yet Mrs. Traynor ran her establishment the way Pie played third base, with excellence and class. May sold good food, big-league booze, and accommodating women.

Pop had heard the hearty laughter of one of May's favorite patrons. Yes, Pop confided to Mom, it had been Babe Ruth himself being poured into a taxicab by a couple of May's lovely ladies.

Pop, smiling, recalled to Mom, "I have seen him before, Alice. Then I thought, 'Oh, oh, the Babe's going to have a tough day.'"

My father's grin widened. That afternoon, hiking back to catch a streetcar home, he had bought a late newspaper. "Today's game wasn't over," he chuckled, "but the Babe already had hit two homeruns against the Browns . . ."

After I zeroed in on the tales of Babe Ruth's pursuit of cold beer and hot women that afternoon in 1927, a year the Yankees' Murderers Row won 110 games and Ruth hit his record 60 homers, I could never hear or read enough about baseball's mostest man. I've asked many questions, too, especially of Waite Hoyt.

Waite was a character in his own right. Asked by his father-in-law to bring a dead body to the family funeral home, Hoyt picked up the stiff, stuffed him into his car trunk, drove to Yankee Stadium, and pitched a winning game. "Obviously," Hoyt told me, "it wasn't too hot that day."

A former teammate of the Babe's, Waite had been driven into Alcoholics Anonymous by spending too many nights trying to keep up with Babe and his bottles. Hoyt would give me endless private commentaries about the Babe drinking from the horn of plenty and enjoying sex with the same guts and gusto as baseball. The Babe was a champion, hands down and apparatus up.

Heck, Babe made even more money than the President of the United States; $80,000 in 1930. But Hoyt always knew that Ruth's staggering salaries helped teammates earn more, too. At bedtime, Waite urged his kids to "thank God, thank Mommy, thank Daddy—and thank Babe Ruth."

As a kid, I knew the Babe only from afar except for one gaped-mouthed moment. I once had a ball autographed by Ruth at the back of the visitors dugout in St. Louis. The bass-voiced big guy had good penmanship.

I was awe-stricken, too, the first time I saw Babe Ruth play ball when I was 10 years old and I persuaded Pop to take me. We sat in the right field pavilion in Sportsman's Park.

Babe didn't do a thing except hit one batting practice pitch far over the towering pavilion, across Grand Avenue and onto a roof. A rouser, according to gawking sports writers. Yet, though striking out twice that day against a cunning lefthander, Walter Stewart, Ruth fanned with majesty. He also contributed a touch of contretemps I've never seen equaled more than 60 years and 5,000 big-league games later.

In the fifteenth inning of a duel between Stewart and Babe's stylish teammate, future Hall of Famer Herb Pennock, the Browns filled the bases with one out. Hit for Stewart? Not when the Brownies had a hot pitcher against a ball club that recently had beat them 27 times in a row.

Dutifully, the Yankee's infield pulled in. So did the outfield, including Ruth, playing left field today though ordinarily a right fielder. Ruth always played left field in St. Louis so that the searing southwest sun filtering through the late-afternoon grandstand louvers into right field wouldn't hamper those prized eyes.

What happened then I can still see now: Stewart looped a fly to short left, providing a profile view for one in the pavilion. The runner on third jockeyed part way toward the plate. If the ball were caught, he wouldn't be able to score.

Not with the Babe's arm. Ruth, only slightly pot-bellied at this point in his abdominal development, broke in on the fly ball with fast, mincing strides. Although he didn't leave his feet, he lunged forward with his glove, hopeful of a shoestring catch, which he didn't make. The ball one-hopped under his glove and rolled slowly a few feet farther toward the distant fence.

I can still see it. The runner, halfway home, broke for the plate and scored the winning run. He waltzed toward the third-base dugout, where his teammates streamed out to greet him.

Ruth, without breaking stride, stepped on third base, pivoted right and ran into and through the St. Louis dugout, which was used by both teams to enter or leave the field. He was the first player off the field. I don't believe I ever saw any other defensive outfielder leave the field at the end of a game before any of the offense.

As a kid, I had a love-hate relationship with the Babe, hating his ample guts for carving up the Cardinals in the 1928 World Series. But I would go out deliberately to see him wearing his number "3." The Yankees popularized uniform numbers in 1929, striping their monkey suits to slenderize the so-called Big Monkey.

Whether homering with towering drives, striking out with Richter-scale seismographic rumbles or popping up, like an express elevator going up a shaft, he was a sight to behold—if looking into the sun didn't make your eyes water. Perhaps apocryphally, Jimmy Dykes insisted Babe uppercut an infield fly so high one day that when Dykes dropped the ball, the Babe reached third base.

My last two playing-field looks at the Bambino, like my first, had unusual aspects. In a rare losing season, 1933, I saw the Babe homer. But the Yankees lost because of an unusual mishap by a 22-year-old rookie in center field.

Years later, that kid, Fred (Dixie) Walker would become an idol in Brooklyn —the "peepul's cherce"—and a friend. But on this day he messed up. When the Browns' catcher, Rollie Hemsley, lifted a routine fly ball to center, Walker charged madly toward the infield. The ball fell untouched far behind him and rolled to the center-field wall for a two-run homer.

Years later when I was a traveling baseball writer and teased him, Walker remembered with a shudder. He'd borrowed Ben Chapman's flip-down sunglasses, although he was accustomed to wearing ordinary smoked specs in the outfield. When he flipped Chapman's glasses, they obscured his vision. He headed south while the ball traveled north.

Dixie smilingly recalled, "I could hear the Babe (in left) yelling, but I didn't know the awful truth until too late. When we headed to the bench after that inning, the Babe chuckled, 'Too bad you didn't stay put, keed. Hell, the ball would-a hit you in the glove—or on the head.'"

Because of that fluke homer, the Browns stayed close enough so that a pinch home run in the ninth inning by Rogers Hornsby tied the game. St. Louis won in the tenth, 7-6. Hornsby's homer provided a dramatic twist. Only recently he had been released by the Cardinals, a worn-down 38-year-old pinch-hitter, to manage the lowly Browns and occasionally play.

When Rog came down out of the third base coach's box to hit, the Yankee bench gave him three jeers. "So this," they crowed, "is the famous National League hitter, 'Mister Hornsby.'"

The Rajah, a righthanded hitter, stood deep and in the far corner of the batter's box, so he could stride directly into a pitch. The Yankee pitcher, one of the best, was Lefty Gomez.

Rog hit Lefty's first offering onto the roof in right-center and he trundled head down around the bases. When he reached home plate, he yelled to the quiet Yankee bench, "Yeah, you bastards, that was the great National League hitter, *Mister* Hornsby."

The next day, Hornsby was accepting bows from reporters. "Pardon me, Rog," a passing Gomez interrupted. Hornsby didn't like it. He scowled. Lefty deadpanned, "Congratulations on the homer, Rog, but, you know, you stood so far from the plate, I thought you were the hitter in the on-deck circle." Oh, such language behind Gomez's back as he whistled his way to the first-base bench.

Vernon (Lefty) Gomez and his wife, June O'Dea, a Broadway singer.

For my final trip to the park to see Ruth play, he didn't. But I took my seat in left field and, once again, the unexpected happened.

That day in late 1934, with Ben Chapman playing center field, Yankees manager Joe McCarthy rested Ruth and moved veteran center fielder Earle "The Colonel" Combs to left. Combs was accustomed to the greater depth in center field. So, racing back on a long drive, he turned, leaped, and cracked his head against the wall's concrete. His teammates carried him off, motionless.

A nosy kid I was, probably a prerequisite for aspiring sports writers. I hurried down under the grandstand just outside the visitors clubhouse. An ambulance wheeled through an emergency gate.

Looking serious and stern, Dr. Robert F. Hyland hurried into the ambulance. There Combs lay, his face whiter than his prematurely graying hair. His collarbone and skull were fractured. Dr. Hyland worked to save the player's life.

And he succeeded. The Colonel credited Doc Hyland with saving his life and concurred when Judge Landis called Dr. Hyland, a daily boxseat holder, the "surgeon-general of baseball."

Combs played only briefly before quitting in 1935, the same year the Babe finished up in Boston. I just wish Ruth had had the sense to quit when he was ahead. Most certainly that was the day in late May when Ruth reached back into his memory bank and went "4 for 4" at Pittsburgh. The last of his three homers became the first ball hit over the towering right-field stands.

With a bow to friend William Bendix and hometowner John Goodman, a true story of George Herman Ruth's life would have been "X" rated—from that time he grew up in his father's saloon, an uncontrollable kid who sipped beer and chewed tobacco at seven, filched nickels and couldn't be handled by an ailing mother or a father for whom he was a cabbage-headed, wide-nosed double.

I could write a book of awe, admiration, and audacity about the gifted guy who would have made the Hall of Fame as a pitcher if not as a hitter. But I'll stick to only a few nuggets delivered to me personally.

For instance, here's an episode involving character actor Walter Catlett, whose voice lives on as the wily wolf in Walt Disney's animated classic, "Pinocchio."

Catlett remembered a snowy January night years ago in Boston when he and two "cupcakes" were entertained by Harry Frazee, then owner of the Boston Red Sox and a theatrical producer. Frazee recently had sold the Babe to the New York Yankees for seed money to produce Broadway's "No, No, Nanette." Proudly, Frazee cabbed his guests to Fenway Park. The cabbie listened as the tuxedoed Frazee talked about "his" park.

The cabdriver followed Frazee out of the cab. Politely, he asked, "You own the Red Sox?" A preening Frazee allowed, "Why, yes, my good man."

"Oh," said the cabbie, "then you're the so-and-so who sold Babe Ruth to the Yankees!" Catlett smiled in recollection and finished the tale. "The cabbie knocked Harry on his ass in the snow and drove off with me and the cupcakes."

One winter when Babe's personal appearance vaudeville tour included a week at the Ambassador Theatre in downtown St. Louis, he phoned young catcher Fred (Bootnose) Hofmann to set up a week's comforts. "So I moved downtown from Mom's," said Hofmann, conveniently a St. Louis bachelor. "I bought the phonograph as he had directed and the records and the bootleg booze.

"The Babe *always* knew where to get the broads. Except for him to walk a few blocks east to the Ambassador a few times daily, we never left his hotel suite at the Jefferson the whole week he was in town. When it was over, I needed a rest cure."

The Babe didn't seem to need many rest cures, except, perhaps, after a bout with Ma Gehrig's pickled eels. Lou's Mom was a Columbia University cook who liked Babe because he liked her cooking. On Sundays, she would produce a pint of pickled eels. Between doubleheader games, Babe would mix the eels with a quart of chocolate ice cream and devour the dubious delicacy.

Said Waite Hoyt, smiling in reminiscence, "The Babe led the league in homers and in burping, belching, and farting his way around the bases."

Hoyt, so close to Ruth that as a Protestant he'd gone to Mass with Babe, always could tell when Ruth felt he'd sinned excessively. "He'd drop a hundred in the collection basket," recalled Hoyt.

Teammates usually called him "Jidge," a version of George. For a time they called him "Tarzan," and he liked that until he saw the full title of Edgar Rice Burroughs' Adonis of the jungle was "Tarzan of the Apes." He knew that behind his back they called him the Big Monkey. Wide-nosed, thick-lipped, the southerner resented the suggestion he was black.

Ty Cobb teased him by addressing him in crossing-field patterns as "Nig." In the 1922 World Series, led by infielder Johnny Rigney with chants of "nigger," the New York Giants tormented the slumping superstar who stormed into the victors' dressing room and stormed at manager John McGraw:

"I don't mind being called sonofabitch, a bastard or even a big prick, but . . . uh, lay off that personal stuff."

Conversationally, Babe could be rough around the edges, even when he was trying extra hard to be smooth. Like the time Wheaties asked Ruth to help them promote the idea that the cereal could make good cookies, too. Trouble was, the Babe pronounced cookies with a cutesy, incorrect "kookies."

They rehearsed him until he pronounced cookie correctly. Then the red light flashed. In person—live and on the air—Babe Ruth extolled Wheaties as a confection rather than just a cereal.

Boomed the Babe, "Try using Wheaties to make 'kookies.' . . . I'll be a sonofabitch, I said it again."

And the surprised radio audience, not so surprisingly, was amused more than angered.

There'll never be another.

The Babe next to the window he broke with one of his three homers in a 1926 World Series game.

4

During the Depression, movies went to double features. The neighborhood flickers offered two-for-one attractions. And if that wasn't good enough, they'd give lady customers a weekly free cup or saucer.

By comparison, baseball invested no effort in making going to the ball park more attractive. No wonder, for instance, the best pre-World War II attendance for Connie Mack's Philadelphia Athletics was only 869,753 in 1925. The A's featured Lefty Grove, Jimmy Foxx, Mickey Cochrone, and Al Simmons during the next few years but never equalled 1925's attendance.

I mention Philadelphia for two reasons— 1) I think Philly might be the best sports town overall, and 2) kindly Connie, the patriarch of Twenty-First and Lehigh, might have been the most reactionary skinflint of them all. He was the last to permit his players to be identified by uniform number.

Not only did the major league clubs not tie in businesses and industries for promotional giveaways or special group nights, but they were giving more information to radio than they gave to those bodies that bellied up to the box office. In some ways, this made listening more interesting than attending.

At Sportsman's Park, hefty Jim Kelly, a golden-voiced round man, used a giant microphone so large he needed two hands to steady it. He stood directly beneath the plate and, using a lineup card, intoned the batting order for the pressbox and nearby expensive lower-and-upper deck patrons. He operated without the benefit of electronic amplifiers.

To inform the other people in the park, Kelly would waddle left and then right merely to intone the batteries. "For Chicago, Malone, pitch, and Hartnett catch. For the Cardinals"— and I can hear Jim's vocal rise and fall—"Al-ex-an-der, pitch; O'Far-rell, catch."

For a player change, the field announcer shouted the name of a pinch-hitter or pinch-runner or relief pitcher. The action often would be over before you knew who did what.

But wait, that's not all. The scorecard itself was coded. Though the players did not yet wear numbers, a number designating them appeared both on the official scorecard and on the scoreboard. To thwart outlaw scorecards, sold two for a nickel outside the park to those who didn't think correct info was worth a full nickel, the club would periodically change a player's number. Only they (and the readers of their official scorecard) would know.

Frisch might be number "4" for a few days, then "14," and by week's end he might be labeled "13." Trying once to save that nickel, I outsmarted myself, a stunt that resulted in my confusing George (Specs) Toporcer for my hero, Frank Frisch. It was the only time Specs played second base in 1928, as he was sent to the minor leagues soon after.

For the 1931 World Series, the Cardinals ended the scorecard hocus-pocus. The ballclub began the practice of placing players' numbers on the uniforms. Pepper Martin, for example, was no. 1, Leo Durocher was no. 2, Frank Frisch no. 3, and Joe Medwick no. 7.

One of the promotions that worked well for the Cardinals was the Knothole Gang. In 1928 I was first eligible for the 10- to 16-year-old free-gate courtesy extended except for weekends, holidays, and special occasions.

The 3 p.m. starting time was standard across the country until broken by the progressive Chicago Cubs, as I recall. The idea was that the majority of weekday customers were white-collar executives who could have a quick lunch, sign their afternoon mail before 3 and stop off at the ball park before heading home.

By city limits, St. Louis was—and is—15 miles long and 7 miles wide. If a kid leaving school at 3:20 from my distance—a four-block walk followed by a half-hour streetcar ride—could make it from the 4500 block south to 2700 north, he would be lucky if the second inning hadn't ended. So, obviously, summer vacation was the time to go to ball games. I guess I averaged one or two a week.

Never one to tarry long for autographs, I followed a ritual en route home. By the time the streetcar reached Grand and

Olive— a midtown midsection some 30 minutes after the game's end—caught in high-hour traffic, newsboys stood boldly virtually between streetcars and automobiles.

Despite radio's new inroads, the newspaper was still the king of slow-poke sports information. They'd doll up Page One for late-afternoon games, flip-flopping the sports section outside, changing the colored front newsprint to peach for the *Post-Dispatch*, green for the *Star*, salmon for the *Times*. (Later, in its Sports Final, the morning *Globe-Democrat* had a quarter-inch blue streak down its regular news front page.)

If newsboys hawked "Brownie boxcar," "Cardinal victory," you knew what that meant. The Browns, as usual, playing two hours earlier back east, would have lost their game. For the Cardinals contest I'd just witnessed, a large hand-set boxscore might show only eight and one-half innings, but a score line dropped in behind the first graph had the final score. A skeletonized play-by-play, yes, but I marveled even then at how fast the newspapers had worked to get the game to their readers.

Toporcer, slightly taller and a bit more slender than Frisch before Frank fleshed out, wasn't quite so distinguishable on the far side of the infield from the left field Knothole section. And he hit left-handed. But you couldn't tell he was bespectacled.

About the time I foolishly tried to save a scorecard nickel out of the two-bits I wheedled from Mom for the ball park—five cents each way on the streetcar and a dime for a Coke—the *Post-Dispatch's* long-time sports editor, John E. Wray, campaigned to give the spectator as much information as the radio audience was getting. For instance, hit-and-error designations by the official scorer were transmitted on radio, but not disclosed to the cash customers.

Temperamental then, too, athletes might be offended if their physical miscues were publicized on the scoreboard or aired within their rabbit-eared hearing. This unseemly censorship boomeranged at least once, older-timers told me, remembering a game pitched against the Cardinals by Chicago's Guy Bush, the Mississippi Mudcat, as they called him. Bush was a swarthy, long-sideburned man who looked like a riverboat gambler.

When the Cubbies engulfed Bush nine innings after the game, obviously celebrating a "no-hitter," agitation and yells from the pressbox prompted the Cubs to look up. Miffed Chicago writers held up one finger, indicating a hit. Angry Chicago players rushed the backstop screen. Catcher Gabby Hartnett even tried to climb it.

Modern scoreboards communicate a plethora of information and even include instant replay—which umpires don't always like. When I was a boy, often there were only two umpires, not three, and never four.

Knothole Gang afternoons at the ball park were filled with delights such as a close-up view of the Cardinals' first World Series hero, Grover Cleveland Alexander, or left fielder Chick Hafey's entertaining kids in the paralleling lower grandstand when the Cardinals extended their infield drill to the outfield.

After catching a few routine fly balls, Hafey would retreat to the wall, 351 feet away from home plate at the foul line, and extend himself with his strong, powerful throws. He drew happy exclamations from the Knotholers when he uncorked a long, accurate, one-bounce peg to the plate.

The Knothole Gang began in 1917 as an offshoot from a free bleacher admission policy for underprivileged kids. It was later refined by General Manager Branch Rickey to include all boys—and ultimately girls, too—with seating provided in the lower left field grandstand wing.

We kids would chant in a sing-song, "We want a ho-mer, we want a ho-mer," when a power hitter like Hafey or Jim Bottomley came up in a critical situation.

Then, too, when a starting pitcher began to waver, we would chant, "We want Al-ex . . . we want Al-ex," a chorus that fell on deaf ears usually because, though starters did double back in a relief role now and then, both Bill McKechnie in 1928 and Billy Southworth in 1929 were reluctant to call on the ancient hero.

But—wait—one day he did come to the rescue, and my mind's eye is 20-20 in recollection. First, the home-town bullpen closely paralleled the low concrete-barrier. So Alexander was at least as big as life when he hurried down from the third base dugout to warm up for a rare relief appearance.

I can see him now, that tall, rangy, sandy-haired pitcher. Stockings white with three thin red stripes made Ol' Pete's knock knees seem more slender. Freckled beneath gray eyes, his sideburns clipped and turkey-wattled at the neck. His face wore no expression. His looks reflected a life style that made him appear older. Why? Well, he was epileptic and an alcoholic, his own worst enemy. But he was one of the greatest pitchers ever. And I had the thrill to see him from so close I could easily admire the single red bird he wore on the left breast in that '28 uniform.

Alexander silently elbowed out of the way another pitcher warming up. He was in a hurry to get ready. His glove, black, was modest even by comparison with the small mitts of the day. So the white ball, by comparison, seemed twice as large.

He threw from a three-quarter righthanded delivery, arm held tight to his side so that as I learned later, he appeared to be pitching out of his uniform shirt. White-on-white does make it more difficult to pick up the pitch, a stratagem that made Alexander even more deceptive than in road gray. Old Low and Away, as pitching teammate Jesse (Pop) Haines always referred to him, snapped off just about five pitches. Then, pivoting on a visual signal from the dugout, Alexander walked briskly to the mound.

Once there, to the joy of the Knothole Gang, he strode to the mound, quickly used five more warm-ups, then retired the side, and as haughtily as when he struck out Tony Lazzeri in that clutch moment of the 1926 World Series, sauntered to the sideline and flipped his glove into foul territory. He relieved only three times in '28 and three more in his final St. Louis season, 1929. My memory of him is a rich and rare mental souvenir.

Even if he hadn't been absorbed in the golden glow of alcohol, I wonder how long Alexander might have gone if he hadn't thought he'd reached and passed Christy Mathewson's National League victory total in 1929.

I've always resented the suggestion that Alexander tied Matty, when it was vice-versa. After a "rest cure" in 1929, he returned in late season 1929, and won game number 373 to pass Mathewson. But that was it. Old Pete went off the deep end and was quietly paid off and eventually traded by a sympathetic Breadon late in the year. After his release, a baseball researcher dug up an extra victory for Mathewson, giving them 373 each.

The next season, Alexander moved to Philadelphia and caught on with his old ball club, the futile Phils. He managed a tough opening-game loss to Carl Hubbell in 1930, 2-1, but the tank of talent was empty, even if Alexander wasn't. The old man bowed out soon after without a victory in three starts and a nine-game appearance that told it all in earned-run average—9.14. If Alex the Great knew he had more ground to cover, more games to win to be the best, I just wonder if he would have held up and stayed up at least a little longer.

Alexander the Great in 1928.

Philadelphia's later great Hall of Fame righthander, Robin Roberts, tells a poignant story. When Robby was an eighth grader at a little red schoolhouse on the outskirts of Springfield, Illinois, a prominent tavern owner brought a famous name for a visit in 1950, shortly before the visitor died.

Introduced, the man got to his feet, and said softly, "Don't do what I did boys. Don't drink."

My own prejudice for Grover Cleveland Alexander stems, of course, from that exciting final game of the 1926 World Series. Alexander sat in the bullpen in a red-jacketed blanket sweater with the collar pulled up and his cap pulled down over closed eyes.

Whether Alex was asleep or not, tipsy or sober, chances are he had engaged in his pre-game drinking practice even though the day before when he'd breezed to his second Series victory, manager Rogers Hornsby had urged him to "take it easy."

After geezer Pete brushed his teeth, as reserve batteryman Ernie Vick told me, Alexander would throw down two or three shots of hooch before heading for a hotel elevator. And if the elevator took a little too long, Alex might meander back to his room for one for the road. He'd hum happily down to breakfast.

When the critical 1926 seventh-game moment came, player-manager Rogers Hornsby wig-wagged from second base— not for either pitcher warming up. For Alexander. Vick nudged him, "Pete, Rog wants you, bases loaded, last of the seventh, two out. We're one-up, 3-2."

Alexander nodded, rose and slowly began shedding that vintage wool sweater substituted for the modern-day jacket. Recalled Vick, smiling, "He took his good ol' sweet time. Pete knew that Tony Lazzeri, though extremely dangerous, was a rookie."

S-o-o, with absolutely no warm-up in the bullpen on a chilly afternoon, jacket cradled over his shoulder, Alexander began his long amble to the mound. Near the shortstop position, Hornsby, who already had announced him, briefed the old-timer on the game situation.

"Well, Rog," said Alexander, "I guess there ain't no place to put him."

Lazzeri hooked one long drive to left, barely foul. Then Old Low and Away struck Tony out on the fourth pitch, a darting short-breaking delivery, which was, of course, down and away. Afterward, Alex would recall, "If he'd hit that one fair, he'd have been the hero, and I'd have been the bum."

With two out in the ninth, no Yankee had reached base against Alexander. Then Babe Ruth walked on a borderline full-count pitch.

After ball four, Alexander, taking a return throw from catcher Bob O'Farrell, advanced a few steps toward the plate and asked umpire George Hildebrand how much he'd missed, if any, with his "3-and-2" pitch. The ump held his hands together, separated by an inch.

"If it was that close," grumbled Alexander, "you could have given it to an old guy."

Happily for Alexander the Great and long-suffering St. Louis, the Babe tried a surprise steal and was gunned out on a Series-ending throw, O'Farrell to Hornsby.

By the 1928 World Series, Alex was so deep in the sauce that pitching opponent George Pipgras recalled that when they posed before the second-game handshake—a photographic tradition in that era—Alex's glow had been virtually replaced by a tremor. When Pipgras stuck out his hand, the wavy-armed Alexander actually missed with his thrust. He didn't miss the Yankee bats though, especially Ruth's and Gehrig's.

Alex was never one for conditioning. In 1925, while pitching for the Cubs, then managed by his old batterymate Reindeer Bill Killefer—and this is Tom Sheehan's story—Alexander once overdid his liquid preparation and wove into the Wrigley Field clubhouse, humming on a day he was supposed to pitch against Sheehan, then with Pittsburgh.

First, Killefer hid out of anger. Next, he raced into the clubhouse rest room, where Alex was seated happily. Snapped the manager, "You're still pitching." Cheerfully, Alex glowed, "Who said I wasn't, Bill?"

Sheehan tells the rest of the story:

"It's a cold day," said Sheehan, "and I warm up early. Alex barely comes out and throws a few, then stops to chat with fans located near the dugout. So I say to myself, 'Well, this is one day you're going to beat the old master.'"

Sheehan paused for dramatic effect. S-o-o? Pouting, he held up one finger. "So Alexander held you to a run?"

Huffed Sheehan, "Hell, to one hit, and he worked so fast and efficiently that I think he was still loaded when the game ended!"

5

　ﻋﺎ

My future, disguised as "Baseball Joe," began calling me early.

By the time I was six, I knew I didn't want to be a teamster like Pop or Grandpa Broeg. I would have loved to be a singer, but Gramp shot me down early.

While in kindergarten, I sang in an Amateur Night Program at a neighborhood movie house. Afterwards, clutching a box of animal crackers, I showed off my booby prize. Grampa, the first Bob Broeg, asked how I'd won it. By golly, I'd sung "Barney Google," a nutty novelty number based on a comic strip.

Upon his request, I gladly gave an encore. Gramp listened, shook his head, reached into his pocket, and handed me a nickel. "Next time you want animal crackers, I'll give you another," he said. "I don't like to see a grandson of mine make a damn fool of himself."

After Gramp died when I was seven, Aunt Millie, the former Amelia Broeg, with whom he had lived, liked to recall that story more than I did. I used to secretly describe Aunt Millie as my "fat aunt," out of her earshot, of course.

Aunt Millie was partial to profanity. The jolly woman loved to needle Louis Thesz, a nice neighbor she called "Louie." He corrected her gravely. "Mrs. Isele," he said, "my name is Louis with the 's' behind." Aunt Millie laughed uproariously at the youthful double entendre.

When Lou was eight and I was six, an older neighborhood kid ran both of us up a back alley. We scurried like sniveling cowards, seeking shelter finally behind the fence where Lou's father, Martin, ran a shoe repair shop. Mr. Thesz was an immigrant.

Martin had been a middleweight wrestler in Hungary, and became his son's first coach. He then turned Lou over to George Tragos, a Greek immigrant with Olympic skills. The physical transformation from when Thesz was 14 to when he was 17 was remarkable. At 14, on a rare holiday from learning his father's cobbling trade, he seemed awkward and gawky.

Three years later, about to enter professional wrestling, he was taller, and his body was as sleek as a tiger. At a friend's house, he offered kindly to wrestle both of us at once. The other guy, about Lou's age, was Gene Lamkiewicz, a Polish kid who was my close neighbor and friend.

Quickly, Thesz grabbed and pinned Lamkiewicz, who then curled up on a nearby chair and purred with joy as Lou played with me like a cat taunting a mouse. Needless to say, I wasn't surprised when Thesz quickly became a local wrestling favorite.

Boyhood friend, Louis Thesz, six-time national wrestling champion.

Even if pro wrestling is now as phony as Santa Claus's whiskers and most rasslers don't know a half-nelson from a Lord Nelson, Thesz could truly wrestle. My old friend, Sam Muchnick, the reformed baseball writer who made a fortune as a wrestling promoter, always regarded Lou as one of the best. Thesz was recognized six times as champion of the National Wrestling Alliance.

At age 74, he wrestled the champion of Japan in Tokyo, where Thesz taught the American version of the ancient Greco-Roman art and was a big fan favorite.

Smiling, he told me, "I honestly thought I could win except that my artificial hip sagged when I was engaged in a complicated double bridge."

In view of Lou Thesz's international recognition as a championship wrestler, that older neighbor kid with the sunken chest earned the rare bragging right of bellying up to a bar and saying, "I chased Lou Thesz and Bob Broeg up an alley. They ran like dogs."

Unforgettable, that Lou Thesz. But then so was Lou Sika, the baseball-batty barber, who introduced me to Joe Matson, the best ball player who never played the game.

Over the years, I've found that immigrants, like religious converts, are deeply dedicated to baseball. Many of the old-timers came to this country at the turn of the century, needing only a nickel for a short beer and a free lunch at a corner saloon, where knowledge of baseball was an open sesame to acceptance and an opportunity to refine the language.

Sika (pronounced Sigh-ka) came in from Hungary in 1907, a diminutive, wiry man who ate a little and walked a lot. Probably why he lived until 95. Poignantly, when Lou was blind and nearly deaf, existing (not living) in a nursing home, I saw him one last time in 1982 to shout the good news—Whitey Herzog's Cardinals were en route to a pennant (and a world championship!)

At the same time Lou began to cut my hair, when I was four, he also began to pour baseball lore into my head. He was conversant on many subjects and not shy about expounding. The name of his barber shop was "Sika's Knowledge College."

After my Uncle Will took me to my first ball game on Memorial Day, 1927, Lou took me to another at his own expense. Boldly, the little man pranced me down past the reserved seats to the dugout rail and beckoned player-manager Bob O' Farrell.

Sika boomed out a "Bob-meet-another-Bob" greeting. I'll never forget the blue eyes on that bulky blond O'Farrell.

A year or so later, taking me to see the Yankees play the Browns, the jockey-sized Sika elbowed us to the visiting Yankees' dugout. He wouldn't leave until Babe Ruth signed my scorecard.

I was stricken in '27 with an emergency ruptured appendix, no piece of cake in the era before miracle drugs. But I've always been a lucky cuss, and six days later my Pop carried me home. While I was in the hospital, Lou Sika brought me a copy of "Baseball Joe at Riverside." The book was the first in a series of "Baseball Joe" stories authored by a number of writers using a common nom de plume, "Lester Chadwick."

Joe Matson captivated me. Hooked by the pilot, I followed Baseball Joe from his boyhood as a 15-year-old kid pitching for the Silver Stars at Riverside (located vaguely in New England), until Matson hung up his smoking glove and bat with the Giants, 13 literary years and 19 calendar seasons later. The books whetted my appetite for baseball and sharpened a writer's most valuable mental "muscles," i.e., the reading "muscles."

As suggested in research by book reviewer Jack Kavanagh of the Society for American Baseball Research, Matson was a "one-dimensional demi-god" who took a fictional journey from Riverside to Yale to the minors to the Cardinals and finally to the prideful Giants.

The authors didn't bother with first names, but you'd have to be out to lunch not to figure the identity of "Mornsby" or "Rheat." The authors did stray, amusingly, when they labeled a character "Rabbit Baskerville" to represent belt-high, basket-catching, shortstop Rabbit Maranville.

Joe Matson outpitched idol "Hughson" (Christy Mathewson) and outhomered "Kid Rose" (Babe Ruth). Matson had 27 strikeouts and five homers in a game! I can't remember if he threw more than 81 pitches. That would be the ultimate perfect game. All strikes. Not one ball hit into fair territory. No foul tips on strike three.

For my memories of Matson—"born in 1894 and died of over-achievement in 1928" as Kavanagh put it—I thank my folks and relatives—and Lou Sika. After I read the first, I relentlessly campaigned to receive additional Baseball Joe books. Many were the birthdays and holidays my wish was granted.

Lou Sika's love of baseball was a magnet pulling me toward my future career. He sponsored a Sunday traveling ball club for which he bought red-striped, tan background uniforms with red "Sika's Barbers" on the shirt front. I know Louie couldn't have had much money, but he had enough for baseball.

He took me on a couple of his team's road trips and let me be the batboy. Once in St. Louis's southernmost public park, Carondelet, the Sikas played a game during which I was hit directly on the forehead with a slicing line foul as I, riding the bench, toppled backwards.

Sika gave me my first baseball bat, a tremendous wagon tongue once wielded by Fred (Cy) Williams, a Notre Dame graduate who had been a home-run hitter with the Cubs and the Phillies.

I'd seen Williams hit against an exaggerated defensive shift toward first base and the right field foul line. I was impressed. How in the hell could Cy swing that big bat fast enough to pull the ball so regularly to right field!

When I grew older, Sika sponsored a ballclub for which I played and managed. Of course, I wondered how he could afford it. But that was Louie. The year before he'd given free haircuts to my Cleveland High School football colleagues when they retired by consecutive championships a rare public high school trophy called the Yale Bowl. A few years later, that patriotic little man gave free haircuts to all service men during World War II.

My athletic background later stood me in good stead as a writer whenever I saw a player carry on after a concussion— "dinged," as they put it, temporarily on what boxing calls "Queer Street."

On a hard, baked field, running the bases as always—hard, but not fast— I got a late hit-the-deck sign at third base and dropped so quickly in a slide that I banged the back of my head hard on the dehydrated diamond.

Groggily I arose, apparently unhurt, but so s-l-o-w-e-d that every step I took, every word I heard or every distance I traveled seemed to be out of proportion. A not-unpleasant dream.

After the game, I seemed to float home to a silent house because Mom and Pop and Freddie were watching a late afternoon Sunday movie matinee. I usually took a cold shower in the basement — hey, you never messed up Mom's house unnecessarily!— and then sat down to what she usually left in her beloved coiled General Electric refrigerator— a ham and cheese sandwich, milk, and her specialty, strawberry pie! In season,

Mom had strawberries for me in one form or another everyday. No wonder I got a schnozz almost as red as W. C. Fields.'

But this night of my concussion, the shower's cold water awakened me as if from a nightmare. Later, meeting my friends at the Virginia Avenue theater for the Sunday night movie, I asked if I had acted or talked differently. No, I hadn't, they said, which could mean I'm always confusing. But I do know that if I'd had a tough play to make, on or off the field, I would have had a hard time coming through.

One Saturday morning at Sika's College of Knowledge, while arranging to pick up his old uniforms for my new team, I walked in when Louie was barbering a man stretched supine, his face covered with a steaming towel.

Second base was the position I loved. Those who played it well were special to me. I begin expounding on my favorites, noting that, yes, Rogers Hornsby was getting old, but there still were Charley Gehringer and Frank Frisch and Billy Herman and Oscar Melillo and Tony Lazzeri and Buddy Myer.

By that time, the man in the barber chair had righted himself and removed the towel from his face. He had a long surname Sika used respectfully with a "Mr." prefix, indicating that the man was a respected and valuable customer. Sounded like Mr. Braunschweiger.

Anyway, Mr. Braunschweiger ripped into me by suggesting profanely that I didn't know my ankle from an elbow because I hadn't even mentioned Fred Dunlap. I was not aware of "Sure Shot" Dunlap, but from Mr. Braunschweiger's scolding, I realized I'd better do some research if I was going to be giving my opinions in public.

Frederick Dunlap, born in Philadelphia in 1859, died in poverty at 43 in 1902, five years before Lou Sika got to the States. Old Sure Shot was a $10,000-a-year player until his career ended in 1897, presumably because by then old Sure Shot was sure to drink shots.

At his peak back in 1894, Dunlap hit .412 and led the league in both home runs, 13, and runs scored, 140. He often played second base without a glove.

Sure Shot Dunlap? Sure, he was plenty good.

But he was no "Baseball Joe."

6

&

Major league baseball made a major leap into the American psyche in 1921 when a Westinghouse radio engineer, Harold Arlin, moseyed into Pittsburgh's Forbes Field and broadcast a very spontaneous radio play-by-play.

Daily broadcasts are continually appealing, especially to the elderly, handicapped, and unemployed. For all, and especially for the confined, the daily ball game is a narcotic, picking up or letting down a fan. Every summer day has a special hook—the baseball game.

From where I view the scene, Cincinnati's and Brooklyn's flaming red-haired Larry MacPhail deserves a sweeping bow for bringing up a lively cornpone kid named Red Barber, first to Crosley Field in 1934, and then to Ebbets Field in 1938.

But, foremost, I always credited Chicago as a city, and the baseball Wrigleys in particular, for first having seen potential value in "giving away" the ball game free. Prior to the Wrigleys, broadcasters in a two-team town aired only their team's home games.

Chicago had the most radio stations airing the Cubs and the White Sox. St. Louis didn't do poorly, either, though the old home town pulled the plug in 1934, in the depths of the Depression, joining cities that barred big-league broadcasts as unfair free-bee competition.

Shamefully, until that red-haired bull-in-a-whiskey cellar, MacPhail, came in from Cincinnati in '38, New York clubs had exercised a four-year radio blackout. MacPhail not only flouted the New York tradition, but he went one step further and sent Barber on the road for the Dodgers' away games.

Road games then were aired only by an announcer ad-libbing and fleshing out barebones ball-and-strike information provided from another city by a Western Union operator. As I recall, WU charged only $27.50 to dit-dot nine-inning service.

Based on the individual broadcaster's knowledge, imagination, and ability to flesh out the ticker-tape skeleton, the clitter-clatter of the game report could be exciting or, lamentably, often boring.

One within range of my pointed ears was pretty good and cuddly, articulating with a warm signature line when the Cardinals or Browns rallied to take a lead. Thomas Patrick Convey would purr, ". . . And the score, oh, the score!"

Thomas Patrick, eventually eased out at KMOX by CBS, did much to jazz up his home-game broadcasts, delivered from the old balcony-chair mezzanine level at Sportsman's Park. Tom even would invite favorite New York and St. Louis baseball writers to take a turn while he took a necessary hike for natural causes.

One day he returned just in time to hear the *St. Louis Times'* Sam Muchnick intone that the count on Jim Bottomley was "two balls." Quietly, Patrick suggested a better way to describe the situation.

Similarly, Patrick's KMOX successor and rival, France Laux, who would win early-day national assignments, was told that the inning-opening litany including a batter first up with the next "on deck" and a third one *"in the hole"* wasn't necessary or nice.

Especially with women listening, as I urged my mother to do during her heavy household chores, which included hand-ironing 21 shirts weekly for Pop, brother Freddie, and me. I told her she'd find Patrick interesting, especially after I watched him do an away game broadcast from KWK's rooftop offices atop the late, lamented Chase Hotel.

My guide to KWK was an uncle, Rufus Schoppe (Shop-ee), married to Mom's sweet older sister, Aunt Maggie. The Schoppes spoiled me, even though Aunt Maggie had a tough, six-day-a-week job as a tedious silk spotter for a dry cleaner. Her pay was $35 a week. Weekends I'd spend with her and Uncle Rufus at their cozy cardboard cottage. She'd whip up "egg bread," South Side Dutch for French toast, and Uncle Rufus' favorite beverage, hot tea.

I'd usually get a Saturday-evening stroll to a movie with one or both. If it was one, it was always Uncle Rufus. We usually would wind up at the indoor-outdoor Melvin Theatre. The indoor Melvin, amazingly, remained one of the rare neighborhood houses still in business in 1994. Like many other movie houses of my youth, the Melvin had an outdoor branch, useful during hot St. Louis summers. The only problem was that silent-movie patrons were annoyed more by buzzing mosquitoes than clattering streetcars.

The day Uncle Rufus arranged for me to see Thomas Patrick put on his entertaining road game broadcast at the Chase, a limited number of persons, mostly kids, formed a studio audience. It was appropriately noisy, the game I "saw," which was lost by the Cardinals at Brooklyn. At the seventh-inning stretch, each "spectator" was given a miniature ice-cream cup and a Coke, both dutifully acknowledged by the host on the air.

As a baseball broadcaster, in my opinion, Tom Patrick couldn't carry Jack Buck's "Ford Frick" award at Cooperstown or Harry Caray's or Joe Garagiola's or Milo Hamilton's. All those broadcasters had St. Louis stints on the air. I'd vote also for Bud Blattner, the former big-league ball player who teamed for a time with Dizzy Dean.

But Patrick was good for his time. He was a pioneer, helping his craft and its future as a bulwark for baseball. Thanks to his friendly, intimate touch, he was a Ladies' Day favorite. The free-gate for women became a promotional weapon second only to the kids' Knothole Gang. When women fans showed up at the ball park as weekly guests, Patrick was festooned with cakes and other yummies. Unfortunately, a ruptured appendix snuffed out his gin-weakened system much too soon in 1934.

Thanks to Patrick, Mom became a fan. She liked it when Patrick would chummy up nicknames, like when he'd call Rabbit Maranville "Bunny." Until she lost her remarkable memory late in her nearly 95 years, she followed the ball club daily on radio, TV, and in print.

Neither Mom nor Pop had much formal education. Fourth grade for Pop, sixth for Mom, but both read daily newspapers from cover to cover. Their diligence crossed my mind when I saw the journalistic arch completed between buildings at the University of Missouri in Columbia. The message was the philosophy of the school's founder and first dean, Walter Williams. Inscribed it reads:

"The Newspaper: Schoolmaster of the Public."

My mom's baseball "Bunny," Walter James Vincent Maranville, originated the belt-high basket catch used by Willie Mays among others, but was regarded as an overaged, dried-out alcoholic when he was called up by the Cardinals late in the 1927 season, 15 years after he'd first come up at Boston and 13 after he had helped shortstop the "miracle" 1914 last-to-first Braves.

Back in 1927, a season the dazzling Frank Frisch played both sides of second base, in effect, after Tommy Thevenow's broken leg brought Class B greenpea Heinie Schuble to play shortstop, Frisch thought an earlier call-up of Rickey's reclamation project, Maranville, might have won the pennant.

Another old teammate, acquired by the Cardinals early in 1928, native St. Louisan Andy High had an affectionate recollection of Rabbit. That '28 year, Rickey's mental gymnastics were worth a gold medal.

To aid in a right-field platoon system, B.R. obtained 37-year-old, lefthanded-hitting George Washington Harper from the Giants to vulcanize the ball club. When three of Harper's 19 homers came in a pennant-clinching series with New York, Harper, a .305 hitter, thumbed his nose at John McGraw!

Perhaps even more significantly, again early in the '28 season, Rickey dealt a hard-hitting young catcher, Virgil (Spud) Davis and outfielder Homer Peel for the Phillies' nimble fast-moving catcher, Jimmy Wilson, a wise guy in handling a pitching staff. It's a possibility that—for a distinct change!—the Cardinals sweetened the financial pot for the underfed Phil as well as picking up Ace Wilson's larger salary.

As for acquiring handyman High, both Rickey and boss Breadon were devious, aware that Rogers Hornsby had little love for either man, and the Rajah had moved into Boston from New York as player-manager. So the St. Louis brass suggested to young writer Ray Gillespie that he tell his friend Hornsby how much Les Bell wanted to play for Rog again. Les tailed off from his .325 season with 17 homers and RBIs for Hornsby's pennant-winners in '26.

The Redbird ruse worked. High came over, filling in occasionally for Frisch at second, but mainly alternating with righthanded-hitting Watty Holm at third. Smiling, too, late in life, Andy recalled how he learned from Maranville at shortstop to play a better third base.

The Cardinals' pennant-winning manager, Bill McKechnie, though only a good-field no-hit former player, was a sharp man who prided himself on position play. So he would motion High from the dugout, telling Andy where to move and how to play.

"I'd be caught between a rock and hard place," said High, later chief scout for the Dodgers. "Barely had McKechnie given me directions, then Maranville would overrule him. So, as he suggested, I moved again surreptitiously. Rab was uncanny."

Handy Andy High in the 1930-31 season.

The Cardinals won the 1928 pennant by two games, aided by a league call overruling the Giants' protest of a game awarded to New York even though Chicago catcher Gabby Hartnett obviously straddled home plate in a rundown without possession of the ball. I remember—and mention—because the victim base-runner was a popular name I'd heard the year before in Memphis, i.e., Andy Reese.

For the victorious Cardinals, sacrificial lambs to the vengeful Yankees of Babe Ruth and Lou Gehrig that fall, little lefthander Wee Willie Sherdel had his finest season of 13 with the Cardinals, 21-10, and Jesse Haines was a 20-game winner again. Ageless Grover Cleveland Alexander won 16.

At bat, a promising rookie, Wally Roettger, hit the ball hard and frequently until he suffered a broken leg. I saw that mishap as a kid, just as I'd seen Tommy Thevenow's similar injury a year before. Oddly, the baseman both times, was little Earl (Sparky) Adams, who eventually played on Cardinals pennant winners in 1930 and 1931.

Seeing Thevenow and Roettger break their legs was tough on my emotions, but McKechnie, coaching third base, was more affected. Years later when Bill was coaching third for the Cleveland Indians (1952) and the Giants' Monte Irvin snapped a leg in a slide, McKechnie refused to take a look. "I've seen enough, Thevenow and Roettger," said gentle Deacon Will.

McKechnie's Cardinals in '28 gave him a pennant to match the one he received three years earlier at Pittsburgh and foreshadowed the two more that would follow at Cincinnati in 1939-40. At St. Louis, Bill had a most productive left fielder in Chick Hafey.

But the bellwether that year was Sunny Jim Bottomley, whose season pleased Mom and just about every feminine fan. He was, indeed, the Ladies' Day favorite, good-looking and cheerful, his cap cocked rakishly over his left eye. And he had a swaggering walk.

Sexy? H'mm, when you're a 10-year-old kid not old enough to feel the urge and surge of the loins, you just don't bother with that. I didn't anyway. All I remember was Jim's bat grip, choked for a slugger, and a slow, easy-does-it swing that masqueraded his great power.

Bottomley, from nearby Nokomis, Illinois, had written Branch Rickey a simple letter asking for a tryout. At his first spring-training camp, viewing a long, slender bat used to stroke grounders and fly balls for infield and outfield practice, he studied the name. Puzzled, he inquired, "Mr. Sherdel, who's this Mr. Fungo?"

Bottomley acquired a crash-course education. His first big-league season, 1923, he hit .371. A year later he had a day no other player achieved for 59 years, until the Cardinals' Mark Whiten in 1993. Jim's "6 for 6" at Brooklyn drove in 12 runs.

Yeah, he was a hitting terror in the mid-1920s, but though he had a few higher batting averages, James Leroy Bottomley never had a season to match the .325 of 1928. Ninety-three of his 187 hits were for extra bases, including 40 doubles, 20 triples and 31 home runs. His slugging average was a robust .628, and he was a going-away choice for Most Valuable Player.

I passionately wanted to attend the ball game and scheduled official awarding of the MVP prize in 1929, featuring the dramatic presentation of $1,000 worth of $5 gold pieces in a canvas sack.

Funny thing, I could find no friend to go with me. Alone, at 11, I hopped streetcars in a complicated triple transfer manuever that eventually got me to Sportsman's Park.

There, with a vista of the ceremony's backside, I watched the presentation at home plate and was rewarded next day with a newspaper front close-up view I've encountered occasionally in Bottomley's photo file at the *Post-Dispatch*.   Sweet nostalgia.

When I worked in the Cardinals' front office as a part-time publicity man the summer of 1939, I saw Bottomley often and developed a friendship with the future Hall of Famer. He finally married, to the disappointment of many ladies in waiting, and endured a second-half season in 1937 as manager of the Browns, entrenched in the black hole of last place. His pleasure and leisure then was his farm at nearby Bourbon, Missouri, for which cooperating old boosters had contributed a milk cow. The contest to name a winner for the bovine beauty brought forth a winner: *Fielder's Choice!*

Sunny Jim Bottomley, a Ladies Day favorite.

In '39, Bottomley worked color on the late Tom Patrick's old station, KWK, teamed with a capable broadcaster, Johnny O'Hara. Bottomley as a commentator often invoked his homespun country humor, best exemplified by an incident one day in the big guy's playing career.

Cardinal trainer Harrison J. (Doc) Weaver, pleaded for a long winning streak. "Naw, Doc," Sunny Jim drawled, "that ain't the way to win. You win two, lose one . . . win two, lose one . . . and when you get up to 100 and 50, you throw the other four games away."

One summer night in '39, at a benefit slow-pitch charity softball game, Jim was playing first base for one side and I was a fill-in for the other. Based on years of not hitting anything that wasn't slow, I'd learned how to hit the soft stuff. Wait on the ballooned ball and, rather then jump out and pull the ball, jab it to the opposite field.

To my delight, I lined the ball just inside the right-field foul line, past the startled Bottomley. I recalled the old star's commentary as I passed him, en route to third base, chuckling when I heard, "Whatcha tryin' to do, Robby," wailed Bottomley. "Kill ol' Sunny Jim?"

The incident reminded me of the story Andy High told about the 1928 Series in which Babe Ruth and Lou Gehrig simply overwhelmed the Cardinals. The Babe hit .625 in four games with three homers. Lou batted .545 with four homers and nine RBIs. After the last Series game, Andy High met the Giants' Bill Terry and Edd Roush, two players of the National League runners-up who had seen the debacle.

They wondered how the Cardinals had pitched Ruth and Gehrig. "Outside" was the answer. Why, reflected the two players who had paid to see someone else play, why hadn't they tried to jam them inside?

"Because," said High, "we didn't want to kill Jim Bottomley at first base."

Mom liked that story. In fact, she grew to like baseball. She even volunteered radio reports. Like the time I asked her to give me a quick fill-in after the 1929 Series opened at Chicago's Wrigley Field.

When I rushed home from school, hurrying into my play clothes, Mom had broken the bad news to a National League fan. The A's had won, 3-1. I wondered, who pitched?

"A man with a funny name," Mom said.

Exasperated, I said, "Oh, Mom, Grove's not funny—Lefty Grove."

No, she was certain it wasn't Grove. So I insisted, "Then there's nothing unusual about George Earnshaw."

She shook her head. Wrong again. Annoyed, hurrying outside to kick a soccer ball or dropkick a football, I suggested that, gee whiz, Mom, if you're going to listen to a ball game, listen.

When Pop came home with the evening paper, he had all the details and startling news. Wily Mr. Connie Mack, the Philadelphia patriarch, was aware Chicago had a heavy righthanded-hitting ball club. He felt they might be fooled by a soft-serving, breaking ball pitcher throwing out of the white-shirted bleacher background. So with Grove warming up in the bullpen as a decoy, the A's manager placed his surprise pitching choice on the warmup slab in front of the dugout—seldom seen sidearming Howard Ehmke.

Outspoken outfielder Al Simmons grumbled. "Isn't that all right with you, Aloysisus?" Mr. Mack asked sweetly—too sweetly—and big Sim grunted an apologetic OK.

That day Howard Ehmke made history. Gaining what would be his last major-league victory ever, the rangy 36-year-old righthander sidearmed 13 strikeouts, then the World Series record.

When I came in from play, tired but hungry, Mom awaited. She named the pitching name she couldn't recall previously. "Wouldn't you say, Robert, that's a funny name," she said with sweet sarcasm, "Ehmke! E-h-m-k-e!"

7

&

Bill Veeck and I agreed over more than one cold one that 1929 and 1930 were the two most captivating years of our youth. The ball was lively, indeed, during these wonderful seasons. Hitters took over the game, swinging heavier bats and making more frequent contact.

Veeck, a 17-year-old kid spending the summer in the Waveland Avenue firehouse across from Wrigley Field, had the best of two worlds in '29. His "Daddy," as Veeck never stopped referring to his father, was general manager of the Cubs. After Pop Veeck acquired Rogers Hornsby from the Boston Braves for five players and $200,000, the Cubbies won the pennant.

One morning when rubbing pitching ace Pat Malone and slugger Hack Wilson out of a hangover from speakeasy schnapps, Chicago's veteran trainer, Andy Lotshaw, "Doctor Lockjaw," allowed as how he'd been a pretty damned good hitter in the minors himself. One word led to another before a grumpy Malone allowed as how Dr. Lockjaw was a slick old oversized windbag who'd rather be rubbing down Bronko Nagurski, anyway. Fact is, Andy couldn't hit the water if he fell out of a boat and . . . .

Well, sir, before you knew it, they were down on the field. Each ponied up a couple of hundred bucks to bet on Lotshaw's outrageous boast that he'd hit one over the fence off Malone, a 22-10 pitcher.

Pat warmed up briefly in the bullpen. Clad in a doc's frock, Lotshaw stepped into the batter's box—and hit Malone's first pitch over the left field wall and into the street.

Malone screamed that he wasn't ready. He needed to warm up more. It wasn't fair. Airily, with a shrug of his shoulders, Lotshsaw picked up the money and returned to his task of mending hung-over heads and battered bodies.

Yeah, those were the days. I judge 1930 as the most delightful season of all, though I was a kid of 12, not permitted out of knickers for another year. National League batters averaged .303. The Cardinals scored 1,004 runs, still a record, and won the pennant. The Phillies finished a dead-last with a 52-102 record even though they batted .315.

In mid-August, the Cardinals were in fourth place, only one game over .500 at 53-52. They dozed, even though Sam Muchnick had teased owner Sam Breadon into making a trading deadline deal for Burleigh Grimes, unhappy at Boston.

An owner who ran through managers like an early-day George Steinbrenner—five in a six-year period of four pennants—Sam Breadon announced he would stick with current manager Gabby Street in 1931. A droll, pipe-puffing former catcher and World War I sergeant, Charles E. Street was best known for having caught a ball dropped off the Washington Monument by famed batterymate Walter Johnson.

When Breadon announced Street was rehired, Brooklyn led the league, followed by Chicago and New York. Suddenly the Cardinals began to win, and the "Robins" waffled. They called the Dodgers "Robins" frequently then in tribute to long-time manager, Wilbert Robinson.

During the rest of the season, I hummed a lively song of the day with an appropriate title—"When the Red-Red Robin Goes Bob-Bob-Bobbin'-Along."

The Cardinals won four of five from Brooklyn at St. Louis, including one victory by Grimes. At the end of August, Joe McCarthy's defending champion Cubs moved into the League lead. At Wrigley Field, an explosive August-ending series symbolized the firepower offense of 1930 and taught a wide-eyed kid a competitive lesson.

Seven-and-a-half games out, the Cardinals battled 20 innings to win a spectacular opener, 8-7, as a result of a game-saving fielding play by Jim Bottomley, 12 magnificent scoreless innings of relief by Syl Johnson, and a pinch single by a little man with a big pinch stick—Andy High.

Ah, hah, the Cardinals were coming. Next day they held a five-run lead into the ninth, then—oops—blew it. Chicago tied the score. In the eleventh, Bottomley hit a three-run homer, but the Cubbies tied it again. Chicago won in the thirteenth, 9-8. The

Cubs flattened St. Louis in the third game, 16-4, helped by two Hack Wilson homers of his league-record 56.

My Redbirds had failed and fallen back. The lesson I learned, as Gabby Street put it, polishing off a reflection that probably goes back to when Pyrrhus was a pup, "Winners don't quit, and quitters don't win."

So bless Uncle Robby's balloon belly, Brooklyn surged and Chicago slumped. By the time the Cardinals moved into Ebbets Field they were only one game behind. Now came a low-scoring, change-of-pace game, which in the high-offense era made news with a capital "N."

This famous game had a comic opera beginning that featured Charles Flint Rhem of Rhems, South Carolina, a town named for his ancestor.

As a short-pants kid, I never liked Flint Rhem too much. Although a 20-game winner as far back as the Cardinals' first pennant year, 1926, "Shad," Flint's nickname, boozed away the greatness expected of him. But he was an imaginative man if not a great pitcher.

Scolded once by Gabby Street for an obvious losing bout with a bottle, Rhem defended himself by drawling, "Well, Sawge, ah was with Alex, and ah figuhed he was mo' potent to the club than me, so ah drunk the fastest and the mostest."

Scheduled to open that key series at Brooklyn, Rhem showed up missing. He reported the next morning and told an amazing story. He had been standing outside New York's Alamac Hotel the night before and had been "kidnapped."

"So help me, Sawge, those guys—obviously gamblers— drove poor Flint over to Jersey and stuck a rod to his head, forcing him to drink cups of raw whiskey, sho' nuf." Not until a reunion many years later in St. Louis did Rhem admit that the kidnapping had been fictional.

Flint's alcoholic indiscretion created a pitching rearrangement and, as a result, a masterful hookup: Bill Hallahan versus Dizzy Vance. The Dazzler, a big, ruddy Florida cracker, had been among the National League's best pitchers for years. Hallahan was a short, stubby left-hander, up and down for several years, at times as wild as Mitch Williams.

Good thing Hallahan pitched with his left hand, because in the excitement leading to the pivotal series opener, reserve outfielder Ray Blades slammed a taxicab door on Bill's right, mashing a finger.

The injured Hallahan pitched a masterpiece and was matched by Vance until Andy High pinch hit in the tenth for injured shortstop Charley Gelbert. Bang! High doubled to right and scored on a single by center fielder Taylor Douthit.

With Gelbert hurt and out of the game, third baseman Sparky Adams shifted to shortstop and High played third. With one out in the home tenth, the Dodgers filled the bases. Al Lopez grounded sharply to Adam's right. Sparky blocked the ball, dropped it, picked it up, and fired to Frisch . . . .

Years later, serving with me on the Hall of Fame's Veterans Committee, defensive master Lopez and a Hall of Fame master still didn't believe it. "I think," he said, "Frisch didn't catch Adams' throw, but just guided it around to Bottomley."

The lightning double play preserved a 1-0 victory, a man-bites-dog score in that run-making merry-go-round. It tied the race, the Cardinals won the next two and, winning 22 of their last 26 games— 39 of 40 from the time they were fourth and 12 out on August 8—the Cardinals reached the final weekend with a championship at hand.

They clinched on Friday. So the season-ending Sunday ticket for which I'd badgered Pop allowed me to eyewitness the debut of a lanky baseball legend.

By now, I needed no assistance when I sought an autograph, which was seldom. Before the final game, manager Street walked to a box seat occupied by St. Louis mayor, Victor J. Miller. I paused close by, taught by my parents not to interrupt.

I couldn't help but hear the mayor wonder aloud about the lanky 20-year-old rookie pitcher warming for the Cardinals that day. Said Street with a mouthful of prophecy, "I believe he's going to be a great pitcher, Mr. Mayor, but I'm afraid we'll never know from one minute to the next what he's going to do."

Which is, I submit, a bull's eye estimate of Jay Hanna (Dizzy) Dean, fresh up from Houston. That first day of Dizzy Dean's big-league career, Ol' Diz, as he would call himself before he threw his first big-league pitch at 19, three-hit lefty Larry French and the Pirates, 3-1. He singled, scored a run and got the game over in an hour and 21 minutes.

A few days later, I saw my first World Series game. After coaxing my folks for a buck for a bleacher seat and the freedom to play hooky, I left the house at 4 a.m. carrying a brown sandwich bag and made a couple of streetcar changes in the half-hour's trip to the ball park. Years later, Mom would wonder how she could allow her 12-year-old son to go out alone in the middle of the night.

I remember standing in a block-long line, awaiting dawn and the opening of the bleacher gates. A band began to play early on the outfield grass. And then the Cardinals appeared in brand-new uniforms.

I eye-witnessed the pivotal play of the pivotal game of the series. With one on in the Philadelphia ninth, Burleigh Grimes faced bulging-biceped Jimmy Foxx, the great first baseman. The last legal spitball pitcher, Grimes, always raised his arms in a stretch position and brought the glove and bare hand to his mouth, concealing the ball.

More often than not, he flicked spit on the ball, creating a scientific situation by which the pitch seemed to fall abruptly off the table, according to descriptions from those in its line of fire. The dipping fast ball nosedived into a sinker.

Square-jawed, cap pulled tightly on his head like a jockey, Grimes occasionally faked the spitter and threw a curveball.That's exactly what Foxx was looking for. As Double-X would explain later, Burleigh had struck him out once with that slow curve, and Foxxie was guessing he'd see it again. I'll never forget watching the ball arch majestically off the slugger's bat far up into the bleachers in left-center.

After the game, a western Missouri judge headed back for Kansas City with a carload of friends and stopped for gasoline on the outskirts of St. Louis. The filling station operator didn't have a radio and wondered about the score. "Jimmy Foxx 2, Cardinals 0," piped the judge, Harry S Truman.

Next morning, when I walked into the seventh-grade classroom at Mt. Pleasant School, the teacher wondered where I had been the day before. "The World Series, Miss Prindable," was my fortunate, honest answer.

Ethel Prindable smiled. "Good thing you told the truth, Robert," she said, explaining that she lived near the ball park on the north side and walking to catch a southbound Grand Avenue streetcar, she had seen me standing in the bleacher line.

Two days later, Hallahan, who had shut out the A's earlier, reverted to Wild Bill in a Series-ending loss at Philadelphia, where the players and their wives piled into a private bus for the short trip to Philly's North train Station. Back in the bus, a big rookie reserve outfielder named George Puccinelli sang softly, yet not quietly, "It's all over now . . . it's all over now . . ."

From the front, captain Frank Frisch growled. Grimes, seated next to him, leaped up, strode to the back and—Sam Muchnick told this one, not Burleigh—the old pro chastised the kid. "Listen, you big bastard, we all know it's over," Grimes scolded, "but we don't have to have it rubbed in."

Without Puccinelli, the Cardinals won another pennant in 1931, this time with an unusual—for St. Louis—12 1/2 game cakewalk. The repeat pennant season was marked by a double rarity. The club's left fielder, Chick Hafey, rangy and rapid, rawboned and rifle-armed, became (1) a serious enough holdout that he did not sign until the season was 10 games old and (2) the first man to win a batting championship wearing eyeglasses.

Hafey was most unfortunately underpaid, a victim in part of the Depression and the Cardinals' tendency to play Scrooge. He became so angry after a spring training salary hassle that he drove his 1929 Auburn from Florida across the Arizona desert to his chicken farm retreat in the mountains of Calistoga, California. His 90-mile-an-hour average speed more than 60 years ago across ribbon country roads still impresses me!

Chick Hafey in 1929.

Hafey sat out until opening day in 1931, then was suspended without pay until management deemed him ready to play, which was ten days later. Seething, he let his bat do his talking. Hafey was perhaps the most potent righthanded pull-hitter ever; Rogers Hornsby thought so. So did Pittsburgh's great-fielding third baseman, Pie Traynor. A lesser talent, Brooklyn's third baseman, Fresco Thompson, once took a lethal Hafey liner in the shin.

Next time Hafey batted, Thompson retreated to a deep third base. The fleet Hafey sized up the situation and beat out a bunt toward third. An inning later when Chick returned to the Cardinals' dugout, a vendor leaned over from the stands and called to him, extending an Eskimo "pie" ice cream delight.

"Mr. Hafey," the kid called out, "compliments of Mr. Thompson. If you'll bunt again, he said he'd send over another one."

Grimes had the courage of a bull dog and if he wanted to hit a batter, he did. Frisch could cream his spitball. And he was nimble enough to dodge Grimes' most intimidating pitches.

Once, in retaliation for a knock-down pitch, Frisch dragged a bunt toward first base, hoping to knock the sturdy Wisconsin lumberjack Grimes on his broad back. Instead, as he strode onto first base, Frisch spiked the pitcher's Achilles tendon and nearly severed it.

When Grimes next faced Frisch's Giants after a spell on the disabled list, Frankie apologized. Still, Burleigh drilled the first pitch into his back. Wincing as he trotted to first base, Frisch whined, "but, damnit, Grimes, I apologized."

Burleigh smiled. "Yes," he said sweetly, "but you didn't smile. I didn't think you meant it."

When Frisch and Grimes became teammates in 1930, they became good friends. With Grimes almost as fiery as Lefty Grove after a loss, Frisch once homered to save a game Burleigh thought was gone. After Burleigh stormed to the clubhouse in the ninth, Watty Watkins homered to tie the game and Frank Frisch, next up, homered to win it 2-1. A young St. Louis Star reporter named Walter W. (Red) Smith—yes, the Pulitzer Prize-winning Red Smith—summed up Frankie's unusual contribution. "It was," he wrote, "the longest home run in history because Frisch talked about it all the way from St. Louis to Boston."

Lefty Grove pitched the opening game of the 1931 World Series for Philadelphia, which undoubtedly would have won its third straight championship, except the Cardinals had a player by the name of Johnny Leonard Roosevelt "Pepper" Martin.

First time up in the Series, the hawk-nosed, wide-shouldered Irish-Indian prayed. "Please God," he asked, and smote the great Grove's fireball for a two-run double. His prayer was fully answered. During a spectacular Series, one of the most glamorous ever, Martin had 12 hits, including four doubles and a homer. He stole five bases, scored five runs and, though hitless the last two games, batted .500.

Happily, I saw Martin's best game, the second one. He was absolutely awesome. Pepper singled in the second inning and stretched it into a double. Next, he shocked the crowd and the A's by stealing third. When Jimmy Wilson lifted an outfield fly, Martin scored, and his Cardinals were one-up.

Later, Pepper singled, stole second, moved to third on an infield out, and when Charley Gelbert laid down a squeeze bunt, Pepper scored again, eluding catcher Mickey Cochrane's diving tag.

The ninth was jammed with drama, and I was a bug-eyed boy with a perfect view of the unfolding panorama. Despite the passage of 60-plus years, I see it all now.

With two on and two down, Cardinal pitcher Bill Hallahan went to a full count on pinch-hitter Jimmy Moore. Both runners took off, and Hallahan broke off a sharp overhanded curve that dipped into the dirt. Fooled, Moore swung and missed. Wilson scooped it up, flipped the ball into his bare hand, and arched it to where third baseman Jake Flowers stood. As an exhilarated crowd began to charge onto the field, home plate umpire Dick Nallin held his ground.

Nallin knew something I didn't. The pitch had hit the ground, and the ump had seen it. So had third base coach Eddie Collins, who raced to the plate and urged the retreating Moore to run to first base. When he got there, Nallin ruled him safe, and one helluva argument broke out.

The field was cleared of fans and, after a lengthy delay, the reluctant Cardinals were forced to take the field. Hallahan returned to the mound.

"Moon" rose to the challenge. Bishop popped a foul down the right-field side, near the temporary World Series seats. Bottomley drifted over, followed by Flash Frisch, galloping in hot pursuit.

Frisch kept yelling, "Plenty of room, Jim . . . plenty of room." Bottomley, heeding the advice, suddenly bumped hard into the low-slung wooden railing and almost teetered into spectators cowering away from him. He reached into the stands, made a backhand grab, and held the ball aloft.

As he trotted off with the Cardinals having won, 2-0, all of us cheering—from near or afar—Bottomley addressed Frisch. "What do you mean, 'plenty of room?,'" Bottomley mocked Frisch.

The Flash laughed and chortled, "You caught the ball, didn't you?"

Afterward, baseball commissioner Judge Landis nudged Pepper Martin in the Cardinals' happy clubhouse and said, "Young man, I'd rather trade places with you than with any other man in the country."

Pepper grinned his toothy, eagle-beaked grin and allowed in his nasal twang of the Southwest, "Why, that'll jest be fine, Judge, just so we can trade salaries, too."

Propitiously, almost prophetically back there at the World Series game I saw in 1931, the Cardinals appeared for the first time with uniform numbers on the back of their flannel jerseys. The red number on the broad back of Martin's shirt was "1."

He was, indeed, "1" of a kind.

Pepper Martin poses with a huge gourd shaped as a bat. At right is Al Simmons.

8

ë.

Pop made sure I lived a carefree youth with plenty of time to play ball. When he was 10, Pop had been forced to quit school. I can recall him saying, "I want Robert and Freddie to enjoy their boyhood. I had none. When they go to work, they'll never stop."

Tall for my age when I was 12 and 13, I was forced to play against public park "seniors" 14 to 16. So outmatched was I the first couple of years, they made me play "bunt short?"

Never heard of bunt short? A poor bloke forced to play between the third baseman and the batter for a lefthanded hitter, between first and home for a righthanded hitter. A bunt short had to be exceptionally alert, because most batters swung late against fastball pitching.

Over the years I got to play with some pretty good baseball and basketball teams, if only because I was smart enough to organize more talented guys to play on teams I managed. Naturally, I reserved a starter's role for myself.

At age 15, for instance, I put together a "midget" division public parks basketball team. Mom cut up the green cover of an old billiard table for our uniforms so we could be the "Shamrocks." In 1933, I was on the city championship team, for which I received (and still have) a thumb-sized loving cup.

Frank Frisch was named player-manager of the Cardinals in 1933. The next day, I went down with some older guys to have a morning workout at Sportsman's Park. Of course, I hoped to see the great Flash, but the tryout was worked by coaches Mike Gonzalez and Buzzy Wares. I hoped Gonzalez wouldn't back me into right field to get rammed by a goat tethered there to help keep the grass short. I never fielded better. The biggest reason: the big-league infield was like a pool table.

Afterward, smiling his silver-toothed grin, Gonzalez said to me in his cracked-ice English, "You fiel' hokay, boy, but you throw like old womang!"

A year later, I somehow earned my way into a baseball school playoff lineup. During the championship game, played prior to a regular Cardinals contest, I had a miserable day on the same smooth diamond. No one had been watching then, but now . . .

If you want to suggest I choked, be my guest. Our Soulard team didn't do very well against a Sherman Park lineup that included two future major leaguers, Joe Schultz and Jerry Witte.

Back in the Riverside Independent League, where I had been scared by a mule at the old Cow Field at age 13, I was a league "veteran" at 16, twice having played on a team good enough to win. Now, copycatting Frisch, I had to have my own team. I persuaded friend Louie Sika to pony up five precious bucks as an entry fee and a half-buck for our side's new ball every game.

Here, by trickery most fair, I was at my most smart ass best. Thumbing the rule book, I came across an archaic requirement that a pitcher deliver the ball with "one foot on the rubber and the other on or in contact with." Hell, even Dizzy Dean was spreadlegging his back (left) foot for momentum. So was our main pitching opponent, Frank Schmieder. I'd tried to get Frank on our team but had failed. Now he was my team's nemesis.

I convinced the umpire that Frank was breaking the rule and that any strike zone pitch we didn't swing had to be called a "ball." The ump enforced the regulation, and by the time I came to bat, Schmieder, teetering unhappily and ineffectively, hadn't got anybody out. In fact, he didn't get the new delivery down for a few weeks, and that gave my team a pennant-winning edge.

But as I approached the plate, Frank had an answer, "Down you go, you rulebook bastard." He hit me twice that day and always threw at me thereafter.

During the summers of America's great depression, our daily ritual at the Cleveland High School campus never varied. Older guys sought jobs in the morning, returned in the afternoon and, with some 20 of us contributing a dime a week each for baseballs, played a doubleheader every afternoon.

The scuffed and chlorophylled balls were sold to us by the Cardinals and Browns at a cost of three for a dollar.

Bob Klasek—called "Lefty O'Doul" because everyone had a nickname—would walk from 4500 south to 2700 north and trundle back with six baseballs in his pockets, a week's supply.

With working men added, we played three games on Saturday. Sunday was reserved for official, uniformed, league games elsewhere.

Great fun, and I'm sure it kept many an older out-of-work guy from going bad. We played all our weekday games without umpires. I recall, if barely, only one fist fight. I opened my mouth to tell a newcoming complainer to quit whining and—wham!— he bopped me.

Here I am at 16—I played because I managed.

I talked big and fought little as a kid. For all of Pop's physical background, he was overly protective. With a flukish high number of football deaths in 1931, he didn't want me to play football. When I sneaked out for freshman football before equipment was issued, my nose was bloodied and I tore my corduroy pants. Both Mom and Pop gave me what-for.

When I began to play soccer, Pop wondered what the sport was like. He'd seen me play a basketball game, so I lied that it was like "outdoor basketball." But one Monday morning the *Globe-Democrat* had two photos of me in action as a goalkeeper. The following Sunday, Pop slipped down to Carondelet park for himself.

At Sunday supper, he asked about soccer again, and I repeated my fib. "Why then," he asked, "were you out cold? I walked onto the field and you were stretched out after being kicked in the head."

"Look, Pop," I pleaded, "I've played close to two seasons, and this one is almost over. Heck, you never even let me roller skate or ride a bicycle for fear I'd be hurt, and really there are no football deaths now, so I hope you'll let Freddie play."

So I finished the soccer season, and brother Freddie was allowed to play football.

I won my one and only organized boxing match—to the surprise of me and my opponent. For a reason I've never understood, a fellow student, shorter, stockier and chisel-chinned, picked on me. Diplomatically, knowing he was taking up boxing at night school, I turned the other cheek until one day, as we crossed paths in the high school corridor, he gave me one insult too many.

I talked back and he took umbrage at my lack of respect. "Tonight," he insisted, "we fight . . . and bring a second." Gad, a duel!

Lining up my friend Tony Kreft as my second, I ate hurriedly on a night Mom happened to have steak rather than hamburger. I told her I had to hurry and why.

Pop wasn't home. She pleaded to no avail. As Tony and I chugged toward the school, Aunt Millie stood outside her house like a railroad flagperson, trying to talk me out of fighting.

No way, too late.

I changed into my gym clothes and stepped into the ring. The night-school boxing instructor refereed. I was scared stiff. But somehow in the midst of the first of three rounds, I came to the happy conclusion that Chisel Chin was a phoney.

If the steak and mashed potatoes hadn't begun to take a gastronomical effect, I'd have knocked out the bum in the third round. Yeah, I was glad the fight was over, but the guy never bothered me again.

As I showered after the bout, Pop charged into the gym. He had skipped dinner, annoyed with me and angry I'd upset my mother. "But, Mr. Broeg," said Tony Kreft, politely, "Bob won the fight."

Parental pride showing, Pop eased off.

Afterward, the family was scheduled to visit Mom's brother, Uncle Will, a doughty Irishman dying of lung cancer. Privately, in his bedroom, I gave him a blow-by-blow re-creation.

I boxed my only fight much better this second time around.

9

To grow up with a baseball player for a hero is good.

To become good friends with him is great.

His name was Frankie Frisch. Trying to imitate him as often as I did over most of my boy and teen years was as ridiculous as Frisch's immediate task of trying to make St. Louis forgive, if not forget, the trade of Rogers Hornsby.

Over the years, while I was growing up taller than Frisch—and skinnier, weaker, and *slower*—kids with whom I played teased me with the nickname of "Frankie Frisch."

Because Frisch turned around at the plate at a time few did, I learned to switch-hit, proving once more that I couldn't hit from either side. Actually, though, in view of my blurred left eye, it did make sense to switch from right to left, avoiding unnecessary head turning to follow those sweeping, roundhouse curves most kid pitchers threw then.

Years later, examined by a neurosurgeon, I learned I'd been born left-handed and had adapted myself into ambidexterity during the process of moving my baby toys from my flawed left visual side to the right.

I always wondered why other guys, even major leaguers, couldn't throw with the off-hand or kick or punt a ball with either foot or slide from the left or right side. Why, even fabulous Jackie Robinson slid on only one side!

How did I imitate Frisch? I wore his number 3 on my uniform, used his batting stance and preliminary wiggle, and, most successfully, perched my cap on the top of my head exactly as he did.

The Old Flash, his own shorthand for the Fordham Flash, was good and funny, charming company. He ranged from humor to ridicule, from gee-whiz humility to self-assured ego. He had the personality to argue shrilly with umpires all game long and drink friendly with them all night long.

One spring in an exhibition, Frisch was spiked in the big toe. His manager, John McGraw, wouldn't tolerate more than a day off. So infection created a problem. Dainty-footed, with small feet for his stocky build, Frisch always had to wear his baseball leather, kangaroo slippers a half-size larger on the wounded foot. As I recall, six and a half.

Conversationally, Frisch's voice was softened with the lack of the 'r' in his New Yawk accent. Both Frank and boss Sam Breadon pronounced the ball club as the "Cawd'nals." Sometimes Frisch would lament in agitation to me, "Crizzsake, Rohbutt, they talk about the slid-ah as a great pitch. Slid-ah, my ass. It's only a nickel curve. The Old Flash could hit one with his beah 'ahm." One moment Frisch could be a braggart. The next he could be genuinely humble and self-deprecating. For instance, one time the Brooklyn Dodgers changed pitchers against the Cardinals (after right-hander Hollis [Sloppy] Thurston had thrown three balls to him).

With lefty Watson Clark taking over, Frisch switched to the right side of the plate and, though he seldom struck out, took three called strikes—"only man ev-ah to take three pitches from each side of the plate without swingin' the damn bat."

Frank Francis Frisch was an amazing anomaly, born with a silver spoon in his mouth, yet a profane man who acted as if he cut his teeth on a brass cuspidor. Two words describe him—intellectual roughneck. He was a scholar and probably the most talented all-around athlete Fordham ever produced, and a leader. Frisch captained the baseball, basketball, and football teams, and also skied and skated.

I heard boys and men cussing when the Cardinals sent hard-hitting Hornsby to New York for Frisch in late 1926.

The city's grand poobahs didn't like it, either. In action unique, the St. Louis Chamber of Commerce denounced Cardinal owner Sam Breadon for having disposed of a championship manager whose batting average for five seasons had been more then .400. Angry citizens not only covered Breadon's Pierce-Arrow automobile agency with black crepe, but they also festooned his handsome west end home with the same. Private club luncheon friends snubbed him, and one sports editor, Jim Gould of the *Star*, vowed he never would cover another Cardinals' game.

The anger was understandable but exaggerated. Truth is, Frisch *was* as great as Hornsby— well, okay, *almost*, discounting my prejudice —and both men wound up in the Hall of Fame. Frisch was a good hitter, Hornsby great. The Flash was a great fielder, Hornsby good, especially pivoting on the double play. Both men could run. Actually, ribbed by a St. Louis writer about Frisch's speed, gambling man Hornsby offered to run Frisch from first to home for a $1,000 bet.

Although equally as competitive as Hornsby, if not more so, Frisch declined. "I thing Rog is probably right," he observed. Frisch was, however, a base stealer and Hornsby wasn't. The Flash was a fourth outfielder, roving far and wide for pop flies. The Rajah was weak on pop-ups.

For all of their rivalry, Frisch would come to Hornsby's defense on fly balls. "Rog," he would say with a devilish smile, "always felt the right and center fielders were paid to do something, too." J. Roy Stockton put it better. "Hornsby was unfamiliar with pop flies," Stockton once wrote, "because he hit so few himself."

The controversial Hornsby-for-Frisch trade resulted from an accumulation of resentment by his predecessor as manager, Branch Rickey, then general manager, and mainly with Big Boss Breadon. The Rajah made the mistake of telling Sam to take an exhibition game and "stick it" somewhere Stockton accurately described as "an utterly impossible disposition." Angry even after winning the World Championship, Breadon made Hornsby an offer he knew Rog would refuse. The trade followed.

Frisch-versus-Hornsby was a daily rivalry from spring training when they carried daily newspaper averages. Frankie hit .376 to .365 for Rog, but hell's bells, you didn't out-hit The Rajah for long. At New York in 1927, as the Giants finished third, Hornsby batted .361 to Frisch's .337.

Frisch didn't hit with Hornsby's power, but he led the National League in stolen bases with 48, at a time few ran. At bat, until he jammed his right hand in September and he couldn't grip the bat, his average would have exceeded his career high, .348. Afield, he was utterly spectacular, virtually covering both sides of second base after shortstop Tommy Thevenow was hurt and a rookie replacement (Heine Schuble) was inadequate. Frisch's record of 1,037 chances acceptance in 1927 still stands for a major league infielder.

Cardinals owner Sam Breadon and my boyhood idol, Frank Frisch.

Frisch was as funny as he was good. One day when Frankie flung himself into first only to have umpire Charley Moran, hands gripping his coat lapels, merely flick his left thumb in a boring "out" sign.

Frisch leaped to his feet, angrily, and shouted, "Uncle Charley . . ."

Moran interrupted. "Don't 'Uncle Charley' me."

Frisch persisted, "Damn it, Uncle Charley, when the Flash busts his damned gut trying to beat out a hit, crizzsake, don't give him that horsefeather little thumb flip."

Next time up, Frisch grounded routinely and strode into the bag an easy out. He remembered, gleefully, that Moran bent over and then up in an earth-to-sky gesture with his right hand and roared, "Y'er out—and does that satisfy you, Mr. Frisch?" The Flash grinned. "That's fine, Uncle Charley," he said, "just fine."

When Frisch returned belatedly from an extended ocean cruise prior to the 1932 season, a disaster was in store for him and the Cardinals. The Cardinals captain wasn't in shape. Some of manager Street's experienced veterans were gone and he no longer leaned on his others for advice.

To the observant eye of Roy Stockton, the Redbirds partied too much that spring. They nose-dived to seventh place, dropping from 101 victories to 72, and Frisch dropped under .300 for the first time since his first full season in the majors, 1920.

Frisch took oral and verbal abuse. I got joshed, too, as among his most ardent faithful. Time and again, he would merely jog out an infield grounder. Fans booed. Sid Keener of the *Star-Times* wrote that Frisch was "laying down" on Street.

To Frisch's professional credit, he submitted that criticism and others negative for his personal clips and files at the Cooperstown's Hall of Fame library. Also, Keener, ultimately director of the baseball museum, remained a good friend who couldn't wait for the Flash's annual visit to the delightful village on Lake Otsego.

Stockton took Frisch aside one day in Pittsburgh before Frank read Keener's original criticism and said, "They're saying unkind things about you, Frank, that seem true."

Startled, Frisch wondered if Street hadn't told the press that he was playing on two hamstring gimpy legs, i.e., Charley Horses? The answer — no!

Angrily, the player took the newspaperman to his hotel room, unbuckled his belt and dropped his pants, displaying two legs taped from knee to groin. "Crizzsake, Roy, on one leg I'm better than Jimmy Reese on two"— this a reference to an infield reserve who lasted only one year with the Cards— "so I don't blame the Sarge. Damn it, I don't want the old buzzard's job. But if I ever manage, you can bet your ass I'll let you know it if I use a player who is hurt." Parenthetically, Stockton recalled that Frisch did.

Street, sympathy on his side, wanted his captain fined $5,000, a whopping sum. Neither club owner Breadon nor general manager Rickey would fine their superstar.

By 1933, when Rogers Hornsby was 37 and out of work, Breadon and Rickey maneuvered to sign him as a player. After the season in 1932, the Cardinals' brilliant young shortstop, Charley Gelbert, had nearly blown away a leg in a hunting accident. Maybe Frisch could play shortstop and Hornsby second in a combination of keystone playing legends.

They tried, briefly, as best summarized years later by Frisch in merry recollection. Said Uncle Frank, "I could go to my right far better than to the left, and Rog liked to play close to the bag to aid his cross-the-chest, double play throws. So we camped around second base like a couple of conventioners . . ."

The result: Trade for light-hitting, sharp-fielding Cincinnati shortstop Leo Durocher. The Lip breezed aboard for pitcher
Paul Derringer, braying for more bucks from "Branch" when
even Mrs. Rickey didn't call the Mahatma by his first name
publicly.

Durocher helped, but not immediately, certainly not in a
July double-header at New York about a month after he had been
obtained. First, King Carl Hubbell, meal ticket of the mound,
shut out the Cardinals in 18 innings, 1-0, and then fireball-firing
right hander Bud (Tarzan) Parmalee powered his often wild hard
one past them in the dangerous twilight of the second game, 1-0.

Over the years, I have retained an appreciation for the
double-dip, 27-inning scoreless skunking that pretty well served
as a managerial swan song for Gabby Street.

In the gloaming of the Sunday second game, fearful
Parmalee might part his thinning hair, Durocher walked away
from the plate. "But you've got only two strikes," shrilled the
umpire. Grumped Lippy Leo, "You take it." Durocher was
forced to return.

In later semi-darkness, the great hitter of old, Hornsby,
walked up as a pinch-hitter and drilled a single to right field. As
The Rajah rounded first base and retreated to the bag, manager
and first-baseman Terry sauntered over and said, "Rog, you've
proved what I've said about you all along. You could hit at
midnight!"

Hornsby was too old for the major leagues' first All-Star
game at Chicago's Comiskey Park, but Frisch wasn't. At 36, he
was the fans' pick to play second base.

I merely listened to that first All-Star game. The Nationals
lost, 4-2, but I glowed under the dim lamps of the Cleveland High
bleacher group afterward that night. Frisch had singled and
homered. Uncle Frank had more ham in him than a hog farm.

"All they remember," he would fake a pout, "is that the
Babe homered. They forgot the old Flash."

Breadon didn't. A couple of days after the All Star game,
the Cardinals owner ousted Street and named Frisch. The player-
manager was a romantic, money-saving Depression-era device.
By the next July, 1934, all eight of the National's managers
played.

By his own admission, Frisch was a better manager when
playing. He was no hypocrite. After Prohibition was repealed, he

made sure beer was provided in the clubhouse. "I hope players will not drink to excess," he said, "but I'd rather have them cool out over a beer in the clubhouse than charge out of a shower and into a bar where they might get into mischief."

In 1933, Frisch said he hoped to use young work horse Dizzy Dean less often. "Mainly," said the Fordham Flash, "I want a hustling ball club, a team that will take the extra base the way Pepper does, a club that will run and slide and play as hard as Pepper does."

Or the way that Pepper Martin's personal inspiration and mine, Frank Frisch, had played most of the time, and as they did his first full season as manager, 1934, when the merry men in red became famed as the *Gas House Gang*.

10

One great lengthy thrill marked my passage from boy to young man.

The Gas House Gang.

Roughnecks. Stand-up comics. Carefree cutthroats. And in 1934, the second hottest summer in the history of St. Louis, they became World Champions.

The Gas House Gang.

As Dizzy Dean said of himself and, by extension, the team—they weren't "the greatest, but they were amongst 'em."

My hero, Frank Frisch, was their leader. Frisch had a pretty good cast of characters, including himself at second base. Pepper Martin, never quite so skilled defensively as his determined zeal would indicate, had moved to third, which he played without underwear and—ouch! —without a jockstrap, too.

Leo Durocher, great glove, weak bat, big mouth, was the shortstop. Fleet Ernie Orsatti, an occasional off-season double for Hollywood silent movie comic Buster Keaton, showboated in center field.

In right, Frisch had Jack Rothrock, a consummate professional and American League retread brought up from Rochester. Rothrock played the team game, hitting behind the runner as No. 2 in the batting order. He didn't miss a game, and his .284 average was deceptive because he hit 11 homers and drove in 72 runs, a robust figure for the second spot. And he gave Frisch what was unique in those days—three switch-hitters in the first five: Rothrock, Frisch and first baseman James (Ripper) Collins.

Collins had labored long in the minors in Sunny Jim Bottomley's shadow. Now the waiting proved worthwhile. The Ripper, who slyly plotted many of the Gang's hi-jinks, hit .333 with 128 RBIs and a league-leading 35 homers. He also batted .367 in the World Series.

Frisch's pride and joy was his young left fielder, Joe Medwick, who reveled in his nickname "Muscles." The Muscular Magyar or Hungarian Rhapsody, as pressbox poets put it, was quick to hit with both his bat and his fists.

Once, Medwick, just coming into his own that year at .319 with 18 homers and 109 runs batted in, tangled in the clubhouse with Collins. Frisch directed teammates to let them punch it out. Then he grabbed both, hugged them and made them shake hands. "C'mon, kiss and make up," growled the Flash, "you're on the same side."

To Dizzy Dean, Muscles Medwick didn't fight fair. As Diz lamented, "You start to arguin' with Medwick and, before you open your mouth, he whomps you."

Medwick did have a short fuse. One day in Pittsburgh—and Durocher loved to tell this one —Joe short-legged it on a fly just inside the left field line, permitting the ball to fall for a three-run double.

In the dugout, Dean lamented Medwick's lack of effort. One word led to a nastier one, until Dizzy, accompanied by brother Paul, clomp-clomped on the concrete with spiked shoes toward Medwick at the far end of the bench. Joe picked up his favorite brown bat and snarled, "Step right up, brothers, and I'll separate you!"

Next time Medwick came up, the bases were loaded. Lo and behold, Joe hit a grand-slam homer over the ivy-covered left field brick wall at Forbes Field. He trotted back to the bench, took a quick drink of water, then filled it with another swig and walked by Dizzy and spit the water on Dean's feet. Joe growled, "Alright, you big meathead, there's your three runs and one more. Let's see if you can hold the damned lead."

Frisch had brought back a former teammate, Mike Gonzalez, to coach the pitchers. Mike had caught Paul Dean at Columbus. "You stick with Pablo, Fronk, she can do," warbled the coach. But again and again and again in the early season, the lanky carbon copy of brother Dizzy was batted out.

Desperately, with the Cardinals hurting—veteran left-hander Bill Walker had suffered a broken wrist and Bill Hallahan was more Wild Bill than Sweet William that year —Frisch tried again. At a Ladies Day game with Mom in the stands in mid-May, Paul beat Bill Terry's New York meal ticket, King Carl Hubbell, 3-2.

That did it. Paul was off and running to a 19-win season. Meanwhile, his young batterymate, promising Bill DeLancey, filled in occasionally for Spud Davis. On Memorial Day at Cincinnati, DeLancey got four hits, including a homer on a change of pace about which Frisch had ragged him.

Reaching the bench, DeLancey plopped down close enough for Frisch to hear him say, "I wonder how the Dutch bastard liked that one?!"

The answer was a lot, because the aggressive catcher was Frisch's kind of guy. Dizzy Dean's, too. When Diz horsed around on the mound, DeLancey would strut out to him and threaten, "When I'm ketchin', 'Great One', cut out that shit."

Frisch would laugh in recollection about Dizzy. "He wondered how a little old infielder like me could tell a great big pitcher like him how to pitch," Frisch would chortle sarcastically. "Hell, he didn't know that I was flashing battery signs to DeLancey from second base, and he'd never second guess the kid."

Economics weren't good, either, when the top average salaries nationally were $8,800 for professional airline pilots and $8,000 for Congressmen. Frisch's $18,500 salary was double the $9,000 paid those 1931 World Series heroes Pepper Martin and Bill Hallahan.

Leo Durocher could bluster about his $6,500 salary, but I have the contract in which Rickey agrees to raise Leo's salary an extra $1,000 if the Lip will meet his obligations to an ex-wife, support their child and pay off numerous debts.

Dizzy, making $7,500 his third full year, threatened more than once to strike because rookie brother Paul, like freshman catcher DeLancey, was getting only $3,000.

Money was a problem. But these Cardinals knew how to have fun. Once while Frisch scorched them unmercifully in New York's visitors' clubhouse, Pepper Martin interrupted, "I've got a question, Frank.

"I was wondering, Frank, if I should paint my midget auto racer white with red wheels or red with white?" A laughing Frisch let that break up his harangue.

Sometimes Martin, using Collins as a navigator, would drop a sack of cold water onto Frisch's bald scalp at a hotel's outside patio. Frank would hustle into the lobby, only to find Pepper seated and seriously studying the newspaper stock market.

Frisch did tell bulging, blue-eyed Collins to stow that portable typewriter for which the Ripper was writing a regular column back home to Albany, N. Y.

But he'd never out-slick Hollywood's Ernie Orsatti, who set up shop that summer for the filming at Sportsman's Park of a baseball who-dun-it movie starring Robert Young and Madge Evans. Before a game, Ernie hit a pitch, rounded the bases and "collapsed," presumably shot by a villainous sniper, i.e., the groundskeeper who once had owned the ball club. The title: "Death on the Diamond."

When the ball club traveled and Orsatti wanted to wander, he would delight in fooling the Old Flash. Ernie would tip and schmooze hotel phone operators and repair to the establishment's supper club. When Frisch would make his phoned bed check, Orsatti would answer the re-directed call from a floor show table rather than from his bed. If Frisch detected background music, Ernie logically explained that, gosh, Frank, he'd fallen asleep with the room radio on—again!

Yes, Frisch the manager took his share of his men's mischief, but they delighted him with their hi-jinks. Especially Ladies Day, when Martin and Dean built a small fire in front of the dugout in 100-degree weather. Said future Hall of Famer Al Lopez coming with his Boston teammates from the cool of the ocean into the cauldron of Sportsman's Park, "Cripes, they'd psyche you even before Diz threw a pitch or Pepper threw a ball at any opposing player who had the temerity to bunt against him at third base."

Pepper had a strong arm and so did Frisch. I'd love it when, ending infield practice, they played "burnout." Maybe Pepper was a diplomat. He retreated away from the faster-reacting Frisch's firing throws before finally climbing into a box seat. The crowd loved it almost as much as the tricky sideline "Pepper" game orchestrated by Pepper.

The game of burnout became burned-up as the players reacted to the Dean brothers' August strike which began when the Dean brothers did not show up for a train trip to Detroit for a fund-raising exhibition. Frisch, who had played 18 tough innings the day before, fined Dizzy 100 bucks.

The pitcher angrily tore up his uniform. A late-arriving photographer asked him to tear another. Dizzy obliged. Club treasurer Bill DeWitt promptly sent him a bill for $36.

Frisch suspended Dizzy. Brother Paul urged the Great One, "Why don't you pop the Dutchman, Jay?" Dizzy sneered, "Let Frisch sew up the uniforms. I hear he's good with the needle and thread." Frisch called a clubhouse meeting, pounded his glove and insisted, "Damn it, nobody, but NOBODY is better than this game."

The Cardinals responded magnificently. Bill Walker returned from his broken wrist. Bill Hallahan came out of his slump. Two pitching geezers past 40, Pop Haines and Dazzy Vance, helped and so did right-hander Tex Carleton, who didn't like Dizzy, anyway. With Pepper Martin hurt, Frisch had moved to third base and placed graceful young Burgess Whitehead at second.

One August day, I managed the price of a bleacher ducat for a doubleheader against Philadelphia. The first game began without Frisch. Commissioner Landis had come to town to make certain the Cardinals weren't taking advantage of the brothers Dean. By the time the hearing ended and the Judge had decided Diz was out seven days' pay plus 36 bucks, third-string catcher Frank (Father) Healy was standing in for Frisch at third base.

By the time 24-year-old Healy came to bat in the first inning — he hit only 13 times that season—Frisch came charging out of the Cardinals' dugout, buttoning his uniform shirt. Frank pinch-hit for Frank, got a base hit and starred in a double-header sweep.

Inspirational, sure, but on Labor Day I sat sorrowfully at the radio in the house of Uncle Will Wiley's widow and heard the Cardinals drop a twin bill at Pittsburgh. They were seven back with only 28 to play, down and certainly out, but . . . .

At Brooklyn, beginning their final eastern swing, Frisch raved, "Don't quit on me, you blockheads. Back in 1921 when I was here with the Giants, Pittsburgh thought they had us buried, and, hell, Pop and Pepper and Bill can tell you about 1930."

They cut into the lead at Brooklyn. Then to New York, where they won three out of four. Back again to Brooklyn to make-up a rained-out double-header. Dizzy Dean pitched a three-hit shutout in the first game. Paul Dean fired a no-hitter in the second game.

Brooklyn manager Casey Stengel moaned, "Eighteen innings coaching at third base, and I ain't seen a friendly face all day." Dizzy's comment became an oft-quoted classic:

"Gee whiz, if I'd-a known Paul was going to do it, I'd-a done it, too."

The Flash couldn't use the Dean brothers every day. But he tried. They pitched five of the last nine as the Cardinals closed on the Giants. They were two out with four games and a wedding to go.

That final week, to general manager Rickey's delight and manager Frisch's annoyance, shortstop Durocher married Grace Dozier, a chic dress designer. Best man Ernie Orsatti juggled the rings during the ceremony.

After the wedding, it was back to the pennant race. Beaten twice at Philadelphia, the Giants lost the next-to-the-last game of the season to the Dodgers. Van Lingle Mungo beat Carl Hubbell, 5-1. The same day Paul Dean won No. 19 over Cincinnati, 6-1. It was the third straight win for the Cards, who were now one up with one to play.

Before the game was over, we knew the Cardinals had won the pennant, a result of an 8-5 Giant loss to Brooklyn. Then Dizzy Dean—"ol' Diz," at just 23 —shut out the Reds, 9-0. The city's reaction reminded me of the 1926 celebration; whistles blowing, sirens sounding, cars honking, rumble seats rumbling.

First baseman Rip Collins led the team in song with an appropriate number from Ruby Keeler's show, "Forty-Second Street." "We're in the Money" meant exactly that, virtually tripling the skimpy salaries of $3,000 minimum for rookies P. Dean and DeLancey.

No wonder, as they told me, the guys whooped it up that night at Jim Mertikas's Grecian Gardens, a lovely restaurant in the disintegrating neighborhood that now houses Busch Stadium.

They could handle anything except florid-faced, 43-year-old Dazzy Vance's "Dazz-Marie," a blockbuster drink that necessitated a king-sized, ice-laden glass with rye, bourbon, Scotch, gin, slow gin, vermouth, brandy and Benedictine, dolloped with powdered sugar, stirred and topped with a single cherry. Nobody dared try it except the Dazzler himself.

The great Gas House Gang drew only 334,866 the entire season, almost a third of it during the final week. Few folks could afford a baseball buck in that depression year. St. Louis' one-year radio play-by-play blackout didn't help either.

I was so needful for the chance to *hear* a World Series game that in an instance of psychosomatic hypnosis, I talked myself into a helluva bellyache while walking toward high school the first day of the World Series at Detroit. I retreated home, not fooling dear Mom. She insisted I swallow a heaping tablespoon of a vile medicine called "paregoric."

But I willingly—ugh!—paid the price.

Before the first game, 30-game winner Dizzy Dean was asked to have breakfast with tycoon Henry Ford at Ford's Dearborn mansion. Ford had purchased the World Series radio rights for a whopping $150,000.

Actor-columnist Will Rogers, the former cowboy who had become Hollywood's biggest box office star, went with Dean as an amused friend of the precocious pitcher.

"Now, Diz," one old son of the southwest said to the younger, "Mr. Ford is a correct person. He'll call you Mr. Dean. So-o . . ."

Mr. Ford answered the doorbell himself, greeting Rogers and "Mr. Dean." Dizzy grinned and blurted, "How ya, Henry, put 'er there. I'm sure glad to be here 'cause I heard so much about you, but I'm sorry I'm a gonna have to make pussycats out of your Tigers."

Young writer Ray Gillespie, also invited, winced with Rogers, but that was Dizzy Dean, all right. That afternoon I only listened—TV came along too late for Frank Frisch's colorful characters —Dizzy draped a tiger skin around his gray uniform with the red number "17." He swiped a pre-game field band's tuba and oom-pahed for the photographers. Then he beat Alvin Crowder, 8-3, in a game that would have been more pleasant for me if Frisch had gotten more than one hit.

Frisch, trying to take pressure off the younger Dean, pitched southpaw Bill Hallahan against the Tigers' predominantly left-handed hitting lineup. It was a good strategy, spoiled only because an error cost the Cardinals a 12-inning game, 3-2.

With my trusty bleacher buck and my traditional middle-of-the-night streetcar ride, I had a seat for the third game. Paul Dean beat Tommy Bridges, 4-1, and Uncle Frank delivered two hits, one of which drove in a run.

The Saturday game, won by Detroit in a 10-4 cakewalk, featured a famed moment when Dizzy Dean, pinch-running for

Spud Davis, tried to break up a double play by compelling Tiger shortstop Bill Rogell to arch his pivot throw over Diz's head. Not if the shortstop has got guts. And Rogell did in a rough-and-ready Series. Bill hit Dean right smack in the forehead with his throw, failing to complete the double play, but . . . .

When they carried off Dizzy on a stretcher — a newspaper headline said, "X-Rays Show Nothing"— brother Paul knew Diz would be all right.Why?

"Because he was talkin' and sayin' nuthin'!"

Frisch tried to defend the obvious second guess for having permitted his most valuable player— and the league's that year — to pinch run. "For one thing," Frisch was quoted, "we have only a 21-man roster. For another, Spud is slow and Dean, a helluva good athlete, is fast."

"For another" —and here the manager threw up hands and sighed — "the hard-playing S. O. B. was down there on his own, running for Davis."

Dizzy spent the night in the hospital. He pitched the next day, but lost a well-played game, 3-1. Brother Paul won the sixth game back at Navin Field. Durocher delivered three hits, and Paul knocked in the winner for a 4-3 surprise that sent the Series to Game 7.

Frisch would recall in a bull session years later that he stalled when entering the visitors' clubhouse, lighting a cigarette, removing a perspiration-soaked sweatshirt and the spiked shoe from the tender foot of the old spike wound. "Who'll pitch tomorrow?" reporters wondered.

"Hallahan," he said.

Frisch, showering late, permitted an argumentative Dean to follow to the water. Uncle Frank recalled, "I wanted Diz to want it badly enough so that he wouldn't sit up and swap stories with Will Rogers or show off for his friends, of which he had too many. Finally, I said, 'All right, Jerome' —Rickey also called Dizzy by his supposed first name —'you're going to pitch.'"

"BUT"— and his verbal but was bigger than his aging athletic butt—"I want you to promise the Old Flash that you'll get a good night's sleep because I'll tell you something, my young friend: You win this damned game and, Depression or not, you'll be able to write your own ticket for $50,000 or more in extras."

Promises, promises, and the climax of an incredible World Series in which the Tigers played rough, but, heck, that was right down the Gas House Gang's back alley. Conversationally and competitively, the merry men in red were more aggressive.

They had heard Detroit's young pitching ace, Schoolboy Rowe, inquire on the radio to his Arkansas sweetheart, "How am I doin', Edna?," and, man, they butchered Schoolie for that one. When Pepper Martin slid roughshod into wounded warrior Cochrane, putting the catcher-manager into a hospital overnight, a newspaper photo caption listed Black Mike as "Our Stricken Leader." The Cardinals' bench jockeys singed Cochrane's jug ears over that one.

Surprisingly, Detroit's silk-smooth second baseman, Charley Gehringer, committed three errors. Frisch hadn't hit and had erred twice himself. Time and again, Detroit's JoJo White, had dumped the old Flash savagely with slides.

Durocher, admiring Frisch's silence, volunteered finally to cover the next time. The manager said "No, let's both cover." When White slid next time, Frisch put chiropractic pressure on JoJo's back, and Durocher plopped heavily on the Tiger's head.

Before the seventh game, as Auker warmed up with the unorthodox ground-scraping delivery that had defeated the Cardinals in the fourth game, Dizzy walked behind him as he crossed the field from the third base side. Pausing, Dean spoke up, "Hey, podnuh, you don't expect to get anybody out with that shit, do you?"

Back at Cleveland High School, as I left one classroom for another, I ran into some students who had been listening to the game. Eagerly, I asked, "What's the score?"

Deadpanned, one said, "Scoreless— and Frisch just hit into a double play."

Liar! Uncle Frank hit a three-run double! The Cardinals scored seven that inning and the World Series brawl was nearly over, delayed only by a seventh-inning fiasco in which Medwick, tripling for his 11th Series hit, tangled feet at third base with Detroit's Marvin Owen and kicked at Owen. That did it for unhappy Detroit fans.

In what Roy Stockton labeled the "Battle of Produce Row," fans from the towering left field stands showered the field with apple cores, banana skins, hard-boiled eggs, leftover lunch and other items that were passed up to the stands by street vendors.

Defiantly, No. "7," Jersey Joe, stood there, hands on his hips, a discreet distance from the fence. Finally Durocher came out to him and put his arm around Medwick's shoulder. "They can't do that to you, Joey," said the Lip. "Don't back off."

Snapped Medwick, "If you're so damned brave, why don't you play left field and let me play shortstop?"

After considerable delay, Judge Landis threw Medwick out of the game, rather than forfeit it to St. Louis. Hopefully, if the game had been close, the commissioner would have acted differently. One thing the Judge did get out of the delay before he acted was an opportunity to study how Pepper Martin spit tobacco from between his teeth. Privately, asked why he had left his front row, chin-on-the-rail seat to talk to a friend a few seats farther from the field, the Judge said happily he had passed along the good tidings that—patooie! — he now knew how to squirt.

As for Medwick, who slammed his glove angrily into the dugout, Detroit detectives face guarded him throughout the rest of the day. They even had dinner with Muscles and Hallahan in their room before spiriting Detroit's Public Enemy Number One into a St. Louis-bound train at midnight.

Frisch added a postscript years later. "You know," he said, "no matter how big and angry that crowd was, if they'd let Joey stand out there with that big black bat, the odds would have been even."

Dizzy and his brother Paul won 53 games —30 for Dizzy in the regular season and 19 for Paul, plus two each in the World Series. A year later, with Dizzy winning 28 games and Paul 19 once more, the brothers Dean were great again.

In my judgment, the 1935 Gas House Gang was a better team then the '34 edition. The '35ers won one more game with rookie Terry Moore in center field.

In 1935, I was visiting my Uncle Rob in Chicago and attended a Fourth of July doubleheader when the Gas House Gang earned its nickname. They swept two from the Cubs and repeatedly bowled over their rivals on the bases.

Both teams took midnight trains out of Chicago that night. Acerbic Chicago sports writer Warren Brown walked through the quiet railroad Pullman and purred to the Cubs, "What's the matter, fellas? Afraid Pepper Martin's on the train? Better stay on your side of the tracks or the Gas House Gang will get you."

With the Cardinals' longest winning streak ever (14) and a Labor Day doubleheader sweep putting them in first place, far ahead of last year's pace, I was thinking repeat pennant. The Cubbies had the last laugh, though, with one of the most remarkable finishes ever. From Labor Day on, they simply never lost.

The Gas House Gang died hard. Down the stretch, the oldest regular, Frisch, nearly 38, and the youngest, Moore, 23, were the hottest hitters. The old Flash, boosting his average from .260 to .294 in a season of limited play, hit .400 in September. Tee Moore had a hot .500 spell until he suffered a broken leg the final 10 days, most harmful because Orsatti's move to center field was damaging defensively.

The Cubs had won 18 in a row and were only two behind when they arrived in St. Louis for a five-game season-ending series. The Cubs were hot, true, but the Cardinals had won 13 of the 17 times these two teams had met in 1935.

I pleaded with Mom that I'd seen the Cardinals win 18 times without defeat. Please, Mom, let me skip school . . . .

The Cubs won the first day and my pleading escalated. Mom finally figured a way I could play half-a-day hooky and I was on my way—with seventy five cents and a borrowed schoolboy band member's pass.

When I arrived at Sportsman's Park, the weather was as damp as the Cardinals' pennant chances. I went to the press gate, more appropriately "pass gate," where band members would pass through. The young man in charge turned me away. "But I play the horn," I pleaded with a forgiveable lie. The man at the gate could have made a helluva St. Peter. The band season was over, he said, and the kids' pass list was suspended.

There I stood, shaken as I fondled the change in my pocket. Let's see — if I spent 60 cents for a bleacher seat, a nickel for a scorecard and . . . uh, used a dime for the several mile streetcar ride home, I'd have nothing for lunch.

Of course I went to the game, hungry or not. But my sacrifice was to no avail. The Cubs won both games and the pennant. The Gas House Gang had run out of fuel.

Afterward, I hung around waiting for Frisch to come out the Spring Avenue exit. Finally, he hurried out, understandably frowning, accompanied by his coach and good friend, Mike Gonzalez. A taxicab awaited.

Throatily—I remember my emotional farewell to the Last Hurrah and the Last Gasp of the Gas House Gang—I grumbled,

"Tough luck, Frank."

I hopped a streetcar with darkness closing in. When I got home, Mom waited. She was both disappointed and angry.

"You and your winning streak," she sputtered, one hard loser to another. "You and Frisch. And you're late for supper!"

The 1934 Gas House Gang: Dean, Durocher, Orsatti, DeLancey, Collins, Medwick, Frisch, Rothrock, and Martin.

11

Two cents for each of four daily newspapers when I was a kid. Everlasting gratitude to Alice and Robert Broeg whose generous use of hard-earned money purchased the world for me.

Shortly after I was born, the *Globe-Democrat* bought the *Republic*, leaving St. Louis with only one morning paper. The *Post-Dispatch* had the *Star* and the *Times* as afternoon competitors.

I was 14 when the *Times* folded in 1942. Even as a kid, I felt the loss. But my heart was closer to the *Post-Dispatch* because of an elementary school teacher.

Mary Culver taught me in third and fourth grades. Miss Culver was a strong baseball fan, fascinated by the baseball stories I wrote for our mimeo school paper. She called me into her classroom during my last term in school and inquired whether I had read Ring Lardner's "You Know Me, Al." I had. Miss Culver nodded and asked if I read J. Roy Stockton of the *Post-Dispatch*?

I grinned. My favorite writer. Well, she knew Stockton's two sisters, both school teachers. If I liked, she thought she could arrange a meeting. "Yes," I answered enthusiastically, "yes."

She did, and I met Stockton sometime later in the ornate lobby of the *Post-Dispatch* building. Tall and handsome at 40, Stockton was smoking a pipe.

J. Roy introduced me to a thin-mustached man a few years older than me. Amadee Wohlschlaeger took me to the busy composing room, arranged a line of type with my name and gave me a weighted copy of the *Post-Dispatch's* traditional Page One wise-cracking Weatherbird.

Stockton rejoined me for the elevator trip to the lobby and asked me to name my favorite player. Why, Frank Frisch. "Mine, too," he said, adding that if I would call him the following summer he would arrange for me to meet the Fordham Flash.

Ah, what a prospect!

In the summer of 1932 I phoned Stockton and he met me at the press gate, but he called me "Norman," obviously thinking of another kid with journalistic aspirations.

He informed me that with the way the Cardinals were floundering, and Frisch in his worst season, and the ball club in a first-to-sixth plummet, he didn't think it wise to invade the clubhouse. Though I was disappointed, I was grateful to see the game. After that I didn't have any more contact with Stockton for many years.

The man who helped me the most was a colorful Cleveland High School football coach, Bert Fenenga, truly a legend in St. Louis. Fenenga grew up in the Dakotas wearing wooden shoes and living in a series of thatched roof houses with dirt floors.

Physically, when coaching football, he cut an amusing sight. Tall, pot-bellied, bird legged, he would come in from practice wearing old canvas football pants, a faded stripe-sleeved orange and blue jersey and white basketball shoes. Many a time, he would step onto the basketball floor and, standing at the free-throw line, arch a hook shot made possible by the damndest stiff arm from the other hand.

A teacher of public speaking, he was forceful when emoting from his desk, whether delivering Lincoln's Gettysburg Address or the emotional lyrics of Edgar Allan Poe's "Bells."

Although he taught all sports, Fenenga loved football and was clever at finding loopholes in the rules. For instance, Fenenga positioned *three* players with their hands beneath the center's crotch. When the ball was snapped, they peeled off in opposite directions, completely flummoxing the defense. Ergo, a change in the rules—only one offensive player can stand behind the center.

Prior to hashmarks, a runner going out-of-bounds required the next play to begin only a yard from the sidelines. Fenenga fashioned an unbalanced line for this circumstance, in which the center, as end man, could be pass eligible.

Or—and this took the frosting if not the cake—Fenenga taught his quarterback to toss up the ball near the sidelines and have his charging fullback fist the ball forward out of bounds. This play was guaranteed to gain several yards, maybe more. You see, until the old coach found the underbelly, regulations only forbade advancing by "throwing" the ball out of bounds, not punching or pushing it.

Coach Bert Fenenga before I met him in 1932.

On the practice field, Coach Fenenga carried a willow switch and, if he saw fit, required a miscreant to bend over and take a stinging flick across the buttocks.

He treated me kindly when I served as first "assistant student manager," then "manager," i.e., waterboy for his Cleveland teams that won successive St. Louis Public High School League championships in 1932 and 1933, clinching a handsome huge silver bowl donated to the school system by Yale graduates back in 1915.

By 15, forced for two years to play with older boys, I now would be too tall for city summer playground softball. But good ol' Coach Fenenga permitted me to slump under the height marker without the usual straighten-up knee to the crotch.

My first time up in the softball league, facing fast-firing Freddie Diaz of the Spanish colony Blow School area, I hit the ball to right-center for a double. At second, I stood there, smiling to myself. "This," I thought, "is what it's all about." And it was.

My senior year in high school, Coach Fenenga let me play on the baseball team and pitched batting practice to me. He prided himself on a change-up, but my slow reactions coincided well with its arrival at the plate and I consistently hit it solidly. Fenenga let me coach third base and used me a few times as a pinch-hitter. And I even got a couple of hits!

One led off a ninth inning of a game in which Cleveland trailed Blewett by four runs in the ninth. We rallied for seven runs. I replaced Charley Buffa at second base for the home half of the ninth. Blewett filled the bases on the windy spring afternoon. With two out and everyone running, I fought a high, fluttering fly ball, but made the catch.

I was pretty full of myself until next day at a squad meeting when Fenenga put the squad into uproarious laughter by reprising — and imitating— my rubber-legged stagger.

But he was a good friend and a brilliant person. In World War II he helped displaced European aristocracy while working for United Nationals Rehabilitation and Relief. Later, he was borrowed from the school system to bail out a bad situation at the Missouri's State boys' reformatory at Boonville. Fenenga and Branch Rickey were close friends. Bridge partners, in fact. The coach suggested I write a piece on the great B. R., general manager of the Cardinals. He phoned and arranged my visit.

My interview with Mr. Rickey in his ballpark office in the fall of 1935 was brief but good. The cigar-chewing, rhetorical master corrected me when I asked about "farm" clubs. "We refer to them as 'subsidiaries,'" said Mr. Rickey.

Branch Rickey explains the finer points of baseball to Pepper Martin.

When I asked him about favorite players, he told me a graphic story about Austin McHenry, a young outfielder who had batted .350 in 1921. A year later at New York's Polo Grounds, Rickey, then manager, watched in dismay as one fly ball after another fell behind his gifted athlete. Alarmed, he took McHenry to a doctor. Brain tumor. At only 27, Austin died.

In my story for the Cleveland school paper, I described Branch Rickey in my opening paragraph as "the smartest man in baseball." I really believe he was— then and before and since— though I never did become one of his many sycophants.

My story prompted him to promise a summer job in 1936, before I enrolled in college the next fall. Mr. Rickey was at a loss as to the specifics. He urged me to see the Cardinals' traveling secretary, Clarence Lloyd, when the ball club returned from spring training on an early April Friday, the day before the spring series with the rival Browns.

Harold Tuthill, covering prep sports for the *Post-Dispatch*, had me cover an occasional high school event. I had known Tuthill virtually from the time I first set foot in old Public Schools Stadium, where city league games were played for years. I high-tailed upstairs to the pressbox and, wondering how I could be so pushy, befriended tubby-tummied "Tut."

In the spring of 1936, Tuthill arranged for me to cover Public High School League baseball triple-headers, Saturdays at the stadium. I'd file brief stories for the Saturday afternoon editions and the first Sunday edition of the *Post-Dispatch*. Then I'd hop a streetcar on Kingshighway for the long trip downtown. There, in the *Post-Dispatch* offices, I'd wrap up the three games.

I'd pick up the paper on Sunday morning and find my work re-written or shortened. The *P-D* was paying me $7.50 a week then, an adequate amount for the times, but they weren't paying space rates.

I also wrote for the *Neighborhood News*, a free-delivery weekly published in south St. Louis by a former printer, Ben Nordmann, and his passel of talented children. I'd met Mr. Nordmann when a friend took me on an excursion boat for a Chippewa-South Broadway Businessman's evening outing. Friend Frank (Bill) Ries told him my hopes. Sneering, dear Ben told me I was a fool for seeking a reporter's future when the only newspaper job worth a damn was in advertising.

Politely, I bristled. Kindly, Mr. Nordmann offered me a chance to write a weekly column for him, 10 cents an inch. You can bet I wrote a column's worth —two bucks— and did so even while away at college my first year.

Finally, hallelujah, April came and I was off to meet with Mr. Clarence Lloyd, per Branch Rickey's request. Cigar pursed neatly, Lloyd didn't know what to do with me. He grumbled when I suggested I could be batboy. "You're too damned big," he snapped.

Finally Lloyd decided he would try me as a ticket-taker. He ordered me to show up the next morning before the first game with the Browns.

I had a job. At the ball park, no less. My ancient Social Security card, which miraculously I've never lost, still lists my employer as the "St. Louis National League Baseball Club."

The "stile boy" with whom I worked, meaning the kid who wheeled the old-fashioned turnstile, was my age. He was a nice young man who eventually became police chief for the City of St. Louis, Eugene Camp.

Traveling secretary Lloyd used me sparingly, because on weekdays the Cardinals didn't draw enough to open many gates. Lloyd gave priority to older people as ticket sellers and takers. I understood.

Lloyd was a working favorite of the established press, a close friend of J. Roy Stockton and Sam Muchnick. He was a master of words who liked to refer to a manager, privately, as a "damager." Or he'd label a newspaper's top boss as the "damaging editor."

Lloyd called the Pirates the "Pie-roots," the Reds the "Red-leggos," and if he wasn't the first to use "Brownies" for the Browns and "Cubbies" for the Cubs, he helped popularize those two nicknames.

When I didn't have duty, I was free to watch all of the game, not just part. When a ticket taker worked, he or she closed out after the official length limit—five innings—and then counted tickets before being allowed to view the action.

I'd fluster occasionally when it came time to count a few thousand tickets. The disastrous words were three, uttered, unsmilingly by Lloyd: "Count 'em over!"

Except for the one game when I trudged up to mezzanine and found two unhappy customers about to rough up the little man. I growled, "Need any help, Mr. Lloyd?"

The men backed off and nothing happened. But that was one Sunday Clarence didn't ask me to "count 'em over."

12

આ

During the hottest summer in St. Louis history, my work day stretched from noon to midnight. The year was 1936 and my work day was split in two by trolley rides. It seemed to me I spent as much time on streetcars as the motormen, but, happily, the Depression ride price for a week's pass was only one buck.

My afternoon job was at Sportsman's Park. In the evenings, I worked at the St. Louis Softball Park at Shenandoah and Ohio. My dollar-a-night job there required my serving as official scorer and announcer for a seven-inning girls game and a nine-inning men's game. My softball park boss was a softspoken little Irishman named Martin (Bud) Loftus.

One of the team sponsors was a former gangster, Herman (Duzzy) Tipton, for whom I'd sometimes hustle up the off-brand cigarette he preferred, Piedmonts. One night Duzzy invited Bud and me to ride downtown with him and we settled into the back seat of his spacious Cadillac.

En route, as we stopped at a traffic light, another car pulled along side. Tipton glanced to his left, then shouted back, "Get down you guys, down on the floor!"

Hesitating, Loftus and I hit the car's carpet. False alarm. I never rode with Tipton again. As for Piedmonts, hey, get your own Duzzy . . . er, Mr. Tipton.

My baseball park experiences were not nearly so dramatic, but far more interesting. On opening day I squeezed into a seat after my ticket-taking duties were completed and saw Lon Warneke and the Chicago Cubs carve up Dizzy Dean and the Cardinals, 12-7. A sad day for Ol' Diz, but, heck, he ended up winning 24.

Next day my ticket-taking services were not needed. So I watched as manager Frank Frisch erred behind Paul Dean, costing a run. Near me, a guy yelled, "Why don't you quit, Frisch?"

When Frisch homered to win the game for P. Dean, 3-2, I couldn't resist.   In a manner most unbecoming a ball club "employee," I jeered for the abashed customer's ears, "Yeah, Frisch, why don't you quit!" Truth is, that home run was the last of the old Flash's career, and he well might have quit because he had little left.

The 1936 Cardinals might have won it all because Joe Medwick flourished at .351 and drove in a league-leading 138 RBIs. Johnny Mize, a hulky giant, underwent groin surgery by Dr. Robert F. Hyland and unseated Ripper Collins at first base. And, speaking of power, bless Leo Durocher's foghorn, The Lip muscled up to his best offensive season ever, .286.

But misfortune struck that glittery All-Star rookie battery of 1934, Paul Dean and Bill DeLancey. Big Dee had been stricken with tuberculosis after his second season and never recovered in a life that lasted only to his 45th birthday in 1946.

Branch Rickey, an astute observer, regarded DeLancey potentially as among the best three catchers he ever saw. Typically, B. R. wasn't always sure of the pecking order, but DeLancey figured among them.

Paul Dean, paid $3,000 as a rookie and $7,500 after his 19-game freshman season, wanted more after winning 19 again in 1935. He held out and was unsigned until the post-camp barnstorming trip back to St. Louis. Always heavy-legged, Paul found it difficult to get in shape.

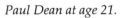

Paul Dean at age 21.

"I don't blame Dutch for the way he used me," Paul said years later in reference to Frisch. "It was my fault. I wasn't in shape even though I won my first five games. I was straining my arm. It popped . . . ."

Afterward, Paul Dean spent more time in dry dock than on the mound. He would only win six more games in the major leagues, none of them in '36.

One day, following a couple hours of rain and the game's postponement, I roamed the empty runways at Sportsman's Park, until, lo, out of the visitors' clubhouse came several uniformed Giants pitchers.

As Carl Hubbell and Hal Schumacher, then Freddie Fitzsimmons and Clyde Castleman lined up to loosen up, I grabbed an empty wooden soda box and sat on it almost close enough to call balls and strikes.

Suddenly, wearing street pants and a white T-shirt covered with the Giants' blue warm-up jacket, the Giants' player-manager, big Bill Terry came out of the dugout. He scowled at me but said nothing. An audience of one, I watched an informal workout.

Next day, the mighty Hubbell, in the middle of an amazing 26-6 season featuring a 2.31 earned run average, went against Roy (Tarzan) Parmalee, who pitched the best game of his career. The contest darkened into a 17-inning gloaming. Newspaper photographers were able to use flashlight shots.

Lefty Gomez (right) ended Carl Hubbell's streak in '36.

In the 17th, on a force play at the plate, a fleet Cardinals runner sped in from third base as Giants catcher Gus Mancuso stretched for a high throw. An eagle-eyed umpire ruled that the runner was safe because the throw had pulled Mancuso off the plate. The Giants argued, but *Post-Dispatch* photographer Jack Gould's photo revealed daylight between Mancuso's foot and the plate as the runner touched home.

Despite hi-jinks and high temperature, the Cardinals led the National League most of that summer. The thermometer exceeded 100 degrees for 13 successive days, and the heat killed 471 people. One proper dowager confessed that when she didn't use her girdle, she kept her tummy tucker in her refrigerator.

At the ballpark, even Dizzy Dean had a logy moment when pitching against a former teammate he liked, Burgess Whitehead. Dizzy threw a lollipop pitch that Burgess lined directly back toward the pitcher.

Dean, ordinarily an A-1 fielding pitcher, took Whitehead's line drive on the right side of his forehead. I gasped as the ball arched high to the left, almost down to the bullpen on the fly. Dizzy made a languid 180-degree pivot while flopping slowly on his keister. He ending up sitting cross-legged in a daze, facing second base. Meanwhile, Whitehead's head bank had turned into a double.

Whitey told me that he was glad he hadn't hurt Dizzy. The Great One himself, forced out of the pitching rotation for a week, was apologetic. "I'm gettin' to be a sissy when I can't get out of the way of a little old line drive."

Whitehead recalled that next time he faced Dizzy, Dean knocked him down, explaining, "We're friends, kid, but not that good-a friends."

The Giants, who had folded to the Cardinals in 1934 and then to St. Chicago in 1935, surged rather than sagged in 1936. They were inspired by manager Terry. After the winning season he retired, won one more as general manager and ultimately went back to a thriving Buick business in Jacksonville, Florida. As one "taught" to dislike the Redbird rival, I found him a most interesting man in our years together on the Hall of Fame's Veterans' Committee before his death past 90.

But he bristled when, using what I like to think is a professional easy-does-it approach, I tried to give him Whitehead's assessment about Terry and his friendly rival, Frank Frisch.

Actually what Whitehead had told me was that he preferred Frisch as a person, Terry as a manager. "They were both
great clutch players," said Whitey, "and Frisch was the more
emotional, but, also, the more passionate. He'd give me a day off.
'Sweet William'"— the sarcasm showed— "never would give a
guy a day off, even when I felt I needed one, but he was the better
manager. Like Leo Durocher, he knew how to anticipate . . ."

When I mentioned to Terry merely that Whitey thought he
was the better manager, but Frisch the more "passionate," Terry's
answer was tart: "Manic depressive," he snapped. "Helped us
win a couple of pennants, but manic depressive." The dictionary
defines "manic depressive" as "one who has a type of mental
disorder alternating between periods of acute excitement and
periods of acute depression."

When Stu Martin couldn't, Frisch tried to play second base
in 1936, but there was a day when the weary old warrior decided
discretion was the better part of valor.

The Cardinals played an exhibition game at Cleveland, and
Frisch felt duty bound to make at least a cameo experience and
rest Martin. But as he watched a dimple-chinned 17-year-old kid
warm up for Cleveland, he began to change his mind. A warm-
up pitch sailed over the catcher and thundered against the
backstop. Frisch turned to rookie outfielder Lynne King.

"Ever play second base?"

"No."

"Well, you are today, kid," said the manager. "The old
Flash is getting too old to get killed in the line of duty."

That day, Cleveland's splay-footed teenager struck out
eight of nine in a wild three-inning stint that convinced the
Indians they had a potential pitching chief. The boy's next outing
was against the St. Louis Browns. He struck out 15. His name was
Bob Feller.

In late September, climaxing St. Louis' part in a 60th anni-
versary celebration saluted in each National League city, Sam
Breadon brought back his 1926 world champions to play a brief
game against the '36 Cardinals before the regular game. For that
fantasy contest, played on an open date in the rival American
League, Hornsby and former star Redbird first baseman Sunny
Jim Bottomley, finishing up with the Brownies, flew in from
Washington for a reunion with old pals.

Unfortunately, though there was a disappointingly small crowd, I was "saddled" with ticket taking in the bleachers. Twice, leaving my post, I bounded up the steps to the playing field level. First, I saw Hornsby hit, which he did only five times officially that full season, hitting .400 —what else! —with two hits. Taking one swing against the Cardinals, The Rajah drove fleet Terry Moore to the center field flagpole, 426 feet from home plate.

I went up the stairs again to see Grover Cleveland Alexander pitch at age 50. He was en route to alcoholic oblivion, a 42nd Street flea circus in New York, and an early grave back home in Nebraska. But for the love of Pete, I had to see Pete pitch, if only briefly.

First up for the 1936 Cardinals, King playing the outfield, drag-bunted the grand gaffer's first pitch toward first base for a single. As Alexander hobbled over to field the ball, the sparse crowd did exactly what I wanted to do—boo the hell out of King!

I'm glad that nonsense of playing former athletes against current performers has gone the way of high-button shoes and low-life tricks—like King's.

The season ended for the Cardinals when Dizzy Dean was beaten by the Cubs' Lon Warneke, 6-3, enabling Chicago to tie St. Louis for second place. I missed the game because I had taken a large step that would afford me the opportunity to study at the nation's first accredited School of Journalism. I had left St. Louis to attend Missouri University at Columbia.

Which meant I missed the one and only big league appearance of Walter Alston, the Cardinals' first baseman that game because Rip Collins was hurt, and Johnny Mize got himself thrown out for arguing with an umpire.

Alston would eventually become a great manager and a good friend. But *playing* in the big leagues was another thing. Big Walt struck out his only time at bat and boxed one of two fielding plays for an error.

I traveled to college in September 1936, escorted by a neighbor who was taking her son for his second year. His name was Fred Kiebler, and he had played on my 1934 Riverside Independent League champions.

One day I cussed him out, but only after I had the breath sucked out of me by the piston knees of a base runner sliding hard, late and high. Temporarily, I thought I'd had it when, briefly, I couldn't inhale what I had exhaled, but I sobered enough to beef at my buddy for his damned lollipop throws. But errors of youth are easily forgiven, and now we were together at Columbia.

Times were tough. To give you an idea, here are prices as researched by editor Steve DeBellis of the *St. Louis Inquirer*, a monthly past-tense newspaper I enjoy.

Prices in 1936 included sirloin steak at 23 cents a pound, three large loaves of bread, 10 cents; spring chickens, three for $1; evaporated canned milk, three for 17 cents; assorted chocolates, 45 cents a pound; top-grade coffee, 32 cents; doughnuts, 18 cents a dozen; bottled beer, ranging from 5 cents to 15; men's suit, $32.75; women's silk slips, $1.75; eight packs of cigarettes, 96 cents; and a new Ford V-9, $495.

So a buck did go a l-o-n-g way. Still, when family financier Mom toted up the score, I was asked to hack it on a dollar a day for room, board, and necessities. Thirty dollars a month was tighter than Branch Rickey at contract time.

I tried. So did Mom. Laundry boxes were mailed back and forth between campus and home. My weekly cleaned laundry included a CARE package, usually a loaf of bread and a few non-perishables. I hadn't been able to get work with many of the other 5,000 plus pre-World War I baby boomers competing for jobs.

Kiebler and I shared a room in a Fifth Street home where Fred had stayed the year before. One night as we sat there studying, we could hear the melodious tingle-tingle of a bell propelled by a Good Humor man. Keeb and I didn't have a cent to spare. He eyed my laundry bag, about to be shipped back with dirty work for Mom.

"How about that?" he said, pointing to the bag.

"Nothing," I said, "except bread."

"So let's make a jam sandwich."

"A 'jam' sandwich?"

"Yeah," said Kiebler, grinning as we did what he suggested. "Let's jam two pieces of bread together."

13

ès

If the women in my life knew I paid for my college keep by washing dishes, they would be surprised.

Although the state legislature had made it "twice" as easy to get into the ol' State U. my second semester by lowering tuition rates from $60 to $30, my new $35-a-month limit was still too skimpy.

So when the Sig Eps, who had "rushed" friend Fred Kiebler and me in September, offered to cut in half our monthly house bill if we washed dishes—$45 down to $27.50 a month—the fraternity had a couple of new pledges.

At a time of no drainboard, which required towel drying, I winced at warm weather spring and fall changes, because tall, narrow-mouthed iced tea glasses augmented the stubby, easier-to-wash-and-dry water glasses. I used up stacks of dish towels polishing scalding-hot glasses.

Extracurricularly, I still had time to assist athletically for the good of the fraternity cause and, more important, to pursue my freshman efforts in writing sports for the Missouri *Student,* now the more flamboyant campus weekly, the *Maneater.*

I watched daily football practices at old Rollins Field and frequently worked briefly afterward with the handsome new line coach, fresh from the University of Minnesota, Phil Bengtson. I fancied myself as a good kicker.

One day, painfully shanking a dropkick effort, I lamented to Bengtson that, criminy, as a kid I knew I often hadn't played with tightly wound new balls, but still . . . .

Phil interrupted with a smile. "Don't you know," he said, "that this last year they changed the rule, *slendering* the ball to help passing. . ."

Bless Slingin' Sammy Baugh's pinpoint passes. The rangy Texas Christian graduate rewrote the record book the fall of 1936 and, as a rookie, propelled the Washington Redskins to the National Football League championship in '37.

The dropkick was accomplished for field goal or extra-point purposes by permitting the kicker to accept a snap from center, drop the ball at a slight angle toward his kicking toe, and then club it airward just as the ball touched the ground. It was used often before the rulebook changed the circumference of the ball and diminished kicking accuracy.

On my first Thanksgiving Day at Columbia, Don Faurot's Missouri team sought to beat ancient rival Kansas. The two schools—and states—had been border-rival cats-and-dogs since ugly Civil War incursions into each other's territory.

When Missouri fumbled early, a Jayhawk dropkicked a three-pointer straight through the Columbia uprights. Missouri, scoring on Kansas for the first time in seven years, won that game, 19-3. I mention it because I've never seen another dropkicked field goal or conversion even attempted, much less accomplished.

This was Faurot's second season at Missouri, and his 6-2-1 record equaled Ol' Mizzou's victories over the five-year period before he arrived.

Perhaps I was homesick. Perhaps it was because I loved my family and Mom's home cooking. Whatever the reason, I ducked into St. Louis many a different way, though never as a hitchhiker. A familial no-no.

I did shock Mom and Pop when a friend and I arrived in St. Louis curled in the trunk of a two-seater. The driver charged us 50 cents each way and propped the truck open with a rope so we could breathe. The only thing we could see was the whirling white of snowflakes. To be sure, the folks had a "don't-you-ever-do-that-again-Robert" fit over that.

At the February conclusion of my first semester, I received an S.O.S. phone call. Uncle Fred was ill, and could I make it home? I waded through snow drifts to the home of a Geology professor, who, grumpily, agreed to give me a make-up final if I didn't return 48 hours later for the Monday exam.

I first rode the Wabash dinky feeder train, coal-stoved and old enough that Lincoln could have used it. At Centralia I indulged in banana cream pie at a small railside hotel before catching the Kansas City-to-St. Louis run. En route home, I skimmed the newspaper, then poured into my textbooks. I always liked to study during day hours so I could minimize my night-time academic effort.

Suddenly, the train pulled slowly into the Mill Creek yard area. It was dark. Overhead on the right I saw the blinking lighted sign of the "Pevely Dairy," a landmark at the southern end of the old chain-looped Grand Avenue viaduct.

I recalled facing that same sign while Mom was telling Pop about having accompanied widowed Mrs. Will Wiley, to a fortune-teller. Pop scoffed, but Mom persisted that she had been told that a dark-complexioned man in her life would die. "And, Bob," Mom said, "the only dark-complexioned man I could think about is Fred." I turned back quickly to the paper's obituary table. There was the name—"Isele, Fred W."

Minutes later when the train pulled into St. Louis's huge Union Station, cousin Charley, Uncle Fred's son, was there. Charley was startled that I knew the depressing truth. Uncle Fred had died after an accident.

Early in February, 1937, I enjoyed a hurried Columbia-to-Kansas City same-night-go-and-come-back trip to watch Joe Louis fight. The foe in Kansas was Natie Brown, whom the famed Brown Bomber barely had beat two years earlier in Joe's adopted city, Detroit.

The man who took me to Kansas City became a fast friend and my campus boss. He was Missouri's new sports information director, Max (Skipper) Patrick, a spectacled, owl-eyed Mississippian who had come to Columbia for journalism.

After my first year at college, it was back to St. Louis for the summer and a second stint as a major league ticket taker and amateur softball league official scorer and announcer.

The Cardinals' season was disappointing. Even though Johnny Mize hit .364 with 23 homers and 113 RBIs and Joe Medwick delivered the National League's last Triple Crown—.374, 31, 114—the Redbirds finished a far-off fourth, and my old boyhood idol, Frankie Frisch, called it quits.

Dizzy Dean still was the noisy bellcow of the ball club, a 10-game winner by the All-Star break. Typically, Dizzy tried to avoid the All-Star game at Washington, but wife Pat and owner Sam Breadon prevailed on him to go to D.C. Breadon even flew there with the great box office attraction.

Rangy No. "17" was within one out of a scoreless three-inning sendoff when the Yankees' Lou Gehrig thumped him for a two-run homer. Lou ranked that All-Star home run as second only to one off Carl Hubbell in the 1936 World Series.

See the impact Dizzy made? What about the impact of the line drive off Earl Averill's bat? Averill, next up after Gehrig's homer, teed off with a smash that broke Dizzy's left big toe. Realistically, Dizzy should have recuperated for a long time, as Dr. Robert F. Hyland urged, but he was competitive. Diz, still limping, rejoined the Cardinals 10 days later in Boston.

The Braves had been easy for Dizzy. Once he had insisted that startled young catcher Bruce Ogrodowski drop a potential game-ending pop foul because Dizzy had bet traveling comedian friend Johnny Perkins that he would strike out the oldest DiMaggio brother, Vince, four straight times.

"Drop it, damnit," Dizzy insisted. "If you want to catch me again, drop it."

Startled, Ogrodowski did. Dizzy fanned the eldest DiMaggio for the fourth straight time and won the couple of bucks he had bet against head-shaking witness Perkins.

A spectator that day, seated in the dugout, Frisch leaped to his feet because Dizzy's game-delaying arrogance came with the potential tying run on base. Frisch hit his head on the overhead concrete dugout roof. He fell back, stunned.

Perhaps the Flash was still stunned the day the limping Diz toed the slab at Braves Field after his injury. But let's be fair and accurate. Frisch had overworked both Dean brothers.

When Jay Hanna went to the mound, he had worked an average of 300-plus innings for five years. Over the last four seasons, he had a 92-39 record plus many saves. If King Carl Hubbell was Bill Terry's "meal ticket," as the press often jeered, Dizzy Dean was Frisch's full-course dinner, soup to nuts. And Uncle Frank was nuts for letting Dizzy pitch that fateful day.

As Dizzy warmed up, favoring the leg, Boston manager Bill McKechnie took the third-base coaching box, McKechnie pleaded, "Don't Jerome . . . don't."

Holding the Braves scoreless into the seventh inning, Dizzy broke off a pitch to Braves' infielder Bill Urbanski and something snapped. He clutched his arm. McKechnie, anguished, wailed: "I told you, Jerome, I told you."

As a pitcher, Dizzy wasn't the same—ever. As a manager, Frisch wasn't either.

Frank had learned a lesson earlier when, with the ball club slumping, he benched rookie Jimmy Brown and Stu Martin as a second-base combination. At Philadelphia, where Baker Bowl's bandbox made hitting easy until the Phillies moved into the Athletics' park in 1938, Frisch returned Leo Durocher to the lineup at shortstop and put himself back in the lineup at second base.

Two of the greats, Dizzy Dean and Frank Frisch.

Next afternoon, according to Brown, Frisch was on second base, fleet Terry Moore on first, and righthanded-hitting Medwick lined a drive to right field.

Frisch, fearing a catch, held up. Moore, with a better view, never broke stride. By the time Frisch reached third base, Moore had rounded second. Coaching third, Mike Gonzalez warbled excitedly:

"She come, Froh-nk, you go . . . she come, you go . . "

As Frisch slid into the plate, Moore slid directly under him, like a two-man bobsled. Frisch, leaping to his feet, brushed off the dirt and, laughing, said: "Any time they can run down the old Flash, it's time to quit. Brown, go to second base!"

When I became friends with Brown, we talked of seeing Frisch's last two plate appearances. Frank was coaching third base. The Cardinals were a run down in the ninth inning and had runners on second and third. Frisch looked into the dugout to decide who to pinch-hit for light-hitting kid catcher Mickey Owen.

From the dark shadows of the late-afternoon dugout at Sportman's Park, someone said in shielding falsetto, "Why don't you hit, grandma!"

Flush with anger, Frisch strode to the bench, picked up a bat, walked to the plate, swung at the first pitch, and bounced a single off first baseman Elbie Fletcher's glove. As the tying and winning run scored, Pepper Martin led the charge from the dugout, hoisting Frisch to his shoulder. What a gracious exit, I thought.

But the next day in a similar ninth-inning situation, Frisch put himself in to pinch-bat against spectacled right-handed Danny MacFayden. Frank cranked the first pitch up the middle, this time an apparent single to center, but Boston shortstop Rabbit Warstler cut across, scooped the ball and pegged to first, where Frisch—out on the play!—pulled up lame.

Goodbye to Uncle Frank. Hello to Mizzou.

Good news! Skipper Patrick took me into the school's P.R. department for 35 cents an hour. I would have done it as a labor of love, but I never turned down a check.

When Washington University of St. Louis came to Columbia for a football game, so did J. Roy Stockton. Missouri won the game, 17-10, and I won a big boost. Almost timidly, I introduced myself to Stockton. No, at first, he really didn't remember that visit to the *Post-Dispatch* office four years earlier, but, yes, he was interested in me.

"Well, you've come this far," he said, smiling. One word led to another, and in a moment of weakness he asked me to send him printed stuff I wrote. Ha! From then on, I face-guarded him through the mail.

Working for Patrick and writing a weekly column for the *Missouri Student* the fall of 1937, I was disappointed in a 3-6-1 detour in Don Faurot's rebuilding. But I was caught up in the coach's efforts. A fire had begun to burn in my heart—and the source of its flames was Missouri football.

For financial reasons, Faurot scheduled three away football games in eight days. Mizzou won against Washington U., Tied KU, and lost to UCLA. I traveled to Lawrence for the KU game. After the Tigers lost, I stopped in at the Sig Ep house at Lawrence and met an old, short man with a bristling mustache— *the* James Naismith.

I cherish that chance meeting and the opportunity to meet and learn from the man who answered the challenge for an indoor winter sport with a soccer ball, a peach basket, and a set of rules so formidable and far-sighted that 11 of his 13 original rules of 1891 still were in existence when we met in '37.

Naismith was a burly, hard-nosed athlete with a master's in physical education, a doctor of divinity, and a doctor of medicine. He almost fit the absent-minded professor mode. Blue eyes smiling behind gold-rimmed glasses, he recalled when kids on campus once asked him to referee an impromptu basketball game, then thought better of it "because the old guy doesn't know anything about basketball."

Naismith talked to me about basketball. "Scoring is important," he said, "but not all-consuming. Speed is. Speed, passing, and the unexpected. "To curb the stall, I'd put in a time limit on the team with the ball. To make the defense come out, I'd penalize the defense after, say, 30 seconds. Or to draw the defense out to the ball, I'd give the scoring team four points rather than two for a basket scored from 30 feet out."

When we talked, he recently had returned from the 1936 Olympics in Berlin, the first time basketball was an official Olympic sport. The great gaffer's way to Germany had been paid only because his pride-and-joy friend and No. 1 pupil, Forrest (Phog) Allen, had levied his oral guns at the ruling Amateur Athletic Union, which then won over the National Collegiate Athletic Association.

Doc Allen, a gifted osteophathist, labeled the AAU as "quadrennial, stuff-shirted, international hitch-hikers." Phog urged a two-foot elevation to 12-foot baskets because, as he wrote in a national magazine in 1937, "Dunking Isn't Basketball."

When nearby Baker University wrote Naismith about hiring the young Allen as its basketball coach, Dr. Naismith informed Dr. Allen, "I've got a joke on you, you bloody beggar," said the muscular egghead, "they want you to coach basketball down at Baker."

Phog bridled. "What's so funny about that?"

"Why, Forrest," explained the man who invented the game to one of the greatest who would ever coach it, "You don't coach basketball. You play it!"

14

Pepper Martin's Mudcats and Branch Rickey's brain irritated the hell out of Frank Frisch in 1938.

The Cardinals' general manager set up a special pre-camp session at Winter Haven, Florida, and instructed manager Frisch to explore moving Terry Moore to third base.

Frisch's reaction was, "For crizzsake, why move the best defensive center fielder in the league?" He had other objections, but they were back burnered when the Flash, teaching rookies how to slide, broke an ankle bone.

Meanwhile, Rickey turned his attention to Dizzy Dean. Ol' Diz was damaged goods at age 27. I happened to be in the ball club's office that Saturday morning when Rickey maneuvered a whopping trade with Chicago.

The shocking news spread quickly. Dean was gone, dealt to the Cubs for right-handed pitcher Curt Davis, lefty Roy Henshaw, reserve outfielder Tuck Stainiback and —harumph!— $185,000, an awesome Depression-era price. Don't forget that Rickey got 20 percent of Cardinals profits.

Obviously, Phil Wrigley, who had taken over the Cubs from his father, was eager to repeat that pleasant Chicago three-season rhythm of pennants—1929, 1932, 1935— and, not to spoil a good story, 1938, too.

Rickey told Wrigley that he was getting a physically sub-par pitcher. P. K. appreciated the caveat emptor. Even though Dizzy proved a disappointment, the chicle-and-chew, double-your-pleasure man was happy. Mr. Wrigley, a shy man, once told me, "Having Dizzy Dean with us was like having a brass band . . ."

During Dizzy's first weekend at Chicago, he used an exaggerated side-wheeling motion and pinpoint control to slow-ball the Cardinals into a four-hit shutout. Terry Moore got two of those hits. "Diz liked me because I saved ball games for him," Moore said later.

A week later in St. Louis, Dizzy faced the Redbirds again. This time he was bombed out early and walked off the field with head down to great applause from the huge crowd.

Frisch, who admired and appreciated Dean, once told me, "I wish to hell he hadn't kept horsing around, trying to come back as a pitcher, but had switched to first base. With his aptitude and attitude, he could have been a great fielder there. And with enough hitting practice, he would have been a good enough hitter."

The practice that drove symphonic longhair Frisch up the musical wall was the cacophony of Pepper Martin's Mudcats, playing country-western and mournful mountain music with guts, if not gusto.

Pepper and Lon Warneke loved to thump the guitar, pronounced "git-tar" by the McNamara of the band. Bob Weiland puffed foggy sound into the mouthpiece of an old brown jug. Fiddler Bill McGee fiddled his violin. Max Lanier played the harmonica, and Frenchy Bordagaray thumbed a washtub.

The Mudcats were too late for vaudeville and too early for television. They were a visual treat with white pants tucked into cowboy boots, the ball club's bird and bat red crests across their blousey shirt fronts and cowboy hats tilted rakishly.

Winning, Frisch could stand them, but not losing. When the floundering 1938 club moved into Rochester for an exhibition game, billboards and handbills proclaimed in large type, "PEPPER MARTIN AND HIS MUDCATS."

In smaller type, as Frisch remembered, the ads proclaimed, "Also, the Cardinals and Joe Medwick and Johnny Mize." Frisch recalled Medwick's angry reaction. "What the bleep is this —a ball club or a band?"

Back in St. Louis, as Frisch would relate to me years later, the manager was at his whining, nasal best when he pleaded to owner Sam Breadon:"Mr. Breadon, I'm the only manager required to travel with an or-CHES-tra."

Smiling, Breadon nodded, called in Pepper and urged him to disband the or-CHES-tra, a high-rent description for low-down noisemakers.

A couple of months later, with the gasless Gas House Gang in sixth place, the club owner called in the manager. Choking back tears, Singin' Sam told his favorite player that after five-plus seasons as manager, the time had come. Frisch tried to help, teary-eyed himself.

"Don't feel bad about it, Mr. Breadon," he said, "I understand."

While Frisch was being fired, I was having trouble getting hired, unable to find paying work except for an occasional five bucks umpiring baseball and softball games. I was the youngest member of the St. Louis umpires association, so seniority was not on my side.

To keep moving my life forward, I struggled with a summer extension course, figuring the extra hours of college credit would allow me more time to work for Patrick when I returned to Mizzou in the fall of '38.

But whether I was in St. Louis or Columbia, I always had time for baseball. The 1938 pennant race captured my attention. League leaders most of the way, Pie Traynor's Pittsburgh Pirates faltered down the stretch. By the time the Buccos got to Wrigley Field the last few days of the season, Pittsburgh's lead— once large enough for the management to build a new press box at Forbes Field— was reduced to a game and a half.

Cubs manager Hartnett decided to gamble with Dizzy Dean in the decisive series. Diz, 6 and 1, hadn't pitched for two weeks and hadn't started a game for a month. Hartnett banked on Dizzy's heart. "I knew they wouldn't scare him." They didn't, either. The Cubs' 2-1 victory meant they could move into first place the next day.

That important game went into the ninth tied with darkness descending. The umpires decided there would not be any extra innings. If the Cubs didn't score, the game would be replayed as part of a final day double-header. Such an event would favor the pitching-rich Pirates.

With two out, manager Hartnett came up to face Pittsburgh's relief ace, Mace Brown, a great breaking ball pitcher. Gabby missed one curve ball and foul-tipped a second. Brown went back to the well and threw a third curve. Hartnett swung and the ball jumped off the bat.

"When I hit it, I knew it was gone," Hartnett told me later. "I felt the blood rush to my head and I was dizzy as I circled the bases." Gabby's famed "homer in the gloamin'" won the game 6-5, and Chicago went ahead.

After the body blow to his Buccos, manager Traynor was so steamed that he waved off a taxi and walked the many miles from Chicago's near North Side to the old Stevens (Hilton) Hotel downtown. Coach Jewel Ens tagged along, as did Pittsburgh sports writer Les Biederman. As he strode through the hotel's revolving door, Traynor remarked grimly, "If either of you had said a damned word, I'd have swung at you."

Pittsburgh Pirates Manager, Pie Traynor.

When the Cubs clinched the pennant in St. Louis the next-to-last day of the season, I rode in with a friend from Columbia. I knew that St. Louis press and radio men would play a brief exhibition baseball game.

I watched from the visitors' first base dugout at Sportsman's Park as Hartnett came in, face flushed from an unforgettable season. Gabby sat there, gripping a giant gourd someone from Arizona had sent him.

In the World Series, Hartnett decided to rely once more on Dizzy's fortitude against the mighty Yankees, led then by young Joe DiMaggio and a veteran first baseman, Lou Gehrig. The Bronx Bombers were bamboozled by Dizzy's corner-cutting control and offspeed pitches. Fact is, he would have carried a three-run scoreless cushion into New York's eighth if third baseman Stan Hack and shortstop Billy Jurges hadn't bumped heads on a slow grounder that trickled between them for a two-run single.

So Dizzy's lead was just a run when Yankee shortstop Frank Crosetti rapped a full-count pitch for a two-run homer. Storming angrily around the mound, Ol' Diz cussed and fussed, finally insisting, "Furthermore, podnuh, if I'd-a had my old fast ball, you wouldn't-a seen the ball." To which they say 'Cro' responded graciously, "Darned if I don't think you're right, Diz."

I listened to the World Series while working and studying at MU and learning to admire Paul Christman.

Don Faurot regards Christman as having made "the greatest contributions" to football at Columbia, where the field is named for Faurot. Wow! What a tribute!

Paul Joseph Christman, son of a *Post-Dispatch* printer, starred at suburban Maplewood High School at a time Faurot redoubled MU's efforts to recruit eastern Missouri athletes even though both St. Louis University and Washington were more competitive counter-attractions.

But Christman, listening to high school end coach Paul Ross, fresh from Purdue as an All-American, decided not to follow the highly recruited Orf twins to Mizzou. The Orfs and members of my old high school, Cleveland in St. Louis, were early backbones of Faurot's success at Missouri.

That success could have been delayed if Christman had not been buried on the ninth freshmen team at Purdue. He was an unimpressive practice athlete.

Christman wrote Bud Orf a letter at Columbia. If you didn't know Roland (Bud) from look-alike twin brother Bob, you weren't alone. Soon the deed was done, and Paul had transferred to Mizzou. By 1938, he was starting at quarterback for the Tigers.

Missouri lost two of its first three Christman-led games. The next contest was against Nebraska, which hadn't lost to Missouri since 1927. Leading Nebraska's cheers was Hollywood's dynamic squirt Mickey Rooney, filming "Boys Town" nearby with Spencer Tracy.

Nebraska grabbed a 3-0 lead, and as the Tigers huddled, carping seniors spoke up until center-linebacker Jack Kinnison interrupted. "Listen, damn it," he snapped, "the kid's calling 'em —and I'll knock on his ass the next guy who speaks up."

Up in the press box, where I sat as a second row eavesdropper behind the *Omaha World-Herald's* sports editor Fred Ware and the *Columbia Daily Tribune's* veteran J. P. Hamel, Ware joshed, "Jake, where's this Christman I've heard so much about?"

Christman completed four straight passes, the last for a touchdown. Hamel bared his buck teeth. "There he is, Fred," said Jake with a grin. "There's Paul Christman."

Christman led the Tigers to a 13-10 upset. Impressed, Ware, who would become the *World-Herald's* managing editor, labeled Paul as the "Merry Magician."

So I didn't invent that nickname for Christman, though I used it. I also didn't nickname Christman "Pitchin' Paul," either. Skipper Patrick did. My best was "Passin' Paul."

Faurot said of Paul, "He was daring, imaginative, yet sensible. I was smart enough to let him call his own plays—even when he'd scare the britches off me by passing three times out of his end zone—*in the same series.*"

Christman led the Tigers to a 6-0 upset over Michigan State the week after the big one at Nebraska. It was a step toward scheduling worthy foes at home, too.

My fraternity brother, football player and friend Mike English, traveled to St. Louis with me and stayed at my house a couple of times, once to watch the Tigers defeat St. Louis University. Mom, who at her spit-and-polish peak ordinarily made you walk on your hands not to dirty the floor, had relaxed in middle age. She actually welcomed guests.

That was good because her Robert needed all the friendship he could get. I had fallen in love and didn't know what to do about it. Though I usually had no trouble communicating, I was constantly tongue-tied in the presence of the Blonde Bomber, a well-scrubbed 4-H beauty I met at a fraternity dance.

Lovesick at 20, I was running second in a two-horse race. The object of my affection preferred another, so my dates with her were few, both in Columbia and in St. Louis. At home, she lived in a north end area difficult to reach except by car, and good ol' Pop seldom entrusted his automobile to me.

Shut out in the Love League, I used Saturday nights of my weekend visits home to see Al Spiegel, auditor of the Chase Hotel. Spiegel often accompanied KWK's Johnny O'Hara to Columbia for football games. Time and again, I wrote Missouri football scripts for O'Hara and appeared briefly with him on radio. In Columbia, he would headquarter at the Sig Ep house.

Time and again, I'd bus up to the Chase and sit and chat with "Uncle Al," as I called him. I'd sip a Scotch or two when talking with Spiegel, then slip into the Chase Club for the midnight floor show of the Big Band era.

When it was time to go home, I was always happy that I'd had a pleasant evening at no cost. But I envied the couples dancing cheek to cheek.

Mike English returned to St. Louis with me for a New Year's celebration. I'm afraid his railroad whistle stop, Monett, Missouri, was too tame for a small town guy who was a city slicker at heart.

Down the street from the Broeg's cardboard cottage was a tavern next door to Louie Sika's barber shop at Virginia and Itaska Streets. The proprietor's wife, Mary, a delightful woman, made delicious steak tartar for raw-meat eaters. Remnants of my old gang hung out there when they could duck out of the house. They were glad to talk football with English.

One night a chunky, freckled man named Tony whom I'd seen only once previously, walked in. A few years earlier he told me he was the only person other than his grandmother whose right palm center crease was a straight line, not broken. When I looked, mine was straight, too. Is there a palmist in the house?

Over the years, mentioning it here and there—as I do now —I've never met anyone else whose hand has an unbroken crease from point pinky past forefinger.

One New Year's Eve, Mike English and I were invited by Ed Frievogel to join his large group. Included was the former team manager, Ed Heggi, a delightful bachelor who had a pretty good job as a General Electric representative in St. Louis.

Interested, Heggi wondered what I might expect to make as a newspaperman? Eager to impress, aware that in those tough times most of the journalistic best were lucky if they made 50 bucks a week, I said— silly boy!— I'd be "happy if I could make a hundred."

Ed crushed me. "Is that all?" He said. It was time for me to get another Scotch.

Before we left the house to celebrate the coming New Year, Mom had plied us with heaping helpings of spareribs, sauerkraut, and milky, butter-laden mashed potatoes. On our way to the party, Mike English and I each chug-a-lugged half of a small bottle of olive oil.

By the dawn's early light, Ed Heggi and many others were long gone home. Still others were passed out or merely asleep. English and I, our stomachs coated so thoroughly, were still on our feet at the miniature bar, drinking, jabbering, as sober as— pardon the expression, your honor — a judge.

We were last to leave, and when we got home we dove into the sack after asking good ol' Mom to awaken us so we could listen on radio as Wallace Duke's remarkable Duke football team sought to finish an unbeaten, untied and *unscored on* season against Southern California in the Rose Bowl. But we forgot to eat first.

Awakened properly, we felt as bust-headed as the Blue Devils must have felt, when in the final 40 seconds of a season of 600 minutes, they were both scored on and beaten. A fourth- string USC sophomore named Doyle Nave passed to Antelope Al Krueger of Antelope Valley, California. Final: Southern Cal 7, Duke 3!

With the first bite of food, I began to feel better. Ditto Mike English. But a few miles from Duke's campus at Durham, North Carolina, there was an emotional and physical letdown.

A Roxboro tobacco farmer with an unusual first name, Zadok, had gone rabbit hunting with his older son, hurrying to get back so they could listen to their Duke favorites. Suddenly, radio side, the father became ill. Then the son. They had handled infected rabbits and suffered tularemia.

The disease was quick and deadly. Before the night was over, Zadok was gone. And there was a serious question whether his son Enos would live.

15

The only time the Blonde Bomber saw me in athletic action, we Sig Eps showed off in basketball, strutting out smoking cigars.

I was six feet tall and weighed 215 pounds.

The B. B. didn't like the fat look. That forced me into a healthier diet and extra exercise. By my 21st birthday in March of 1939, I had lost 20 pounds.

The world was turning ugly. The fascist Franco had won power in Spain. Hitler's legions had goose-stepped into Czechoslovakia. But everything was cozy in Columbia, population 17,000, with a university enrollment of 5,000 and a couple of convenient girls' schools, too, Stephens and Christian (later Columbia) College. Ol' Mizzou never had it better than this era of conference basketball, baseball, and track and field championships.

I wrangled a summer job with *The Sporting News*—Baseball's Bible— published in St. Louis. With streetcar and lunch fare, that $12.50 a week wouldn't go too far, but — eureka!—the baseball Cardinals' Ed Staples came to town and offered me a job in the Publicity Department. TWENTY bucks a week and a chance to watch the Cardinals for free. But, wait, Ed. What about *The Sporting News*?

Staples told me not to worry; he'd handle it. But he blew it, as I learned when I got a letter of concern from mentor J. Roy Stockton. Stockton wondered what in the hell I'd done to tee off Spink.

I wrote Spink an abject apology. In return, I received a terse note I'll never forget: "My dear Bob: As you grow older, you'll realize you've got to consider the feelings of others."

That was all.

When I reported to the Cardinals, Staples saw to it that his "other" young employee had all direct contact with the fire and brimstone boss of *TSN*.

J.G. Taylor Spink (center) flanked by Joe E. Brown (left) and Jimmy Conzelman.

The "other" young man was a skinny blonde whose Christian name—Vaughan—wasn't memorable. But by his nickname and surname he became known as one of the most astute baseball men: Bing Devine!

"Der Bingle" went to work for the Cardinals the day before I did. His intentions were to work in baseball. Mine were to have a newspaper career. We formed one helluva fine front office double-play combination.

Staples and his secretary had one office on the mezzanine level of Sportsman's Park. Devine and I were sandwiched in a small room nearby. We did much of our work in an adjacent sloping alcove. Hunched over, we cranked out press releases for the Cardinals and their 30 farm clubs on an old mimeograph machine.

We were busy with so many "subsidiaries," because Branch Rickey had a theory that the more players a ball club looked at, the more likely it would find talent.

So Devine and I often had to deduce how the club was doing from the cheers or groans of the fans. Occasionally we'd find time to watch an inning or two.

One of my favorites was Enos Slaughter who came to spring training after nearly dying of the tularemia that took his father's life. Enos had painful lumps under his arms and suffered from dizzy spells, but he righted himself to a whopping .320 season.

Frisch's managerial successor, Ray Blades, seemed brisk and brusque. But the former outfielder was ahead of his day in his use of his bullpen. Southpaw Clyde (Hard Rock) Shoun relieved 53 times.

Blades was a crafty Rickey copy-cat. In exchange for broadcasting privileges, radio stations gave us brief sound bites to advertise the next day's pitchers.

Once, when I went in the visitor's clubhouse, Leo Durocher of the Dodgers was more aggressive than usual. The Lip felt that Blades had used advance information unfairly. Profanely, Leo ordered me out of the clubhouse. I held my ground. One word led to another. Durocher pushed against my feet with his spiked shoes. I shoved him away. He charged back. I squared off. Only an alert Brooklyn trainer averted a fight, leaping in, "Jeepers," he shouted, "Leo, you can't fight this kid."

When I returned to the front office without the next day's Dodger pitcher, I told the story. In glee, gossip Staples flew upstairs to spread the news. Soon I had to accompany him to the owner's office and tell Mr. Breadon.

The incident had no negative repercussions for me, and the season held no pennant for the Cardinals, although a large surge stirred a town spoiled by earlier successes.

Soon it was time to go back to university life. Against what I thought was formidable competition, I had applied for an $18.50-a-week job as the Columbia correspondent for the Associated Press. In my corner were Paul Mickelson, J. Roy Stockton, Jake Hamel, the managing editor and sports editor of the *Columbia Daily Tribune*.

One afternoon I was summoned by phone to the Cardinals' clubhouse to meet Paul Mickelson, formerly a baseball writer and national AP sports columnist, then chief of the wire service's bureau at Kansas City.

When I burst into the clubhouse, all I could see was Pepper Martin grinning with a playful headlock applied to the curly auburn locks of a man doubled over. When I asked for "Mr. Mickelson," Pepper let go with a grunt, and the man was—as they called him at the AP — "PRM."

Paul Roosevelt Mickelson, a handsome, lightly mustached man, was suave, polished, and a helluva great newspaperman. Hallelujah! The job was mine! Mickelson urged me to be in Kansas City in early September for detailed directions from his state editor, Ed Mills. I said I would, happy for the chance, glad also not to need any more financial aid from my folks. The sum seemed so huge, I told Paul Christman I was probably making more money than he was.

But I gulped at the challenge of the job.

Sure, covering sports would be a piece of cake for me. Yet I also had to write a weekly farm column and didn't know anything about agriculture. Highway deaths and court cases, especially at a time blacks were seeking admission to Missouri, weren't easy to contemplate. At the time, Ol' Mizzou was segregated. "Dixie" was the athletic fight song.

Hardly had I accepted the AP job when I received a phone call from the university's business manager for sports. Virgil Spurling needed a new sports information director because Skipper Patrick had suddenly decided to return to a similar job at his first alma mater, Mississippi State.

Spurling spelled it out. If I would drop out of school the fall semester, he would pay me $30 a month. But, I interrupted, "Gee, Virg, I'm not going to college not to go to school." All right, he suggested, reconsidering, reduce my academic load and he'd give me 25 bucks a month because he was sure I'd . . .

I *knew* I could do the P. R. job. I *hoped* I could do the AP job. Spurling's pay offer was better and the chance to travel with the football team was inviting. Earlier that summer, I'd spent a long lunch hour filling in *Collier Magazine*'s Kyle Crichton for what would be a feature piece about colorful likely All-American Christman. I knew we had a winning football team. I wanted to be close to the action.

But when I closed my eyes, all I could see was the note I had received from Taylor Spink. Sighing, I swallowed a dose of life's castor oil and passed on the job offer.

The same late afternoon I hung up sorrowfully from Spurling, a young friend of mine named Mark Cox and his bride drove up to my folks' house, en route to Champaign, Illinois, from her family's home at Jefferson City, Missouri. Cox, a senior when I had been a freshman, now worked for a man he liked, the legendary Bert Bertine at the *Champaign Courier-Journal*. But Bertine seemed settled in, and Mark was looking. Quickly, I detailed Virgil Spurling's phone call and offer. Mark immediately called Spurling and got the job.

Me? I had a couple of hundred bucks and an itching need to buy my first automobile. Pop went with me to a used car lot. I was quickly enamored of a 1934 Chevrolet Cabrolet green convertible complete with a rumble seat and slightly worn leather seat linings.

"You are," Pop insisted, "buying another young man's problems." But he left the decision up to me.

So I had snazzy wheels by the time Cincinnati came to town for a Sunday double-header. The 40,807 crowd, second largest ever at Sportsman's Park, was nearly 7,000 over capacity.

Where did those standees go? Everywhere, including on the playing field. Ropes were stretched on the sidelines and into the outfield. The situation was complicated, because city police reversed their previous policy and stayed outside the park. Among the civilians helping hold back the crowd were club owner Breadon, ushers, groundskeepers, and players. Yeah, and me. I worked next to Pepper Martin, not playing that day.

My focus was completely on my work, so that I didn't realize the first game had begun until a whining sound passing over my head attracted my attention. I looked down and—oops! — was in fair territory, only a few feet farther back than third baseman Don Gutteridge.

Gutteridge was extremely deep, because the batter was slow afoot and a dangerous hitter. Right-handed slugger Ernie Lombardi, a future Hall of Fame catcher, had zinged the ball over my head and into the ducking crowd for a loud foul.

A second look confirmed that no matter where I stood, fair or foul, I was in the gun sights of the big bat Big Lom waggled with a golfer's interlocking grip. Aware the crowd was settling, I spoke up to the boss. "Mr. Breadon," I said, "I don't know about you, but I'm getting the hell out of here." In his best Southwest twang, Pepper Martin piped, "Me, too." We all retreated.

Soon it was time to go to Kansas City.

Arriving there on a sleepy Sunday morning, I was startled when I walked into the *Kansas City Star* office and found the AP's huge office agog with the kind of excitement that made me wonder whether —cripes! — those movie version, rush-rush, newsroom scenes weren't so phoney after all. The man I was supposed to see, Ed Mills, editor of Missouri state news, was tied up.

Hours later, my confidence wavering in my fitness for this pressure profession, Mills came to my bench and apologized. He was too busy and would have to mail my instructions to Columbia. I asked him, "Is this a typical Sunday in the AP?"

Mills arched a brow. "Then," he said, "you don't know. Britain has declared war on Germany."

At Columbia, in the *Daily Tribune* office, I operated from a broken-down desk that had been the AP's chair for many others, including Hal Boyle, who would win a reputation as a World War II correspondent and, ultimately, as a homespun national columnist.

Boyle could make jokes, but I was the joke when I went out for my first assignment. I was tipped by the AP's state capital bureau that a kid riding a mule, en route from Cardwell, Missouri, to Columbia for enrollment, had stopped and met the governor. He would be trundling in to Columbia soon on Highway 63.

The dumb-like-a-fox kid from the cotton country looked bigger than his four-legged friend. He had the right answers in a good, bright, brief interview. He planned to lend "Rosie" to a Columbia-area farmer "because me 'n Rosie grew up together and if I left her behind, she'd up and die."

I raced back to the office, over-eager, dashed off a short human interest story scheduled to be transmitted during the 10-minute break each hour when the two-state Missouri-Kansas hookup cut loose for originating news from St. Louis, Jefferson City, or Columbia.

I broke the circuit with an item from "CM," short for Columbia. And then, trying too hard or, if you prefer, choking up, I was stunned by the sensitivity of the keyboard. I produced gibberish. Ignoring Mills' instructions from Kansas City and Hamel's advice at Columbia, I hadn't practiced punching. In one word, my story was—a mess!

Next day I received a note from division news editor Mickelson at Kansas City, capped by the zinging sentence "Who punched that story —you or the mule?"

With the state skeet shoot scheduled over the weekend just off Highway 40, north of Columbia, I breezed out there Sunday in my green gasser, top down, September sun beating on my felt hat, fashionable in a long-sleeved shirt buttoned and a four-in-hand tie. I wheeled off the highway onto a dirt road, short of the skeet course.

As I turned right toward the sound of guns firing, my car and I were rained on by mysterious objects. Suddenly I realized — gad!—I was in the line of skeet pellets. Hurriedly, I wheeled away, returned to the highway and drove up to the proper skeet entrance, prudently parking out of sight.

Sauntering in, I inquired casually if anything unusual was going on. One of the middle-aged scorers spoke up. "Yeah," he said, "some silly sonofabitch just drove into the range."

Secrets don't last. A few days later, a "wire brightener," included reference to the effect that Bob Broeg, campus correspondent for the AP at Columbia, had beaten war correspondents to service under fire by wandering into the "wrong" end of a rifle range.

On a more serious note, a black Kansas University graduate, Lucille Bluford, applied to Missouri's famed School of Journalism. Previous efforts to achieve law school eligibility for Lloyd Gaines had failed. But if the MU Jay-School was so great and its faculty so superior, as advertised, how could black Lincoln University at Jeff City be equal? Slyly, in a losing cause, the Missouri Board of Curators arranged for MU faculty members to rotate to Lincoln, so Ms. Bluford lost her case.

I didn't know a legal tort from an apple tart, but a kindly Boone County judge named Dinwiddie practically held my hand as he guided me through the mystery of a writ of mandamus.

To keep the AP man out of the rival paper's UP office, Prof. Eugene Sharp assigned me to write the daily sports column for the six-day-a-week Journalism School newspaper.

I can remember Jake Hamel's amusement at my first AP weekly farm column. The lead paragraph began, "'The use of Korean lespedeza as a foraging crop is spreading in Missouri like a three-alarm fire.'"

Jake nodded. "Pretty good column, Broeg," he wrote, flashing teeth that were too prominent, "but I wonder how many farmers will know about a three-alarm fire."

By the time Nebraska came to town for a pivotal game in bluebird weather—Mark Twain always said he missed "Mizzourah in October" —the Tigers had rebounded from a 19-0 shutout at Ohio State.

Before the game, Coach Faurot fed his players their pre-game meal of peaches, tea and toast at a private dining area near where I sat at my *Daily Tribune* sidewalk window, head down at the typewriter.

A tapping noise drew my attention. A grinning Paul Christman stood outside. Assistant coach Phil Bengtson had taken Christman, the Orfs, and other Catholic players to Mass. Now they were joining the rest of the squad at "Duck" Mallard's nearby Harris Cafe. I gave Christman a two-hand grip as a salute of good luck. He winked.

I returned to work but quickly felt a tap on my shoulder. It was Christman, who'd found his way inside. With the back of his hand cupping the side of his mouth, he stage whispered, "I've got a scoop for you, kid. I'll pass those bums out of the stadium by the half." By halftime Christman had passed for three touchdowns, en route to a 27-13 upset.

Later in the season, Christman led Mizzou to a 7-6 win over Oklahoma that brought the Tigers the league championship and their first bowl bid—against Georgia Tech in the 1940 Orange Bowl. Tech's hocus-pocus offense beat Missouri, 21-7.

For me, Pitchin' Paul was the cherry on the top of the ice cream sundae.

Mizzou All-American Paul Christman.

16

ን

Since only one person in 50 had an automobile during the Depression, I was under the delusion it was better to be amongst the "ones" instead of the "forty-nines."

My Chevy convertible increased my popularity and earned me a choice assignment during Journalism Week. I was asked to escort two top International News Service men to an evening auditorium session.

One was Barry Faris, managing editor of the Hearst wire service. The other was a wiry little Irishman named James Killgallen, father of Dorothy Killgallen.

When I went up to their hotel room, Killgallen poured me a drink. I heard Faris gruffly bark on the phone, "No, damn it. I don't want him on the Rex. The damned Italians might turn him over to Hitler."

Afterward, as introductions were completed, I timidly asked Mr. Faris to explain. He said he'd been talking to his home office and "they just don't think. Our Vance Packard, a helluva reporter, is in Hitler's doghouse, and he's going back to Europe, but I don't want him on an Italian ship. Mussolini and Hitler are too friendly."

After the evening session, the two men wanted a drink and invited me to come along. We talked about sports. I didn't know then that Killgallen once wanted to have Burleigh Grimes rubbed out by the Big Guy (Al Capone).

When I left Killgallen and Faris, it was so late that I was surprised when I pulled up in front of what should have been a darkened fraternity house. The lights were on and the guys were listening to the radio. Why? The Germans had invaded the Lowlands.

Next morning I stopped early at the Jay School to drop off my column. The two INS men were leaving in a hurry. There would be no speaking engagement by Killgallen.

Faris shook his head. "Got to get back to New York," he said. "The Germans have invaded the Lowlands."

Yeah, I knew, Germany had decided on an end-run around France's mighty Maginot Line. I'd heard it from the fraternity brothers when they were listening to the radio early this morning and . . .

Faris looked at Killgallen and swore. "I'll be damned," he said, "here's an AP kid out in the boondocks who knows what the hell's going on in Europe, and New York doesn't even call me 'til morning. Wait 'til I get back."

That money-sucking car kept me from ducking into town for the Sunday game of the old weekend spring series with the Browns. With a couple of other guys, I got no farther than Kingdom City, 20 miles east of Columbia, when the so and so coughed to a halt. While the other fellas hitched a ride back to Columbia, I spent the day— and, of course, as usual, my money — in the job shop at that highway bus stop.

When the Cardinals sputtered early in 1940, I lost the chance for another summer in the club's P. R. Department. Owner Breadon's retrenchment included my $20 a week.

Sam understood the economics of owning a ball club. Breadon's nephew and assistant Bill Walsingham once told me, "A close second can be more profitable because it excites the fans, but, losing, you don't have the salary pressure you get from a championship team." I hate that philosophy.

The Cardinals owner had an ongoing salary hassle with slugger Joe Medwick. After Medwick's National League triple crown in 1937—237 hits, 31 homers and 154 RBIs— the player had defiantly demanded, "Now what did I do wrong this time, Mr. Rickey?"

Breadon insisted he just as soon would "throw the $2,000 out the window." Medwick zinged him back. "If you threw that $2,000 out the window, your arm still would be holding it." So Medwick and his salary were dealt to Larry MacPhail and Brooklyn in 1940 for players and cash. But none of the money was earmarked for my $20-a-week salary. I didn't have a summer job.

Paul Mickelson came to my rescue. He arranged for me to meet the National Semi-pro Baseball Congress' creator, Ray Dumont. So I began an early Sunday morning drive to Kansas City. My car threw a rod. A farmer towed my green cash sucker to a ramshackle repair shop. The car was in trouble, but I had to keep going. A streetcar took me to my appointment.

Dumont was short, dumpy, full-cheeked, and hawk nosed. He had a sloping forehead covered by fine, vanishing hair. Although he combed that remaining hair furiously with thin, feminine hands, he liked to keep his hat on.

When Ray talked, he mumbled much of the time, his mouth trying to keep up with his nimble brain. He smoked thin, cheap cigars and had to re-light them often because he drooled. Dumont worked himself up like a pinball machine on "T-I-L-T." His guttural voice spoke rapidly and those big blue eyes opened wide, as friendly as a St. Bernard's. He was entirely different from what I expected, but he hired me at $20 a week, and set a start date in May.

Meanwhile, my five-year-old green Chevy convertible was no longer a part of my life. The repair charge was $35. Instead of paying, I gave the mechanic the damned car. For me, it was addition by subtraction.

When the semester ended, I was bound for Wichita on a day train across the hot Kansas wheat fields. A great summer awaited! Hap Dumont was a joy to work with and for. In 1935 he had the idea to "go National," as he put it, meaning establishing a semi-pro tournament for teams and towns outside the purview of professional baseball.

Hap promised Leroy (Satchel) Satch $1,000 personally if he would bring his Bismark, N. D. "coloreds" to Wichita. At the time Hap talked, he didn't have the 1,000 bucks, but he was good for it, just as he promised publisher J. G. Taylor Spink of *The Sporting News* that he wouldn't take a nickel out of the first National Semi-pro Baseball Congress Tournament if the St. Louis publisher would help advertise it.

The Dumont-to-Spink-to-Paige double play combination paid off in a small profit with a large future. En route to the first championship, Satch struck out 60 batters in four games, still a record for the annual tournament.

Wichita became to the baseball "National" — Dumont put it with emphasis—what Louisville is to the Kentucky Derby and Indianapolis to the Speedway's "500." And if you think the center of Kansas' Sedgewick County is a hayseed, hick town, excuse me. I don't share the view at all.

Dumont's boyhood boss, Pete Lightner, sports editor of the *Eagle*, liked to tell about the time, engrossed in thought after a late afternoon session at the bank, Dumont waded through the snow to his office at Goldsmith's. Minutes later, stunned, he phoned the police to notify them his car had been stolen!

The cop on the desk knew better. "No, Hap," he said, "it's right where you left it—right in front of the (police) station in a no parking zone. And that's the second time this week."

Hap was a promotional master. To draw attention to "the National," Dumont installed a jack-in-the-box microphone under the ground near home plate, so the umpire could step on it and make announcements. Good idea except when an ump forgot to lower the mike before a blue-language exchange with an irate manager.

Dumont experimented with a game in which the batter could leave home plate either for first base or third. He played a Kansas State sunrise game with free coffee and doughnuts and free admission to anyone who would come in pajamas. He put in a 10-run rule, wisely copied, that ended games in which one side had that sizable lead after five innings. To move up action, he enforced a 20-second rule between pitches and 90 seconds in a change of sides by installing a klaxon, whose ugly squall was both effective and embarrassing.

Me, George Sisler, and promotional master Raymond "Hap" Dumont in 1940.

Once Hap announced that he would play a game without lights. That one attracted General Electric. He painted uniforms, ball, bat, gloves, and bases with phosphorescent paint. In a preliminary test, Hap found to his dismay that it just wouldn't work.

Shrewdly, using no seeds for his double elimination tournament of 32 state champions, Dumont would rely on his own judgment, seeking early pairings by which strong teams quickly would eliminate the weak. First, offering only limited team travel mileage, he didn't want Depression-era teams sitting around wasting hotel or travel money. So he'd bring back a losing team quickly. Second, stronger attractions built box office returns and, hopefully, an extra night's play if the champion suffered a defeat.

Dumont once persuaded a friendly Wichita manager to try plastic helmets in a Kansas State tournament game. Mickey Flynn's Wichita Civics wore 19-ounce plastics shaped like football headgear.

The majors really didn't get plastic helmets until the early 1950s. But, shucks, Hap Dumont had 'em earlier, as he did so many things in his role as baseball's Rube Goldeberg, the gimmick guy of the game.

Working the tournament for him was a dawn-to-dawn patrol job. Oh how I enjoyed it! Mom shipped my white-jacketed summer tux so I could emcee the opening night in style.

Summer formal as nifty emcee for Dumont at Wichita.

When the summer was over, I left Wichita with an unexpected $200 bonus from Hap. It was time for another semester. One midnight as friend Howard (Buck) West and I listened to the romantic midnight strains of Cincinnati's high-powered WLW, quietly playing soft music and poetry, Buck told me that, cripes, why didn't I try to find a girl with journalistic interests.

I told West the J-School gals I knew were bags. He disagreed. Why, in the basic course for juniors in journalism, he sat next to a most attractive young woman named Dorothy Carr.

Next morning, as I sneaked a last-minute smoke before an 8 a.m. class, a tall, full-lipped blonde, high cheekboned and firm chinned, stalked hurriedly down the campus toward Neff Hall and breezed past me into the building. Bless my romantic soul, I told Bucko that night that, yeah, he was right.

I asked sports information director Mark Cox if he knew Dorothy. Cox's student assistant, Art McQuiddy, spoke up and said they were good friends. Timidly, because my efforts with girls tongue tied a glib guy, I wondered if smart ol' Art could arrange a date?

Out of my bonus from Ray Dumont, I had ordered and just received a custom-made, covert-clothed, three-piece tan suit. Nice. That morning I'd stopped in and bought a new hat. So I was ready, but startled and surprised, when just before the kickoff of Missouri's opening football game the next day against St. Louis University, McQuiddy came up and piped: "You're set for tonight —7:30!"

Dorothy Alice Carr had agreed as a favor to roomie Grace Sparn and to friend McQuiddy. She inquired about me to a woman friend who had just returned to campus after a year's absence.

"Oh, yeah," the Texan replied, "I know him. A nice, fat guy!"

In advance sorrow for obviously having been hooked on a blind date, Dorothy did what she seldom did. She sipped a couple of Scotches with Sparn and Gracie's parents before she returned belatedly to the sorority house. I stood there, hat in the hand, talking with McQuiddy's mother.

Before introductions were made, Dorothy nodded and dashed upstairs to powder her nose. Mrs. McQuiddy followed her.

Ah, that lovely woman. Moments later she came downstairs, smiled and whispered, "She likes you."

The first date was unusual. We joined Mark Cox and lovely wife, Tootie, for a drink. Mark invited us to a Kappa Sig kitchen. Paul Christman wanted a couple of drinks, and he didn't want everyone to know about it, most certainly coach Don Faurot.

In a blazing late September sun that afternoon, Christman had passed for three touchdowns in an entertaining 40-26 victory over Dukes Duford's St. Louis University team. The big guy was pink cheeked and red necked from the afternoon sun as he sat with his future wife, Inez Potter.

It was a delightful evening, and Dorothy enjoyed it enough that she kissed me goodnight and invited me to an afternoon introductory tea reception for the sorority's freshman pledges. I floated away with more self-esteem than I ever had known.

17

ᨠ

When I graduated after Christmas in 1940, the *Post-Dispatch* still had no opening for me. The Associated Press assigned me temporarily to their Jefferson City office. Howard Flieger was my new boss.

Flieger was pale and frail. He typed his stories like a classical pianist plays the piano. I marveled at his crisp, clean writing under fire. Cripes, I wondered, if a man this capable were only a "correspondent," how great were the great ones? Hah! Within a year, he was covering the White House!

During my infancy days on the state capital press corps, Governor Lloyd Stark held a party in the Executive Mansion. The No. 1 Missouri citizen tingled an ice-filled drink and suggested to Flieger, "this reminds me of belled cattle in Switzerland." Flieger tinkled his own drink, nodded, and said, "but it really reminds me, Governor, that I need another Scotch and water."

Flieger gave me Fridays and Saturdays off, requiring that I begin my work week at mid-day Sunday. Almost every weekend I'd flee my sleeping room on the second floor of a Jefferson City business school and bus 30 miles to Columbia to spend time with Dorothy Carr.

As the low man on Flieger's five-person totem pole, I was hired primarily to "punch" copy. Having finally mastered the lightning reaction of the delicate direct keyboard at Columbia, I was completely lost with its direct opposite. The tape machine used at Jeff City required more forceful and faster "punching."

Finally, working alone one Sunday back from a happy weekend at Columbia, I became a passable puncher. My work assignments included editing bare bones copy for a "pony" report that went daily to several small Missouri newspapers. I worked there for several months until my temporary assignment was over. Needing a job, I hooked up again with my friend Hap Dumont.

The night I left for Wichita by train, Howard Flieger brought me up sharp. "Remember how bad you were punching at the beginning?" he said, as I shuddered. "We were so hard pressed then that I had to appeal to Paul Mickelson. And he told me that if you didn't improve by the following Sunday, he would send in a professional (commercial) puncher to take your place."

A week later my friend Mickelson called me. He had put my name into what amounted to an AP waiver list, i.e., a thumbnail sketch of potential staffers caught between engagements. Boston had claimed me.

Boston! "Yeah," insisted Mickelson, "the big leagues, but you can do it. Take it and do us both proud."

With a gulp, apologizing to Dumont for checking out unexpectedly, I traveled home by train for a tearful farewell with my family. En route to New York, I stopped off at Chicago to see Dorth and to meet her father, a quiet, shy, widowed electrical engineer. Mr. Carr had been student water-bucket man for Ol' Mizzou early in the century. And he was a baseball fan, so I had that going for me. Some day I hoped to get to know him better, and his daughter, that leggy lovely headed for her senior year.

Homesick and in love, I arrived at Boston in the late afternoon, just in time to step into the old *Boston Globe* office that housed the New England division headquarters. A hunt was on for a rapist killer and immediately they had me helping run down tips and rumors phoned in by area newspaper correspondents. They didn't know that I didn't know "Hav'ril" was spelled "Haverhill," that "PEA-body" was pronounced "Pea-BODY" and . . . uh, well you get the idea.

By mealtime, I got the message that you didn't need the last syllable if you wanted a "hamburg" or a "frankfurt." If you wanted a milk shake, you'd better ask for a "frappe." And you'd better wake up, son, and realize that the hustling desk man they labeled Frank "Hot" was really Hart.

Guess I sounded different, too, as I learned the ropes as a night side rewrite man, 5 p.m. to 2 a.m. In my free time, I went to—what else?—baseball games.

Before I left St. Louis, sports editor Ed Wray and mentor Roy Stockton had told me to look up the Braves' club president, Bob Quinn. Quinn had built nearly an American League pennant in St. Louis in 1922 and had established many friends.

Running the Braves now on a string and a prayer and some of manager Casey Stengel's money, Honest Bob had a ball club so bad that the only .300 hitter, pinch-fielding center field veteran Johnny Cooney, couldn't have hit a home run if he had batted from second base.

When I met the 72-year-old Quinn, he told me, "Bobby, I feel so good I could jump out this window." That would have been a floor-and-a-half flop to concrete.

The manager also gave me a warm greeting that prompted a good friendship. Charles Dillon (Casey) Stengel played high school sports at Kansas City Central with Missouri University's basketball coach, gentlemanly George Edwards. Coach Edwards had a message of good cheer for me to give to his boyhood buddy.

Ol' Case was 52 when I met him. Gosh, he seemed older. Yet his growling, gravelly voice had the power of a young bull. He extolled Edward's versatility on their baseball and basketball teams, demonstrating how he (Case) had hid behind a church basement pillar to receive a pass from good ol' George for the winning basket.

Prominent for the other Boston team, the Red Sox, was wide-hipped, crabby, graying Lefty Grove, struggling—and succeeding—at age 40 to cap a great career with 300 victories. And then there was Ted Williams, who daily did 75 regular push-ups and 75 more on his fingertips. I was privileged to be there when Williams hit .400, now a much more magical figure then it was a half century ago. After all, Bill Terry had hit .401 a decade earlier, 1930, and I'd grown up in a decade, the 1920s, when Ty Cobb and Harry Heilmann did it and George Sisler twice and, cripes, Rogers Hornsby had *averaged* .400 for five seasons, 1921 through 1925.

Time has magnified the magnificence of Teddy Ballgame's accomplishments, climaxed by his final day heroics. With a .3995 average, "The Kid," as they called him, ignored manager Joe Cronin's kind suggestion that he sit out the final double-header at Philadelphia. After all, they would move up the fraction to .400.

The night before, nervous, he almost tied his doubleheader record. Once, as a kid, Williams wolfed down a shortcake and a malted milk, 13 ice cream bars and 11 bottles of soda.

Philadelphia catcher Frankie Hayes wished him well, but warned Ted he wouldn't get a "blankety" break because Connie

Mack threatened to run his battery out of baseball if they eased up. Bill McGowan, who would rate as Williams' favorite umpire and many others', too, fussed at the plate, dusting it off, and said without looking at Ted, "To hit .400 a hitter has got to be loose. He's got to be loose . . . "

He was. The floppy-armed, leggy hitter with the eye of an eagle and the selection of a patient parent when assessing pitches did it royally. He went "6 for 8" in the double-header. .406!

The Yanks were en route to another world championship. Joe DiMaggio hit safely in 56 straight games. The July 17th night Joe Dee's streak was stopped in Cleveland, a gabby cab driver told Joe he had a "feeling" the streak would end. When DiMaggio and his early day protector, Lefty Gomez, left the cab at the lake front stadium, Gomez grumbled, "Why in the hell did you tip him? The guy was trying to jinx you."

I got Gomez's number from the *Boston Globe* and called him to ask for an interview. Reluctantly, he agreed, but only if I could meet him at Harvard, where he played squash to stay in shape.

Once there I told him that I just had left the office and heard unfortunate news. Beautiful comedienne Carole Lombard had been killed in Indiana in a plane crash on a War Bond tour.

Gomez plopped onto a nearby bench. "She's — was— such a good friend of my wife and me. Clark Gable's wife, you know?"

To this day, I can remember straddling the bench, looking over Lefty's shoulder as the rivulets of rain streaked down on the dressing room windows behind the ballplayer. If I said they reminded me of tears, you might think I was hokey, but they did.

My tears in 1941 were for the running Redbirds, called the "St. Louis Swifties" by *New York World-Telegram* cartoonist Willard Mullin. Billy Southworth had built a young team of greyhounds. They reacted to his spit-and-polish discipline. Coaching third base, Southworth even wore sliding pads!

If you came aboard this earth after sliding pads abandoned ship, they were strapped at the waist and thighs like a western gunslinger's holster, worn primarily to keep players from rubbing the meaty parts of the flesh in painful sliding contusions, i.e., "strawberries." Wet with sweat, they were too damned hot.

So were the Dodgers under ex-Redbird Leo Durocher. The Flatbush faithful were acting up persistently and comically at Ebbets Field, self-styling their team as the "Bums."

Not my favorites, of course, but the nation's, and the sentimental butt of radio jokes regularly. Pitcher Kirby Higbe seemed to summarize their style best. In Brooklyn patois, he was called "Higglesby."

One time when his wife intercepted a steamy love letter from a feminine fan who obviously knew him too well, the pitcher issued the most outrageous denial. Said he to her, mister to missus, "There must be another Kirby Higbe."

To my dismay, the Dodgers won the pennant that year. I saw lefthander Howie Pollet's big-league debut, happy at Boston to greet old friends Roy Stockton, Leo Ward and older players I knew best from my years working at the ballpark.

But it was another day at Braves Field when a pitch from Boston left-hander Art Johnson skulled my friend Terry Moore and sent him to the dirt, a victim of a fractured skull. I raced from the rooftop pressbox to the playing field. There, watching as doctors hovered over Moore, I listened to Johnny Mize, standing by with bat in hand, as the big slugging first baseman muttered:

"That's the final straw . . ."

Cardinals first baseman and single-season home run record holder Johnny Mize.

In a showdown series in St. Louis, the Durochers took two out of three. Brooklyn's "Peepul's Cherce," Dixie Walker, was pivotal in the critical decisive third game of the series, a duel between Whitlow Wyatt and Mort Cooper. Mort had a no-hitter until the eighth when Walker doubled. From second, Dixie dexterously pilfered catcher Walker Cooper's curve ball signal.

Surreptitiously, Walker wig-wagged the information to the next hitter, Billy Herman.

Banjo-eyed Billy, knowing the curve was coming, drilled it to right-center, where Johnny Hopp was no Terry Moore. The ball landed for a run-scoring double and a 1-0 Brooklyn victory.

That did it, and, with me as an unhappy witness, the Dodgers clinched the pennant at Boston with a victory over Casey Stengel's kissing-cousin Braves.

After a series in St. Louis, Case told me, "Your club has got a new one—kid with a funny name—and he's going to be a great one. He hit the crap out of Tobin's knuckler and he lined another hit off a dead fish. You'll hear about him, *Brogue!*" I figured he meant the unusual name I'd seen in the late season box score— someone named Stan Musial.

I listened to one game of the Dodgers vs. Yankees World Series from an unusual position. At the invitation of the AP's Tom Horgan, I rode Boston Harbor in his 24-foot ketch, listening to his radio. During the ninth inning of an apparent Brooklyn victory that would have won the series, I sat perched on the shallow bulkhead of Horgan's boat.

When Mickey Owen missed a game-ending third strike to Tommy Henrich, setting up a four-run Yankee reprieve, I was so startled I slipped backward and my hind side was baptized.

When baseball was over, all I had were movies and mail to help me forget St. Louis and Dorth. I couldn't afford the cost of a long-distance call. Four bucks out of only $32.50 a week.

Pardon my whine, but I wasn't writing enough sports. I did cover a Boston College-Manhattan football game at Fenway Park, drawing a kind word from AP sports editor Herb Bunker in New York for a parallel in likening B. C.'s Teddy Williams dashes toward the right field bleachers as a takeoff on *the* Ted Williams.

I became a boating "expert," covering a crew race on the Charles River among Cornell, Navy, Wisconsin, and the Massachusetts Institute of Technology. And I bulletined a track and field event, the Boston Amateur Athletic Union, in which fabulous Cornelius (Dutch) Warmerdam exceeded 15 feet in the pole vault when he was far superior to any competitor. With present equipment and methods, Warmerdam well might have been like Russia's Sergi Bubka, a 20-foot vaulter.

Once the *Post-Dispatch* asked if I could cover a football game between Missouri and New York University at Yankee Stadium. Traveling by early train, I got to the hotel suite occupied by my old publicist pal, Mark Cox. Don Faurot invented the Split T formation, and his team, using it well, was bound for the Sugar Bowl. The Tigers shut out New York University, 26-0.

Afterward, thrilled at alma mater Missouri's success, columnist Bill Corum of the *New York American* wanted to take Cox and new line coach Harry Smith out on the town until their midnight train trip from Penn Station.

Me? I was delighted to tag along to the famed Stork Club and then the private wine cellars of the "Twenty-One Club." Finally, we stopped at a new first-class "saloon" recently opened by a former bartender, Toots Shor, who became as colorful as his crumb-bum greeting. What a night!

World War II sneaked up on all of us soon after. Sleepy-eyed after a long Saturday night, none of us knew where the hell Pearl Harbor was! Earlier in 1941, I'd been drafted, but my bum left eye got me a 4-F label.

In Boston, I'd become collared in the sports editor's dog house. His Jekyll and Hyde mood swings, as he came in early with a curt greeting and then returned long-fanged from a long liquid dinner, were tough to take. Once he called me a vile name and we almost came to blows. He was a nasty drunk, and I don't like to be pushed. It was time to move on. But how? And where?

With the war on, Wichita's two-man bureau was jeopardized. Paul Mickelson needed a ready-made one-man replacement. He asked for me.

My Boston bureau chief called me in, smiled, and broke what he considered good news. New York AP would have to okay the transfer, a formality. I wrote the folks and Dorothy. I'd get to see them, if only briefly.

I packed my steamer trunk and gave up my place to live. Every day lasted too long. Finally, the date of departure came and the bureau chief had me drop by his office. New York's approval had not yet arrived. He phoned them from the privacy of his office.

Seconds later, he walked out, frowning, "The general manager (Lloyd Stratton) turned down Mickelson's request. Called it inexpedient."

A regular melodrama. Stranded on a snowy day. Hauling my belongings in a trunk. Heartbroken, I found a flea-bag place to live and awaited spring and the soothing salve of baseball, hopeful of getting more sportswriting opportunities.

Casey Stengel always made me feel better. In 1942, he came back from Sanford, Florida with another woeful team despite the presence of two big-name players, catcher Ernie Lombardi and outfielder Paul Waner, now 39 years old.

At times, by his own admission, Waner saw three balls at the plate and picked out the one in the center. One day at camp, the veteran outfielder asked Stengel about an advertisement on the right field fence. He couldn't make it out. Stengel's eyes widened.

"The ball isn't the same size, either," suggested Waner. It's size now? Stengel wondered. "Oh, about the size of a ball."

"About the size of a ball," exclaimed Casey, "well, how in the hell big did it used to look?"

Gravely, said Waner, "As big as a grapefruit."

Waner was within reaching distance of 3,000 hits. Eddie Collins and Tris Speaker had achieved this distinction in 1925. The last National Leaguer to reach the milestone had been Waner's famed Pittsburgh predecessor, Honus Wagner, retired since 1917.

Aware of hitters who had *not* achieved the Mt. Everest of hitting—Babe Ruth, Lou Gehrig, Rogers Hornsby, George Sisler, Bill Terry, Al Simmons and, oh, so many other great batters— I became obsessed. The AP assigned me to follow Waner's assault.

From afar, I winced in a game at Pittsburgh's Forbes Field, where obviously P. G. would have loved to deliver the clincher. With a runner on first, Waner grounded to deep short and when the shortstop's throw to second base was too late for a force out, the scorer called the play a late fielder's choice rather than an appropriate infield single.

Back at Boston, playing Cincinnati, Paul grounded to deep short. Eddie Joost juggled the ball briefly. Palms down, first base umpire Tom Dunn signaled, "Safe!"

In the press box, Gerry Moore of the *Post* planned as scorer to hold out his forefinger in the familiar "hit" sign gesture. But — lo! — standing on the bag, looking up to the cozy close press box, Waner shook his head and brushed his arms sideways. He didn't want it.

A couple of days later, Waner lined a shot between the legs of pitcher Rip Sewell and into center field. As Paul reached base, Stengel waddled out of the Braves' third base dugout and Pirates' manager Frank Frisch trudged to first base. Waner had done it!

My brief stay in Boston was unusual from a standpoint of individual accomplishments, e.g., Williams' .406 batting average, Lefty Grove's 300th victory, Waner's 3,000th hit and, indeed, a *pitcher* hit four home runs in succession!

That honor belonged to the Braves' Jim Tobin. One day "Old Ironsides" delivered a pinch homer. Next day he pitched and won by hitting three homers.

Meanwhile, the young Cardinals rookie with the funny name, Musial, skidded in the Grapefruit League. But Stengel wasn't fooled. With a knowing wink, he told me, "Your fella is going to hit— for the next 10, 15, maybe 20 years."

Although Brooklyn broke strongly from the gate in 1942 and the Cardinals trailed, Stengel liked the St. Louis Swifties. He also liked to deliver monologues if anyone would listen.

"I hafta say that club is amazing," said Casey. "They don't steal many bases, but, my, those jackrabbits are so fast that they pressure my infielders and outfielders into hurrying." He pantomimed juggling the ball as if playing with a hot potato. "They force errors and turn singles into doubles, doubles into triples."

Cutups Casey Stengel and Frank Frisch.

By early August, though winning often, the Cardinals still trailed the Dodgers by a dozen games. Stengel steamed after a comic opera contest, the worst beanball battle any of us had seen. Whit Wyatt, already 13-3, owned 10 straight over a ball club that hadn't beat him in four years, but his head-hunting awakened the Braves and infuriated Stengel.

Wyatt knocked down Boston's leadoff batter, Tommy Holmes, with his first pitch. Twice against the Braves' only power hitter, Max West, control pitcher Wyatt forced West to hit the dirt. The Boston bench began to trade insults with Durocher and his side. When Wyatt came up, the Braves' Manny Salvo, back from a sore arm, forced Wyatt to go down. When Manny came up, Whit retaliated against him.

In Boston's sixth inning, Wyatt threw three pitches under West's chin, then walked him, and Max carried his bat to first base. So when Wyatt batted in the seventh, Salvo plunked a pitch into the rival's ribs. Angrily, Wyatt took two steps toward the mound, then threw his bat at Salvo. Both benches cleared. When Wyatt brushed Salvo's arms with a pitch in Boston's seventh, another fight nearly began. The result set up the winning run for the Braves, 2-1.

Afterward, Stengel was furious, "If I had a ball club as good as his, I wouldn't throw at a club as lousy as mine. They don't have to pull stuff like that to win." Pouring himself another beer, he nodded to me, "This race isn't over. This fella's club has been winning steadily. No, Brooklyn ain't in yet. And I know other clubs have got it in for 'em. I talked to (Frank) Frisch and (Jimmy) Wilson and the rest."

So the Cardinals had an opportunity to make their move. So did I.

I had written to Roy Stockton regularly, bracing myself not to expect a reply. One letter told him of my troubles with my supervisor, including our near fight. His answer came surprisingly quick.

"Dear Bob: Well, it seems to me you've come a long way before you met your first sonofabitch . . ."

My mentor was right. Until my problems with the AP's divisional New England sports editor, everyone treated me royally. I am a lucky guy.

The rest of Stockton's note told me the *Post-Dispatch* had no opening on its sports staff, but why didn't I try the rival *Star-Times*? The sports editor, Sid Keener, had a young staff, most of which was on the move as a result of the war. Suggested Stockton: "Go with Sid and beat our ass. Make the *Post-Dispatch* hire you."

Okay. I wrote Keener, a feisty, fiery little man who could praise highly or criticize with enthusiasm in his dual role as sports editor and columnist of the "other" St. Louis afternoon newspaper.

I cannot tell a lie. I told Keener a lie. I told him my salary was $50 a week.

Keener was suspicious of any guy who wanted to leave Boston. Ray Gillespie, Keener's right-hand man whom I knew, advised him that, cripes, Sid, this is the kid's home.

So Keener wrote that he just had lost his best baseball writer to service. But no one could expect 50 bucks. His best would be $42.50.

Wow, $7.50 more than I was making plus I could live at home. I accepted and phoned Mom to get the spareribs, sauerkraut and mashed potatoes ready.

Before I left, I said a fond farewell to Casey Stengel.

"Some day, Case," I told him, "you'll get a good ball club and prove you're a good manager. Some day your ship will come in."

18

Back home again in St. Louis in 1942! The war made it the worst of times. The Cardinals made it the best.

Don Drees was covering the Redbirds for the *Star-Times* so I was an "inside" man for the sports staff. The bulk of my work was copyreading, re-write, and making sure the newspaper's agate-type baseball play-by-play was correct.

The '42 Redbirds were the best of the Cardinals' 15 pennant-winners and one of the most well-balanced ball clubs in baseball history. They were blessed with tremendous team speed, an excellent defense, and pitching talent both rich and deep.

This team represented the complete triumph of Branch Rickey's farm system. In '42, Rickey was a lame peacock—like a duck, only more egotistical. He had been notified his contract as general manager would not be renewed, but he was a prize catch for any ball club willing to pay the financial—and psychological—price. Thanks in part to a 20 percent share of player sales profits, Rickey, a past master at hoodwinking the buyer, earned $80,000 in 1942.

Members of the talented '42 Redbirds: Ray Sanders, Walker Cooper, Mort Cooper, and Enos Slaughter.

But Breadon was no longer willing to tolerate Rickey's questionable manpower shenanigans. The scotch-sipping, barbershop-harmonizing Democrat didn't want the teetotaling, psalm-singing Republican around any longer.

The 1942 Bums left the gate in first place and never did fold. After the Boston beanball flare-up I had witnessed, the Brooks won 30 of their last 47 games, a pennant pace, but not quite so good as before they began to fire up their foes.

But when the cream rose to the top, it was colored Cardinal red. About the time I was preparing to make my move, Billy Southworth's St. Louis Swifties made theirs. When they returned to St. Louis in mid-August for a 22-game stand—still eight and a half games back—young outfielder Harry Walker added a novelty number to their collection of clubhouse phonograph records.

Spike Jones' clattering hillbilly number, "Pass the Biscuits, Mirandy," became the victory song. Mort Cooper, stalled repeatedly at what he regarded as a lucky number, changed from his "13" and began to win. After every victory, he borrowed the next highest jersey number. The road runners were off and running.

When the Dodgers came to town and lost three out of four, the lead was reduced to five games. By the time I was on my way home, the deficit was just two games, and the Cards were in New York to play the Dodgers.

I entered the Cardinals' clubhouse at a time few writers did. To my dismay, the Redbirds were grim and silent. I went up to the pressbox, sat down next to Stockton, and shook my head. P-r-e-s-s-u-r-e.

The Dodgers felt it, too. They were so tight, their spiked shoes squeaked. Mort Cooper held them hitless for five innings, drove in the first run off rival Whit Wyatt and won his 20th game, 3-0. Next day before I had to leave for St. Louis, Whitey Kurowski hit a two-run homer off Max Macon, and Max Lanier made it hold up. Winning 29 out of the last 34, the Cardinals had drawn even with only 14 games to go.

Musial's grand slam homer off Pittsburgh's Rip Sewell— off whom he had hit his first homer at Forbes Field the previous September—produced a 4-3 final week victory. The lemon of the Grapefruit League, living up to Casey Stengel's predictions, hit .315 that year, second only to Enos Slaughter's .318.

My job at Boston had started at 5 p.m. But now I had to catch a 5 a.m. streetcar in St. Louis for the half-hour trip downtown to the *Star-Times*. But I was happy on all counts except for a delay in seeing Dorth. From a graduate assistant's job in journalism advertising, Miss Carr had moved to the editorial staff of Meredith's *Better Homes and Gardens* magazine in Des Moines. We'd have to wait.

But not the road-running Redbirds. By the final day of the season at Sportsman's Park, they owned a game-and-a-half lead, two up on the decisive defeat side. Although manager Southworth wisely said a ball club shouldn't think pennant until it was 30 games over .500 —you know, 90 and 60 with only a few to play — team captain Terry Moore wouldn't go that far.

Hailed time and again as the ball club's "inspiration," by Slaughter, Musial, and Walker, Moore explained to newsmen and announcers his reticence. "We're not saying a thing," he said. "I've not only been on four second-place ball clubs in seven years, but back in 1935, we didn't do a damned thing wrong and lost. Chicago won 21 in a row."

The 1942 Dodgers would know what the 1935 Gas House Gang felt. Durocher's dudes finished with a flourish, a 104-48 record, including, as mentioned, their last eight. But in the opener of the Cardinals' final day double-header with the Cubs, slick young lefty Ernie White pitched effectively, and the Cardinals clobbered Lon Warneke early.

As Warneke took the traditional short cut to the showers, exiting through the third base home dugout, he snapped to his former teammates, "All right, you bastards, there's your lead. Now, let's see you hold it."

They did. When the game-ending fly settled in Musial's glove, the Cardinals were two up with one to play. They won the last game for victory No. 106 and 43 of the last 52.

In the World Series, the Cardinals faced the mighty Yankees, who had lost only four of 36 games in a romp through seven previous Series appearances.

The Bombers won the opener, 7-4, while I worked "inside" the *Star-Times*. I was on hand for the second game, and the Cardinals won 4-3, thanks to some great defense. Enos Slaughter threw out a tying run.

When the Series moved to Yankee Stadium, that great defense permitted Ernie White to become the first pitcher to shut out the Yanks in Series play since Jesse Haines back in 1926 Musial went back for one good catch and later, when Stan slipped in left center on a Joe DiMaggio line drive, Terry Moore leaped over the fallen Musial to make a brilliant backhanded catch.

Slaughter completed the frosting at the finish when King Kong Charlie Keller lofted what seemed likely to be a decisive three-run homer. Enos raced back to the low barrier in right field and, timing his leap, caught the ball just as an orange, thrown from the stands, blurred across his vision.

Slaughter told me: "Moore raced in, beefing to (umpire) Cal Hubbard, who said that, yeah, if I hadn't caught the ball, he would have called Keller out. But that would have been the day —an American League umpire costing the Yankees a World Series ball game in Yankee Stadium!"

Next day, proving that they could score as well as pitch and field, the Cardinals won a wild one, 9-6. When Southworth ordered a suicide squeeze play, batter Marty Marion missed the sign. With fleet Moore charging home from third, Marty swung away as Terry virtually skidded to a halt. As the bat swished in front of his handsome Irish phiz, Moore yelled, "Hey, Marty," then tagged home plate with a grin because Marion's swing resulted in a single.

Yankees manager Joe McCarthy took umbrage at the "little guy" in the Redbird dugout, diminutive equipment manager Morris (Butch) Yatkeman. When captain Moore took out the lineup card for the fifth game at New York, American League umpire Bill Summers told him, apologetically, that the Yankees objected to Yatkeman's presence in the dugout.

"Little Butch," exclaimed Moore, glaring at the Yankees' messenger, jut-jawed third base coach Art Fletcher. Simmering, Moore nodded to Summers, then addressed Fletcher. "Listen, Chisel Chin, tell Mac there ain't going to be no 'tomorrow' in this Series."

There wasn't. Whitey Kurowksi wrapped a two-run homer around the left field foul pole in the ninth, providing Johnny Beazley a 4-2 lead going into the last of the ninth. But the Yankees died hard. Joe Gordon singled and Redbird second baseman Jimmy Brown muffed Bill Dickey's grounder.

Redbird benchwarmer Frank Crespi exhorted trainer Harrison J. "Doc" Weaver to apply the "double whammy" against the Bombers. Weaver bared his teeth in a combination sneer and snarl, put the back of his left hand on top of the right and pointed the little fingers of each hand toward Gordon.

After the next pitch, catcher Walker Cooper gunned the ball to Marty at second, behind the runner. Out! The deed was done. Jerry Priddy popped up and pinch hitter George Selkirk grounded out.

Cardinals trainer Doc Weaver applies the double whammy successfully from the bench.

The Cardinals' world championship made my homecoming even happier. So did Sid Keener's assignments.

At the time, no St. Louis newspaper covered Missouri regularly. With no Sunday paper, this economy made more sense for the *Star-Times* than the *Post-Dispatch* and *Globe-Democrat*. Keener assigned me to cover the homes games of both Washington University and St. Louis U.

Both local universities then were in the Missouri Valley Conference and had good coaches. Washington had Tom (Kitty) Gorman and St. Louis U. was led by Dukes Duford.

Their 1942 game was played on Thanksgiving at St. Louis' Walsh Stadium. Dorothy had come in from Des Moines to meet my folks. She and Pop watched together as St. Louis U. won a resounding 26-0 victory.

Dorth's visit enabled her to finish a job switch that—happy days! —would put the two of us in the same town for the first time since I left Columbia for the Jeff City AP job almost two years earlier. Miss Carr would switch jobs two weeks hence to become assistant news editor of the American Red Cross' 17-state midwestern office, headquartered in St. Louis.

A week later, handling copy at the sports desk as Georgia's Frank Sinkwich completed a Heisman Trophy season against rival Georgia, I was startled by the hectic bell ringing of an AP "FLASH." A "BULLETIN" was frequent, a "FLASH" rare.

This one conveyed the information that President Roosevelt had barred enlistments in the Navy and Marines for the first time in their history, putting both in Selective Service, from which Army obtained most of its manpower. I shrugged, interesting, but . . .

That second Saturday in December, Dorth came in on a morning train from Des Moines. She had found an apartment in University City. But I drove her to our house in Pop's car for breakfast. Wasn't it wonderful we were finally going to live in the same city?

While we were eating, I received a phone call.

"Brogue?" said the voice.

"Yes, this is Bob Broeg."

"This is First Sergeant Butler, " roared the voice of the top enlisted man at St. Louis' Marine recruiting office.

"Oh, yes, First Sergeant Butler."

"You still want to get in the Marines?"

Startled, I said, "Uh, y-e-a-h."

"Well, get your ass down to Union Station by midnight Monday. You got to be movin'."

First Sgt. Butler must have hated President Roosevelt's week-old edict, barring Navy-Marine enlistments. With a 10-day period of grace expiring December 15, top Marine brass must have decided to approve every Tom, Dick and Robert who had requested to enlist in the Corps.

And, yes, I had asked.

So before returning to our happy brunch, I went upstairs to my room, rooted out a present, a woman's watch, and walked into the kitchen. To Dorth, I said, "Merry Christmas!"

My announcement and explanation brought a stunned look from Dorothy. Mom teared up, walked out of the room for a moment and returned with my Christmas present: six beautiful white shirts, engraved with green "RWB" initials, a gift I wouldn't wear for nearly three years.

I was extremely apologetic when I phoned Sid Keener with the news. The best I could give was two days' notice, not two weeks. Keener told me to forget it, because, yeah, war was sure hell, but could I work Monday before leaving Monday night?

I never saw Union Station as packed as it was the night I was sworn in and shoved off on a late train for the Marine recruiting station at San Diego.

A couple of dawns later we pulled into "Dago," as they called it, and saw a rickety wagon at the station with a sorry looking group of guys.

Who were they? Our Marine driver knew. They were last-minute rejects, kids who had shown previously unrevealed physical unfitness after arriving at camp.

I shuddered. What a hell of a way to slink back home. When the Navy corpsman in charge of visual tests got to me, I covered my left eye and, of course, I read with 20-20 acuity. But when he covered my right eye and wanted me to read with the left, I paused. He ordered me to take a step forward.

I walked slowly until I was flush with a distant wall. The corpsman blurted with the nicety of military language, "What are you, a f - - - - -g clown?"

Before I could plead that I wasn't Emmett Kelly, the corpsman had screamed, "Captain!"

A medical four-striper appeared. The corpsman stated his disgust to the officer.

The captain asked to see my service record book, a military passport by which a service man hopefully stays out of trouble. The doctor opened it, turned the long, slender book sideways, then showed a tissue stapled in.

"Waivers, corpsman," the medical man said. "The man signed them — on his eye and feet."

The corpsman read the tissue insert, thanked the officer, and said with a sigh, "War sure is hell, ain't it, Captain?"

19

When I returned from boot camp in February of 1943 to become a recruiting sergeant in St. Louis, I was lean and trim and filled with great admiration for the Corps.

Living in St. Louis meant I had access to Mom's culinary best — her rich, tangy lemon meringue pie still is best ever — and to the apple of my romantic eye. I met Dorth after work that first day when she came down the O'Reilly building elevator.

There I stood, sun-kissed and boot-haircutted, wearing the Marines' forest green. Dorth took one step forward, stopped, raised her head and laughed. Her greeting? *"The green Marine with the red nose."*

My proposal came on Valentine's Day at a Billiken basketball game and she accepted, suggesting a late fall wedding. I bid for an earlier date, because I had read that if a couple married before July 1, they could receive a full-year's benefit for tax purposes. We were married on June 19, 1943.

Dorth and I on our wedding day, June 19, 1943.

Dorth was hardly a great sports fan, but she had educated ears and was willing to learn. I took her to the Browns' home opener against the Chicago White Sox. I was well aware that the Spalding Company had manufactured an ersatz ball, called the "balata," a poor green-tree substitute for precious war-time rubber. We watched Luke Appling loop a couple of soft foul balls down the right field line. Munching peanuts, Dorth asked:

"What's wrong with the ball? I didn't go to many games in Chicago, but the ball didn't sound like a rock. Appling's foul ball used to go farther." She was right. The balata was a dead ball bust.

I don't think many women were subjected to a honeymoon like Dorothy Carr Broeg. The day after the wedding, with her Cub fans father and grandfather in town, we sat in steaming heat through a doubleheader between the pennant-bound Cardinals and sixth-place Cubbies. Next day, a Monday, the Marines generously gave me off. Dorth had to work her 9-to-5 at the Red Cross office.

One day Dorth and I went to a game and saw what amounted to man-bites-dog news. In the process of a Redbird doubleheader sweep over the Dodgers, Brooklyn right-hander Les Webber irritated the mighty Musial, en route to his first batting championship. Webber decked Stan with the first pitch, then forced him to back away from three high-and-tight deliveries.

For the only time in his career, Musial had had enough. On Ball Four, he started to the mound, but he was restrained by catcher Mickey Owen and plate umpire Al Barlick. A fight was averted, if only briefly. Next up, big Walker Cooper grounded out and apparently stepped intentionally on the foot of Brooklyn first baseman Augie Galan. Walk was tougher than brother Mort and meaner, too.

Trailing the play as catcher, Owen saw the spiking and raced, fully geared, toward Cooper. Just as Walker turned, Mickey leaped. One catcher caught the other, fully geared, like a trapeze artist. Coop slammed Owen to the ground. Both benches emptied, police were called, and Cooper and Owen were ejected.

One day I was notified I'd been unexpectedly transferred to Marine headquarters in suburban Washington. It was tough to leave my bride of only a few weeks.

Why was I reassigned? The Marines, usually to their disgust, are second-class citizens as part of the Navy. General

Littleton Waller Tazeleton Waller asked me: "Could I help produce for the Marines something superior to the Navy personnel magazine?"

Cripes, though I hoped to write for magazines, all I'd ever actually done was read them. I hardly knew a page layout from a basketball lay-up. But one is wise not to falter or stammer in front of the brass. Besides, I recognized the name of an artist the general said would do our color covers. Alex Raymond was the artist, and his "Flash Gordon" was one of the best newspaper cartoons of the time.

So I nodded, held my breath, and took over temporarily, a momentary staff of one. I did all right against the backdrop of a sobering sound. Every day I heard "Onward Christian Soldiers" played during funerals at Arlington National Cemetery, located directly across the road.

One day I was interviewing a good-looking, well-coiffed man named Bonham, who was the Red Cross director. When I mentioned that my wife happened to be assistant news director of the ARC's midwestern office, he wondered "if my feelings would be hurt" if he found her qualified for the same job in Washington? Joy! Sure enough, Dorth soon joined me in Washington.

Sports? Although, as in St. Louis, servicemen were admitted free to sporting events much of the time, I still used my BBWAA pass to renew acquaintances and meet new friends in the press box, including the *Washington Post*'s gifted Shirley Povich.

Through former sports writer Dick McCann, General Manager of the Washington Redskins, I arranged for a season ticket. Dorth didn't like cold weather, but I wasn't about to miss a chance to see rangy Sammy Baugh. Baugh was the passer who best seemed to take advantage of the slenderized ball.

As deep man in the single wing, Baugh pinpointed passes with a rifle arm. The leggy Texan's punting was a sight to behold, particularly his artful quick kicks.

I love football, but baseball is my main passion.

For the 1943 World Series, travel had been altered so that three games would be played in Yankee Stadium and the next four in St. Louis if necessary. Old boss Sid Keener offered to get me a Series press ticket and to share his hotel room at the New

Yorker if I could get away from Washington. I requested a few days' furlough.

The experience was one of my fondest, an oasis in a time of strife. Meat points were tough to get under rationing. So was good whiskey, but the hotel dredged up the finest in food and drink for Cardinals traveling secretary Leo Ward and his friends, one of whom was the manager of St. Louis's outdoor Municipal Theatre and its indoor American Theatre — Paul Beisman.

Aware of my interest in show business, Beisman told me a little story. "The Theatre Guild has come up with a new concept, and I've just put $1,000 in it. It's a different weave of music out of the book. Rodgers and Hammerstein did it — 'Oklahoma.'"

As for the Series, well, heck, when former boss Keener asked for a suggested pre-Series paragraph lead, I thought the fact that the Yankees were favored over the world champions was most newsworthy. As in most instances, the bookies were right.

The Cardinals had won 105 games, seven more than the Yankees. As in 1942, the Redbirds lost the Series opener, 4-2. But the next day belonged, heroically and tragically, to the Cooper brothers. Their father, Robert, a mail-carrier in western Missouri, dropped dead of a heart attack. Mort pitched and won, 4-3, then departed for home. Brother Walker caught and joined the funeral wake later. The Yankees won the next three games, clinching the championship in St. Louis against Mort Cooper, who had rejoined the team, on a two-run homer by Bill Dickey.

Dickey was in a glow riding the elevator in the Chase Hotel after the Yankees' championship celebration. A slightly built service man addressed the tall catching veteran and said, "Bet you don't know me, Bill."

Dickey smiled a tipsy smile. "I can't think of the name," one ball player said to the other, "but I know how we pitched to you."

Any baseball fan worth his salt yearns for spring training to begin and dreams of being there. I was no exception, even if getting there wasn't easy.

Effective in 1943, the Eastman-Landis line, named for the national director of transportation and the baseball commissioner, limited spring training for baseball. Ball clubs had to train north of the Ohio River and east of the Mississippi.

Some unusual "addresses" appeared as training sites, like Bear Mountain, New York, where the Brooklyn Dodgers operated for new club president Branch Rickey. The Washington Senators trained on the University of Maryland campus at College Park.

In 1944 and 1945, I did whatever I could to "be there" at the Washington and Boston camps. One Sunday morning in 1944, I took a trip to Georgetown University, where the Boston Braves trained under a new manager, Bob Coleman. Casey Stengel and most of my friends were missing. Ol' Case had been struck down by a taxi as he crossed Kenmore Square. He suffered a fracture of one leg so severe, that in a baseball uniform the leg looked as if a baseball were stuck in the sock.

Boston sports columnist Dave Egan, whose attacks on Casey and Ted Williams make today's critical columnists seem like Sunday school teachers, gleefully suggested that Boston's man of the year was the cabbie who hit Ol' Case!

"My" team, as Stengel would say, won a third straight pennant in a breeze. They still had Musial, the brothers Cooper, and the first player ever to win a Most Valuable Player virtually with glove alone, Mr. Shortstop Marion. A second-season veteran, Harry (The Cat) Brecheen, was 16-5 and a new one, Ted Wilks, was 17-4 before he became "The Cork," nicknamed aptly as a rally-stopping reliever. The Cardinals also brought back 40-year-old Pepper Martin.

One day Martin played right field next to Musial. Stan, a good outfielder, lost a fly ball in the sun. Kerplunk! — the ball hit him on the head and bounded away. Stan was dazed and embarrassed as Martin raced after the ball, fielded it and fired back to the infield. Solicitously, Pepper came over, put his arm around No. "6" and inquired, "Ya all right, kid?" Musial nodded affirmatively. Martin doubled over and flopped to the ground, "You don't mind if I laugh, do ya?"

The best laugh that season was enjoyed, of all people, by the St. Louis Browns, who won their first nine games in 1944. That fast start of club general manager Bill DeWitt's carefully contrived roster of castoffs and cutthroats, 4-F's, and players able to escape from war plants, created a fascinating feeling for many, including me. If the Browns won the pennant, St. Louis would have a unique Streetcar World Series. I writhed in desire to see at least part of it.

I've always had good breaks, but I couldn't believe it when, smiling around his pipe, a boss major approached my desk.

IBM research had kicked out the fact that only four members of the Baseball Writers' Association of America were in the Marines. The other three were in the Pacific, presumably all combat correspondents. So the Marines' entertainment monthly, *Leatherneck Magazine*, wondered with permission approved if I'd like to cover *all* Series games at their expense?

My hopes soared high for a Brownie final-day victory after manager Luke Sewell's swashbucklers did the impossible, winning three straight from the third-place Yankees. The final-day showdown contained high drama.

First, an apparent gambler phoned Washington's Emil (Dutch) Leonard at the Detroit hotel, where the Senators would finish against the Tigers, offering a "bribe." The Dutchman recommended one of Stockton's utterly impossible dispositions. Leonard beat the Tigers, 4-1.

The Brownies' largest single-game crowd ever in St. Louis, more than 37,000, shoehorned into Sportsman's Park. A warplant wonder, Chet Laabs, flew in from Detroit for the showdown. With the Series kielbasa in the frying pan, the Pole poled two homers. Shortstop Vern (Junior) Stephens hit one and Sig (Jack) Jakucki, the grizzled guy who had angrily draped a semipro ump off the bridge at Wichita's Arkansas River, turned in a pennant-clinching 5-2 victory.

For a few precious moments, I'm sure many folks back home forgot the war or, rather, cried that the father didn't live to see the Browns win or that a brother, son, nephew, and dear friend was tied down in a European hedgerow or Pacific foxhole or far off in a ship of war.

The Brownies, whose 89 victories matched the fewest to prevail in the old 154-game schedule, almost pulled off a Series upset over the 105-game threepeat Cardinals.

I told the folks that, if they didn't mind, I'd spend most of my hours downtown at a hotel. Even though cousin Charley Isele saw to it from his butcher shop that Uncle Bob and Aunt Alice didn't suffer, still basic red stamps for meat were rare.

For the Browns' home date "press parties," owner Don Barnes killed the fatted calf. I still don't know how he did it or how he tapped into the best beverages, but, ah, me, not to reason or ask why, but merely to sigh and try. As I stood with wide-eyed amazement at the lavish display, I heard a familiar graveled voice. Casey Stengel hurried toward me. He had won the American Association pennant at Milwaukee.

"Brogue," began Ol' Case, still remembering the name, if not how to pronounce it, "I hafta say we won 'cause your man Bill Norman helped me. Played like you said he could."

The Browns played terrible defense in the 1944 World Series, probably because the field was worn out. Despite their 10 errors, they came within one incredible play of an upset over the first National League team ever to win 100 games in three successive seasons. The key play came up in the second game after the Brownie's Denny Galehouse had outdueled Mort Cooper in the opener, 2-1.

In the tenth inning, the Browns threatened. George McQuinn doubled, and Mark Christman, next up, bunted along the third-base line. The Redbirds' pitcher, reliever Sylvester (Blix) Donnelly, lunging to his right, fielded the ball while running toward third base. Blix pivoted and threw blindly to third, low and right into McQuinn's sliding spikes. Mac tagged himself out.

In the eleventh, Cards pinch-hitter Ken O'Dea, batting for the light-hitting second baseman, Emil Verban, singled home Ray Sanders. The 3-2 score evened the Trolley Series. If the Browns had won in 10, rather than lost in 11, they would have had a three-love lead because they won Game Three. No World Series team has overcome a three-game deficit. As it was, the Cards won in six.

At the finish, full of figurative beans and a winner's Series share, frail Cardinal second basemen Emil Verban, "3 for 3" that day and .412 overall, detoured by way of the first-base club box before fleeing through the home dugout on the opposite side. He said something to Brownie owner Don Barnes.

Why? And what? "Because," snapped Emil saucily, "the Browns gave our wives lousy seats when they were home team. So I asked the owner how it felt to be sitting behind a post."

After I returned to Washington, combat correspondent Bob Burrill and I were talking sports over a precious beer one night. Army had just handed Notre Dame the Irish's worst defeat in history, 59-0. I suggested that this was an unforgettable blow.

Burrill noted that others had suffered humiliation over the years, too. Such as? The Washington Redskins, skinned alive by the Chicago Bears just a few years earlier in the NFL's championship game, 73-0 . . . Uh . . . Roy Riegels' wrong-way run in the 1929

Rose Bowl game . . . Fred Merkle's famous boner when he failed to touch second base for the New York Giants in 1908 . . . Gene Tunney cut into red, white, and blue ribbons by a light-heavyweight, Harry Greb in 1922.

Yeah, I got the picture, like Sam Snead's blow-up in the U.S. Open in 1939. Heck, a guy could write a book.

We looked at each other. Hell's bells. With the blessing of Dorothy, who must have recognized what she was getting into long before she said "I will," I spent numerous evenings researching at the Library of Congress.

The resultant 262-page book, *Don't Bring THAT Up!* subtitled "Skeletons in the Sports Closet" was my first. Trouble was, publication was delayed so that it didn't come out until April, 1946, at which time nobody wanted to read. Not even me.

When the European phase of WWII ended on V-E day in June, 1945, the Marine Corps issued a Letter of Instruction. Many regular Marines who had been wounded were now ready to come back to work in the States. Billets were necessary. If previously a Marine had been found not capable of combat, he could be re-examined now, either to go overseas or to go home.

Maybe if I got out now, I could qualify for an appealing job. Dorothy listened and agreed. I decided to go for broke, figuring that if they thought I was damaged goods earlier, they wouldn't want to send me out now.

But when I checked in at headquarters for a test of my fitness for combat duty, I think the Navy four-stripe medical captain, an internist, must have wondered what in the blazing hell this 27-year-old technical sergeant had been doing high and dry on the Potomac instead of in the bloody high tide at Tarawa or on the drab mountain ash of Iwo.

When he sat down to sign my request for reassignment or release, he stopped his pen in mid-air. He looked down at the memo by which the opthamologist recommended my dismissal. Suddenly he stormed toward me and grabbed my left forehead and cheek.

"Let me see that eye," he growled, pressing his fingers into my face. Suddenly, he let go and stalked back into the office and plopped into his chair. I'm saying to myself, "Sign that, you sonofabitch, sign it." I'm glad he did, and I'm glad I served in the Marines. Semper Fidelis.

But now where would I go? H'mm, I made my contacts. To the *Post-Dispatch* through Stockton. To the *Star-Times* through Sid Keener, who offered $60 a week. Paul Mickelson, in New York as general news editor for the Associated Press, offered a job in the sports department at $75 a week. Hap Dumont at Wichita repeated that he would match my best offer.

But where the heck was the *Post-Dispatch*? Finally a telegram arrived. At long last, my quest was successful. The *Post-Dispatch* made me an offer. And for SEVENTY-FIVE dollars! Which would go a lot farther in St. Louis than New York.

I said to my wife, "You know what — you don't have to work any more!"

20

æ

If Red Smith, who worked for Sid Keener at the *St. Louis Star* from early 1928 through most of 1935, had not been such a gifted writer, the closest I would have gotten to the *P-D* could have been the newsstand.

My mentor, J. Roy Stockton, urged the *Post-Dispatch* to hire Red but was rebuffed by the *P-D's* long-time managing editor, Oliver K. Bovard. Why? Because Red had done such a masterful job covering a rural woman's first reaction to the big city that Bovard thought the gifted young writer had made up the tale.

So Red ended up in New York writing first for the *New York Herald-Tribune* and then for the *New York Times*, which syndicated him nationally. He became the best known Smith since the cough drop brothers.

And I ended up in the sports department of the *Post-Dispatch*. Where I was busy working on August 13, 1945, V-J Day.

Pop had go to bed early, because as a sales supervisor — "route boss," he had to replace a young squirt unable to make it the next day. Was his employee anticipating a hangover?

Mom, Dorth, a neighbor woman, and I began to celebrate with a bottle of Scotch. In the midst of the haw-haw and hurray, I broke into tears. They were startled. This was no time to cry.

Oh, yes, for joy, if you knew, as I did, that brother Freddie, five years my junior, and a Marine, had little or no chance of surviving the invasion of Japan. In an amphibious invasion, after the first wave of rifle Marines were boated to a beachhead, the second wave were the radio men, of which Freddie was one. Instructions transmitted over their radios directed naval gunfire. They were sitting ducks.

So, girls, if the foe could knock out those men, they could blind the big guns. Before I could finish the tale of heavy general casualties of JASCO members, the women were crying.

Thanks to Harry Truman's decision to drop the atomic bomb, brother Freddie would go on to a great life. Since Dorth and I were childless, Freddie and his wife gifted Mom and Pop with their only grandchildren.

Freddie got out of the service too late for the 1945 football season. He transferred to St. Louis U. from Missouri U. because Pop was ill and played two years.

My work for the *Post-Dispatch* provided me with a variety of sports assignments in '45. One Friday night in 1945 at a press cocktail party preceding the Missouri-Oklahoma football game, OU's new young president, George Cross, stood there, glass in hand, and said, "I'm going to build a football team that is going to help me build a great university."

He did, and they did. Hardly had Missouri won the 1945 championship, 14-6, when war-time Oklahoma coach Dewey (Snorter) Luster resigned. Don Faurot recommended war assistant, Jim Tatum, for the vacant head coaching slot there.

Tatum got the Oklahoma job and recruited Faurot's other assistant, Charles (Bud) Wilkinson. Tatum lured many seasoned war veterans to Oklahoma, including some who were discouraged from Missouri by Faurot.

My candidate for the most noble coach of all was St. Louis University's Dukes Duford. Duford was best described by NBA and LaSalle University coach Ken Loeffler. "His soul," Loeffler said of Duford, "is as warm as his big, brown St. Bernard eyes."

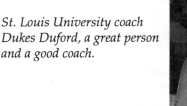

St. Louis University coach Dukes Duford, a great person and a good coach.

When the 1945-1946 basketball season opened, Duford pointed to a tall, skinny kid with black, curly hair and said, "If we give that kid enough help, he'll be an All-American."

I scoffed. "C'mon, Dukes, St. Louis isn't a basketball town," but Duford was as right as rain about Edward Charles Macauley — "Easy Ed," who would two years later lead a home-grown St. Louis-area team to the National Invitation Tournament championship, at a time when the NIT was more prestigious than the NCAA.

En route to the NCAA championship in the 1945-46 season, Henry's Iba's Oklahoma Aggies came to town, led by Bob Kurland, the Jennings giant who left town for the glamor at Stillwater. With freshman Macauley playing the senior Kurland head up, St. Louis played the Aggies pretty well as part of a doubleheader at the St. Louis Arena before a then-staggering crowd of 13,000 paid. Washington U. featuring dandy medical student super athlete, Stan London, played Tulsa in the other game.

One day in February of 1946 my boss asked the oddest question: "How many white shirts do you have?"

"Plenty," I told Stockton.

"Well," he responded, "do you think you could tear yourself away from your desk and cover the Cardinals?"

Does a bird like to fly?

Ordinarily, John Edward Wray, who remembered the Browns when they were American Association champions back in the 1880s, would cover American League Browns and Stockton himself would be with the Cardinals.

Wray, 70, was about to step down as sports editor, and management wanted JRS temporarily in the office. Stockton urged the warmth of St. Petersburg for Wray. But a combination of cataracts and glaring Florida sunlight made that inadvisable.

Dorth ironed all my white shirts and my brother Freddie rushed me down to Union Station in Pop's car. So began the most interesting and exciting years of my life. For the next 13 years, I was a "baseball beat" writer, usually assigned to cover the Cardinals.

The good moments far outnumbered the bad.

During my first spring training as a beat reporter, I was saddened by what the war had done to so many fine players. Wounds, age, and rustiness took a heavy toll.

But I was delighted by many sights: Red Schoendienst playing left field with a towel around his freckled neck, Joe DiMaggio hitting a home run for the rival Yankees, late-arriving Stan Musial leaving a false thumb in a handshake.

Our favorite watering trough was the Sundown Club, which had lively music and a breezy bartender. A young and giddy writer could see super-stars DiMaggio and Musial standing back-to-back at the bar.

Once the *Post-Dispatch* asked me to drive down the spooky Tamiami trail at night to Miami Beach and investigate the spending of dubious war-time gains.

Thousand dollar bills were numerous. Pot-bellied old timers who had sold scrap metal illegally at a time of national need were strolling the beaches with young, beautiful, curvaceous, blond opportunists. Other men and their wives were having the first bountiful time of their lives at the gaming tables.

At the Colonial Club, I saw a scrawny old gal, who looked as if she'd never worn high-heel spiked shoes before, show considerable aplomb at roulette. As she reached across the table with her right hand to post a distant number, her left breast escaped her low-slung gown. Without a "pardon my titty," she tucked it back in with her left hand.

My story on the "vulgar display of wealth" was happily good enough for the first page of our Sunday *Everyday* magazine. The situation—and life—was best summarized for me by restaurant entrepreneur Jack Larkin.

"Son," said Larkin, "you'll find here—and elsewhere—that men mumble and money talks!"

Over the years I grew to love St. Petersburg. Hey! Who doesn't like spring training?

For years the Redbirds stayed at the Bainbridge Hotel in St. Petersburg, where, as Roy Stockton put it so well, noting the nearby Atlantic Coast railroad tracks, "the train runs through your room every morning at 7."

In 1946, the men who had contributed much of their short-lived athletic careers to the war effort were back, including captain Terry Moore and road roommate Enos Slaughter. Some were damaged goods, like Johnny Beazley and lefty Ernie White. The club's best minor-league pitching prospect, big John Grodzicki, came back with a limp and a dropped right foot, a result of a bullet that struck a nerve in the buttocks when he descended with a parachute battalion.

Sam Breadon, running his own store, unwisely began to deal away players. Veteran hustler Jimmy Brown was "gifted" to Frank Frisch at Pittsburgh for a price. So many players went to Boston — Mort Cooper, Johnny Hopp, Ray Sanders, and later Ernie White and Danny Litwhiler — that I nicknamed the Braves the "Cape Cod Cousins."

Boston's Three Little Steam Shovels, owner Lou Perini and two contracting partners, were willing to spend money to make money. The Braves' manager now was Billy Southworth, who had walked away from the insecurity of managing short term for Breadon for a fleshier, long-term contract at Boston.

Pridefully, Breadon made no effort to keep Southworth. As successor, Breadon tapped Eddie Dyer, a virtual unknown.

"The Old Lefthander," as Dyer liked to call himself, was a knowledgeable minor-league manager and organizational troubleshooter. When he came to the Cardinals as manager, expected to win, Breadon threw him a nasty curve by selling the league's best catcher to the New York Giants for a whopping $175,000.

The loss of the power-hitting, take-charge catcher W. Cooper was grievous. The Cardinal players privately bad-mouthed the team's owner. Breadon compounded his mistake by trying to hurry 20-year-old Joe Garagiola into the majors and by expecting George Sisler's son, Dick, to provide muscle at first base.

Garagiola had hit a king-sized homer in the Philippines that so impressed the locals they placed a plaque on the outfield fence. A radio report from the scene portrayed Joey as a Paul Bunyan in bloomers.

Young Sisler, big and strong, had played winter ball in Havana, for a team owned and managed by Cardinals coach Mike Gonzalez. Dick hit so impressively Gonzalez predicted the hulking hitter would "hit 30 home rung —ceench!"

That "ceench" haunted the good Señor throughout the season, Gonzalez's last in the big leagues. Reduced soon to spear-carrying, Sisler hit only three home runs and struggled at first base.

The Cardinals were in trouble. In early June, Dyer asked Stan Musial to go to first base — "for the good of the club."

21

ࢠ

While World War II rounded third base early in 1945, the Brownies trained at Cape Girardeau, Missouri. There they helped put on a War Bond sale at a pancake supper. Manager Luke Sewell and coaches Zack Taylor and Fred Hofmann served flapjacks to the fans with a flourish until it was time for the playing-field brass to eat.

Sewell winked at Taylor and invited Bootnose Hofmann to go out and entertain the ladies. Luke and Zack would serve him.

Indeed. Between one well-buttered pancake and the next, they inserted a thin paper napkin. Again and again they did the same — pancake, butter, napkin, pancake, butter, napkin. They soaked their concoction heavily with syrup and brought the tall tempting stack to a hungry, beaming Hofmann. With Sewell and Taylor watching amusedly, Bootnose cleaned his plate with gusto.

"Best pancakes I ever ate," he glowed. "Give me another stack." His taste buds. His stomach. His decision. Our entertainment.

Too bad I traveled too little with Bootnose. But I did log more miles with one-of-a-kind Red Schoendienst.

When Eddie Dyer took over as Cardinals manager in 1946, he immediately labeled Schoendienst as "my No. 1 utility player," drawing a quiet hard-feathers retort from the throaty voice of the 23-year-old kid from nearby Germantown, Illinois. Dyer's point was, of course, how could he take seriously a player who hit only .278 against war-time pitching?

The young Schoendienst reminded me of Huckleberry Finn. As a schoolboy, he often skipped classes to fish and hunt. As a baseball player, he was a natural. But with Kurowski at third and Marion at short, he had no position. I suggested second base.

"I don't want to play second," Red snapped. "Damnit, Red," I said, remembering my own athletic aspirations and my fondness for Frank Frisch, "second base has a short throw, which would help your arm, but you have to cover two bases and . . . "

When Kurowski needed more time to get ready after a long spring training holdout, Red played third base expertly. When Marion was hurt, Schoendienst moved to short. By then, I think manager Dyer, too, had the notion that Schoendienst was better than he had originally surmised. Dyer began playing Red at second and okayed the trade of Emil Verban to Philadelphia as part of a three-way exchange for catcher Clyde Kluttz.

The other second baseman, Lou Klein, could read the writing on the outfield wall. In May, Klein leaped to Mexico along with the staff's top starter, Max Lanier, and relief pitcher Fred Martin.

At the time, Lanier roomed with Schoendienst, who had moved into the regular lineup. Max left an explanatory note. It wound up, "and keep hitting those line drives, Red."

The offers from Mexican League financier-sportsman Jorge Pasquel kept coming. Stan Musial turned down a $50,000 cashier check's bonus and a $25,000-a-year contract for five seasons if he would give up Lil's Pennsylvania pierogi for Pasquel's hot tamales.

My task as a reporter trying to cope with the shock of the Mexican League challenge to American baseball was complicated by a national railroad strike that threatened to strand the Cardinals in New York.

Hustling Leo Ward lined up a chartered DC-3 for Cincinnati and a game for the next night, a Friday, and a sellout crowd anxious to see the Reds' rangy rookie pitching sensation, Ewell Blackwell, go against Cat Brecheen. Marooned in Buffalo, the Reds resourcefully had hurried back to the O-hi-o in taxicabs.

Ward's plane could take half our group. The rest of us would go by bus under the direction of coach Buzzy Wares.

The Friday flight was forced to land some 50 miles short of Cincinnati. From there, with a police escort, the Cardinals traveled by taxis to Crosley Field. The cab carrying Musial and a few others had a hood problem. The cabbie suggested one of the players lie across the hood like an overgrown ornament.

Said Musial, "Oh, no, you don't. You lie on the hood." So with Stan driving, peering out the left window to see around the cabdriver, the cab finally arrived at Crosley Field.

A crazy day in a crazy season of crazy developments.

There was an effort by a Boston lawyer named Robert Murphy to unionize the ball players. The Cardinals listened, but declined, though, as mentioned, three left for Mexico and others like Moore, Musial, and Slaughter were solicited. Actually, at Pittsburgh, Murphy came close to achieving his goal when the Pirates threatened to sit out a night attraction. That is, until pitcher Rip Sewell stood up and said he had signed his contract and was going out to the pitching rubber, alone if necessary. Next, old friend Jimmy Brown said he'd go, too, and ultimately the team played.

So Murphy failed. His only consolation might be that extended meal allowances and other courtesies extended players are still labeled "Murphy money."

Brought up in a union family, I have full respect for what my father did as a founder and later as working president of Teamsters' No. 611. Personally, I've not been a good union man. I liked my job too damned much to put a dollar sign anywhere near it, but I always pay my union dues.

But I am—was—sympathetic to ball players. For example, Lanier was earning only $10,000 after a career of 78 victories and 53 defeats. No wonder he took what seemed like a king's ransom to go south of the border.

Forty-two players were making fewer than $5,000. Heck, as a young newspaperman I was making more money than some big leaguers and could look forward to a longer career.

With many other players jumping to Mexico and the Mexican League bankrollers making offers, the Lords of Baseball were prompted to ask the unusual: "What'll it take, fellas, to keep — or make — you happy?"

I saw brief little items in the press here and there, various clubs asking for one or more of (1) more meal money on the road, (2) a minimum $5,000 salary, (3) club responsibility for handling players' personal luggage from train to hotel, ball park, etc., (4) buses from train to hotel or ball park rather than awkward delays and scrambles for taxicabs.

What did the Cardinals want? I asked them on a rainy day in Manhattan. Yes, what?

Why, at that very moment I was told, shortstop Marty Marion and his roommate, trainer Doc Weaver, were working on a pension plan in their New York hotel room, kibitzed by captain Terry Moore.

Marion was a mastermind, a super-salesman who had learned promotion in his brief college days at Georgia Tech. Doc Weaver was thinking about retirement for himself and other long-toothed gaffers like the coaches, Buzzy Wares and Mike Gonzalez.

I found the Marion Pension Plan detailed and practical: Deduct two bucks a day from each player's salary, matched by management. Add the profits from the annual major-league All-Star game and World Series radio money. And if the overall amount wasn't adequate, schedule a mid-season game between natural rivals: Cubs vs. White Sox, Cards vs. Browns, Yankees vs. Giants, Red Sox vs. Braves, Phillies vs. Athletics, etc. The goal: A $100-a-month pension for 10-year veterans at age 50.

Happily, when I wrote a long, detailed open-date story for the Tuesday *Post-Dispatch*, my AP alma mater (St. Louis chapter) thought enough of the concept to distribute it nationally. We all read it the next day in the New York papers.

The concept caught on quickly. Men the caliber of Tom Yawkey, Phil Wrigley, Larry MacPhail, and the Cardinals' Sam Breadon applauded the thought and encouraged further effort. Players set up an informal committee and elected the Dodgers' Dixie Walker and Yankees' Johnny Murphy as representatives.

The pension story was the most significant I ever wrote. From that sheet of yellow legal secretary paper grew a giant.

It was a death stroke for the Mexican League. As for the National League, the Cardinals stayed in the pennant hunt largely because of Musial and young pitching perfectionist Howie Pollet.

When Musial moved to first base, the Cardinals picked up from a slump that dropped them seven games out by the Fourth of July, but in a mid-July series with the Dodgers in St. Louis, the Cardinals swept four straight.

Musial's hitting won three out of four at home. When the Cardinals played in Brooklyn shortly after, he was still hot.

Having dinner with Leo Ward after one game, I wondered about a noise I'd heard whenever Musial batted that day at Ebbets Field. Said Ward, "They were chanting 'Here comes the man.'"

"That man," I corrected, using an expression of the times.

"No," Leo insisted, *"The* Man."

So I began to refer to him as Stan (The Man) Musial. As you may have noticed, it caught on.

Musial never really cooled off in 1946. He hit .365, including 50 doubles, 20 triples, and 16 homers among his 228 hits. He had speed, power, and what athletes call "class." Musial became my favorite player of manhood, just as Frank Frisch had been the favorite of my childhood. Ridiculously, I called him "Banjo," or "Banj" for short, a synonym used by Rogers Hornsby in devastating reference to Punch-and-Judy slap hitters.

I covered virtually the entire 1946 season by bus and streetcar. It was one thing to switch buses from Southwest on Kingshighway to Vandeventer and take a short walk to the ball park on Dodier Street. Happily, because sports editor Ellis Veech of the *East St. Louis Journal* drove downtown to the bridges, I had a post-game ride to the *Post-Dispatch* offices. But if I didn't finish my work at the *Post-Dispatch* by midnight — and I did seldom — I had to wait an hour for an owl-car Southhampton streetcar.

Pop knew a veteran automobile salesman who owed him one and arranged for me to buy a new black Chevrolet coupe. It was double ugly with the gas spout sticking out the side and nothing behind the driver's seat except a ledge. But, ah, to me it looked like Cinderella's carriage.

Shortly after I bought the car, Dorth and I stayed overnight at Columbia after Ed Macauley led SLU to a victory over Ol' Mizzou in basketball. Our trip was interrupted by shocking news. Pop had a stroke. The early morning phone call sent me rushing down the old narrow-ribboned highway 40 from Columbia to St. Louis at reckless speed.

Pop was lying on his bed with his face distorted from a life-threatening brain hemorrhage. I couldn't stand it. I backed away and into the hallway, weeping silently.

What had I ever done for my father? Oh, I'd caused him no trouble and, sure, he was pleased at "By Bob Broeg," my byline with his name, but — again! — what had I ever done for him?

Mom used to say Pop held back only 10 bucks a week for his lunch and for gasoline. He'd passed up so many things for me.

If only Pop could live and I could have another chance to show my love and gratitude. Thank God he did, and I did. Pop recovered enough for me to take him to good restaurants, movies, and ball games. Privately, Mom told me how pleased he was. Once, ailing, he said to her that, gee, Alice, I hope I don't die when Robert is on the road, so that he has to come home.

My Pop, Bob Broeg.

I mention my second chance, friends, hopeful you'll not need an extra-inning opportunity to show life's appreciation to your parents. Learn, please, from a lucky guy.

St. Louis and Brooklyn ended the 1946 season tied. The first playoff in history was necessary. (That game back in 1908, Cubs versus Giants at New York's Polo Grounds, merely had been a replay of the tie game when umpire Hank O'Day blew the whistle on Fred Merkle's failure to touch second. *Replay*, not a *playoff*.)

Both the Cardinals and the Dodgers lost that final day of the regular season. The tension of their upcoming playoff spoiled what was intended to be a "victory" party honoring Sam Breadon. At a dinner at Ruggeri's, Roy Stockton emitted a zinging zap concerning Breadon's player sales and other frugalities. "It looks, Sam," said the boss from the lectern, "as if you sliced the baloney too thin this time."

With the Cardinals and Dodgers tied for the best-of-three playoff, National League president and Frick hooked Breadon and Dodgers' manager Leo Durocher on a phone for a coin toss. The Lip won and awarded the first game to St. Louis. Durocher boasted that he wanted the home field advantage and, besides, he told eastern writers with a wink, there would be no more than two games.

There weren't, but not the way Leo had figured. Even though the Cardinals had won the season's series from the Dodgers, 14 games to eight, the Brooks had won three of the last four. This time—straight up — Leo figured to start young Ralph Branca against Howard Pollet.

Pollet, returning from service, had been a masterful 20-game winner, leading the National League in most innings pitched, 266, and lowest earned-run average, too, 2.10. Now he was pitching with a bad back and a great heart.

Batting champion Musial contributed a triple, but hitting heroes in the 4-2 playoff opener were Terry Moore and kid catcher, Joe Garagiola, who had come up in May.   I called Joe "Gargonzola" because he was the biggest cheese on The Hill.

After a train trip to Brooklyn for game two, extra-base hitting by Moore, Musial, Enos Slaughter, Erv Dusak, and pitcher Murry Dickson, gave the Cardinals a six-run lead. It was whittled to two before reliever Harry Brecheen came in with the bases loaded and struck out little Eddie Stanky and big Howie Schultz. The 8-6 game clinched the pennant, making it four for Musial's first four full seasons.

Their opponents were the Boston Red Sox, who had five .300 hitters to the Cardinals three—Musial, Kurowski, and Slaughter. For Boston, Dom DiMaggio and Johnny Pesky were table-setters for the clean-up crew of Rudy York, Bobby Doerr, and the distinguished Mr. Ted Williams, back from service with a .348 average, 38 homers, and 123 RBIs.

Two of the game's legends, Ted Williams (left) and
Stan "The Man" Musial.

Teddy Ballgame and the Bosox got a bad break before the Series when they played a couple of games against an All-Star team of American Leaguers. In one, Mickey Haefner, left-handed knuckleball pitcher of the Senators, nicked Williams painfully on the right arm. Having said that—and with due respect to a great hitter who belatedly became a good friend — I reject the suggestion that both Williams and Musial were inept in the 1946 Series.

Williams had only five singles and one RBI in 25 official trips, .200. Musial hit 22 points higher with six hits in 27, but four hits were doubles, one a triple, and The Man drove in four runs.

When Dyer copied Lou Boudreau's "Williams shift," Kurowski made a good suggestion. Because Marion ranged long-armed and legged like an octopus, Kurowski suggested Marty stay on the left side of the infield. Whitey hopscotched directly beyond second base so that Red Schoendienst could move into the hole next to Musial.

The strategy worked or, putting it another way, Williams didn't test it too much. In the Series things got so bad for Williams that in the fourth game the slender slugger beat out a bunt. The sports headline of the afternoon *Boston American* tabloid screamed: "TED BUNTS!"

Something that bothered Williams other than his injury was the crafty pitching of St. Louis left-handers, led by Series hero Brecheen. I learned something about The Cat from a gambler I almost met before the Series at Herb (Curly) Perry's after-hours' watering trough. Perry tried to introduce me. The geezer scoffed. He didn't want to talk to sports writers. Before I could tell him to go spit in the notion, he explained:

"You guys don't know anything. I've made up my own mind ever since I saw Pete Alexander drunk as a skunk and then go out and win. I've got my own notion: Your man, Brecheen, is more than a .500 pitcher (15-15) no matter what the figures show, and he'll prove it."

Right, ancient sir. The Cat kept Ted off balance with breaking balls down and away and pitches up and in. Williams went 1-for-8 against Brecheen.

In the first Series game, the Cardinals led until the ninth when a bad-hopping grounder by Mike Higgins skidded through Marty Marion's legs. And with two out, Tommy McBride dribbled a slow single between Kurowski and Marion, tying the score. That cheap hit had an ugly postscript.

*Marty Marion, 1944
National League MVP.*

Dyer, calling the signals for his kid catcher, had flashed a fast ball sign to Garagiola. Joe relayed it to Pollet. Howard shook off the signal. Dyer gave it again. So did Garagiola. A head-shaking Pollet refused once more: Dyer shrugged. Pollet served a slow curve that fooled McBride, all right, but Tommy dribbled it in the seeing-eye no-man's land between third and short, his only hit in five tries. Dyer, of course, second-guessed himself even more than Pollet.

In the tenth — wow! — Rudy York hit one over the top of the hot-dog stand at the back of Sportsman's Park bleachers. The 3-2 final, Boston, saw a head-hanging heavy-hearted Dyer call it the "worst defeat I've ever had."

The Cardinals won game two behind Brecheen. The Series moved to Boston where the Red Sox won game three and the Cardinals tied the Series by winning the fourth game.

In game four, Enos Slaughter made himself felt during an easy Cardinals victory. He had four hits and uncorked a tremendous throw to the plate, nailing what seemed a sure-thing run after a catch, yet, in reflection, a stupid out considering St. Louis's long lead. When Boston writers marveled about the throw, Slaughter growled, "I ain't concedin' nuthin.' Don't they run in the American League?"

Boston won game five, putting the Red Sox only one victory away from their first World championship since Babe Ruth was a pitcher in 1918. Bosox hurler Joe Dobson creamed Slaughter painfully with a late-inning pitch. Enos' right elbow swelled horribly and he had to leave the game.

En route by train back to St. Louis, the Cardinals' gifted team surgeon, Dr. Robert F. Hyland, told the right fielder he was through for the series. Unusual action could cause the blood clot to move toward the heart. Slaughter snorted to the trainer, Doc Weaver, "Get me, ready, Doc, I'm playin'."

Throughout the night and into the day, hourly, the devoted player and tireless trainer alternated hot-and-cold packs. For game No. 6, to the surprise of many, Slaughter not only was in the lineup, but he got a hit, a run, and made a good running catch against Williams. Brecheen won again, and the Cardinals forced a seventh game.

Boston started Dave (Boo) Ferriss, a 25-game regular-season winner and author of a Game Three 4-0 shutout over Murry Dickson, his opponent again.

Dickson had a rocky beginning and quickly gave up three hits, providing the Red Sox a brief lead, 1-0. Then Dickson, a 15-6 regular-season pitcher, completely shut down the visitors until the eighth, by which time Schoendienst, Musial and platoon left fielder Harry Walker had provided a 3-1 lead.

Suddenly, in the eighth, Boston pinch-hitters Rip Russell and George (Catfish) Metkovich singled and doubled to put runners on second and third with none out. Dyer switched to Brecheen, who had won the day before. The Cat retired Wally Moses and Pesky, but DiMaggio drilled a game-tying double off the right-center field fence. Dom pulled up at second, lame, and left for pinch-runner Leon Culberson.

With Culberson in DiMaggio's center-field slot and veteran Bob Klinger pitching, Slaughter, still swinging gingerly, led off the home eighth with a single, but two outs later remained at first base.

Slaughter was in motion before Harry Walker swung and lifted a fly ball to medium left-center, where, as Enos reasoned, fleet defensive genius DiMaggio was *not* playing. By the time Slaughter touched second base, he said to himself, "I'm going all the way."

Eddie Dyer had listened earlier in the Series when Slaughter groused that third-base coach Mike Gonzalez had held him at third when he thought he should have scored. Eddie soothed his right fielder, "All right, Eno, all right. If it happens again and you think you can go, go! I'll take the responsibility."

That was all Slaughter needed as he raced toward third, head down and digging hard. When he turned the corner,

Gonzalez flapped his arms. Neither second baseman Doerr nor third baseman Higgins could communicate what was happening to shortstop Pesky, waiting for Culberson's throw-in on what seemed little more than a garden-variety single.

Whirling with the ball in his hand, Johnny was surprised and off-balance. His throw to the plate was weak and late. Slaughter slid grandly — and safe! The crowd gasped, then roared.

In the ninth for Boston, York and Doerr singled with none out. With a sacrifice in order, Whitey Kurowski made a good play on Higgins' bunt and threw quickly to Marion at second for the force.

Enos Slaughter scoring the winning run for the Cardinals in the eighth inning of the seventh game of the 1946 World Series.

After Roy Partee fouled out, McBride's grounder bad-hopped just enough to roll up Schoendienst's right arm. Red trapped it in his armpit. Captain Moore yelled from center field, "Throw the damned ball, throw it." Like a magician pulling a rabbit out of his sleeve, Red flipped a Series-ending throw to Marion at second.

I always resented that arbitrarily, unfairly and unromantically, the official scorers called Walker's game-winning hit a double. Harry, hoping to distract a throw as he watched Slaughter round third under full steam, did reach second. But, as he agreed, it was a single, not a double, as I insisted to the official scorers. They didn't listen. Too bad.

Heck, wouldn't history treat the Paul Revere ride of Enos Slaughter more dramatically if, as most certainly happened, the big-butted buzzard from Carolina scored the winning run from first base on a *single!*

A great finish to a great baseball season.

Another important reason 1946 was a memorable sports year for me was the athletic accomplishments of my brother. I sat in the Billiken stands, having asked off St. Louis U. assignments after Fred transferred from Missouri U. to St. Louis when Pop became ill.

Others wrote glowingly of Freddie's excellence on the quarterback option, borrowed by Billikens Coach Dukes Duford from Don Faurot. Bob Morrison, one of the *Post-Dispatch*'s finest reporters ever, wrote glowingly that Fred Broeg, "turning the flanks like Montgomery at El Alamein," directed an upset victory over Detroit University. The *P-D* bannerlined Fred Broeg's name across the top of the main sports page on a Monday I wasn't even there.

Freddie and good ol' Dukes went out in glory, For two straight weeks, with no face mask, Fred Broeg had suffered a broken nose. Now, as he jump-passed from the 10 to the 2, setting up a touchdown that beat Duquesne, 14-13, a tacker's elbow popped the nose again.

Blinded by bleeding, Freddie rushed to the bench, where trainer Bob Bauman swathed him with a towel. Duford, patting the quarterback's shoulder and trying to watch the next play, said sorrowfully:

"Gee kid, I'm sorry. Is that the same one you broke last week?"

22

Guilty, racially, I sat on my hands as a young man, a follower, not a leader, while my beloved home state fought to maintain the separate-but-equal education charade. My university, like my grade and high schools, was segregated. Athletic teams wishing to compete against Mizzou had to leave black players at home when they played at Columbia.

By the time I was a student and Associated Press reporter, I was embarrassed when New York University was forced to leave home its best running back, an Afro-American, in 1940. And I winced at the time a triangular track meet between Missouri, Notre Dame, and Wisconsin had to be aborted because the Badgers insisted on bringing their black athletes. But I merely mumbled my discontent.

Happily, because of boxing's Joe Louis and the contributions of black soldiers in World War II, segregation gradually lost its psychological hold on America.

I was glad when Jackie Robinson became the first Afro-American to play in the major leagues since 1884, the year Moses Fleetwood Walker, a catcher, and younger brother Welday Walker, an outfielder, briefly played for Toledo when the American Association was a major league.

But before Robinson could swing a bat in "organized ball," the euphemism used to label white professionalism, much careful ground work already had been done by Branch Rickey, whose conscience and connivance broke the insidious barrier.

When Albert "Happy" Chandler was sworn in as a replacement for the late Judge Landis in 1945, I was asked by the *Post-Dispatch* to cover his first press conference in Washington. At the *P-D*'s request, I casually asked about the future of the Negro in professional baseball. Chandler's answer was more wish-wash than evasion, and I so noted in my story. Chandler had a king-sized ego but was no fool.

He knew the time had come.

Ousted by Breadon from the Cardinals, B.R. had moved his battered felt hat to Montagu Street in Brooklyn. Bless the Mahatma's cerebellum medulla, he had honest misgivings, true, but he also was looking for another competitive advantage. Just about everybody else had caught up with Rickey's farm system.

Tish-tishing New York bankers' laments that Col. Larry MacPhail had spent too much money, Rickey insisted he couldn't end scouting, like most clubs. The war wouldn't last forever and he wanted to sign teenage prospects and — humph! — maybe a black player or so . . .

No one told him no. By the time B.R. was ready to go public, there wasn't a helluva lot the bigots could do about it. He tapped Robinson for Montreal's farm club in 1946 and, in 1947, Jackie came to the Dodgers. Thick-legged, pigeon-toed No. "42" faced animosity on his own ball club.

But player resistance was relatively weak. They had no union then. No arbitration. No grievance procedure. If a player didn't play, a player didn't get paid.

Dodgers president Branch Rickey signs Jackie Robinson to a one-year contract.

As for the Cardinals — and this is important to me— some of the world champions didn't like it, but *none* conspired to strike against Robinson. The team, many of them still my friends, received an unfair rap. This injustice has never been corrected. It's time the wrong done to them was made right.

The problem was initiated by their hot and bothered club owner, Sam Breadon, groping for the reason behind his team's slow start. One day he had a fearful thought that his players might boycott games in which Robinson played. Breadon was already worried about attendance in 1947, because he had given many pay hikes, vaulting Musial, for example, from $13,500 to $31,000.

After manager Eddie Dyer's guys divided their first four games, they lost nine in a row. The 2-and-11 record panicked Breadon, a fan at heart. He wondered, "What was wrong with his Cawd'nals?" He fantasized a possible reason: Were they distracted by the presence of the black player at Brooklyn? And he wondered in fear: Would they strike rather than play against him?

If you believe sportswriter Roger Kahn, or others who have skimmed the surface over the years, you would bet that sports editor Stanley Woodward of the *New York Herald-Tribune* unearthed a diabolical scheme when he confronted National League president Ford Frick by phone in May, 1947.

It really happened like this. A nervous Breadon flew to New York to converse privately with team captain Terry Moore and player representative Marty Marion.The owner, ignoring the fact that he had helped emasculate the team by selling players, asked the two leaders their opinion of the manager. Moore and Marion gave Dyer a vote of confidence.

While in New York, Breadon visited National League president Ford C. Frick. Breadon was concerned that his players might not play against the Dodgers with Robinson in the lineup. He had no indication from Moore and Marion that this was even being considered.

Frick told Breadon the obvious. If the players refused to play a game for *any* reason, they could be barred for life.

A couple of days later, Breadon phoned Frick from St. Louis to say everything was settled. "'A tempest in the teapot,'" Frick quoted Breadon. "'A few of the players were upset and were popping off a bit, but they really didn't mean it. Just letting off a little steam.'"

Personally, all I'd ever heard was a relentless lobby gumbeater, Harry Walker, quoting brother Dixie of the Dodgers, i.e., "Fred" saying this and "Fred" saying that.

Frick picked up the story in his autobiography:

"Six weeks later, a New York newspaper attended a private dinner at the home of a Cardinal official. In the course of the dinner conversation, the (Breadon) incident was casually mentioned. The newspaperman called his office and relayed what he had heard. The next morning the incident, enlarged and embellished, was headlined across the sports page of a New York morning newspaper.

"The implication was that a widespread rebellion of National League players had been headed off at the last minute by the iron-fisted threat of drastic action by the league office. The story forgot to mention that the headlined incident had occurred six weeks earlier, and by the time the story had been published, the three or four players who had said they would never play against black players already had done so.

"Because of that ill-timed publicity, the Cardinals were unfortunately marked publicly as the great dissenters when, in reality, their players adjusted more quickly than many of the other players who were more vocally vehement in their clubhouse condemnations. . ."

Yes, Stanley Woodward could foul up, and he did with that inaccurate eight-columned banner headline. To this day, the New York press has never set the story straight. How irritating! How unfair!

One day early in the 1947 season, I sat on the bench next to Dyer before a series with the Dodgers at Sportsman's Park. Robinson took the shortcut to the visitor's locker room through the home side's third-base home dugout. As No. 42 breezed by, Dyer greeted cheerfully, "Hiya, pal." Jackie turned, smiled and said, "Hi, Eddie."

As Robinson loped toward the visitors' bench, Dyer said, "I've got to keep him happy, pal. Jackie's like Frank Frisch. Get him mad, and he'll beat you by himself." By now, you ought to know that when Frisch's name is mentioned, I certainly wouldn't forget.

The headline and story established a climate wherein conclusion-jumpers like Woodward (and others) tried to make a mountain out of a molehill when Enos Slaughter spiked Jackie at first base. Was it intentional? Slaughter said no. Twice the year before he had put gritty little Dodger second baseman Eddie Stanky into drydock. Nobody said anything.

A hard-playing hustler, Country didn't like the racist rap. A few years later when Monte Irvin moved from the outfield to first base for the Giants, playing out of position prompted Monte to awkwardly cover first with his foot extended over the bag. Rump-running fireballer Slaughter almost stepped on it. As he returned past Irvin, Eno growled:

"Damnit, Monte, watch your foot. They're still on my ass for cutting Robinson." I checked Slaughter's story out with Irvin. One Hall of Famer grinned about the other. "That's exactly what Enos told me," said Irvin.

Roger Kahn unfairly accused Garagiola of spiking Robinson. But I have searched my memory and I do not recall any occasion in which Joe nipped Jackie.

The only thing close happened in 1950 when bunting for a sacrifice in an early-season game, Joe ran hard to first base and found Robinson, now the second baseman, with his sturdy, football-calved leg extended across the bag. Trying to avoid the leg, rather than step on it, Garagiola leaped and caught a toe on Robby's leg. Joe fell heavily on his left shoulder. The injury required surgery. So Garagiola deserves a plus, not a minus, for his interactions with Jackie Robinson.

Another hero of mine, Stan Musial, took an unfair hit in 1947 when a *Collier's* magazine piece by Kyle Crichton suggested that success had inflated The Man's ego. Crichton insisted that when Musial stiff-armed him during an early-season visit in the New Yorker Hotel, it was because Musial had been beaten physically by Slaughter.

Reportorial responsibility took a whipping then as it had from Stanley Woodward. Oddly, both stories broke the same weekend.

The mighty Musial's lack of contribution had been a major factor in the Cardinals' stumbling start. The true reason became evident when he was felled by an attack of appendicitis, which forced him to pass up a scheduled interview with Crichton, who decided to forgo truth and take revenge by claiming Slaughter had beaten him physically.

But, happily, as appendicitis-stricken Musial lay naked on his hotel bed, his body was unbruised and unmarked. Three St. Louis reporters crowding into the hotel room were inadvertent witnesses.

The real question was whether Stan should undergo surgery in New York, as the hotel physician suggested, or risk a burst appendix en route by train to Pittsburgh, or fly to St. Louis to see Dr. Hyland?

Musial chose St. Louis. At Lambert Field, Dr. Hyland waited with an ambulance and whisked Stan to St. John's Hospital. Doc Hyland suggested a compromise. He could operate now, he said, or, if Stan permitted, Hyland could freeze the appendix and tonsils until after the season. Musial opted for the delay, and weak, wan, and still unmarked from any physical violence, returned to the lineup a few days later.

Hit by hit, he inched up his average from .188. When he reached .300 by Labor Day, the Cardinals held a cheerful party in the clubhouse. By this time they were back in the race, largely because of Musial, who finished the season at .312, with 19 homers, and 95 RBIs.

1947 also marked the return of Joe Medwick. When Joe was dealt to Brooklyn early in the 1940 season, the hard-boiled slugger became persona non grata in his St. Louis. He embittered union fans by joining best friend Leo Durocher and taunting strikers when they rode to the garment factory in which Mrs. Durocher was an executive. Now Ducky-Wucky became the worst, a hated Dodger.

He never swung the bat with his previous authority after the Cardinals' Bob Bowman beaned him in an ugly 1941 scene at Ebbets Field. Joe bounced from Brooklyn to the rival New York Giants to the Boston Braves and back to Boston. At the end of spring-training in 1947, the New York Yankees gave him a pink slip.

Married to lovely Isabelle Heutel of a prominent South County family, Medwick sulked in his Sunset Hills home. At not quite 36, Joseph Michael seemed to have reached the end of his playing career.

But Dyer reckoned that he needed most a right-handed bat for pinch-hitting and part-time play. Manager talked with club owner. One thing about Sam Breadon. He could forgive, if not forget.

One Sabbath morning prior to a doubleheader, Breadon and Medwick agreed to terms. Seated with me in the pressbox that afternoon was the coach of the St. Louis professional basketball Bombers, Ken Loeffler.

In the late innings when Dyer needed a pinch-hitter, Medwick waddled out of the dugout, swinging a couple of bats, and the field announcer droned:

"For the Cardinals, No. 21, Joe Medwick batting for —" a hush of surprise fell over the crowd and then a roar. Muscles hadn't had a bat in his hands for weeks, but off Fritz Ostermueller, one of the polysyllabic portsiders who always humiliated the Cardinals, Medwick hit the first pitch against the right-center fence for a double.

As he stood there at second base, the crowd that had hated him now screamed for joy. Loeffler beamed and said, "That's one of the most exciting things I've ever seen."

Me, too.

I also remember one getaway Saturday afternoon at Philadelphia when Medwick, pinch-hitting, stepped up to the plate. Then he stepped out and pointed his bat to the Phillies' bench, jawing angrily. On the next pitch he belted a game-winning homer.

I had to hurry to get Joe's actions and remarks to lead off my story. "Yeah," he blurted, "that big-mouthed Ben Chapman popped off at me as a has-been, and I told him I'd hit one upstairs."

With Musial hitting, the Cardinals were winning, but rumors circulated that Breadon might unload the team. He had been club president since 1920 and major owner the vast majority of those years.

Dyer urged the owner to talk with the team. Singin' Sam hadn't been in the clubhouse since Rogers Hornsby insulted him 21 years previously. Mr. Breadon told the players he wasn't going to sell the ball club, but where there's smoke — unless it's in a pitcher's fastball — often there is at least a faintly flickering flame.

The Dodgers, winning two games fewer than in 1946, won the pennant in 1947 by a five-game margin. With Robinson the National League's first official Rookie-of-the-Year, and Roy

Campanella and Don Newcombe ahead, Brooklyn was now the team to beat in the National League.

For Sam Breadon, Robinson's success and the reports that Rickey had more black talent on the way could have been among reasons why the club owner decided to hang it up after 27 seasons as chief honcho, the last 21 of which included nine pennants and six world championships. He was in ill health.

I honestly wonder whether Mr. Breadon thought St. Louis was ready to handle black players. The city that had been a Yankee arsenal, festooned by southern sympathizers in the Civil War, lagged — along with the state of Missouri — in equal rights.

Jackie Robinson, ejected, exchanges grins with rival Cardinals.

Fred Saigh, a 40-year-old lawyer, went to work to acquire the Cardinals, well aware from conversations with Breadon that Sam wasn't feeling well.

Breadon owned 78 percent of the Cardinals and had about $2.6 million in undeclared cash reserves, a million earmarked for a stadium. Uncle Sam said, okay, build a park or declare. Saigh suggested the obvious —sell for capital gains.

Fred recognized that while he wasn't Breadon's version of a buddy, Robert Emmet Hannegan fit that criteria. Hannegan, a former baseball and football player at St. Louis University, was Postmaster General for a man he had helped to the presidency, Harry Truman.

For $3.5 million, the two men bought out Breadon, entitling them to the $2.6 million in the cash drawer. Although the Cardinals did not own Sportsman's Park, they did own several minor league ball parks and franchises. Saigh and Hannegan mortgaged the baseball real estate and used Saigh's leases on the Railway Exchange and Syndicate Trust buildings as collateral to borrow $60,000 for a short-term loan and—presto, by November of 1947, they were the proud owners of the Cardinals.

At the last moment, Breadon witnessed weepy-eyed staff members lamenting the sale. He hadn't realized how much his male and female employees cared for him. He asked a tearful "Miss Moiphy," his personal secretary, to get Hannegan on the phone and told Bob he had changed his mind.

"But Sam," Bob pleaded, "I already resigned from the president's cabinet." So, "S. Breadon," as he always signed himself, stepped out.

Saigh got 70 percent of the stock, but played second fiddle for a year before buying Hannegan's shares after the 1948 season for a million dollars. Bob would be dead within another year at 49. Mrs. Hannegan remained grateful to Saigh for easing the rest of her long life.

I am loath to close this chapter without an update on racism in baseball. Hall of Fame Dodgers manager Walter Alston surprised me with an off-the-record comment some 20 years after Brooklyn broke the color barrier.

A couple of times I noted a late change on the lineup card posted in the dugout. Said Alston in response to my query, "I'm not supposed to have five black players in the starting lineup and I forget now and then, so I have one of my coaches double check."

I'm not trying to embarrass the O'Malley's, but what goes around comes around. Unlike the charges against Slaughter and the Cardinals, this story is true.

Trust me. I may be tactless sometimes and blunt. But I don't lie.

23

ও

I couldn't help but agree, albeit reluctantly, when Cleveland's Lou Boudreau won the 1948 *Sporting News* Player-of-the-Year award even though Stan Musial, my main man, had the greatest of his many great years.

In a one-game playoff for the American League pennant, the 31-year-old Boudreau did the best pressure single-game "managing" I ever saw. Lou went "4 for 4" at Boston's Fenway Park, including two home runs.

I consider that game and situation perhaps the most captivating of my writing career. Boudreau had the greatest pennant-winning playing contribution of a manager since Tris Speaker hit .388 in 1920 to lead the Lake Erie Tribe to the winner's circle. Cleveland did not win again until Boudreau's magical game 28 years later.

Of course I thoroughly enjoyed Musial's great season, one of the finest any major league player ever had. Sure, many have hit for a higher average than .376, but Musial had the maximum overall power season of any player since the jackrabbit ball era of 1929-30.

He missed tying for the top in homers by one rained out home run. If it had counted, he would have won the Triple Crown that year — batting average, homers, and RBIs — and in addition have been the *only* player of this century to lead the league in runs, hits, doubles, triples, and slugging percentage.

What a year!

1948 was also when I learned the hard way that work and drink do not mix. I liked to tip a few with Ken Loeffler, who coached the St. Louis Bombers. The Bombers were part of the Basketball Association of America, formed late in 1946 by the topflight indoor athletic buildings in the country.

Loeffler was an engaging guy, an intellectual roughneck, a strong man, a pianist, and a poet who reminded me of Frank

Frisch. I liked to be in the same room with Loeffler and another many-splendored man, Jimmy Conzelman. Dry-witted and high-humored, James Ryan Gleason Dunn had taken a stepfather's name in appreciation of Dr. Conzelman's efforts for his mother and the family.

An excellent football player at Washington University, Jim swivel-hipped through pro football's Roaring Twenties, finding time for all of life's pleasures. He was a middleweight boxing champion at Great Lakes during WWII and a songwriter and pianist. Nobody could pound out and sing with Jimmy's gusto "I'm the Only Man in the World Who Can Take a Biscuit Apart and Put it Back Together."

If only Conzelman and Loeffler could be with me at the same party! One night stockbroker George Newton set up a late-evening cocktail whoop-it-up, inviting both Conzelman and Loeffler. I was thrilled to be included.

Trouble was, Newton scheduled it for a week night when Loeffler's Bombers were playing the Boston Celtics. The basketball game ran so late — a triple overtime victory for St. Louis — there was no chance to write before going to the lavish Newton apartment. I also had the problem of a 6:30 a.m. shift at the *Post-Dispatch* the next morning.

Fascinated by the repartee of Loeffler and Conzelman, I drank more Scotches than I intended. All at once, I'd had way too many. Dorth drove me downtown, stopping at an all-night cafeteria for more black coffee.

By the time she dropped me off at the *P-D*, I must have looked as bad as I felt. The man in charge of the sports desk, Herman Wecke, nodded and watched me struggle to put one word after another.

I finished my story very late and now faced that 6:30 a.m. stint on the copy desk. Sober enough now to know how badly I felt, I knew I had to work until 2:30 p.m. Instead, when Stockton came in about 8:45, Wecke took him aside. JRS walked over to me. "I think you ought to go home," he said to my combined embarrassment and relief. I never drank again when I worked.

I did drink with managers and coaches, sources of great information, but seldom with players. Too often after night games on the road by the time I finished my work, the field foremen were ready to saw wood. With no TV or only test patterns in my hotel rooms, I began to know nearby bartenders too well, because I'd drop in here and there for two or three beers.

In hindsight, that was a big mistake. But it would have been worse, I felt, to get too close socially with the players. That included Musial. The Man was a giggling guy whose love for music and magic would have made him a happy addition to the Gas House Gang and Pepper Martin's Mudcats.

Stan could play a slide whistle, thump clubhouse chairs with aluminum coat hangers and mouth a big-league harmonica. In baseball vernacular, Stan was loosey-goosey. That's the best way for baseball players to be, according to the theories of manager Eddie Dyer. "Unlike football, an emotional, stiff-wristed game," said Dyer, who played and coached both sports, "baseball requires loose wrists."

That's what Musial had in 1948 from the first time he picked up a bat in spring training. Stan was strong and healthy after having undergone surgery to remove his appendix and tonsils. He even felt strong enough to move his hands down to the knob of the bat, rather than choke-grip an inch. He felt the switch would not hinder his bat control. Obviously, he was correct.

As spring training ended in 1948, new owner Bob Hannegan and I sat alone one evening after dinner. I reminisced about the 1941 "governorship steal" session in Missouri when, fresh out of college, I learned so much at Jefferson City. I told Bob that I thought at the time his involvement in the incident had finished him politically.

But before I could tell him how wrong I had been because President Roosevelt had named him Internal Revenue collector for eastern Missouri and then national IRS chief at Washington and Democratic national chairman, Hannegan interrupted.

"Well," he said, acting as if I'd stung him in recollection, "at least I kept Henry Wallace from becoming president."

Hannegan explained that virtually everyone thought that he had maneuvered to get Harry Truman on the 1944 presidential ticket as one Missourian helping another. His real thrust, he said, had been to curb Wallace. "We're liberal in the Democratic party," Hannegan told me, "but not *that* liberal."

With agreement from other party leaders that FDR's frail health made the vice-president a likely future occupant of the White House, Hannegan wheeled and dealed from convention headquarters in Chicago.

Finally, the president himself called. Wearily, FDR said, all right, all right, he'd get rid of Wallace. But who could replace him? Hannegan mentioned the president's White House advisor and former South Carolina governor, Jimmy Byrnes, and liberal Supreme Court Justice William O. Douglass and the man whose committee on excessive war spending made his name — Truman — used often in headlines.

Hannegan remembered FDR's saying almost patronizingly, "Oh, yes, little Harry."

Later when Hannegan was asked to submit a possible candidate's memo to the White House, he listed Truman's name first. "Still," Hannegan said thoughtfully, "the decision was FDR's. You know, a lot of folks are on Harry now, and many of the men he appointed to jobs have embarrassed him. No one really gives him a chance this year (against Thomas E. Dewey), but he not only dropped the 'A' bomb, saving many lives, but he also came up with the Marshall Plan and moved to save Greece and Turkey and recognize Israel.

"I'm betting money he's going to win the 1948 election and, further, I believe history is going to record Harry S Truman as a great president!"

If I may move from a great prediction about a great president to a great player on his way to a great achievement, Musial reached a milestone on May 24. He got hit No. 1,000 in a game at Chicago. I came in just as a photographer had him exercising the silly custom of kissing his bat.

I needled him. "C'mon, Banj," I said, "if you're going to talk about hits, how about 3,000?"

His eyes widened. Three thousand! Uh-huh I told him I'd seen Paul Waner do it five years earlier. He remembered. I wondered if he could guess the other six players.

He named Ty Cobb quickly, but groped and then mentioned Rogers Hornsby and Babe Ruth and Lou Gehrig and . . . When I shook my head no each time, Stan exclaimed, "You mean, none of *those* great hitters."

I told him, "But you can." Musial rolled his eyes as he looked up from his locker seat. "Why — uh — that's 200 hits a year for 15 years," he said.

Or fewer hits a year if a guy could play longer, I suggested. He nodded and said softly: "You know, you play this game for money and to win, but little extra incentives don't hurt. Keep reminding me. Way ahead or far behind in a game, it'll help my concentration."

I laughed and appointed myself vice-president in charge of Musial's base hits. I kept reminding him, usually 100 hits at a time.

Boston had the '48 bunting just about wrapped up — "bunting," archaic for pennant — when the second-place Cards went there for the last time. Nemesis Warren Spahn had a chance to clinch the pennant on a brisk September day. The wind blew rapidly toward the Charles River in right field.

Musial, physically under par, just had come in from a couple of punishing defensive days at Brooklyn and at New York. Playing center field, Stan had taken a double away from Robinson with a somersaulting catch. Then he stole a triple from Pee Wee Reese with a backhanded catch. Finally, on Tommy Brown's bid for a game-tying two-run bloop hit, a sprinting Musial dived, saving the game but jamming his wrist. At the Polo Grounds, leaving his feet for another excellent play, Musial bruised his right hand and re-injured his left. So both wrists were taped at Boston on this day the Braves needed a win to clinch the National League race.

I was standing with Musial before the game and pointed to a starched flag flying over the bandbox right-field bleachers at Braves Field.

"Lovely day to hit," I suggested. Angrily, Musial ripped tape off both wrists. His first two times at bat, Musial singled and doubled off Warren Spahn, who was forced to take an early shower.

Off former Redbird right-hander Charley (Red) Barrett, Musial timed a change-up and, as he put it, said to hell with the wrist. He pumped the ball into the right-field seats for a home run into the "jury box."

In the sixth inning, facing a second southpaw, Hard Rock Shoun, Musial singled to left. By now, Musial and the bench were aware of his record five-hit opportunity.

Ex-Redbird farmhand Al Lyons pitched to Musial in the ninth. Lyons missed the plate twice. The loud taunting of the Cardinals' right-field bullpen could be heard upstairs in the pressbox. They challenged the gutless so-and-so to get the ball over the plate.

The pitch would have been another ball, up and away, but Musial reached for it and grounded a seeing-eye single into the hole between first and second. Another 5-for-5, his fourth of the season, tying Ty Cobb's record.

The Braves, forced to wait another day to clinch against someone else, rooted greedily for Cleveland to win the American League pennant rather than the rival Red Sox. More seats in the Indians' stadium, you know. To many a romanticist, including me, a first all-Boston Series would have been more appealing.

But Cleveland's shortstop-manager, Lou Boudreau, had other ideas. A basketball star from Harvey, Illinois, and an immediate predecessor of the University of Illinois' basketball Whiz Kids, Lou quit college to join the Indians in 1938.

By 1942, at only 24, the former Illini was brash enough to ask and receive the manager's job from owner Alva Bradley. So Lou really wasn't Bill Veeck's choice when the open-shirted burrhead came out of the Marines with fire in his eyes and acquired control of the Indians.

Cleveland Indians "Boy Manager" Lou Boudreau.

But Bill stayed with Lou. As a result, Cleveland — and baseball — enjoyed a legendary season. The Indians were greatly helped by homer-hitting Joe Gordon and Ken Keltner. Larry Doby, the Tribe's first black player, contributed. So did the ageless wonder of black-league baseball, Satchel Paige.

When Veeck suggested Paige, Boudreau insisted on a private look-see. Lou caught the stork-legged, bullet-headed 42-year-old master. Next, he batted against Paige in practice. Lou did hit .355 that year, stroked 18 homers, drove in 106 runs, wheedled 98 walks, and struck out only nine times.

So when he said Paige would do, he wasn't thinking of gimmickry, though Cleveland's pennant race participation and Veeck's genius for promotion drew a fabulous 2.6 million to their lakefront stadium. The Tribe's gate in 1948 was equivalent to about 5 million in attendance now.

Paige contributed a 6-and-1 record and 2.43 earned-run average. Reformed infielder-outfielder Bob Lemon achieved his first of seven 20-game seasons in nine. Fireballer Bob Feller was slightly under his peak pitching with 19 victories, but Steve Gromek was a plus with 9-3 and the surprise package was the 20-7 season and league-leading 2.43 ERA of a big handsome rookie left-hander, Gene Bearden.

Because I was on my way to Boston by train the last day of the 1948 season, I missed the chance to see Dizzy Dean, 36 years old, portly, and five years out of professional ball, pitch for the Browns against the Chicago White Sox the final day of the 1947 season.

It was a rich box-office gimmick — the way Babe Ruth occasionally pitched season-ending games for the Yankees — and resulted from Diz's carping radio comments about the horse manure of Bill DeWitt's last-place Brownies. DeWitt's banjo eyes lit up cash-register bright with an "if-you-can-do-better-show-us" approach. Thanks to the kindness of the Cubs' Phil Wrigley, releasing Dizzy off Chicago's voluntary retired list, the deed was announced and the date set.

Dean shut out the Chicago White Sox for four innings on three hits and a walk. At bat, Ol' Diz whacked a liner to left and, sliding hard into second base, came up limping. At this point, seated in a dugout next to manager Herold (Muddy) Ruel's third-base dugout, wife Pat Dean leaned over and yelled into the dugout, "Crizzsake, Muddy, get him out of there before he kills himself."

Damn, I hated to miss that, and I lost also the last-day windup of Musial's mightiest season. Railroading with Stockton for the World Series, I wrote a season's wrap-up on The Man for *The Sporting News*, planning to drop it off in a stop at Cleveland's Union Station. There, as I charged up from the train tunnel to the station lobby, I emerged to a stunned and lighted sight.

Not only was the station rotunda unexpectedly crowded, but there was an eerie silence. "Why?" I wondered, dropping my Musial story in the mailbox. Someone mumbled, "The Indians lost and the Red Sox won." The two teams ended the regular season tied for first.

The American League had only a one-game playoff, unlike the National League's best-of-three. It would be at Fenway Park the next day and, happily, the boss and I were on schedule to see it.

At Boston, checking in hurriedly at the Kenmore Hotel near Fenway Park, we walked the short distance to Jersey Street. I was pumped up with excitement. "Gee, Mr. Stockton," I said, "this is great. I'll bet Boudreau gets at least a couple of hits."

I was thinking how hot a player he'd been, and how cool he was when the chips were down. He was also able to make excellent managerial decisions under pressure. After Bob Feller lost the windup to Detroit the day before, the stunned Cleveland club huddled momentarily in the clubhouse, where Boudreau quietly discussed his pitching problem. He had fallen with Feller Sunday. Bob Lemon had pitched Saturday. Southpaw Gene Bearden had pitched Friday. You know, you weren't supposed to pitch left-handers in Fenway with that short, leering front porch in left field. Still . . .

Second baseman Joe Gordon spoke up. "Skip," he said, "you've been calling them all season, you call it." Boudreau nodded. The manager opted for the left-hander, but, please, keep it quiet, guys, so the kid can get some sleep on the train.

Red Sox manager Joe McCarthy also made a most surprising starting pitching choice. He gave the ball to little-used righthander Denny Galehouse.

Boudreau caught a break even though regulars Gordon and Bob Kennedy, zonked with booze and sleeping pills, overslept on the train and almost missed the game. Next, boldly, the manager used a first baseman, Allie Clark, who had never before played the position. Both Veeck and vice-president Hank Greenberg protested, but Boudreau wanted one more righthanded bat.

Lou's own magic wand put the Tribe on top in the first inning when he homered. With the score tied in the fourth, Lou's second hit was followed by Gordon's single. In the press box, some of us wondered whether Ken Keltner would sacrifice. The next batter was the lefthanded-hitting Doby, who had hit .301 with 14 homers.

Instead, Keltner "decoyed" the Boston pitcher. "He leaned over the plate, which he never did," Galehouse told me, "so I didn't need Tebbetts to wig-wag me to jam him inside on the second pitch. But Ken leaned back and tomahawked the ball up and over for a three-run homer — and that was the last pitch I made."

The Tribe's 8-3 triumph, after which lame-legged Veeck hotfooted across the field to hug Boudreau, led to a private celebration party that night at the Kenmore. Private, yeah, but, wearing a golfer's white, slouchy golf cap and a silly grin, Bearden wandered the lobby floor that night and the next.

Cleveland breezed through the World Series in six games. Bearden won two games. After the playoffs, the world championship seemed almost anticlimactic.

24

For everything there is a season.

The first 1948 World Series game at Cleveland's Lakefront Stadium, won by the Indians, 2-1, on Larry Doby's home run, was over in 91 minutes. Media and baseball people convened in a hospitality room for the joy of mingling.

Cardinals' P.R. maven Bing Devine dropped by my table. "Have you heard the good news?"

Missouri 20, Southern Methodist 14! The Tigers' stunner over a great team with 16 straight victories came a week after Ol' Mizzou had whipped St. Louis U. in the last game the schools would play.

Billikens' football coach Joe Maniaci, a former star with the Chicago Bears, had an imperious air, like a latter-day Mussolini. Before the Missouri game, Maniaci had haughtily slapped on his team's bulletin board a message to the effect that, if MU used the option play, the Blue and White would turn the Black and Gold into black and blue. *St. Louis Star-Times* reporter Jim Toomey, a St. Louis U. fan, but a newspaperman first, printed it.

Faurot, unhappy that St. Louis had fired Dukes Duford, a man he admired, didn't have to say much to his players. They were ready. Before the crowd had settled, quarterback Bus Entsminger pitched off the option for one long-gaining touchdown. Next series, faking a pitch, he ran for another. Two offensive plays, two scores.

The 60-7 final didn't reflect the fact that over the years St. Louis had equally divided 21 games with Missouri, 10-10-1. It also didn't reflect Boy Scout Faurot's usual efforts to avoid embarrassing an opposing coach or team.

After Mizzou followed its success against the Billikens by upsetting SMU, Roy Stockton assigned me to travel by train with the Tigers and cover their next game—against Navy in Baltimore. The Middies weren't very good, and Missouri jumped to an early 35-0 lead.

Using offensive players on defense in the second half, Faurot watched the Midshipmen score two touchdowns. Navy's future admirals cheered lustily at Babe Ruth Park, which was what old Memorial Stadium was called. Afterward in Faurot's suite at the Lord Baltimore Hotel, the coach accepted congratulations and fended off grouchy alumni suggestions that he had been too generous. An even more impressive victory would have helped weekly ratings.

When they had all left, Faurot told me, "As a former Navy officer, I wasn't eager to pour it on. Besides, we were lucky early to have such a large lead. You see what happened—we won, and yet the Middie players and crowd were happy."

Faurot arranged for Mizzou's players to go by train from Baltimore to Washington Sunday morning and watch the Redskins play at home against Philadelphia and old teammate Ed Quirk.

The Tigers would also have an opportunity to tour the White House and maybe — just maybe — if president Truman wasn't too tired after finishing his last give-em-hell campaign stop, the First Family might visit with the kids from their home state.

Faurot, meanwhile, would return by way of College Park, Maryland. He had been extended a courtesy car by his friend and former split-T pupil, Jim Tatum, serving his second season as head coach of the Terrapins after leaving Oklahoma.

Faurot invited me to be his passenger on the early-morning auto trip. We arrived at Tatum's house early enough to awaken big Jim, who was hungover from post-game drinking and a one-point night-game loss to Duke.

Tatum, already a disciple, wanted to learn more from Faurot about the Split-T. Don scribbled a few diagrams hurriedly on some drug-store napkins. I nervously studied the clock, knowing the schedule for the team's arrival at Washington. Hey, Don, we better get going!

Too many "we-better-go" moments later, Tatum phoned assistant coach Warren Giese, who drove Faurot and me at breakneck speed into nearby Washington. By the time we screeched to a halt at the White House gates, a bus carrying the Missouri players from Union Station already had arrived.

President Truman was not only back, but would be happy to meet the Tigers. Faurot snapped to his players, "Hurry up, fellas, the president is a busy man, *too!*"

The meeting with Mr. Truman, wife Bess, and daughter Margaret didn't last long. Personally, I got only a brief handshake.

To Faurot, Truman whispered with a smile, "As commander-in-chief, Don, I shouldn't say this, but I'm glad you beat Navy . . . "

Ah, these were the salad days for Don Faurot. If only it hadn't been for Oklahoma and Bud Wilkinson . . .

By the time Missouri went to Norman, ranked fourth with the Sooners sixth, Missouri was favored, having lost only to Ohio State in their opener. Oklahoma's opening-game loss at Santa Clark would be the last in Wilkinson's second-longest winning streak.

NBC sent in its star radio sports announcer, Bill Stern to broadcast this "Game of the Week." Stern was considered number one. But I didn't agree. Though his voice was gripping, I felt Stern didn't have the football expertise of CBS's Ted Husing.

Husing had made himself with a correct call of "Clyde Van Duesen, Clyde Van Duesen" in a rainy-day cavalry charge to finish in the 1929 Kentucky Derby. Everybody else thought it was the favored Blue Larkspur.

Gravelly voiced Clem McCarthy had called that one wrong for NBC, but when Stern needled him, Mac had a comeback. He knew Stern had corrected many a miscalled touchdown-scoring football run by inserting a late make-believe "lateral" to the correct ball carrier. Cracked McCarthy, "You can't lateral a 1,200-pound horse."

The regular Oklahoma announcer, Curt Gowdy, was not happy about Stern doing the broadcast. Gowdy was obnoxious about Stern the night before the game at a press party in Oklahoma City.

Oklahoma was obnoxious to Missouri during the game, though the Tigers scored first and the score was 7-7 at halftime. In the second half, the cream came to the top — the Crimson and Cream of Oklahoma.

The Sooners caved in a Tiger punt return man early in the third quarter, recovering a fumble at the Tigers' 30, and then their quarterback Jack Mitchell used an unusual play that reflected

Wilkinson's wizardry. On a T-formation spinner — striding neither left nor right — the future Arkansas and Kansas coach ran directly through the middle for a touchdown. Four touchdowns in 12 minutes humbled Faurot and Missouri 41-7.

Despite the loss, 1948 was a good season for the Gator Bowl Tigers and for Easy Ed Macauley and his Billiken basketball teammates. They won the NIT in the spring and went against NCAA champion Kentucky in the Sugar Bowl basketball tournament the next December.

Kentucky basketball coach Adolph Rupp insisted no gamblers could touch his players "with a 10-foot pole." The Baron's cliche was as bad as his judgment. To earn illegal payments, some of Rupp's Fabulous Five sought to shave the margin of victory against St. Louis.

But they got less than they bargained for because Lou Lehman, one of St. Louis U.'s two top subs, threw in a basket that gave Billikens a 42-40 victory. Tainted, yes, but earned by honest players giving their best.

I covered the game from a seat high in the stands. I was on vacation and had planned to watch the tournament, not expecting to work. So I was stunned when the Bills' new athletic director, Bill Durney Slattery, phoned me with a message sent to him by telegram from Stockton in St. Louis.

JRS didn't even know where I was staying. The message asked Broeg to "pull out his typewriter" because the managing editor had been mesmerized listening to St. Louis' victory over Bob Cousy and Holy Cross in the tournament semifinals.

I had no typewriter and no place at the press table. I made up a scoresheet and worked from my seat in the stands. No, I didn't appreciate the assignment and was resentful that management had cut corners by not sending Bob Morrison. But I liked my job and feared Stockton as much as I respected him.

At the game's happy end, I made a dressing room visit and repaired to the downtown Western Union office, where I borrowed a typewriter.

The story was as obvious as my red nose. Led by captain Denny Miller and featuring All-American Macauley, the team was composed of all St. Louis-area kids—regulars D. C. Wilcutt, Joe Ossola, Bob Schmidt, and two masters off the bench, Lehman and Marv Schatzman. The roster also included Ray Obie, John Cordia, and my own cousin, lanky Bill Wiley. So I wrote about the Sugar Bowl championship won "by kids from the sidewalks of St. Louis."

Boss Stockton not only liked it, but so did the bigger boss, managing editor Ben Reese, who passed along his compliments to Stockton, who passed them along to me by way of Durney-Slattery *again*.

JRS still didn't know where 'n hell I was staying, but he wanted me to know that he'd told the M.E. to read Broeg more often.

My next assignment involved my friend Ken Loeffler and the St. Louis Bombers. Loeffler was not a pleasant fellow to all, especially to his players. At a time when Ebbie Goodfellow was an affable coach of the American League Hockey Flyers, Loeffler proudly referred to himself as "Meanfellow."

Loeffler recognized that post-war basketball would be "extended college play" and require close supervision. When Michigan's basketball coach made a disparaging remark about the new pro league, Ken suggested that he would play the critic for "room, board, books, tuition, cash, or whatever else they're giving at Michigan."

St. Louis Bombers basketball coach Ken Loeffler.

Because ownership of the Arena and the basketball Bombers was penny-pinch tight, Loeffler insisted his players ante up their own pre-game meals for home games — steak, unbuttered baked potato, salad, and melba toast. He housed them for naps on Army cots in a hideaway cavern in the Arena.

With only one star, Indiana's talented Johnny Logan, a former Army captain sharp with the two-handed set shot, Loeffler prevailed through his two seasons as coach by relying on resolute defense and a weaving offensive routine. Any player with height on his side was required automatically to take his shorter defensive antagonist into the pivot position.

The year before, 1947, St. Louis and Chicago got down to the final game tied. With seconds left, St. Louis lost a one-point lead when center Bob Doll tried a crosscourt pass. The Stags' Tony Jaros intercepted and put it in for the win.

In 1948, the Bombers and Stags again went down to the final game tied. Chicago opened a 15-point lead in the second half. With no shot clock, victory for the Stags seemed inevitable. The Stags went into the basketball equivalent of the pre-vent de-fense in pro football. But the Bombers got a field goal here, a basket there, a free throw, another bucket.

Suddenly, St. Louis was on a roll and Chicago couldn't mesh when the Stags tried to go back on the attack. The Bombers reeled off 23 straight points. With seconds left, as a time-out ended, Loeffler watched Belus Smawley of Appalachian State waddle away from the St. Louis huddle with his head down. Ken heard Smawley drawl: "Ah'd like to see 'em catch us this time!"

In the happy, steamy dressing room, Loeffler shouted, *"Nunc pro tunc."* How's that? His grin widened. "Latin for legalese — nunc pro tunc — now for then — this year for last year."

Afterward, an impromptu victory party at a Chicago bar found the fast-talking eastern coach laughing and joking with players, who seemed somewhat reserved in his presence. Finally, a couple of drinks later, he sidled over to a piano, and sad-faced, began to play softly. I walked over and detected a tear.

"Look," said Ken Loeffler, motioning to his happy warriors, "they're happier that I'm gone." Sighing, pausing, fingering the keys, the coach said softly, "Well, at least I've got a unified team — they all *hate* the coach!"

I covered the seven-game championship series against Philadelphia's eastern conference champions. With his team down 3 games to 2, Loeffler invited me to sit in with his players at their Game 6 pre-game meal at Philadelphia. The professor blueprinted his plan for victory. He would play cat and mouse, hold down the score, and win at the end. Loeffler planned to use little Francis (Buddy) O'Grady to control the ball. The coach figured his only man-for-man edge was forward Acriel (Ace) Maughan. He assigned Ace to tightrope the end line against a weak defender who tended to overplay him to the inside.

"Somersault" Maughn, as I called the acrobatic athlete, had a great night, as the Bombers implemented Loeffler's plan with precision and understanding. They won 58-55, and now needed a seventh game win back home to bring home the championship. At St. Louis, they finally drew a good crowd at the big Arena. Unused to playing before a large home crowd, the Bombers were rattled and lost discouragingly and decisively.

Loeffler had been promised a $1,000 bonus by owner C. D. P. Hamilton, who blithely reneged. Hamilton meant well, but had a horrible habit of constantly referring back to the Depression era and the Cardinals' early success.

"You've got to keep them hungry," he would too often say, mimicking Sam Breadon and Branch Rickey. He kept Loeffler so hungry he eventually left the team and, unfortunately, St. Louis.

Ken had the right name for the sports scrooge: "C.D. Peanuts Hamilton."

25

The Redbirds of the early championship years brought as much joy to Harry Caray as they did to me. We both became fans, but when we were working, I could let off steam privately before tackling a typewriter. Reacting live and on the air, he did not have my advantage.

Harry fanged the jugular of Eddie Dyer and Eddie Stanky, the smartest baseball man I ever met. But I was offended more by his unfair assaults on my profession, as was my friend and rival, Bob Burnes of the *Globe-Democrat*. Caray often would begin his evening sports show with: "*Despite what you have read in the newspapers*" or "*Even though you haven't read this in the newspapers . . .*"

When a newspaper reporter heard the above often enough, an adverse reaction was inevitable. "The Canary," as many called Caray, didn't have many friends in the print media.

But I, for one, *was very* impressed by the time, effort, and talent he applied to his radio work. In fact, the first time I met Caray was when he asked me to share his microphone on a KXOK radio sports show during the 1944 World Series at which I was a curiosity, a uniformed Marine covering the World Series for *Leatherneck Magazine*.

After watching the way Harry planned and segmented his program, I told him I thought he'd be a great success. He raised bespectacled eyes in delighted surprise. "Because," I continued, "you're the first damned radio guy I've seen work."

Most local radio sports reporters merely repeated virtually verbatim press releases written by promoters such as Sam Muchnick (wrestling) or Jack Van Pelt (horse racing and boxing).

Caray was a hard-working original and also an enthusiast with the ability to make a poor game good and a good one great. His biggest break came when Sam Breadon opted in 1947 for a network that would require exclusive rights from the Cardinals.

Breadon picked Caray and Gabby Street over Johnny O'Hara and his spectacular partner, Dizzy Dean.

Street, a former good-field, no-hit catcher for fabulous Walter Johnson at Washington, began to pontificate daily about young catcher Joe Garagiola's throwing difficulties. The Old Sarge harped so much about proper techniques, that every so-and-so and his sister became engrossed in the catcher's return of the ball to the mound or second base. I said it then—to Street and others—and I say it now. I detest the second guess and do not think it reflects well on the character of the second guesser.

After a Cardinals game at Brooklyn, Street's self-supposed omniscience earned me a spotlight I didn't appreciate. The Cardinals Ron Northey hit a long ninth-inning drive atop the center field fence at Ebbets Field. It bounced back on the field, but the press box had the impression it was a game-tying home run. As Northey jogged toward second base, third-base umpire John (Beans) Reardon, rushed over, flashed the circular over-the-head homer motion and quipped, "Whatcha running so fast for, Tubby?"

When the Brooklyn outfield retrieved the ball and threw it in for a play at the plate, Northey was called out. Umpires Jocko Conlan and Larry Goetz agreed the ball hadn't left the playing field. The argument was loud and long, causing me to delay writing my story until the train ride home reached Philadelphia and a waiting Western Union man.

Huddling with Northey and manager Dyer, I came away feeling that Reardon was too much a standup guy to avoid denying either the homer sign or his comical comment. So the story I dropped off at North Philly said, in effect, that the Cardinals believed they would have a strong chance of winning the protest Dyer had lodged. The train continued its trip to St. Louis.

When it pulled into Union Station late the next afternoon, I was met by KSD radio's Harold Grams, paired with my boss, J. Roy Stockton, on a daily 6:15 broadcast. The town was confused and wanted an explanation at a time the radio men didn't travel. Commenting on his ticker-tape broadcast of Northey's alleged homer, Street had insisted you never could overcome an umpire's judgment. The *Globe*'s morning story had been indecisive.

Hardly had I repeated on radio my reasons for believing the

protest would be upheld when National League president Ford Frick did just that, allowing the run that tied the score, 4-4.

Having no radio broadcasters on the road added romance to a news reporter's coverage — especially the clubhouse afternoon-paper aspects of a night game. But when Caray and Street did travel with the team and broadcast road games, there were more difficulties, like, for instance, Labor Day weekend when the 1948 Cardinals and Pirates were playing each other in the midst of a four-team pennant race involving St. Louis, Pittsburgh, Boston, and Brooklyn.

With two men on and none out in the Cardinals' first inning, and Musial, the hottest hitter in the league, at the plate, Dyer set the runners in motion. Stan hit a hot line shot for which shortstop Stan Rojek leaped and made a great catch, setting up an easy triple play.

On the train after the defeat, we sat in a club car while Caray huffed that Musial should have bunted. Street drawled that, yeah, he thought a bunt was in order. Before I could blast the idiocy of the suggestion, retiring team captain Terry Moore stepped in. I've never heard Tee Moore as angry, but that was Caray for you. He has an ability to draw out emotion, whether positive or negative.

Harry can create crowds, if not help win games. He can help managers lose favor, too, as new owner Fred Saigh found out. Saigh became the sole owner when Bob Hannegan's uncontrollable blood pressure became too much for the former Postmaster to bear. Saigh gave his partner a remarkable $1 million return on his 30 percent of their original $60,000 cash investment. Hannegan died within a year, secure in the knowledge that his widow was financially taken care of.

Fred Saigh (right) greets Dodgers President Branch Rickey.

Saigh resents any suggestion that the sale of any ball player helped buy out Hannegan, but it's true that shortly after the payoff, it was announced that little right-hander Murry Dickson had been sold to the Pittsburgh Pirates, owned then by a friend of Hannegan's, Democratic Chairman Frank McKinney.

Despite the absence of Dickson, the 1949 Cardinals matched the victory total of the championship season of 1946. After a stumbling start, they played with a championship consistency that brought a record 1,430,676 attendance to a small ball park.

Howard Pollet rebounded from arm trouble and compiled a great 20-9 season with a sparkling 2.77 earned-run average. The rest of the pitchers were fine too — George Munger, Harry Brecheen, Al Brazle, a kid named Gerry Staley — and especially the rally-stopping Ted Wilks. The Cork won 10 games and saved nine.

Hannegan's final act as club president was to give a plum assignment to Bing Devine. Der Bingle, long-time minor-league business manager, had been recalled to serve as the Cardinals' P.R. person in 1948. Hannegan made him general manager of the top farm club at Rochester, New York.

Saigh offered me the public relations job as Devine's successor. "No," I told him, "but thanks."

Saigh's salary offer, $10,000, was generous, but I was making about that as a writer, counting my work for *The Sporting News* and magazines like the *Saturday Evening Post*. The club owner suggested I could continue my freelancing, but I shook my head. No, because as a club employee, I would lose credibility. Besides, I was doing what I *wanted* and was perfectly satisfied with being a sports writer traveling with a big league ball club.

Except for Stockton, the *Post-Dispatch* office was virtually empty when I walked in after turning down Fred. I repeated the conversation to JRS. Surprise! The sports editor was angry that I had turned Saigh down cold. Stockton wandered away.

Moments later, I answered a call from the managing editor's office. Big Ben Reese and J. Roy Stockton didn't like each other, but, fortunately, both liked me. Reese said sweetly, "I understand my friend Fred Saigh is trying to steal you from us. What will it take to make you happy?"

"But I *am* happy, Mr. Reese." He nodded and asked again what it would take to make me happy. I told him once more that I *was* happy.

Pausing, the barrel-chested M.E. said, "Well, suppose we make you happier with a $20-a-week raise!"

Twenty bucks a week! Jiminy crickets —$20 in 1949 was like $200 now.

Back in the sports department, JRS saluted me for having kept my big mouth shut. "If," he said, "you had said, 'Oh, Mr. Reese, $2.50 a week or $5 or $10,' I'd have wanted to kick your ass, but, ah, yes, $20, that's nice."

Either the Cardinals or the Dodgers would have burned up the league without the other in 1949. The two clubs finished 15 games ahead of the pack, and the Cardinals displayed a blistering offense. Until Eddie Kazak suffered a broken leg, this blond third-base rookie whose last name is a palidrome, hit over .300. Second baseman Red Schoendienst, hit well over .300 until late-season fatigue revealed a health problem. Bad-backed Nippy Jones at first base also hit .300, and the 1-2 punch of Stan Musial and Enos Slaughter was devastating.

Stan the Man, hitting over .500 for the second straight season against Brooklyn, batted .336 against the National League, with 36 homers and 123 RBIs. The Old War Horse, Slaughter, competed with Musial and Jackie Robinson for the batting title. J. Robby won it with .324, four points ahead of Musial, six in front of Slaughter, whose career received an indirect boost from Doc Weaver, the Cardinals' colorful old trainer.

Weaver was an inventor who looked for ways to improve player productivity. He devised a gauzed nasal filter, permitting allergy victims to breathe easier despite dust on the diamond. Other Weaver inventions included air-foamed rubber innersoles which made him a hero with umpires, floor walkers, and cops.

In 1949, Doc teamed with Gene Sutton, a chiropractor who believed that from cradle age many people's legs deviated in length. Sutton could tell at a glance when someone had one leg shorter than the other. Although he never proved it to me, he also claimed he could eyeball whether a lady's left or right breast sagged more.

Sutton could maneuver feet like an auto gear shift. In each arch, he would insert a felt diamond-shaped pad of different thickness, compensating for any difference in length. Using a special benzene coating to avoid blistering, he would figure-eight the foot with tape.

When he finished and you stood erect, you seemed and felt taller, straighter and — take my word for it — more (ahem!) manly. Gene had time for me only a couple of times a week.

He replaced the tape every day for the players under his care. As a result, Jones' back didn't ache, Slaughter ran with even more vigor, and Wilks was at his overpowering best.

If the Cardinals had won the 1949 pennant, Gene Sutton might have made a great stride toward preventive medicine, his true lofty aim. He wanted to set up shop at St. Petersburg and show that proper foot alignment and taping could help athletes avoid injury.

One of Sutton's most successful projects, Nippy Jones, figured in 1949's most bizarre baseball incident. This was the year that Mexican League players Max Lanier, Fred Martin, and Lou Klein came back to the Cardinals. Other returnees to National League teams included a Cuban left-hander named Adrian Zabala.

Pitching for the New York Giants against the Cardinals, Zabala was leading 3-1 with a Redbird runner on base. The Cuban cunnythumb served up a pitch that was belted by Jones into the left-field bleachers for what would have been a game-tying home run. But, umpiring the bases, Jocko Conlan had flung up his hands in a "balk" sign. Under rules at the time, the homer was obviated. So Zabala was awarded a 3-1 victory.

In the gloomy dressing room, Dizzy Dean burst in, pushing back his cowboy hat from a face growing considerably rounder. "Ah always knew ah quit this game too danged soon," roared Ol' Diz. "Imagine, callin' back a 'home run' ball!"

One day on the road, traveling secretary Leo Ward, who customarily wore Countess Mara ties, had on a bow tie. It looked so much neater than my sloppy four-in-hand. Gee, if I only could tie one of those. "Easy," coaxed Leo. He stood behind me in front of a mirror and we practiced until I got it. Ever since I've been fit to be tied—bow-tied.

My clothing decisions had no effect on the close pennant race between the Dodgers and Cardinals. Musial's bat was another story. The Man pummeled the Bums and helped earn the Cardinals a long stay in first place.

Once after walking Stan, Preacher Roe barged into a Cardinal clubhouse meeting next day to assure Dyer, "Skip, ah learned how to pitch to Musial. Walk him on foah pitches and pick him off base."

Aware that in the transition from a fireball pitcher to a cute one, Roe had picked up a slick illegal spitball, Musial always tried to stop the cunning cuss from getting two strikes on him. Once Terry Moore, coaching third, detected Roe loading up a spitter and called out a warning. Preach changed to a slow curve, high and inside. Musial, falling back from the plate, virtually one-handed it over Brooklyn's short right-field fence.

But Elwin Charles Roe won decisively in pivotal games against the Cardinals. In the last series at Brooklyn in 1949, after yielding a first-inning two-run homer to Musial, Roe out-dueled Pollet, 4-3.

The Cardinals owned a game-and-a-half lead as we trained east for the last two series of the season. St. Louis had to play Bill Meyer's sixth-place Pirates and Frank Frisch's last-place Chicago Cubs.

Hosting a group of out-of-town writers in the diner while rain poured down outside, Leo Ward pointed out that "if we were rained out all of our five games and the Dodgers won all theirs, we'd *still* win the pennant by percentage points."

With the opening night game rained out and Leo's calculations 20 percent unfolded, I ate dinner with Pittsburgh's grizzled manager, Bill Meyer, a courtly son of the south from Knoxville. His Dixie background made Bill favor the Cardinals, but he growled ominously:

"I think my club might have favored your club, but on that Labor Day weekend over at your place, Slaughter woke us up." Meyer was referring to Slaughter's pell-mell slide into second baseman Danny Muraugh.

"Furthermore," said Meyer, "I think your club is tired. I don't think you'll win it here anyway."

That same night, former road roomies and hunting buddies, Harry Brecheen and Murry Dickson, had dinner together. Said Dickson, "I hope you win, Cat. We can delay our hunting trip, but you're not going to beat *me*!"

Dickson had already beaten the Cardinals four times in 1949. Why did we trade him if it wasn't for the money? Sure, he had been a disappointing 12-16 in 1948. But I'd learned something one night that year eating with Brecheen and Dickson.

Murry, giving up home runs too frequently, had been victimized by a long one that day at Brooklyn. He complained about a rabbit in the ball.

Brecheen nodded. "The ball is livelier, the fences here are shorter, but, Murry, the real problem is you're trying to pace yourself and that can't be done any more. I go as far as I can, as long as I can, and if that's not enough, they've got to bail me out."

That crucial series in 1949 saw Pittsburgh win game one. Then in game two, the Bucs', Dickson beat Gerry Staley, 7-2, and with Brooklyn having won a rain-shortened doubleheader that day at Boston, the Cardinals were out of first place — for the first time in 43 days.

Still, if they won at Chicago on an open date for the Dodgers, the Cardinals would be tied with two games to go. But a 6-5 Chicago victory meant Brooklyn was one up with two to play.

The next day the Dodgers lost at Philadelphia, so the door was open. But the Cardinals were futile against Chicago. Even the umpires couldn't — or wouldn't — help. When Slaughter lifted a high foul and a fan reached out and grabbed it, plate umpire Jocko Conlan called the batter out for the fan's interference. The Cubs' 3-1 victory meant Brooklyn need only win the final day.

That Saturday night in Leo Ward's suite at the Knickerbocker Hotel, the traveling secretary had planned a small victory party. A couple of his old friends had come in from St. Louis. Stonily, the four of us sat in the room, numbed, when the suite doorbell rang, the door opened, and a hat sailed into the room, followed by Cubs manager Frank Frisch.

"I wanted to see if I was welcome," Frisch said softly and then, sneering, he snarled, "for crizzsakes, when you can't beat humpty-dumpties like I've got . . . my God, you don't deserve to win the damned thing. Give the old Flash a drink."

The next day the Redbird bats awakened, but it was too late. Led by Musial's two homers, they clobbered the Cubs behind Pollet, 13-5. The Dodgers blew a five-run lead and needed 10 innings to win the pennant. I would have strongly preferred Leo Ward's five rainouts.

En route home on a quiet train, I finished my obituary piece for the next day's *Post-Dispatch* and walked into the manager's private compartment, where Dyer sat with his wife. I expressed regrets and said, "You know, Colonel, considering the hearts we broke in 1930, 1934, 1942, and 1946, I guess we had one coming. But I wonder when we're going to get this close again." Dyer nodded in agreement.

A stunned Eddie Dyer at the end of the '49 season.

It was a sad sports fall all around for St. Louis. After the 1949 football season, the Billikens gave up football because the sport lost too much money and coach Joe Maniaci's lack of academic responsibility had compromised the Jesuits. New St. Louis U. president, Paul C. Reinert, also dismayed by the sport's financial losses, put down his academic foot and St. Louis U. has never played varsity football since.

Losing football was sad. But what happened to Gene Sutton was tragic. The Cardinals' fizzle had prompted *Collier's* to jettison a piece staff author Bill Fay had written about the innovative chiropractor.

Gene, regarded as a clubhouse nuisance by narrow-minded manager Dyer, was fired. A national sporting goods' company that previously had encouraged him financially announced abruptly it had changed its mind.

Divorced, mentally down, Sutton turned to a bottle and then a gun. He blew out his brains.

Gene's ideas had been ahead of his time. Now his time was over. Doc Weaver and I were crushed.

26

಺

Moments after arriving home from Chicago following the Cardinals' 1949 fold, I telegraphed Casey Stengel at Yankee Stadium: "CONGRATULATIONS. THE SHIP CAME IN. SEE YOU SOON."

When I arrived in the manager's office in New York to cover the Series between the Yankees and Dodgers, I heard Stengel's loud, guttural voice. Jovial Jim Dawson of the *New York Times* nudged me forward through the jostling reporters until we arrived at the front, and I saw Casey's craggy face.

"Case," called Dawson, correctly rhyming my last name with egg, "this is Bob Broeg of St. Louis."

Stengel looked up, and grinned and roared, "The hell it is. It's Brogue of Boston. The man on the streetcar. The ship came in . . ." Casey remembered my Back Bay farewell seven years earlier and also our occasional rides from Braves Field on streetcars that dipped underground to become subways.

Casey celebrates the first of five Yankee championships in 1949.

After Brooklyn and New York swapped 1-0 victories in the first two games, the Series quickly became a Yankee cakewalk, particularly after Branch Rickey couldn't persuade Preacher Roe, winner of Game One, to pitch again with short rest.

I was annoyed when Dodger manager Shotton turned uncooperative in announcing his pitchers, huffing that it only helped the gamblers. I had a nasty comeback for "Kindly Old Burt."

"Mr. Shotton," I said, "the gamblers are so damned smart they know your pitcher before you do, but I have an obligation to the readers, especially from out of town, to make certain I'm right."

Speaking of an obligation to the readers, during the 1949 baseball season I became uncomfortable with *Post-Dispatch* Managing Editor Ben Reese, because he had become pals with Fred Saigh, often sitting in the owner's box. I felt, in effect, that the growling-voiced managing editor was looking at my typewriter over my shoulder. Fortunately, he liked what he read.

When assignments were being made for the 1950 season, Reese must have told Stockton he wanted me to cover the Cardinals. Fur flew and when everything settled down, Reese compromised by having Stockton assign me to cover the Browns. Stockton told me what had happened and then, removing his pipe and pursing his lips as he did when annoyed, fastened his blues onto mine and said firmly:

"I told Reese I can outwrite *any* sonofabitch on my staff!"

Minding my manners, I did the best I could with the Brownies, who had operated too long on a financial shoestring. The American League club's owners, the DeWitt brothers, sought a new lease from the Cardinals in 1950, claiming the old arrangement was forfeited because of the National League club's title change at the time of Breadon's sale.

At only $35,000 per and half the maintenance, the lease seemed awfully cheap. During the court case, one of Saigh's directors, blabber-mouthing, announced the near-miss Nationals had made a million bucks in 1949.

In fact, 1949 was a year of box office records for both the Cardinals and St. Louis's Municipal Theatre, a 12,000-seat outdoor oasis in public Forest Park. The box scores: for the Cardinals, nearly 1,450,000 admissions. For the Muny, nearly 900,000.

For the Browns (blush!) *only* 270,000. No wonder the Brownies felt they needed another gimmick.

Over the years, the Brownies had tried a one-armed out-fielder, Pete Gray in 1945, and they had tried early in 1947 to use black players Hank Thompson and Willard Brown. Trouble was, Hank was too young, and Brown was too old.

So on the train trip to Los Angeles in 1950 to the Browns training camp I wasn't surprised to be introduced to another Browns "gimmick"— New York psychologist Dr. David Farrell Tracy.

A double-chinned, round man from Gloucester, Massachusetts, where his father had been a fishing-town grocer, Doc Tracy attended Tufts College for two years. During his World War I Army service, when he was a hospital patient in London, David was quite impressed by the efficacy of hypnosis against battle shock.

After WWI, he had gone to where we were headed now — L.A. — and earned a doctorate in metaphysics from the Divine College of Metaphysics. If that didn't sound too impressive, the New York lecturer and practitioner listed himself as married to Florence Wey, associate editor of *American Journal of Medicine and Surgery.*

One-armed marvel Pete Gray in 1945.

Doc was a showman. His brown eyes bulged farther than Browns' owner Bill DeWitt's blues. Tracy had a slight yellow tic in one orb that made it look like a gimlet eye— the better to see you with, grandma. He didn't think he could make a pennant purse out of the second-class baseball citizens, but he was confident he could ease pressure and build confidence.

Using hypnosis, he had been successful in curbing his patients' excessive smoking and drinking. He even taught dentists to minimize the "ouch" out of their drilling.

But baseball has its own realities, not all of which are susceptible to a degree in metaphysics. As Buck Crouse at the Chicago White Sox told linguist Moe Berg, "That damned curve ball don't care how much education you got or ain't."

Hanging around with Doc Tracy was a lot more fun than watching the Browns camp. Poor ol' Zack Taylor was trying to make chicken salad out of chicken feathers. Gangling first baseman, Don Lenhardt, could hit the long ball. Quiet Sherman Lollar could catch and right fielder Ken Wood could throw.

As for pitching, well, that had been a Brownie problem since I was a pipsqueak. The Browns' best pitcher was a chunky young right-hander named Ned Garver. And he was horrible in camp. From day one, Ned worked on his control, trying to nip corners and missing so often that, as the saying goes, time and again he walked the park and then served up one that cleared the bases.

Roy Sievers was the Browns' most valuable asset. As a 20-year-old rookie in 1949, Sievers hit .306 with 16 homers and 91 runs batted in. He was the American League Rookie of the Year.

But DeWitt squeezed the $5,000-minimum first-year man by offering an increase to only $8,000, prompting a holdout that finally brought Sievers to camp dissatisfied and out of condition. For one who had watched winning baseball, I was dismayed at the failure to grasp basics by members of the Browns' staff. In one instance, the third-base coach, with a Brownie runner on third, another on first and none down, held the man at third as a St. Louis hitter grounded into a double play.

I argued that the man on third had to go, giving up one out rather than two and, if possible, hope to stay in a rundown long enough for the runner on first to reach third and the batter to get to second.

Over a beer, the coach shook his head. I asked for his choice as the wisest American League manager? He mentioned Bucky Harris, then at Washington. Fine, and I bet $5, payable at the All-Star break when we'd both be in St. Louis, that Bucky would back me. He did.

One good reason to be with the Browns was to see the City of Angels flex its developmental muscles after WWII. Another was to enjoy the hospitality of the Browns' traveling secretary, Charley DeWitt, to whom every night was New Year's Eve.

The DeWitts were lavish with the press, I report with some embarrassment as a sports writer who has tried, wherever gracefully possible, to pay his own way. But there was *no* way I could keep up with even a short-pocketed ball club's treasury. When Charley was handling finances, the Browns paid cash for virtually everything, seeking the 10 percent discount often offered.

Spring training with Charley Dewitt in 1950 and 1951 meant LaCienaga restaurants like Lowrey's famed prime rib, Murphy's corned beef-and-cabbage special, and others.

The Browns' housing address was Hollywood. The hotel was the good, solid second-class Hollywood Plaza, just a few feet from famed Hollywood and Vine. Just across Vine street at the corner, Red Nichols and his Five Pennies played. A couple of doors south of us on Vine was a bar where gifted Joe Venuti played "Hot Canary" on a hot violin.

Next door was a branch building of CBS. Hurrying out one morning, I knocked Harry Morgan on his keister. If I sound like a name dropper, I am. If there's still a bit of a little boy in the man — an *old* man — again I'm guilty. I was delighted running into Barry Fitzgerald in the Hollywood Plaza Hotel. And I met the Wicked Witch of the West. Margaret Hamilton was a pleasant conversationalist.

The Browns' business address was in Burbank, California, out on Olive Street Road, past the Disney Studios. One day, with former St. Louis soprano Helen Traubel— a Brownie fan from the days when her father ran a Jefferson Avenue drugstore near Charley DeWitt's insurance agency in St. Louis— munching a hot dog in the stands, Bing Crosby showed up with his young twin sons just about the time our package of cheeseburgers arrived.

As end man in press row, I tried to lob one to Ray Nelson of the rival *Star-Times*. Should I underhand . . . no, better a soft overhand flip. Alas, en route, the sandwich napkin fluttered, the restraining toothpick came out, and the cheese, catsup, mayonnaise, and meat separated from the bun, and, well, the mayo and the rest of the goop hit Nelson smack in the face.

Those were the days and the nights. One evening, tardy enough to have missed my playmates, I cut from the Plaza's lobby into the side of an adjacent bar, a long rectangular place named "It" by originator Rex Beach in honor of flapper movie-star wife Clara Bow.

As I stepped into the bar's tight corridor, a familiar body whizzed past me. Seconds later, big Al Simmons, one of baseball's greatest hitters ever with the Philadelphia Athletics, introduced me to a balding man I recognized immediately. It was Bill Frawley, movie actor, best known later as neighbor "Fred" in Lucille Ball's great "I Love Lucy" TV series. I *knew* Frawley was a great baseball fan.

Both men were deep in their cups. Simmons was in town as a coach for the Cleveland Indians, who had come from Tucson, Arizona, for a series of exhibition games on the Coast. Old friends, Sim and Frawley were gabbing about the proper way to go back on a fly ball. First, Simmons raced the length of the bar. Next, Frawley. They appealed to me for an opinion. Not tonight, Josephine.

My memories of my first-ever trip to the West Coast are rich. I remember the trip to San Bernardino and the short run down the express highway to Pasadena, where I ogled the idle Rose Bowl, remembering football games I'd heard from there, as far back as Roy "Wrong Way" Riegels' famed run in 1929.

First prize for frivolity goes to a St. Patrick's Day party at the actors Friar's Club honoring Pat O'Brien. The brief formal dinner ended quickly. The best attractions were in the club rooms, where I swapped football stories with Jimmy Phelan, who had been at Missouri about the time I was born; and listened to Walter Catlett tell the one about the cabdriver knocking Harry Frazee on his duff for having dealt Babe Ruth from Boston to New York; and saw the screen master of drunk waiters, Vince Barnett, volunteer his favorite act.

Above all was Bill Thompson, wearing a kilt, participating in one funny episode after another, as amusing as his voice impersonations on the "Fibber McGee and Molly" radio show.

Thompson, rubber-legging with too much Irish joy, finally took a pratfall and . . .

Well, shortly thereafter, Pittsburgh's screwball baseball broadcaster, Bob Prince, came up with a favorite toy as a good-luck charm for the Pirates. He called it the "green weenie." The designation always made me smile. Because when Thompson took off his kilt, his rump was as bare as when the doctor first paddled it at birth, but I don't think Bill was born with a green ribbon tied around his . . .

In 1950, neither the Browns nor the Cardinals had a very good season, although Musial hit very well. My favorite baseball memory involves Alfred Fred (Red) Schoendienst, who had run out of gas late in '49.

Red turned the corner dramatically in 1950, and I updated the *Saturday Evening Post* piece they had bought about the Cardinals second baseman. They set a publishing date.

Fans and players talked then about *"Post* luck," meaning the Curtis publication's knack for having good things happen. This time fate's shotgun was loaded with good fortune, and the *Post* was shot square in the ass.

Late in the 1950 All-Star game at Chicago's Comiskey Park, Red sat on the bench between former teammates, Walker Cooper and Murry Dickson. "I wish the old man would give me a chance," said Schoendienst, referring to National's manager Burt Shotton, "and I'd put one up there."

The switch-hitter motioned to the distant left-field stand's upper deck. Shotton finally rested Jackie Robinson, and Red teed off on Detroit left-hander Ted Gray. His homer won the game in the fourteenth inning, 4-3.

The next day the *Saturday Evening Post* featuring my story on Schoendienst hit the stands!

My reaction was the same as the publisher's.

Yes!!!!!

27

In 1951, I saw a Lilliputian play major-league baseball and a Giant become a legend.

The year began when Fred Saigh fired Eddie Dyer and named Marty Marion as manager. The change didn't help the Cardinals much, because what they needed was more talent. No manager can win without it.

Musial had talent, of course, and continued to hit wonderfully well. Stan's roommate, Red Schoendienst, was also effective. "We're filling the room with base hits," quipped The Man. But the Cardinals finished 15 games behind the Giants.

They weren't helped by a flu bug that bit deeply during their first eastern swing. Musial was sidelined and needled the skinny manager about the solid blue socks Marion had affected for use with the road uniform.

"Know what, Marty?" said Musial. "They're Mourning Socks."

Eddie Dyer (left) and Fred Saigh as Dyer resigns as Cardinals manager. J. Roy Stockton (left) and the UPI's Stan Mockler in background.

I skipped the ball club's first swing so I could speak on sportswriting at alma mater Missouri's annual Journalism Week. Among a few hundred students in my audience, about a dozen hung around afterward. I took them across the street to the former Pop Given's restaurant, where, as far as I know, we originated the Thank God It's Friday Club in the late 1930s.

Among the several who went along were two young men who would play an ongoing role in my life. One was a fifth-year senior, Joe Pollack, and the other was Dave Lipman. Both eventually played major roles at the *Post-Dispatch*.

Because I didn't take the trip to Cincinnati, I missed a fist fight between broadcasting's Harry Caray and the *St. Louis Star-Times'* W. Vernon Tietjen. Both wore thick glasses.

Later, after gossip had given me the details, I needled Tietjen that it had been a double no-hitter, fistically speaking. He assured me there had been at least a foul tip.

On June 15, J. Roy Stockton's right-hand man, Lloyd McMaster, awakened me. McMaster told me that, oh, yes, the Cardinals had traded pitcher Howard Pollet and catcher Joe Garagiola to Pittsburgh for outfielder Wally Westlake and pitcher Cliff Chambers. That brought me to full attention, sorrowing for the loss of a pitching pro, Pollet, and the kid catcher of whom I was most fond, Garagiola. It worked out for Joe, though, because playing with the Pirates gave him some great comedy material. For instance, after batting .274 for the 1952 Pirates, dead-last with only a 42-112 record, Garagiola said of his team, "When we got rained out, we'd throw a victory party."

McMaster had another piece of news. "Today," he brayed, "the *St. Louis Post-Dispatch* bought the *St. Louis Star-Times*."

You could have heard the lint fall out of my navel. What would happen to my friends who wrote for the *Star-Times*? That's what I asked Ben Reese shortly thereafter. Mr. Reese had retired as managing editor and moved to New York to serve with the American Press Institute in its offices at Columbia University's Pulitzer Building.

We met at the Polo Grounds and Reese listened to me commiserate for the reporters out of work. Finally, he said, "You've sobbed enough for the other side. Just think what would have happened to the *Post-Dispatch* if the *Globe-Democrat* and *Star-Times* had merged."

The *Post-Dispatch* had me stay on the road with the Cardinals at the All-Star break. Minus All-Stars Musial, Schoendienst and Enos Slaughter, the Redbirds played their Allentown, Pennsylvania, farm club on Monday, and then on Tuesday took the field against a soldiers' team at Fort Lee, New York.

Before the trip Marion asked me: "How would you like to manage these two games?"

Flat-footed fools plod in where angels fear to flutter. Sure, what the hell, I'll make a horse's tail out of myself. Sandwiched between Marion and coach Terry Moore, I received an early lesson when the count reached "2 and 0."

"Hit or take?" . . . Uh.

C'mon, think a pitch in advance so the sign can be flashed by Moore to Ray Blades, coaching third base. And what about "3 and 1" on the third-place hitter, to Hal (Hoot) Rice. Do we send the runner on first? . . . Uh, sure, why not?

I managed a winner, anyway, in both games.

Cardinals owner Fred Saigh desperately wanted Marion to manage a winner. Saigh was alarmed by the presence of Bill Veeck, the new owner of the St. Louis Browns. Veeck's plan was to irritate and harass Saigh enough so the lawyer would move the Cardinals to another city. Like Baltimore or Milwaukee.

Veeck delighted in prodding the Redbird club owner wherever possible. Bill was always looking for a gimmick to upstage Fred. He came up with a helluva stroke of marketing genius.

After conceiving and designing his most famous stunt, Veeck used his public relations man, Bob Fishel, to search for an appropriately short person. He rejected several, but finally found 3-foot-7, 65-pound Eddie Gaedel, pink-cheeked, cherubic and, yeah, damned cute. Eddie came to town, won Bill's approval and signed a contract for $100 and expenses.

If Veeck hadn't tipped me and I hadn't buttonholed *Post-Dispatch* photographer Jack January, there would have been no picture as captivating as the one January took by sneaking out onto the playing field and kneeling a few feet from the batter's box.

When Gaedel flew back into town that morning, he was spirited to Veeck's apartment. There, borrowing young Bill DeWitt's boyhood uniform, to which a number had been attached, Veeck went over the ground rules with the 26-year-old. Friskily, Eddie swung two small bats.

"Whoops, hold it," Veeck admonished, "you're *never* to swing that bat. *Never*. I'll be up on the rooftop, directing the entertainment, and in the Marines I was a crack rifle shot . . . "

Gaedel nodded. He understood the message and was whisked downstairs into the Cardinals' empty clubhouse.

Before the first game, the approximate crowd of 20,000, real b-i-g for the Browns, was given free cake and ice cream. Between games, with Veeck directing from the roof, the production began. Aerial bombs exploded, spewing miniature flags onto the field. Old-fashioned autos and high-cycled vintage bikes paraded. A hand balancer performed at first base. My old boyhood soccer friend, Bill Keough, bounced as a professional trampolinist at second base. A juggler performed at third.

Four Brownies walked onto the field — Satchel Paige on the drums, Al Widmar with a bull-fiddle, Ed Redys with an accordion, and Johnny Berardino shaking the maracas.

Suddenly a giant papier mache cake was wheeled onto the field. The band played "Happy Birthday," and out from the cake's top layer popped a short man with a fractional number on his back. Quickly, he raced into the home team's third-base dugout and disappeared. The crowd laughed happily. Wasn't that a clever climax!

Climax! Haw!

After Detroit went down in the first inning of the second game, the field announcer droned: "Attention, please! For the Browns, batting for Frank Saucier, number 1/8 — Eddie Gaedel."

The crowd gasped as Gaedel came out swinging his little bats. I held my breath. Would the hot-tempered Ed Hurley, umpiring at home plate, permit the charade? Forewarned and fearing the worst, manager Taylor came loping out to the plate waving a telegram from American League president approving the contract of Edwin F. Gaedel.

Hurley shrugged and motioned Gaedel to the plate. Detroit manager Red Rolfe protested feebly, not liking the comic-opera scenario, but willing to go along. His bench needled Eddie.

Hurley beckoned Bob Cain to pitch. The left-hander motioned for catcher Bob Swift to come out for a conference. Could he lob the ball underhanded? Swift didn't think so. The catcher asked if he could lie down behind the plate. The pitcher didn't think Hurley would permit their adding to the farce.

Eddie Gaedel

So Swift went back behind the plate, kneeled, and Cain, trying to get the ball down low enough, did what Veeck had hoped. He walked Gaedel on four pitches.

Eddie triumphantly threw the bat aside and dashed to first base. Jim Delsing came out to pinch run for him. As Jimmy stepped on first base, Gaedel grandly slapped the new right fielder on the rump and raced back toward the dugout. The crowd loved it.

When Fishel told me that Gaedel had to hurry to catch a flight back to Chicago, I urged the P.R. man to bring Eddie up to the press box. Fishel agreed and, after Gaedel had showered, we were introduced. "You know, Eddie," I told him, "now you are what I — what lots of us — always wanted to be."

"What's that?"

"An ex-big league ball player."

Forgive my envy, Eddie, but the bottom line is that the story of your moment in baseball is my personal all-time favorite.

As for the most spectacular moment in sports I've ever personally witnessed, that would be . . .

But let me set the scene first. Leo Durocher's New York Giants, an early favorite in 1951 after The Lion's overhaul, appeared to die early with 11 defeats in the first 13 games, but didn't quit, even when 13-1/2 games out in mid-August. Their 16-game winning streak made it a two-team race.

Still, as Dodgers' manager Charley Dressen ungrammatically put it after a borough rivalry series, "The Giants is dead."

Playing my own game with Dressen when Brooklyn came to town for its last visit, I asked him who would start the World Series. Most baseball people would consider such speculation bad luck, but not Chesty Cholly. "Roe," he said flatly, "the Preach."

The Giants followed Dressen to town. The final game of the series was a rainout. Fred Saigh's public relations' director, Jim Toomey, who had left the *Star-Times* in time, had an idea. The Cardinals were scheduled to play the Boston Braves the next night, but if the Giants wanted to stay over, why not offer New York a day-game opportunity?

For the first time since 1883, a major-league ball club played two opponents the same day. As usual, Warren Spahn subdued his Cardinal cousins at night, but during the day the Birdies dealt the Giants a painful defeat.

No matter. The Jints were en route to an episode called "The Little Miracle of Coogan's Bluff," referring to the stone heights above the Polo Grounds at 155th Street. They won 37 of the last 44, including the final day. The hunter caught the hunted. The Dodgers and Giants were tied for first place.

Stockton and I entrained east, deciding not to fly even if meant we would reach Ebbets Field in time for the playoff opener. We listened to a radio play-by-play of the first game, won by the Giants, 3-1. New York's third baseman, Bobby Thomson, hit a run-scoring fly ball and a home run off a big right-hander, Ralph Branca.

The Dodgers won the second game 10-0 at the Polo Grounds and here we all were again—a one-game showdown for the pennant. I guess I was as excited as the players and hopeful the Giants could complete their Cinderella comeback.

For seven innings the game was a tense 1-1 duel between the Giants' Sal Maglie and the Dodgers' Don Newcombe. Both had pitched shutouts in their last regular-season start. Then, suddenly, in the Dodgers' eighth, Brooklyn scored three runs off nemesis Maglie. Newk, on the other hand, never seemed better than when he fanned the side in the Giants' eighth.

I was responsible for writing a running account of game action when Alvin Dark began the Giants' ninth with an infield single. With Gil Hodges holding Dark at first base, entirely unnecessary with a 4-1 lead, left-handed contact hitter Don Mueller pulled a ground ball that flicked off the first baseman's glove for a hit. If Gil had been playing off the bag, Hodges, the best right-handed fielding first baseman I ever saw, would have surely sucked up the grounder.

With runners on first and third, Monte Irvin popped out. Then left-handed-hitting Whitey Lockman thumped a double to left, scoring Dark. Mueller had to hurry to avoid Andy Pafko's throw to third base. Don jammed his ankle. The game was delayed as he was carried off on a stretcher. Clint Hartung pinch-ran for him.

Meanwhile, manager Dressen of the Dodgers wrestled with a problem. When he asked pitching coach Clyde Sukeforth about his potential relievers, Carl Erskine and Ralph Branca, Clyde told him Erskine was bouncing his overhanded pitch. So Dressen decided to replace Newcombe with big Branca.

Now Thomson was at bat, more controlled and settled because of the delay caused by Mueller's injury. Bobby respected Branca, but knew he could hit him. After all, he had smacked a homer and run-scoring fly off Ralph two days earlier, hadn't he?

Branca's first pitch I'll never forget — a fast ball right down the pipe. I groaned to Stockton, "Criminy, boss, Thomson is not going to get that good a pitch to hit again." Branca threw his second pitch up and in, attempting to move Thomson back off the plate. To me, the ball seemed guided, rather than thrown hard.

Thomson leaned back and tomahawked the pitch with a quick, compact swing. The ball zoomed quickly to left field, just a bit deeper at 271 feet than the 257 in right.

Time and again, I had seen low line drives go into the lower right-field seats at the Polo Grounds, but not to left. This one — in my split-second judgment— was perhaps a double off the fence, scoring maybe only one run because left-fielder Andy Pafko could really throw and . . .

Home run!

Although I didn't hear Russ Hodges' radio report — "Giants win the pennant, Giants win the pennant" — or Ernie Harwell's pronouncement on TV, this I *do* know:

For a good split second, there was silence as if the crowd, like me, had to count . . . three . . . four . . . dammit, five . . . the Giants are champions!

Thomson's arithmetic was faster than mine. Halfway toward first base, the lanky Flying Scot began to leap gracefully like a gazelle. He circled the bases in triumph, his progress noted closely by the competitive Jackie Robinson, hands on hips, making damned certain that, unlike Fred Merkle in the same ball park 43 years earlier, Bobby didn't miss second base.

As Thomson neared third base, Eddie Stanky, the scrappy New York second baseman, surged out of the first-base dugout, raced toward third and tackled manager Durocher, who was coaching third.

With that one swing, Robert Brown Thomson won my gold star for the most thrilling smash of the century.

The basher of baseball's biggest blow, Bobby Thomson.

28

ða.

Bill Veeck liked to make a fan's visit to the ball park fun. He might surprise the ladies with orchids or offer free cans of peas and corn. Or saddle a fan with a squawking caged chicken. Or, on a hot night, deliver a 100-pound hunk of ice to a spectator's seat.

When Saigh, trying to play "can-you-top-this," sought to give away an automobile, as Veeck did previously elsewhere, a local Irish magistrate with an avowed love for the Browns wouldn't let the Cardinals indulge in an illegal lottery.

Veeck puckishly draped huge photos of Brownie players, past and present, above the concessions stands in the grandstand runways. First time the Cardinals were home, Saigh draped the photos with red covers.

Fred would place players on waivers to send them to the farm system. Veeck would claim them. Saigh probably got his best advice from his smart P.R. man, Jim Toomey. Cracked Toomey, "Let him have them, Mr. Saigh. He'll run out of money and patience."

Both Saigh and Veeck, recognizing that a new national toy — television — affected attendance, wanted a share of revenue from those clubs who televised their homes games, notably New York. They argued that the visiting club provided 50 percent of the talent necessary for a game, yet received none of the TV revenue that reduced attendance. The Cards actually paid more money to the Giants and Dodgers when they came to town than vice versa.

Typically, because league president Will Harridge and the Yankees' George Weiss didn't like Veeck, the American League voted down the cheeky Marine veteran's request. But the NL approved Saigh's.

Veeck, always a tough act to emulate, brought an aged Satchel Paige to the Brownies and placed a rocking chair in the bullpen so the pitching legend could rock until needed.

Sometimes Bob Fishel, stationed on the dugout roof, held up large cardboard signs to the crowd so they could vote "yes" or "no" on questions like: Bunt? Steal? Hit-and-run? Philadelphia manager Connie Mack shook his shaggy old head. God, what was the grand old game coming to?

In 1952, Veeck replaced Zack Taylor as manager with Rogers Hornsby, who was under a cloud for his horse-racing gambling. Previously, as Brownie manager, Rog used a cashier's check to pay off a loan. Boss Don Barnes asked whether the check had come from gambling. Hornsby huffed, "Well, at least I don't extort big interest from widows and children." Fired!

In '52, Rog still was bigoted. He drove Paige hard in spring training until the ancient mariner complained, "What you trying to do, Mr. Hornsby, get ol' Satch ready for baseball or the U.S. Army?"

Hornsby was harsh even on one of his favorites, bespectacled rookie catcher, Clint (Scrap Iron) Courtney, who was goaded into a rail station race against athletic Milton Richman, United Press baseball writer from New York and fell while running, cutting heavily into his arms and forearms. Hornsby coldly made Courtney catch a painful doubleheader the next day.

When Rog wanted to change pitchers, he didn't walk to the mound, take the ball from the pitcher, pat him on his fanny, and summon a replacement. Hell, Hornsby whistled to the plate umpire, calling time. With one foot on the dugout step, he motioned to the mound for the pitcher to take a long walk and, at the same time he beckoned the bullpen for a replacement.

After an early June game at New York when umpires ruled fan interference on a foul ball hit by the Browns, Hornsby argued feebly. He *never* gave umps much trouble. From St. Louis, however, listening to the ball game, Veeck thought Hornsby should have protested. Traveling Secretary Bill Durney Slattery went to the edge of the dugout at Veeck's behest, and passed along Bill's beef. Rogers' answer was crude and rude.

Veeck flew to Boston to meet the team and meet with Hornsby. One Hornsby expletive after another led to Rogers' immediate cessation of employment with the Browns. The players ceremoniously presented Veeck with "An Emancipation Proclamation" plaque.

Baseball promoter Bill Veeck in 1952.

The Browns increased their attendance 100 percent, but whoa! They still drew less than any other team in the majors, only 518,000. The Cardinals dropped to 913,000, even though their first season under new manager Eddie Stanky was statistically a good one.

Maybe St. Louis wasn't a two-team town. Or maybe the fans didn't like Stanky. Curious guy, Eddie. He expected his players to give the same personal drive and dedication he gave to the game. Few did.

Stanky's team-game concept was brilliant. If a hitter failed to take one shot toward the opposite field with a runner on first base, swinging and missing when going to right or popping up or flying out to the right side, the malfeasance cost him a couple of bucks. Later, the manager threw the money into a private party for the players.

One early-season day at Chicago, playing second base, Stanky was late covering first base, and the batter was safe.

Shortly, thereafter, with the Cardinals losing by, oh, 4-to-1 in the fifth inning, the mighty Musial struck out and did not take the field.

Doing play-by-play, hemmed in by changing-edition deadlines, as were Chicago P.M. writers, I needed to know why and I needed to know *now*.

Why remove Musial? Was he hurt? We appealed to a press box attendant, to ask field announcer Pat Pieper to find out. Pat trundled over to the visitors' dugout, then came back to phone the press box attendant.

Politely, I heard the gentle graybeard say, "Oh, Pat, I can't tell them that."

"What, Jurgy?" I insisted.

Lowering his head, he said softly, that Stanky had told the press to indulge in the physically sexually impossible. I stormed out of the press box, down the winding stairs, circled the catwalk up to Wrigley Field's visitors club house and found trainer Doc Weaver working on Musial. Stan had twisted a knee. I was red hot. I told them I was going down into the dugout to have it out in the midst of the game. Weaver and Musial restrained me.

Doc insisted. "Don't, please don't. Stanky is hot now and has just fined Harry Brecheen for ignoring a pitchout sign."

I took their advice and hurried back to the press box to insert Musial's injury in my running account. But I kept the Brecheen fine information to myself for subsequent *Post-Dispatch* use only.

Veteran *Globe-Democrat* baseball writer Mike Haley suggested guardedly we double-check the four-letter Anglo-Saxon vulgarism Stanky reportedly had directed to the press box.

After the game, Haley, who seldom visited the clubhouse, accompanied me. Stanky sat there in the clubhouse with his head bowed. I asked curtly, "When Pat Pieper came over to inquire about Musial, did you tell him to tell the press to . . ."

He looked up and nodded. "That's all," I said, spinning out of the club house, accompanied by Haley. I headed downtown to do my overnight, planning to skewer the skipper, aware that when Eddie was a minor-league rookie, teammate Brecheen, an older player, had stepped forward for him in a tense situation.

You see, I had a hearts-and-flowers' piece. Stanky, angry at himself for failing to cover first base, had taken it out not only on the press, but also on St. Louis playing favorite Brecheen, fining the man who had befriended him.

Well into my story, I got a phone call in my hotel room from traveling secretary Leo Ward. Stanky, in Leo's suite, wanted to see me. I wasn't interested and said so, but friend Ward persisted. So I charged to the sec's suite. There sat Stanky, starting to make an explanation. I interrupted him.

"You know," I said, "you're great at putting women 'on a pedestal,' especially your own wife. I'm not so damned gallant, but my wife happens to be here, visiting her father in Oak Park, and I'm supposed to take them to dinner before our night train to Pittsburgh and . . . "

Softly, Stanky broke in, "You always said a man is entitled to a fair hearing." H'mm, yeah, I guess so. The manager continued. Sure, he'd fined his old friend, Brecheen, but only because The Cat had been the first pitcher to transgress after Stanky had imposed an automatic fine for missing a sign. "Actually," said Stanky, "he fined himself."

I wheeled out of the room, calmer, and toned the piece enough to explain the manager's tantrum, but not enough to spoil a good story.

Throughout the season, short on starting pitching, Stanky relied on an angular left-handed veteran, Al Brazle, and a rawhided right-handed rookie, Eddie Yuhas.

Alfie, flinging sidearmed rather than throwing, used a dinky curve and quick-dipping sinker to make even good left-handed hitters bail out amateurishly, i.e., Dixie Walker, Tommy Holmes, and Earl Torgeson.

When Brazle fanned Torgeson four times in one game, the rugged left-hardhitting Braves' first baseman paid the Cardinals' clubhouse a visit the next night at Sportsman's Park. He yelled for Brazle, then threw him a plaid street cap and a matching plaid jock strap, and yelled, "Here's for both your heads, you prick."

In an aside to me, Torgeson huffed, "Let's see you print *that*."

I nodded that I would, at least watered down for a family newspaper. I fudged and wrote that Torgeson threw in two plaid caps and told the loosey-goosey left-hander that they were for both his heads.

The Redbirds fell short of pennant-winning Brooklyn, eight games ahead, and Stanky's alma mater, the Giants, four in front.

The Cardinals' hope was that a well-publicized long drink of water, Wilmer (Vinegar Bend) Mizell, would be as good as Dizzy Dean.

Mizell's well-publicized debut brought club president Fred Saigh to Cincinnati for one of the most memorable nights of my newspaper life. The press learned Saigh faced an income-tax exchange charge; Mizell, after a wild hesitant start, lost a 2-1 duel; and an umpire attacked a ball player!

In an argument at home plate, Hemus got into it with plate umpire Scotty Robb. Stanky, rushing out in an effort to save his player, shoved Solly aside and, gesturing with his hands in the manner of Durocher, took up the conversational cudgel. Suddenly, Robb pushed the manager away, whipped off his mask and raised it as if to conk little Eddie on the head.

Stanky stepped back in astonishment. In the press box, I winced, aware that the new president of the National League, Cincinnati's former general manager Warren Giles, was watching from a box directly below, providing Giles the same silhouetted view we had upstairs.

I feared the worst for the man who bit the dog. Sure enough, Giles soon announced his decision, fining Hemus $25, Stanky $50 and Robb an amount "in excess of both," probably $100, yet amounting to a heavy slap to the umpire's dignity. In a huff, Robb promptly quit the job.

Fred Saigh came a long way in a hurry after buying out Breadon with Hannegan, then setting up his dying partner's family finances. In the process, he ran afoul of the IRS. The investigation we learned about on that June night came to a climax in January, 1953.

In a surprise judgment handed down by federal jurist Roy Harper, one-time business manager of a Cardinals' Class "D" farm club at Carruthersville, Missouri, Saigh was fined $15,000 and sentenced to 15 months in prison. Even though the area's district court was regarded as the nation's toughest, the prison term caught lawyers old and young by surprise.

I recall Saigh's staggering a few feet in protest toward the bench, pleading that his aged mother would be alone. Judge Harper snapped at the 47-year-old executive, "You're a lawyer. You know the meaning of 'nolo contendere' (no contest)."

With a 10-week period before incarceration, Saigh faced a need to divest himself of his interest in the ball club, either by sale or by placing it in the hands of others. Representing the *Post-Dispatch*, I flew to New York, not with Saigh, but I had dinner with him at a restaurant operated by a colorful character of whom I was fond, Herb (Curly) Perry.

When I took Saigh to his establishment, just off Lexington on 49th street, Perry was at his cheerful best. "Don't let it get you down," Curly commented. "Take a sun lamp with you and get a good tan."

Saigh, smiling, somehow took the gauche gaffe in stride. Next day, too, he was at his best after a lengthy meeting with the commissioner, who came out, arm around Saigh's shoulder, and announced that Fred would sell.

Saigh's only complaint — other than shock over the prison term — was the orchestration by which it looked as if he were seeking the highest bidder rather than one from St. Louis. Fact is, he turned down an out-of-town offer $500,000 in excess of the reported $3,750,000 he received from Anheuser-Busch.

Gussie Busch, the brewery big-wig, didn't know a foul from a mallard, because his priority was the family, brewery, and animals. Busch didn't recognize all the goodwill his purchase would earn him and the brewery.

At a 6 a.m. press conference designed to favor the *Post-Dispatch*, crack cityside reporter Selwyn Pepper and I witnessed the changing of the guard. By the time I left, I'd promised to drink no beer except Budweiser. This at a time when Budweiser trailed Schlitz nationally and was third in the St. Louis market to Stag and Falstaff.

Stag, bottled by the western branch of the Griesedieck family across the river at Belleville, Illinois, had come out of WWII a big seller. Friend Mel Price, the East Side congressman, had done extremely well with his stock. I congratulated him and wondered why the success? Previously I'd seen and tasted Stag only when playing an occasional softball game in Illinois.

"Because," said Price, "it's good, but also because you, me and many of us in service came out wanting to drink and not get drunk. Less alcohol, I'm sure."

I checked that one with the bartenders at Ruggeri's. They agreed. Stag froze more quickly than other brands. So when Stag was advertised as "dry" beer in the 1940s, it was, in effect, what now is a popular "light" beer.

Saigh recognized the huge boost the Cardinals would give the brewery. When Fred sold out, he asked banker Jim Hickok to come up with about 25,000 shares for him at under $20 a share. A few days later, Hickok phoned with the availability of a block of 28,000. Buy!

Without Saigh's ever buying another share, stock splits over the past 40-plus years have boosted the little man's holdings to 1,089,000, largest outside the immediate family. I speculate that Saigh's initial investment of approximately $500,000 is now worth nearly $50 million.

One of Gussie's first acts as owner was a foot tour of Sportsman's Park. He hurried in and out of rest rooms and concessions stands, afterwards rasping, "I'd rather have my ball club play in Forest Park."

At this time a brewery spokesman, John L. Wilson, temporarily Busch's right-hand man, made a stupid bid, an offer of $800,000 to Veeck for the ball park, $1.1 million if the Browns left town. Sounded as if, like Harry Caray, they were trying to alienate American League beer drinkers . . .

Ultimately, Veeck — or his creditors — got the $300,000 extra, but only because Bill couldn't see bucking Budweiser's beech-wood bank account. He opted for his former minor league town, Milwaukee, which had begun building a stadium.

But hold it! Boston had minor-league rights to Milwaukee.

On my birthday — March 18, 1953 — at St. Petersburg's Vinoy Park, the National League approved Boston Braves' owner Lou Perini's request to move the old Beantowners' long-standing National League franchise to Milwaukee. The last-previous franchise move had been 1902, second season of the American League, when Milwaukee gave its Brewers to St. Louis as the Browns.

With mayor Tommy D'Alessandro of Baltimore seeking a ball club, Veeck played footsy with the Maryland metropolis whose Orioles had been the swashbuckling champions of the previous century's Naughty Nineties.

But the American League hated the impudent Veeck's guts and turned thumbs down. Not on Baltimore forever, but *this time with Veeck.*

I honestly don't think I saw the lame-legged lame duck again until the Browns were sold to Baltimore interests after the

1953 season in which, not surprisingly, attendance by fans who knew they were no longer wanted slipped to 291,000. Aware instinctively of what Veeck faced and with only tapped-out resources, I felt understanding and sympathy for him.

The man who stood tallest that summer was the Browns' publicity director, Bob Fishel. Early, pleasantly, he set the ground rules. "Look," he told Bob Burnes and me, "Veeck is my friend and my boss. You are my friends. If we can meet, talk, have fun, and forget for whom I work, great."

Saigh was out, Veeck was out, Busch was in.

Gussie was a Peck's Bad Boy whose favorite class in school was "Recess." Will Rogers taught him to ride and rope, which was fine with Busch, because he liked action. He learned quite a bit about fast fillies during his fast-track youth.

He learned, too, as he told me, how to beat the drums for Budweiser. Gus would roll into a bar and order a round in a voice even more distinctive than mine. Winking, he explained, "About every dozen bars, I'd switch to a Scotch to warm my belly, then back to the beer."

Gussie had pizzazz, charisma, seat-of-the-pants genius. When he didn't know a guy's name — he didn't bother to learn most of the time — Busch's gravel-voiced "Hiya, *pal*" had the same public impact as Dizzy Dean's "podnuh."

By the time I met Busch, he had been forced out of his playful way of life by the unexpected death of his older brother Adolphus, whom he idolized. He had been married twice. One of his wives died very young, still a girl really, and he'd long been divorced from the other. Both women had mothered two children by him.

Shortly before the brewery and Busch got into baseball, Gussie had been on a European trip in search of schnauzers when he stopped at a quaint Swiss inn and met Trudi Buholzer, the innkeeper's daughter, who became the third Mrs. A.A. Busch Jr.

I had some great moments with the beer baron I always called "Gus" after he growled at me, "Cut out that Colonel crap, pal, and call me Gus."

Not "Gussie," the tender nickname used by many, or the "Augie" label misapplied by many and, of course, not "August," favored by his son, who has done even more for the brewery than the "old man," which is saying something.

August Adolphus Busch Jr. — why 'n hell didn't they make it August *Anheuser* Busch, just like why didn't Mom make my full handle Robert *Wiley* Broeg rather than Robert William? — figured prominently in my life.

He rode a special train to Milwaukee for the opening game of the 1953 season, his brewery's first as owners of the Cardinals, and Miller Brewery's first backing of the Braves.

The Braves won that opener unusually in 10 innings, 3-2. Warren Spahn was the winner that day and regarded that victory as one of the most significant of his 363, a record for a left-hander.

The win was achieved in the tenth inning on the only homer hit all season by rookie center fielder Bill Bruton. Bill's long drive might have been caught by Enos Slaughter except that, coming down with the ball, Slaughter crunched his bare elbow into the steel cyclone-wire prongs of a fence that had not yet been covered. The ball popped out over the barbed barrier.

A couple of nights later, the Cardinals made their home debut, the first for Gussie Busch and the brewery. The press box elevator didn't work. Pre-game aerial bombs failed. Missouri governor Phil M. Donnelly, scheduled to throw out the first ball, had a sore arm and couldn't, and Irish tenor Phil Regan, a movie actor under contract to the brewery, had a sore throat and was unable to sing the national anthem . . .

You can bet Gussie Busch's sweet life, as he always put it, that the Big Eagle was not satisfied. He was never willing to settle for anything less than top cabin.

Busch assigned Anheuser-Busch corporate heavyweight Dick Meyer to upgrade the entire Cardinals operation, on and off the playing field. And Gussie ordered his scouts to find and sign young Afro-American baseball talent.

He wanted the best, by God, and he wanted it sooner rather than later.

29

⁂

Gussie Busch found it difficult to tolerate a bad hop either on the ball field or in a beer bottle. His will to win would not accept imperfection. By 1954, he was busy trying to build a better ball club and sell more beer.

Busch, already competing with Miller Brewing, always gloried in his victories, whether banging down a card triumphantly with a shout of "Gin!" or strutting in his saddle holding a blue ribbon, or handling a handsome coach-and-four at Grant's Farm as if he were a cowboy stagecoach driver; Gussie had to be first and best.

Meanwhile, Jolly Cholly Grimm's Milwaukee guys were being lionized in the upper midwest, especially 23-game winner Warren Spahn and 21-year-old third baseman Eddie Mathews. The Braves attracted more than 1.8 million spectators, who drank a lot of Miller products.

"What would it take for the Cardinals to win?" Busch asked. Stanky, put it simply: "better players." Okay, buy 'em. Busch was shocked when the Giants' Horace Stoneham laughed at an offer of $1 million for Willie Mays, and the Dodgers' Walter O'Malley shook his double-chinned jowls negatively at a $600,000 bid for Gil Hodges.

If he couldn't buy stars, Busch was willing to spend money on promising prospects. The Cardinals bonused $65,000 in 1953 for Dick Schofield, a spry little high-school graduate from Springfield, Illinois.

Stanky, trying to put the kid at ease in Brooklyn when he joined the Cardinals straight out of high school, assembled all the shorter players and, privately, measured them on a scale in the visitors' clubhouse. Stanky asked me later, "Guess who, next to me, was the smallest guy?" I suggested, "Slaughter?" Snippily, Eddie added, "Well, how come you never have referred to him as 'little' Enos Slaughter?" "Because," I said softly, "legends aren't little!"

Enos Slaughter was a legend, true, but he was a crabby legend. I learned early to let Bosco's bitching go in one ear and out the other, but I would commiserate with him only to the point of politeness. Once he lingered in the St. Louis clubhouse, sounding off about the official scoring that had taken a hit away from him in a game won by the Cardinals.

His grousing got to me. "Bosco," I said, "I don't do the official scoring, don't get paid for it, and won't take any abuse about it." Well aware of how important his public image was to him, I added a zinger. "Suppose," I suggested sweetly, "I wrote for tomorrow's paper that the great team man, Enos Slaughter, was upset because he wasn't credited with a hit in a *winning* game!" He slammed the door on his way out.

Slaughter ranked only behind Musial and Red Schoendienst as subjects I wrote the most about over the years for the *Post-Dispatch* and various magazines, especially *The Sporting News*.

To use one of J.G. Taylor Spink's favorite expressions, I'm just about the only S.O.B. the editor and publisher of *The Sporting News* didn't fire. Spink was a helluva newshound and a great editor, though I don't know if he could write his name.

If he wanted a story written about a person or situation with which I was in disagreement, I would write using his name, not mine. Happily, that didn't happen often.

Of course, I always wrote stories about Musial under my own by-line. Stan was usually winning or in contention for the batting title, and his personality made him a popular subject. In 1954, however, the battle for hitting supremacy was between Brooklyn's Carl Furillo and Red Schoendienst.

Schoendienst, finishing at .342, suffered a nasty injury while beating out an infield hit in a night game at the Polo Grounds. Alvin Dark, the Giants' regular shortstop, was filling in at second base. Dark charged the ball and, firing hard on the run, handcuffed first baseman Whitey Lockman. The ball hit Schoendienst's left eyebrow as Red turned to look. Red went down, hard and in pain.

I groped through dimly lit areas under the stands to find the first-aid room. Red lay on his back, an ice pack over his eye, coddling a bottle of beer brought to him by Frank Frisch, then doing pre- and post-game TV shows. Two doctors hovered over Schoendienst, buzzing in frantic conversation.

I spoke up. "Hey, Doc," I said, "didn't Red tell you he always has trouble with his left eye, spots in his vision?" They sighed in relief. Fearing serious damage, they hadn't known that Red had been hurt when he was a Civilian Corps Camp kid during the Depression. Another kid, hammering nails into a post, hit one into Red's left eye.

With Schoendienst and Musial as twin pillars, Busch searched for ways to improve the team. The Cardinals spent wildly in the minor leagues for a quick-fix. Gussie insisted that the team sign black players. The Cardinals' first was Tom Alston, a defensively gifted Ichabod Crane at first base. But Tom couldn't hit. Lefty Memo Luna, son of a Mexican border-town mayor, couldn't throw much harder than stringbean Alston could hit. And Vic Raschi, a great competitor for championship Yankee ball clubs, had dropped off enough that he wasn't worth the $75,000 purchase price.

Tom Alston, the first black player to appear on the Cardinals' roster.

Busch was never remotely close to being a quitter. He kept searching for answers. The stocky beer baron was extremely leery of planes and relied for his long-distance transportation on a modernized motor bus and a private railroad car. When he traveled with the team, his train car was attached to the players' Pullmans.

I loved it when the "Chief," as publicist Al Fleishman called Busch, came out from his inner sanctum to drink Budweiser with the media. If you asked for a "beer" rather than a "Bud," you were fined 50 cents.

Once at Ebbets Field, I sneered in Busch's presence at the Barnum-and-Bailey circus ads lining the walls. St. Louis's Sportsman's Park was the same. It often looked as if the left fielder were trying to play fresh with the bare backside of a curvaceous mattress-company model.

By pleasant contrast, I suggested that Gussie note the plain green restfulness at the Polo Grounds, where the only ad was a Chesterfield cigarette sign above the scoreboard. I suggested that could be a Budweiser sign in St. Louis. Busch liked that.

After acquiring Sportsman's Park from the Browns, he hammered through his brewery board a $2.5 million ball park improvement for 1954. Busch wanted to call the park "Budweiser Stadium," but Ford Frick said no. Sportsman's Park would become *Busch* Stadium.

A new adjunct to the scoreboard in left field included a giant eagle — the brewery's symbol — and an animated red-hued bird that flittered happily whenever the home-team smacked a home run. Since there weren't many of those, Stanky asked publicist Jim Toomey to chart fly balls off the *right* field screen, home players and visitors. The Brownies had screened the area in 1929.

And there was Harry Caray. How the Canary could warble for the fans. How he could sell beer. Dick Meyer asked me about him. I said I didn't get along with Harry, but "keep him anyway." Later, at a time I was trying to get along with Caray, I noted petulantly that, cripes, I'd come to his support. Caray put me in my place. "If," he said, "you could have got me my job, I wouldn't have wanted it."

One job was lost just before the 1954 season opener. The Cardinals traded Enos Slaughter to the New York Yankees — and wow! — the ball club and A-B phones sounded like a pinball machine on "Tilt."

A beetle-browed young outfielder from Arkansas, Wallace Wade Moon, showed up at the Cardinals' St. Petersburg camp when he was supposed to report to Omaha at the Triple-A spread. Obviously, the 24-year-old master's degree graduate from Texas A&M impressed manager Stanky. The decision to unload Slaughter gave Moon the right field job.

At nearly 37, Slaughter had slowed down, all around, though his .291 batting average in 1953 wasn't bad. But when Dick Meyer called him off the field before a Sunday exhibition game at Sportsman's Park and told him he had been sent to the Yankees, ol' Eno shocked Meyer and the press. The veteran's tearful balding head, buried in his handkerchief, touched many. As he left the ball park belatedly and ran into Musial across the street, they cried together.

Enos Slaughter, brokenhearted after being informed of his trade to the Yankees.

Moon became the National League Rookie of the Year, beginning spectacularly by homering his first time at bat. He was shifted to center field for a series at Chicago's Wrigley Field, where I urged him to take extra fielding because of the wind. He shrugged. No need. H'mm, that day he misjudged two first-inning fly balls. The Cubbies posted "8" that inning and won a wild game, 23-13.

Another time at St. Louis, lining a drive down the right-field line, Moon rushed halfway to the bag, stopping to argue fair ball when he thought umpire Bill Jackowski had ruled foul. So, yep, they threw him out at first from the outfield.

I had a rare Sunday off when the Cardinals played a doubleheader that season. I was at home preparing for dinner when Bob Burnes phoned me to say, *"Your* man blew it!" With the bases loaded in a tie game and Ray Jablonski at the plate, Stanky, coaching third base, sent Moon on an unsuccessful steal of home. The Cardinals lost the game.

Sight unseen, I told Burnes, "I don't believe it. I don't believe Stanky would take the bat out of Jablonski's hands. Eddie has pumped too much confidence into Jabbo as a hitter."

I didn't see Stanky until Tuesday night. Typically, he tried to take the blame, but I persisted. Okay, okay, he didn't send Moon, but don't write it. Horsefeathers! I hurried out to Wally and talked about the blunder for which the manager had taken blame. But, insisted the player, the manager didn't want the player to talk about it.

"Wally," I said, indignantly, "you're a popular player. Stanky isn't a popular manager. Don't you think the public would forgive you quicker?" He nodded, weakly, so I wrote a short sidebar item. But, you know, denials never seem to eradicate accusations, as proved by Joe McCarthy, the senatorial demagogue, not the Yankee manager.

Early in the 1954 season, Stan the Man hit five homers in a doubleheader, missing a sixth only because he didn't pull one drive that Willie Mays caught against the center field flagpole. When Musial returned home happily, 13-year-old blond son Dick greeted him. "Gee, Dad," said the kid, "they sure must have been throwing you fat pitches today." Jack Buck, joining broadcaster Harry Caray that season, cracked, "Gee, does Stan do this every Sunday?"

Musial also figured in the All-Star game played that summer at Cleveland's huge stadium. He singled twice in a wild game, won by rallying Americans, 9-7, on a bloop single by Nellie Fox after Red Schoendienst had been thrown out on a steal of home.

Musial made a quick return trip to Cleveland for a home run hitting contest at which, as Branch Rickey would put it, the "inner conceit" of the superstar manifested itself.

Musial wanted to hit more homers than his fellow contestants Larry Doby and Al Rosen. Stan asked the Cardinals' traveling batting-practice catcher, Greg Masson, to pitch to him. If Musial won, Greg would get 100 bucks. Doby and Rosen, given 10 swings apiece, each hit one or two out of the park. Musial hit seven out of 10 for homers and hit the top of a fence with another. The crowd roared.

Cleveland's mayor proudly presented Musial with a miniature loving cup. The star trotted into the clubhouse, put the peewee prize in his locker, fished for his wallet and pulled out a "C-note" for Masson. Greg accepted, smiling happily. He broke up Musial when he cracked: "You're a great hitter, Stan, but a lousy economist, giving up 100 bucks for a $10 trophy."

In mid-season 1954, Musial made his annual position switch for the good of the ball club, moving back to the outfield. By then, Ulysses Brooks (The Bull) Lawrence, son of a Pittsburgh policeman, had stepped in as the ball club's first meaningful black player, posting a 15-6 pitching record for the sixth-place team.

The new first baseman, Joe Cunningham, a happy-go-lucky guy, could play defense, and he broke in at bat most impressively, hitting three home runs in his first two games, two of them off left-handed Redbird nemesis Warren Spahn. Joe tailed off a bit, though, and one night in Cincinnati, I watched him fuss around in the batting cage and suggested a different stance. He tried it and homered the first time up, prompting an Associated Press writer who'd heard my "expert" input to write a wire-brightening box item. Well, it sure beat wandering into a skeet-shooting range.

I was living the good life, doing what I wanted, happily married, making a living from baseball and the Cardinals. But I had fallen into some debilitating habits and my health was in jeopardy. One thing was sure: I needed to quit smoking three packs a day.

I'd tried. After a sedentary day, I covered a minor basketball game and, afterward, stared at the office ceiling collecting my thoughts. Nothing came from the typewriter until, reluctantly, I pulled out the day's first cigarette and took a couple of puffs.

For too long when I wasn't burning candles at both ends with Veeck or other night owls, I'd frequently finish dinner, pull out a typewriter and research notes, and blending beer and peanuts with heavy puffing, punch out a magazine story.

Staying briefly with Mom and Aunt Maggie because Dorth was on a trip, my insides burned even more than usual because of Pop's recent death. This was only 1954, but Washington University's Dr. Evarts Graham had already linked smoking and lung cancer. Please, I pleaded to myself. This was not the way I wanted to look and feel.

I decided to stop that night while watching "The Robe" with my mother and aunt. I kept wondering how those early Christians could give up their lives when I couldn't give up a filthy habit! Afterward, I took the ladies to Ruggeri's for a late snack. When I came out of the rest room, I wondered if Mom had noticed anything, figuring, naively, that, no, she hadn't. She almost crushed me with her cheerful, "Why, yes, Robert, I just told Maggie that you had given up smoking." *Given up*! Come now, Mom, don't paint me into a corner.

That night, staying in their spare bedroom, I couldn't sleep. My nerves were so atingle that poor Mom had to turn off all the clocks. By dawn, still wide awake, I was up and dressed, awaiting Dr. Bill Missey at his office.

He asked if I thought I'd suffered a heart attack and, yeah, I did wonder. He gave me an EKG test, read the results, and said my ticker was tocking fine. He knew I was withdrawing from nicotine. "Here's a sleeping pill," he said, "go home, get a good rest, and good luck." I did that. That did it. I never smoked again.

That made me and my mother and Dorth happy, but the Cardinals didn't make Gussie happy, finishing sixth, despite Musial and Schoendienst and Cunningham and Busch's best efforts. The New York Giants won the National League pennant and upset the Cleveland Indians in the World Series.

The outcome of the Series was foreshadowed in the opening duel between the Indians' Bob Lemon, and the Giants' Sal Maglie. With the score 2-2 in the eighth, two on, one out, lefty Don Liddle relieved Maglie to face left-handed-hitting Vic Wertz.

If you believe most reports, Wertz hit the ball so hard it might have wound up in the Harlem River. Actually, it was a helluva long wallop, but it wasn't the greatest catch I ever saw Willie make. At the crack of the bat, Mays raced toward the stands in deep right-center. Then, like a football receiver timing a catch or a catcher slowing to camp under a ball, Willie eased just a bit, caught the ball and, whirling, uncorked a long, strong and *accurate* throw to shortstop Alvin Dark.

If Mays had missed the cutoff man, the runner who had tagged up at second could have scored — easily! Instead, he was forced to stop at third. So, with right-hander Marv Grissom taking over from Liddle to retire the side, Don sauntered to the Giants' bench and, winking in relief, commented, "Well, I did *my* job — me and Mays!" With the game tied into the home tenth, pinch hitter James Lamar (Dusty) Rhodes looped Lemon's first pitch just inside the right-field foul pole, only 257 feet down the foul line.

The game was so exciting I felt like celebrating with a cigarette. But I didn't.

30

Baseball fields had been pockmarked with gloves until the 1954 rules changes banned players from leaving their gloves on the field during their team's turn at bat. I don't recall a single game lost because a player of one side tripped over the other's glove.

The new rules banned all foreign objects from the field and thus eliminated the time-honored custom of spreading bats in front of the dugout.

Among the "foreign objects" forced off the field were photographers, which unfortunately limited the angles of action photos, no matter how sophisticated cameras became.

Umpires were not banned by the new rules, however, even though there were times both players and managers felt it might be a good idea. For instance, when the opposition had the bases loaded and the batter hit a short looping fly that outfielder Ralph Kiner appeared to trap. Young umpires Hal Dixon and Tom Gorman raced to the spot.

"Catch" signaled one. "No catch," signaled the other. The runner on third base scored, the man on second took third, but the runner on first saw the "catch" signal and ran back toward first. Somewhere in all the confusion he was tagged out to end the inning and begin the argument.

Plate umpire Larry Goetz, one of the best ever, upheld the catch call and the double play, but ruled that the runner on third had scored. In fact he never tagged up.

After the game, Goetz refused to let the press talk to the two embarrassed young umps, but when asked to describe what had happened, he answered by saying, "horseshit umpiring!"

I learned through the grapevine that Warren Giles was about to fine Goetz. "Warren," I said, "please don't. Goetz completely humanized the situation with his frankness." Giles, a former Missouri Valley Conference football referee, changed his mind.

Once when Philadelphia was visiting St. Louis, the Phillies won a 10-inning, rain-delayed marathon in the first game of a doubleheader, 11-10. The second game of the doubleheader didn't begin until 6:48. Neither manager Eddie Stanky nor umpire-in-charge Pinelli was aware of a league change that expunged previous restrictions against using lights to finish the second game of a doubleheader that began after 6 p.m. So with darkness descending before the second game reached the required five-inning minimum length, Stanky directed his Cardinals to stall when they came to bat in the top of the fifth trailing 8-1. St. Louis catcher Sal Yvars incited a fight with Phillies first baseman Earl Torgeson. A free-for-all ensued. Even Terry Moore, the Phillies' new manager, and little Stanky dove into the fray.

When order was restored, Pinelli ordered the game forfeited to Philadelphia. The decision was cheered by the hometown crowd, angry at Stanky.

Giles immediately suspended Stanky and came to town for a hearing, after which he lengthened Eddie's suspension to five days and fined him $100. Yvars was suspended for three days and Torgeson two. Giles didn't penalize Pinelli, who should have known the rule had been changed. Stanky, meanwhile, at the behest of boss Gussie Busch and aided by publicist Al Fleishman, crafted a public apology and promised to cool down. With Stanky seated in the pressbox, the Cardinals won five in a row under coach Johnny Riddle.

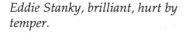

Eddie Stanky, brilliant, hurt by temper.

I always felt bad about having brought to public attention — and to Busch's — the final transgression leading to Stanky's dismissal early in the 1955 season.

Harrison J. (Doc) Weaver had just died in St. Louis. A light-hearted rah-rah guy, gadget-wise, and a musician at heart, Doc had done one last service for the ball club he joined in 1927. "Bucko," as Branch Rickey called the fullback he coached in college, persuaded the departing Browns' great trainer, Bob Bauman, to join him with the Cardinals.

Doc died in St. Louis at a time the ball club was in Cincinnati — and arrangements were made for key veterans to return to St. Louis on Monday's opening day for the funeral. Left-handed rookie pitcher Luis Arroyo summed up the grief, "Who now will play the mon-do-leen?"

In Cincy that disastrous weekend, the Cardinals played miserably, especially while blowing the extra-inning opener of a Sunday doubleheader. As the Reds' winning run scored, cocky little Dick Bartell, coaching third base, gave manager Stanky an up-your-bucket salute.

After the second game, Stanky cautiously kept his right hand concealed on a bus ride to the railroad station. After some detective work, I discovered that in the clubhouse between games, Eddie had lashed out in anger after Bartell's insult. In Stanky's wrath, he backhanded three condiment containers. The mustard crashed into the mayo and the mayo into the catsup. Glass broke and the manager bloodied his hand . . . and his reputation.

I wrote about the mishap with a light touch of sympathetic amusement, but the episode was ill-received by Busch and his advisors. As we played at Chicago, they huddled in St. Louis.

The Cardinals that year were in a "force-feeding" mode. Wally Moon was a sophomore, Rip Repulski a third-year man and three rookies — Bill Virdon, Larry Jackson, and Ken Boyer — were in the starting lineup as was young shortstop, Alex Grammas.

Boyer, the handsome younger brother of Cloyd, and older brother of Cletus, was potentially a great hitter. He seemed — in my book — a possible Hall of Famer. He might have been the best third baseman. Trouble was, though he stood far back in the batter's box, he did not, like Rogers Hornsby, stride into the ball.

I asked Rog to take a look at him from the Wrigley Field press box. Hornsby was impressed with what he saw and said, sure, he'd be glad to talk to the kid. I hurried to the clubhouse to tell Boyer, certain he'd be happy to learn from a .358 career hitter. You know, Ken, instead of just standing back, he can show you how to stride into the pitch and . . .

Boyer interrupted with a slight smile. "Thanks, but no," he said. "I can't go into the ball. I was almost killed with a pitch in Houston." H'mm, even "afraid" of the pitched ball, an ugly way to put it, Boyer still hit .287 for 15 years, with five over .300, eight seasons of 20-to-32 homers and six with 90-to-109 RBIs.

After the series with the Cubs, I ate dinner with Stanky on the train home. "Trouble with you, 'Genial,'" I said, using his own self-applied nickname, "you're just like Frisch."

Stanky's sharp blue eyes widened. He didn't like Frank because he thought the Old Flash's cutting comments about players Eddie managed — "spring training is a country club without dues" — were especially cutting.

I nodded. "Frisch's humor is ridicule, Genial, but so is yours. Trouble is, his is more humorous. You're a mental carica-turist. If you thought my main weakness was my red nose, you'd call me 'W.C.'"

"Yeah, all the way." He laughed, but it really wasn't funny. Neither was the fact that when we got off the train, Edward Raymond Stanky had been fired.

The next night, Stanky actually orchestrated a weird press conference held at Grant's Farm at which he passed along the managerial baton to Harry Walker. Stanky said quietly, "And I would have managed this team next year for nothing . . ."

During the off-season, Red Schoendienst was quietly inci-sive as usual. "Whether Stan is in the infield or outfield, our outfielders — especially Moon and Repulski — don't throw well enough. Too often the other guys get a man on second base, not first. Not even a good pitching staff, which we don't have, can get two if the other guy's on second."

New manager Harry Walker was the choice of Bing Devine, called in from Rochester by Dick Meyer to run the store because the latter's time was more valuable at the brewery.

Harry didn't do well as a manager because 1) as a 37-year-old player, he could pinch-hit only occasionally (five for 14), 2) he wearied players the morning after many night games by attempting to force-feed understanding and 3) he relied too much on players who had succeeded for him at Rochester.

Triple-A players! Not major leaguers!

The Hat wasn't helped, either, when a Stanky-launched stratagem failed. Jim Toomey's "balls hit off the screen chart" boomeranged. In 1954, the Cardinals had hit the screen almost twice as often as their opponents, 35 to 18.

Musial, hitting 35 homers in '54, had been denied 10 more. So Stanky had asked that the homerun barrier be removed in 1955. Trouble was, the foe hit 28 "new" homers in 1955, compared to the Redbirds' 24.

At the 1955 All-Star game in Milwaukee, Musial was hitless into overtime. Although Leo Durocher substituted freely, The Lip stuck with Stan the Man. When Musial came to bat in the 12th inning, Yogi Berra, catching, moaned about his number of squats behind the plate.

"Gee, I'm tired, " groaned Yogi.

Plate umpire Bill Summers, beet-red American League veteran, also said he was tired.

"Me too," said Musial, not turning his head, swishing his bottom for relaxation, brown eyes fixed on lanky Frank Sullivan's right arm. The Boston Red Sox pitcher threw.

Musial swung and began a four-base drift around the bases. By the time he reached home plate, Berra was long gone. Summers was there for the formality of making certain Musial got a foot on the plate before National Leaguers, happy with their 6-5 victory, carried him off. Durocher was delighted.

Managing the Dodgers or Giants, Durocher used to fuss that, damnit, he didn't care whether he got beat by Slaughter or anyone else, just so it wasn't "the big guy." As a result, Leo's pitchers often threw at and hit Musial.

Once when Durocher roared, "Hit him on the '6'" and lefty Windy McCall did, brash young Mr. Jackson offered to low-bridge McCall. Stan said, no, with thanks. Next time up, he hit Windy's first pitch onto the Polo Grounds' towering right-field roof.

Musial was the sole box office draw for too many losing *seasons* for the Cardinals and losing *teams* for St. Louis. Then Ben Kerner came to town early in 1954.

Kerner brought his Milwaukee Hawks into St. Louis for a mid-season exhibition. The attendance opened his eyes, and with the encouragement of *Globe-Democrat* sports editor Bob Burnes, Kerner decided to switch cities.

I could write a book about Ben Kerner, especially if permitted to include his colorful, owl-eyed, cigar-puffing young promotional whiz of an aide Marty Blake. Kerner gratefully gave Blake not only a pat on the back, but $50,000 when Marty left the Hawks to become the No. 1 purveyor of professional basketball talent.

The Hawks' Robert E. Lee Pettit played both ends of the court with admirable team contribution and incredible durability. He was a crowd favorite who deserved to be a role model for kids.

I covered the St. Louis Hawks' first exhibition game at Pinckneyville, Illinois, against the Ft. Wayne Pistons. Victory over Charley Eckman's division champions was psychologically s-o-o important.

On the bus ride, Kerner promised a steak dinner if the Hawks won, hamburgers if they lost. We won and ate steak. Until the league stopped it, Kerner used little incentives like a pair of pants or a sports coat for exceptional individual or team effort.

Primarily a baseball writer, I missed some exciting Hawks basketball games. So I was in Kansas City, returning to St. Louis with the Cardinals in April, 1958, when I heard the big news that the Hawks had won the NBA championship and that Pettit had pumped in 50 points. Mimicking a line I'd heard Kerner use time and again, I wired him from KayCee:

"I DON'T SEE WHY ANYONE EXCEPT PETTIT EVER SHOOTS. CONGRATULATIONS."

St. Louis Hawks All-Stars Len Wilkens (left) and Bob Pettit.

One of Kerner's biggest boosters was my friend Gus Busch, who astutely stepped in after Falstaff fouled up the radio rights. Ben had signed with Falstaff for only a pittance. So when the Hawks sneaked into a first-place division tie, their soaring popularity gave Kerner a chance to switch to Anheuser-Busch.

Thereafter, Kerner often played gin rummy with Busch, usually at Grant's Farm. Gus warmly hailed Kerner with a growled nickname — "Hawk." By then, A-B had moved up in the Lager League. Earlier I teased Gus that Falstaff beer seemed to get a dollar's advertising value for every penny, while A-B seemed then to spend a buck for a cent's worth.

Busch begrudgingly agreed, "pal," but Falstaff began to falter in critical judgments, and Anheuser-Busch began to score, though not necessarily with the appointment of Frank Lane as the Redbirds' new general manager.

Busybody Alphabetical Spink of *The Sporting News* sold Busch on Lane, who had come up rapidly through the baseball ranks after World War II. The former physical-fitness faddist, who loved to referee the coldest football games bare-armed, ran the Kansas City Blues, then in the American Association, and then the Chicago White Sox. He was, Spink insisted, the man Busch needed to provide aggressive front-office leadership. Lane was not a believer in the Cardinals' "force-feeding" mode. He thought the way to win was to trade, trade, trade. With carte blanche approval from the Brewery, just about every move Lane made that first season seemed suspect — and for good reason.

Except his first move. His new manager was Fred Hutchinson. Over the years I've been impressed by many men. High among them was the ruggedly handsome, curly-haired Hutchinson, extremely competitive, short-fused and hot tempered, yet able to keep his fury impersonal.

Over the years, I've learned not to be concerned with whether a ball club wins or loses in spring training. Seldom do Grapefruit League records have any meaning. But in 1956, I agreed with scouting and farm director Joe Mathes, who thought that Hutch's young ball club played as soundly as their Grapefruit leading 21-11 record indicated.

En route to St. Louis, Hutch told me he'd give first shot at shortstop to fleet Don Blasingame, a rookie, but would play Alex Grammas opening day. "I know about opening days," Hutch said thoughtfully, almost with a shudder. At Seattle, he had been a boy wonder, a professional pitcher right out of high school and a big leaguer at only 20. "One day on the bench will be enough to calm down the kid."

The Cardinals started well in the regular season. Then Lane dispatched versatile Solly Hemus to Philadelphia for Bobby Morgan. Why? "Because he gives us more protection at shortstop," piped Lane, at about a time Hutchinson and all agreed that Blasingame would make a better second baseman. Trouble was, Morgan couldn't play short.

Lane then dealt lefty Harvey Haddix to the Phillies for an old friend, 40-year-old Murray Dickson, and right-hander Herman Wehmeier, best known for his inability to beat the Cardinals.

But my heart sank the deepest the mid-May afternoon when long-faced Jim Toomey called me into the New York hotel suite to announce that Lane had traded shortstop Grammas and pinchhitter-outfielder Joe Frazier to Cincinnati for infielder-outfielder Chuck Harmon. "Wait, that's not all," said Toomey, announcing that as of the *Post-Dispatch* release date the next afternoon, the Cardinals were sending Bill Virdon to Pittsburgh for another center fielder, Bobby Del Greco. Del Greco, a rookie about whom I knew little and wished I'd known less, couldn't carry the NL Rookie-of-the-Year's bat and wasn't that much better a fielder.

Press and public winced at Lane's deals — in St. Louis, at least — but reaction was cyclonic when Trader Frank dealt popular Red Schoendienst. The switchboard at the ball park and brewery lit up just as in the case of Enos Slaughter. Lane, having dealt away two shortstops, had figured out that his team, now losing, was in dire need of a shortstop. To get Alvin Dark, he gave up Schoendienst. Deal after deal, the Cardinals grew worse, and the promising season faded away, although Musial, as usual, did not fail to deliver.

At the D.C.'s Touchdown Club luncheon the day before the 1956 All-Star game at Washington, J. G. Taylor Spink of *The Sporting News* presented a handsome giant grandfather's clock prize, now displayed at Cooperstown, to the Player of the Decade, Stan Musial. To decide the award, *The Sporting News* polled players, manager, coaches, umpires, and the press. Stan modestly accepted, "I can't field like DiMaggio, hit like Williams, run like Robinson or pitch like Feller, but I appreciate the honor."

The next day Ted Williams hit a home run. Rummaging through the records, the *Washington Post*'s Bob Addie intoned over the loudspeaker system, "And with that homer, Ted ties Stan Musial with four . . ."

As Addie spoke, Musial swung and hit one into Griffith Stadium's left-field stands, bringing a chuckle from the press when Addie corrected. "Check signals," he cracked, "Musial just untied that record!"

The new team on the block, Milwaukee, came to St. Louis the final weekend a game up and with a chance to clinch, but the Cardinals won the first game and created a first place tie. The Cardinals won game two to put Brooklyn back into the Series after Musial doubled off rival Spahn in the 12th and Rip Repulski skipped a game-inning hit off Eddie Mathews' glove. Crushed, angry, and in tears, Spahn flung his glove at AP photographer Jack Hogan.

By beating the Braves, who had a larger park than bitter rival Brooklyn, the fourth-place Cardinals cost themselves a few hundred dollars each in World Series shares. "So don't ever question baseball's integrity," Spahn grumped.

Gussie Busch had some choice comments about Frank Lane at the Knights of the Cauliflower Ear's pre-training salute in 1957.

Growled Gus: "Frank Lane better come close this year and win next or he'll be out on his ass!"

31

Spoiled by three satisfying decades of rooting and writing winners, I was ill-prepared when a plague settled on my sports house in the 50s, and both Missouri and the Cardinals became perennial losers.

During his first 12 seasons at Mizzou, beginning in 1935, Dan Faurot's teams won 74 games, lost 39, and tied seven. Faurot's prize pupil, Paul Christman, summed him up as "a coach who wins the games he should and, now and then, one he shouldn't."

But his final seven years netted a 27-40-3 record. Faurot announced before the 1956 season that it would be his last and he would become full-time athletic director. His close friend and assistant, John (Hi) Simmons, best known for his success as coach of the 1954 College World Series champions, wished, with delightfully drawled profanity, that "blankety-blank good ol' Don

The Ol' Master of Ol' Mizzou, Don Faruot.

hadn't been so blankety-blank darn generous" sharing the secrets of the Split-T formation.

Two coaches, primarily Oklahoma's Bud Wilkinson and
Maryland's Jim Tatum, mastered Faurot's invention and stuffed
the spheroid down Missouri's gullet.

I thought Tatum shafted Faurot and Missouri horribly in
the season-ending 1954 game at Maryland that hastened Don's
demise. The Terps were great; Missouri so-so. But the Tigers had
won the bread-and-butter Kansas game. Tatum sweet-talked
Faurot into moving their match from the season-opener to Thanksgiving and national television. With Maryland seeking an Orange Bowl bid, I urged the pennywise coach-director to tell the
players that if they gave a good showing at College Park, Mizzou
would train them to New York for a day's stay and a Broadway
play.

No, no, Faurot insisted, the players would much prefer to
be home with their families for Thanksgiving. My retort was a
tart suggestion that there sure'n hell wouldn't be much turkey
left if the players didn't reach St. Louis by plane until 8 p.m.!
Final score: *Maryland 74, Missouri 13.*

A stunned Faurot told loyal tub-thumper Bill Callahan, "I
feel as if someone has kicked my stomach into my backbone."

Me, too.

During Faurot's final season, 1956, things went so badly
even the officials seemed determined to hasten his retirement.
At Nebraska, Tigers tackle Frank Czapla separated the Husker
quarterback from the ball with a crushing tackle, but the referee
surprisingly ruled that the squashed player was in the act of
passing the ball. Awarded one more play, Husker halfback Willie
Greenlaw lobbed an option pass for a touchdown that gave the
game to Nebraska, 15-14.

A week later at Columbia in a bowl-bid game, Missouri led
Colorado late by a touchdown. As the Tigers stopped what
amounted to the visitors' last drive, the referee dropped his
handkerchief, leveling a 15-yard penalty against Tigers tackle
Paul Browning for having swung at Colorado's John (The Beast)
Bayuk.

Browning held up his bare forearm to show the ref the teeth
marks where Bayuk had bitten him. The referee, one of the best,
Cliff Ogden, shrugged it off. Cliff sniffed to the complaining
Faurot, "He could have bit himself, Coach!"

Up in the press box, Colorado's P.R. pixy, Fred Casotti, summed it up in headline style: "BAYUK BITES BUFFS INTO ORANGE BOWL."

Faurot's coaching career ended against Kansas, where the Tigers trailed late until reserve quarterback Dave Doane tied it with less than a minute remaining.

The Jayhawks returned the ensuing kickoff to the 20. On the first play, KU quarterback Wally Strauch was sacked. Kansas coach Chuck Mather thought the new line of scrimmage was the 9, but, in fact, it was the 4. So when the KU coach called for a reverse, Tiger tackle Chuck Mehrer barreled his 230 pounds into the end zone and bear-hugged ball-carrier Robinson for the game-winning safety. Final, 15-13, MU.

Quipped Columbia business man Alec Estes, "You win some, you lose some — and now and then one washes up on the beach."

Like, for instance, the 1955 World Series, the first ever won by the Dodgers. The Brooklyn Eagle headline trumpeted: "TO-MORROW FINALLY CAME TODAY."

One of the Series stars, Dodger captain Pee Wee Reese, aided my voting for the National League's Most Valuable Player award that year. Brooklyn center fielder Duke Snider batted .309 with 42 homers and a league-leading 136 runs batted in. Catcher Roy Campanella hit .318 with 32 homers and 107 ribbies. Both deserved the MVP award in my judgment, but which? Privately, I asked Reese.

Said the "Cap," "Snider is my roommate and my close friend, but I believe I'd have to give it to Campy again."

I did, but if I had voted Snider first and Campanella second, rather than vice-versa, they would have wound up tied, a rare distinction.

In mid-summer of 1956, Frank Lane went too far when he sought to deal Stan Musial to the Philadelphia Phillies for Robin Roberts. Stan's business partner, Julius (Biggie) Garagnani, told an A-B executive that Musial wouldn't report.

Truth is, Stan would have gone, if traded. But Gus Busch did not like the thought of trading Musial. Through Dick Meyer, Busch told Frantic Frank that Musial would stay put and, further, that any future trades would have to be cleared with the Big Eagle himself.

In the '56 Series, Yogi Berra, like Campanella a three-time Most Valuable Player, single-handedly destroyed a great pitcher's confidence. Don Newcombe was a Paul Bunyan of the toeplate. In 1955 he had been 20-5. In 1956 he hiked his won-and-lost numbers to 27-and-7. But to the barrel-chested Berra, big Newk was little more than a batting practice pitcher. Honestly, I felt sorry for Don.

In the second inning of the second game of the 1956 World Series at Ebbets Field, Berra capped a five-run surge against Newcombe with a grand slam, knocking out the giant. In the seventh game back at the diamond dollhouse on Bedford Avenue, Berra blasted Newcombe for a two-run homer in the first. Two innings later, Yog, the best badball hitter since his boyhood idol, Joe Medwick, golfed one off his ankles over the right-field screen for another two-run round-tripper.

Before the Yanks won easily, big Newk stalked out of a quick shower and in a hurry to find a drink, popped a parking-lot attendant who was slow delivering his car and quick to criticize his pitching.

Don Newcombe stalks off angrily after a game in the 1956 World Series.

Drinking hasn't always hurt World Series hurlers, as Pete Alexander demonstrated, and a Peck's bad boy, Don Larsen, dramatized by pitching the only World Series no-hitter and perfect game.

Personally, I can't get over Larsen's achievement. I never in my career saw a regular season no-hitter. Yet I did personally witness Larsen's in the spotlight of a World Series.

I wasn't close enough to hang around with the good-looking 6-foot-4 guy. But the teetotaling Richman brothers got a good story because of their friendship with Larsen.

Milton Richman, sports editor and columnist for United Press International, and younger brother Artie, a *New York Daily Mirror* writer, were deep-dyed New York City boosters of baseball's backward Browns. They first knew Larsen when he was a 7-13 rookie with the Browns. So they were close enough and loyal enough to be his barside companions the night before he entered baseball folklore.

He pitched a two-hour, six-minute masterpiece and needed only a home run and one good catch by Mickey Mantle, to outduel Sal Maglie, 2-0.

I'll never forget the ninth-inning drama. With two out and the crowd screaming, he faced lefthanded-hitting Dale Mitchell, a good batsman pinch-hitting in Maglie's place.

Ball one, outside . . . strike one, called . . . strike two, swinging. . .

Aware that this would be the last plate umpiring assignment of retiring Ralph (Babe) Pinelli, the old Cincinnati third baseman, I turned from my typewriter to the boss in our Stadium auxiliary press seats. "Mr. Stockton," I said, "Mitchell better start swinging now. . ."

Don Larsen presents Yogi Berra with the glove Berra wore in Larsen's "perfect game." Larsen had it bronzed to commemorate his World Series achievement.

Sure enough, the next pitch was wide to the third-base side, outside and obviously a ball. Mitch took it, but Pinelli threw up his hand in a third-strike call and sprinted toward the umpire exit. Berra bounced up, raced out to the mound, and leaped into the big pitcher's arms, like an oversized kid greeting papa.

Mitchell complained, but there was no one near to hear. Donald James Larsen, a journeyman pitcher for seven clubs, with 14 seasons and an 81-91 career, wrote his name into the World Series record books. No pitcher will ever do better unless he does it twice.

In 1957 the Cardinals made a pass at the pennant for the first time in eight years. So the season was exciting. There were the brothers McDaniel and, as always, Stan The Man Musial.

Opening day on a muddy field at Cincinnati's Crosley Field, Musial, ordinarily a poor spring hitter, opened with a perfect "4 for 4." I was delighted as I charged into the visitors' clubhouse afterward. The great hitter I ridiculously called "Banjo" was grinning.

Aware I wouldn't write what he said, he noted that the effective right-handed slider, a short, quick-darting curve that came with the trajectory of the fast ball, had bothered him and Ted Williams. To handle the pitch in toward his fists, Stan had stepped back off the plate a bit more.

"I'm giving up a bit the chance to go to left field on a ball away from me and I guess the pitchers will catch on," said Musial, "but until . . . " Until it was too late, meaning never, because at nearly 37, Musial upped his average to a seventh batting championship, .351. Early, he noticed that he was seeing the ball better after giving up smoking. Hank Sauer, who replaced Red Schoendienst as Stan's roommate, smoked heavily. Briefly, so did Musial.

With Busch spending beer money on bonuses, $50,000 went to Von McDaniel, younger brother of Lindy McDaniel. Another $25,000 went to a home-town pitcher named Bob Miller, who had pitched for St. Louis' national junior American Legion champions in 1956.

Von McDaniel was big, strong, and handsome with a gleaming 4-H smile, the country cousin from cotton-choppin' country. Miller, also 18, was slighter and pimply faced, the nervous city slicker. Both looked like what they really were—recent high school graduates. McDaniel was one of the brightest,

single-season phenoms ever. Bob Miller, the baby-faced inno-
cent, became a serviceable career pitcher and coach.

Miller in 1957 was just about what you would expect. He
pitched only five games all season, a total of nine innings, with a
whopping 7.00 earned-run average.

Von McDaniel's year was one to be envied by "Baseball
Joe." Fred Hutchinson, once a kid pitcher himself, was sensitive
to youthful prospects. But the manager impulsively had Lindy's
kid brother warm up during a hopelessly lost June game at
Philadelphia. Surprisingly, the kid pitched four perfect innings.
A few days later in a game apparently lost at Ebbets Field, Hutch
had Von warm up again.

Oops, the Cardinals rallied suddenly and were in front.
Shockingly, Hutchinson stayed with the boy. With three innings
to go, protecting a one-run lead in a stadium where the Cardinals
hadn't been able to do well for seven years, Von kept the ball
down and over the plate.

In the Dodgers' ninth, Pee Wee Reese bunted safely, bringing up menacing Duke Snider. Shortstop Alvin Dark rushed in
to calm the kid. "You know who this is, Von?"

"Sure," was the solemn reply, "Mr. Snider."

Mr. Snider politely grounded out, and Von McDaniel was
a game-saver. Personally, I was so keyed up that after writing
extra stories for the *Post-Dispatch* and *The Sporting News*, I went
to an all-night movie on Forty-Second Street to watch Errol Flynn
as General Custer in "They Died With Their Boots On."

Hutchinson tried to conceal that he would pitch the pearly-
toothed phenom five nights later against Brooklyn in St. Louis.
He didn't fool anyone. Sportsman's Park was packed.

The crowd saw a thriller. McDaniel led young lefty Danny
McDevitt into the sixth, 2-0, but the Brooks filled the bases with
none out. The bubble would burst for sure, but, no, Elmer Valo
tapped back to the pitcher. Calmly, Von threw home to begin a
double play. And when he got Gino Cimoli to tap back to him,
he was en route to a two-hit shutout. Later, the box office baby
pitched a one-hitter against Pittsburgh.

The "Me 'n Paul" reminiscence of the Dean brothers wasn't
lost on anyone, especially with Lindy matching Larry Jackson's
staff-leading 15 victories. The storybook season had humorous
twists, like the night Musial called me over and asked Lindy to
repeat what he just had told Stan the Man.

Dizzy Dean, flanked by Lindy McDaniel (left) and Von McDaniel.

"Oh," said the young starter who would become a great reliever, "I said that if you don't walk anybody and don't give up any home runs, it's going to take a lot of singles to beat you . . ."

The All-Star game was played in St. Louis, and at the break the Cardinals held a slight lead in a five-team race. Old friend Casey Stengel, managing the American League, winked and said, "Looks as if we may be back here in October."

But St. Louis' Bob Scheffing, managing the Cubs, turned loose a couple of young pitchers named Dick Drott and Moe Drabosky. They each beat the Cardinals twice in a nine-day span, once here and again there.

In between, Milwaukee also swept the Redbirds three straight in St. Louis. The Braves were on the warpath after having acquired the man manager Fred Haney wanted — Red Schoendienst. Fact is, when Milwaukee acquired Red from New York, Haney wanted to name him captain.

"No, no," cautioned Schoendienst. "You've got your own established players," said Red, thinking of Warren Spahn, Eddie Mathews, Joe Adock, and young super-star Henry Aaron. "But I'll take charge for you."

At a clubhouse meeting, addressing his outfielders, Haney, who once had managed the losingest Browns' team ever (1939), put it on the line bluntly. "I'm tired of you bastards missing cutoff men or throwing late to the plate. I want you to throw every f——ing ball to Red."

With the Cardinals losing nine in a row and the other contenders also slumping, Milwaukee's 10-game winning streak gave the Braves a whopping lead. When the Cardinals rubber-legged into Milwaukee for a return series, Hutchinson told his players to get lost for the night, including the McDaniels, who were shepherded by other bible-quoting teetotalers, Dark, Vinegar Bend Mizell and Hal Smith.

"At least," Hutch quipped to the 4-H boys, "you can get double-thick malted milks."

For a hot-tempered guy who could demolish a clubhouse, Hutch was a pretty good psychologist. Next night, he listed a lineup that included reserves, his coaches, and equipment manager Butch Yatkeman, giving everyone what each needed most —a laugh. Musial, hitting one of his 29 homers, beat Juan Pizarro and turned the pennant rout into a race.

Because I had hernia surgery at the start of the season, I had been advised to avoid trains and fly so I wouldn't have to worry about luggage. I knew Stan had trouble sleeping on trains, so I urged him to fly, too. He balked. I suggested huffily that he could afford it and, besides, Ralph Kiner of Pittsburgh was flying alone. Musial shook his head. "I belong with the ball club," he insisted.

Team play was the reason his consecutive-game playing streak ended in Philadelphia. Trying to protect the runner by hitting behind him, Stan swung awkwardly at a pitch high and away. He tore his shoulder muscles and suffered a hairline fracture. Best diagnosis — out the rest of the season.

Sixteen days later, he assured Hutchinson he could play. Pinch-hitting, he punched a basehit to the opposite field. Noting that he could play first base, where few throws are required, he moved back into the lineup, and handyman Joe Cunningham moved to the outfield.

With Musial hitting for average, if not for power, the Cardinals closed the gap against the Braves. However, during the last Monday night of the season, a Hank Aaron home run won the pennant for the Braves in extra innings.

Hutchinson put his arm around Musial and said, "Go home, Stan, take the rest of the season off. I'm going to look at some kids. Hell, the way you're hitting now, hurt, they couldn't catch you if we played all winter."

This was, if you will, one of the greatest seasons a 37-year-old player ever had. Not only the average, .351, but, also, as determined by Jim Toomey, Musial drove in 102 of a possible 171 runners in scoring position, i.e., second base or third.

Frank Lane labeled the 57 Redbirds as "the courageous" Cardinals. Seated on the press roof for day games, shirtless and wearing sunglasses, radio at his side and newspapers flipping from his hands like kites into the wind, Lane made quite a sight — and sound.

If too many of his men faltered at the plate, he would bellow, "How can the ball *stand* it?" And, more directly and at times audible to a frustrated hitter or pitcher, his shout — frequently heard at the bench — would be a roared:

"Get the s-o-n-o-f-a-b-i-t-c-h out of there."

The worst I'd seen — or heard — had been at a game at Brooklyn, where Hutch had committed a boo-boo. After bringing in the left-handed Mizell to strike out left-handed-hitting Snider in a tenuous situation — three-run lead, one-out — he permitted Vinegar Bend to face the right-handed muzzle of Gil Hodges. Sure, Gil banged a game-winning grand slam.

Lane couldn't find Hutch at the ball park, so he bounded the hotel steps two at a time, seeking his elusive prey. By the time Hutch made it to a midnight train, the manager weaved toward us so loaded that coach Terry Moore had to walk with the zig-zagging skipper to keep him from taking a header onto the rails.

Having come close per Busch's dictum, Frantic Frank might have seemed secure for another year. But shortly after season's end, the Cleveland general manager's job opened. Lane asked for his release.

"Here's-your-hat-what's-your-hurry?" was Busch's farewell to the Mad Trader.

32

೩

My friend, Bing Devine, a man who didn't drink, smoke, or chase skirts, replaced Frank Lane as general manager of the brewery-owned St. Louis Cardinals. Like Frantic Frank, Der Bingle had guts.

His first move was to refuse a "very fair deal" offered by the Philadelphia Phillies: outfielder Richie Ashburn and pitcher Harvey Haddix for the Cardinals' Ken Boyer. Confided Devine, "I'm banking what little reputation I have that Boyer will be a great player at third base."

During the near-miss 1957 season — for the good of the cause, enabling Eddie Kasko to play third base — Boyer had volunteered to play centerfield. His batting average dropped from .306 to .265.

If Boyer moved back to third, who would play center? Devine engineered a deal while eating dinner with Cincinnati skipper Birdie Tebbetts and general manager Gabe Paul — three St. Louis pitchers for two Cincinnati outfielders, one of whom was centerfielder Curt Flood.

As we returned by train from Devine's deal at the winter meetings, a *Post-Dispatch* messenger met me at the station. Would I come to the office rather than go home? The reason: Frank Broyles, who had brought back enthusiasm to Missouri football in just one season, was reportedly leaving for the University of Arkansas. Could I double check? I reached Broyles at home and he confirmed his imminent departure.

After writing the story for the *P-D*, I sat back and remembered how it had been when Faurot retired in December of 1956 and was hailed at a fete in Columbia.

Broyles had been handpicked by Faurot after 14 candidates had been interviewed over a two-month period. Don had turned down a veteran Michigan State assistant, Bob Devaney, whom he regarded as too old.

But Don liked the lanky, 32-year-old redheaded Frank Broyles, a great three-sport star at Georgia Tech and one-time Baylor and Florida assistant. Broyles came to Mizzou after six seasons under Bobby Dodd at alma mater Georgia Tech. The personable Presbyterian deacon Broyles— Scotch-Irish-German — must have reminded Faurot of himself. Frank didn't smoke, drink, or swear, either.

Broyles, trim though nibbling incessantly on candy, minutes, grapes, orange slices, and sipping eight soft drinks a day, drove himself, his staff, and his players with a velvet-glove approach. He emphasized three "E's" — enthusiasm, encouragement, and execution — and he re-emphasized an old saw that "statistics are for losers."

After a 7-7 opening game tie with Vanderbilt, Broyles coached the Tigers to an exciting 5-1-1 record, including a 9-6 upset over Colorado. With Broyles' team having flown back to Columbia immediately after the game, I had to await a morning flight to St. Louis from Denver. I recall walking Mile High City on a nippy night, buoyed by the high altitude and a couple of drinks, yet aware that Ol' Mizzou was too hot not to cool down, especially with Oklahoma coming to town for a first-place fight.

The Tigers were crushed by the Sooners, 39-14. I don't think the young coach had the same enthusiasm for Missouri after that loss.

Next, Broyles unwisely relied on a six-man line that failed to stop Kansas State's Split-T, 23-21. And at Lawrence, with regular quarterback Phil Snowden hurt, Frank tried to sit too long on a one-point lead, relinquishing short-yardage, first-down gimmies too often. A long run set up a winning field goal for Kansas, 9-7, with 48 seconds to go.

Two successive narrow season-ending defeats were hard to take. Belatedly joining Broyles and his Bengals at loyalist Pete Carter's Kansas City restaurant after the KU game, I told him the 5-4-1 season had been stimulating and promising. He merely grunted.

Within two weeks he had answered Razorback AD John Barnhill's job offer with a flip, "What took you so long, Barnie?"

Having recruited hard and fast, including MU's first two black players, backs Mel West and Norris Stevenson, Broyles was quoted out of Little Rock as having said, "They're living on Cloud Nine up there . . ."

Dan Devine, with Stan Musial the special journalistic joy of my mature years as a sports writer, became the new Mizzou coach and soon a good friend. Maybe too good, considering the need for balance between newsprint personal and professional views. As my wife Dorth suggested, Devine looked like a corner druggist, but his soft-spoken words had the power to inspire.

Daniel John Devine was a champion. When Missouri came courting, he had a season to go on his contract at Arizona State University. After his 1957 Sun Devils went unbeaten, Devine had many suitors and wasn't interested in Missouri. But out of respect for Faurot, he came to Columbia for a look-see.

An airline stewardess dropped hot chocolate on the fastidious man's suit. When his plane arrived late, he was met in Kansas City by a group of aggressive, back-slapping, fawning well-wishers, a type he abhors. Then, while riding to Columbia with Faurot, Don's car ran out of gas.

"So there I sat at 2 a.m.," Devine told me, "cold, alone in the dark, wearing a topcoat too thin for a midwestern winter, wondering what in the heck I was doing in Missouri in the first place."

The unflappable Faurot hailed a truck driver, got a lift to the nearest gas station, and finally made it to Columbia, where Dan spent the night at Faurot's house. Early the next morning, Faurot gave Devine another thrill. They drove the narrow, corkscrew road from Columbia to Rolla in a heavy fog.

Chuckling, Devine said, "You know how Don is, light-fingered and heavy-footed behind the wheel, talking a mile a minute about the job when, honestly, all I kept wondering was whether I'd live to see my family again."

The university's president and board were waiting for them in Rolla. There, Faurot and university president Dr. Ellis, sold Devine on Mizzou. The history-teaching prexy even kicked up the stingy Faurot's salary offer to a bit more than the $15,000 Faurot had offered. Not bad when you've coached an unbeaten season for $12,000.

Dan'l, as I tabbed him early, had grown up third eldest in a family of nine in small town Wisconsin. To ease the family's financial pain, he left home to live with an aunt and uncle in Proctor, Minnesota, a suburb of Duluth on Lake Superior.

Devine was an intense competitor as an athlete and man, chomping carrots and practicing eye exercises so he could pass

Air Corps depth-perception tests. World War II wound up with Lt. Dan Devine in the Pacific as a B-12 bombardier.

After the war, he returned to college at Duluth, became a star running back, and got married. By the time he graduated, his life was well-organized, a plus in his approach to coaching.

"When you've got infant twin daughters who awaken in the night, and you don't know whether the crying one needs a bottle or a diaper change, you had better be well-organized," he told me.

I can imagine the sting when the superintendent of schools at International Falls, Minnesota, said Devine, applying for a coaching job, didn't have a "big enough name."

Cradles clamped atop their 12-year-old family car, the Devines drove 750 miles to Jordan, Michigan, a fishing resort town. There Dan achieved two unbeaten seasons with a team that hadn't won a game the year before he arrived.

So did Devine begin a coaching career that, by the way of an assistant's role at Michigan State, and head coach at Arizona State, brought him to Missouri for the 1958 football season.

That same year the mighty Musial climbed the highest baseball hitter's mountain, meeting the challenge I had carrot-sticked for him in 1948.

What I saw during the 1958 baseball season was delightful. The Brooklyn Dodgers had moved to Los Angeles and the New York Giants to San Francisco. For the first time, like it or not, ball clubs had to fly.

The Cardinals' first stop would be San Fran. En route, I sat behind Musial and Sam Jones, whose face showed his acute fear of flying. Stan didn't help by loudly chirping, "I can see the headlines, Sam: 'PLANE CRASHES. MUSIAL ONLY SURVIVOR.'"

The Giants played at Seals Stadium, a cute little park with a chummy left-field fence and a trolley ride to the barrier in right. With a capacity crowd and an over-full pint-sized press box, I sat in the club's third-base seats with general manager Bing Devine and one of his old favorites, insurance man Taylor Douthit, center field star of the Redbirds' first pennant winners.

Musial went "4 for 4." Ty Cobb expressed delight that a player he earlier had picked as the best, all-around, still was in good shape with pretty good legs. To Stan, the terrible-tempered superstar confided, "Rest your legs, Stan, and drink a little wine.

My last couple of years, I'd sip wine in bed and eat my meals in my hotel room to conserve my legs."

Stan's philosophy was "easy-does-it." He felt that "good hitting means physical relaxation, mental concentration, and don't hit fly balls to center field."

Musial faced another challenge at Los Angeles, where the Dodgers played at football's famed Los Angeles Coliseum. The left-field wall had a giant screen on top and was extremely close to home plate. Right field, except sharply down the foul line, was deeper than at San Francisco.

I watched at the batting cage as the Dodgers and Cardinals switched swats. Duke Snider lingered to boo-hoo to Musial. The Duke pointed to the right-field fence, a far cry from Brooklyn's Ebbets Field's short front porch.

Stan added, "Duke," he said, "if you can't beat it, join it." And then, stroking mostly up the middle and to the left side, Musial gave L.A. what he'd given Frisco: "4 for 4."

If the Musial of early season 1958 had kept that same, easy, level stroke all season, would the grand geezer have hit .400? Back in 1950, Musial had a robust hit total that put him well over .400 early — he always figured a hitter would have to be *over* .400 going into September — but he slipped and fell rounding first base.

When he tried to get up, he couldn't. To himself, Stan said, "Thank god for the restaurant." Recovering slowly, he finished with a league-leading .346. Thereafter, he wore an elastic knee brace.

Stan's restaurant partner was Julius (Biggie) Garagnani, active in Democratic politics and a maven of maloprop — "tell me the name of the magazine you wrote about Stan, so I can *prescribe* to it." He was an astute restaurateur and an honest man, if sometimes stubbornly optimistic. Before the season started, he scheduled a large private celebration party in early May for Musial's 3,000th hit.

By that Sunday, Musial had 41 hits in 21 games, an outrageously gifted total, but still two short. At the premature celebration, I complained to Garagnani, "Cripes, Big, what'n hell did you think The Man was — a damned machine!"

After the party, many of Musial's friends and fans entrained to Chicago for a two-day series against the Cubs. This would be the Redbirds' last team trip by train — memorable!

Musial got one hit in the first game at Wrigley Field. Back at the Knickerbocker Hotel, manager Fred Hutchinson called for an impromptu press conference at the bar.

He-man Hutch laid it out for St. Louis writers and radio men. "I could bullshit you guys," he said, "and hold Stan out tomorrow, saying he's got a bellyache, but I'm going to level with you. He told Terry Moore he hoped we'd win tomorrow, but that he hoped he'd walk four times, so he could save No. 3,000 for St. Louis."

Hutch paused, crunching on ice, as he always did, leading to Joe Garagiola's favorite nickname for him, The Big Bear. Hutch continued, "You know, I'd hate to see 6,000 or 7,000 see him get it where when there's a 30,000 sellout for St. Louis Wednesday. So unless I need him, he's not going to play tomorrow."

Sam Jones and the Cardinals trailed in the sixth inning, 3-1. With one out and a man on second, Hutchinson beckoned to the right field bullpen, where Musial was sunning himself.

Fewer than 6,000 persons were there when Stan zeroed in on a sweeping outside curve thrown by Moe Drabowsky. Musial hit a solid liner between left fielder Walt Moryn and the foul line.

A stand-up double. Hit number 3,000. The Man had climbed the mountain. He had reached the goal I had articulated for him ten years earlier.

Photographers rushed onto the field. Base umpire Frank Dascoli retrieved the throw-in and handed it to Musial. Hutchinson trundled out of the bullpen, shook Musial's hand and then pulled him for a pinch-runner.

"I goofed," said Hutch later. "Once he had his 3,000th hit, I should have left him in." Musial stopped by a boxseat and kissed a trim blonde woman. He was asked later if he knew her. "I hope so," he said, laughing. "That's my wife."

The Cardinals won 5-3. Their trip home—their last train trip home—was historic. A chartered bus rushed the team to the Illinois Central tracks on South Michigan, just below the Loop area.

The dining chef had whipped up a decorated "3,000 Hit" cake. Broadcaster Harry Caray pulled out handsome cuff links for Stan, suitably engraved, and Musial bought a magnum champagne bottle for winning pitcher Sam Jones.

The train slowed, then stopped at Clinton, Illinois, so Stan could say a few words to about 50 well-wishers. Nearly an hour later, twice as many fans greeted him at Springfield, Illinois, singing, "For he's a jolly good fellow. . ."

The jolly good fellow spoke briefly and then went back into the parlor car, where, amid friendly chatter, he fell asleep. He had reason to need rest because he hadn't slept much the night before.

An old friend's wife, Molly Pizzica, weary, had left their party to go to bed early, asking a blundering bellman to let her into her room. Later Stan and his party couldn't find her. So they, and Chicago's gendarmes, spent most of the night trying to find Molly.

"Where's Molly?" was the question oft repeated. No answer was found. Finally the search was left to the police and Lil and Stan went to their room.

Near daybreak they were startled to receive a phone call from Molly herself, asking where her husband was. Molly had never left her room — the wrong room.

Did Stan fall asleep while sunning in the bullpen before his pinch-hit appearance? I don't know, but when he awakened from his nap on the train, Musial took Molly's hand gently and asked, "Where's Molly?"

About that time the train pulled into a jam-packed Union Station. Dick Meyer and Bing Devine were there, along with a band and a crowd that had waited two hours.

Cheered wildly, Musial finally stopped the applause by suggesting, "Now I know how Lindbergh felt."

A foghorn voice interrupted, "What did *he* hit?"

Musial, mindful of the lateness of the hour, surveyed the crowd and saw so many small fry in the audience, that he felt compelled to announce, "No school tomorrow, kids."

Next night, before the SRO crowd, Stanley Frank Musial made hit number 3,001 one to remember. First time up, he smashed Glen Hobbie's initial offering onto the right-field roof.

Home run by a home-town favorite!

By *my* favorite!

33

Any suggestion that the sports editorship of the *Post-Dispatch* was my goal is incorrect. Painfully aware a guy had to pay his dues as a desk man, I merely wanted to write. Mostly about baseball and, to a lesser degree, football.

In 1958, J. Roy Stockton decided to retire as sports editor of the *Post-Dispatch*. Although from time to time Stockton had indicated my time would come, I was disappointed during spring training when he told me he was leaving, and I was officially "it." The announcement was scheduled for July 1, 1958 when JRS would step down.

At the time, I was national president of the Baseball Writers' Association of America. For a quarter century, the BBWAA had rotated the presidency, and 1958 was St. Louis's turn. The *Globe-Democrat*'s Bob Burnes, a nice guy and my drinking partner, had nominated me.

Nineteen fifty-eight was the golden anniversary of the writers' association. The BBWAA was lucky — not to get me — but to get Dorothy Carr Broeg, who, with Mensa mentality and plenty of time on her hands, rewrote the half-century old constitution under the guidance of the national's long-time secretary-treasurer, Ken Smith of New York.

Me? I made a limited banquet circuit to New York, Cleveland, Boston, and Milwaukee dinners, explaining how the BBWAA was born, after years of ball clubs stiffing writers by allowing cronies and celebrities into the working press facilities.

At the 1908 World Series, the last ever won by the Cubs, writers sat so far back they couldn't recognize Tinker, Evers, and Chance, much less the guy at third base, St. Louis's Harry Steinfeldt. And when Detroit forced the reporters to watch and write from the rickety grandstand roof in rain and snow, the scribes had it up to here. They met at a Detroit hotel and organized an association that for many years thereafter controlled press boxes.

My only speaking mishap was at Cleveland. I sat at the head table between my old drinking pal, Bill Veeck, and the Cleveland Browns' famed football coach, Paul Brown. Veeck swiped my notes and sat there and grinned as I tried to recall my speech from memory.

Veeck embarrassed me, sure, but I was mortified that in this 50th anniversary celebration year, St. Louis hadn't had even an annual formal chapter meeting. In fact, there had been no meeting of any kind since a fist fight broke out in 1927.

Would the St. Louis chapter endorse a dinner? Would Beowulf Q. Phan, to use one of Stockton's synonyms for John Q. Public, give a hoot about a dinner honoring baseball writers? My guess was that the fans didn't care. So why not establish awards in writers' names for future dinners, but for that golden-anniversary dinner, honor a so-called All-Time St. Louis team?

Stockton shrugged his shoulders. If I did the work, it was okay with him. Burnes already was doing a radio sports show on KMOX as well as seven columns a week for the *Globe-Democrat*, plus numerous goodwill speaking engagements.

So it was up to me — and my wife.

There was the problem of money, but I got an early lift. Ben Kerner, owner of the basketball Hawks, noted that if we would hold the dinner the night before the National Basketball Association All-Star game at the St. Louis Arena, he would buy 150 tickets to entertain visiting owners, players, writers, etc. Bing Devine guaranteed 10 tables of 10.

Slyly, hoping I wouldn't offend Burnes and other Browns' fans, I tried to balance a proposed lineup that included the obvious, George Sisler at first base, but also Hank Severeid as one of the two catchers, Ken Williams as left fielder, Johnny Tobin as utility outfielder and Urban Shocker as one of the four pitchers.

Shocker was dead, and also the Cardinals' Grover Cleveland Alexander, but the other proposed pitchers, approved by Stockton, Burnes, and *East St. Louis Journal* sports editor Ellis Veech, were Dizzy Dean and Jesse Haines. Ol' Diz certainly could help the box office.

The rest of the team included Stan Musial in right field, Rogers Hornsby at second base, and Frank Frisch at third base — no way I could leave off the old Flash — Terry Moore in center field, Red Schoendienst as the extra infielder and Bob O'Farrell as the other catcher.

Flanked by two of my favorites, my boyhood idol Frank Frisch (left) and Stan Musial, the player I greatly admired as an adult reporter.

O'Farrell would have to be brought in from Waukegan, Illinois, Hornsby from Chicago, Frisch from New York, Severeid from San Antonio, Texas, Williams from distant Grant's Pass, Oregon, Haines from Phillipsburg, Ohio, and Dizzy from Phoenix, Arizona, but, dawgonnit, podnuh, Ol' Diz couldn't make it. A conflict.

Bud Blattner broadcast the basketball part of the night's program, and Joe Garagiola was supposed to be at the mike for baseball, but he was snowed out. Stockton and Burnes spoke briefly. I made my BBWAA presentation.

Baseball commissioner Ford Frick attended the dinner and made the greatest speech I've ever heard. His turn didn't come until 12:40 a.m., whereupon the commissioner rose to his feet and said, "Thank you, ladies and gentlemen, for inviting me — and good night!"

As deservedly the most embarrassed about the length of that wee-hour fiasco, I wasn't embarrassed financially because, happily, we did clear about a thousand dollars. The staggering result of that first St. Louis baseball writers dinner — and now we're among the few cities that still have them—is that it not only stayed alive, but flourished to the point we achieve almost automatic 2,000-seat sellouts and make enough money to provide journalistic and athletic scholarships.

When I left the baseball beat in mid-season to assume my duties as sports editor, I was not leaving a promising season—or team. Except for Musial's 3,000th hit and hot stroking by Ken Boyer and Joe Cunningham, there hadn't been much. Pitching was subpar from the time Von McDaniel's bubble burst in spring training.

Happily, Ford Frick didn't go into his song and dance at our long dinner.

I've got my own theory as to what happened to the likeable phenom. From childhood, his life in rural Oklahoma had been a cycle of baseball, harvest, basketball, baseball, harvest, basketball. But after his rookie year with the Cardinals, Von spent all winter at college, hitting the books, not the bricks.

The youngster became physically soft. So during spring training he was confronted with the double whammy of poor physical conditioning and the dead-armed weakness caused by the debilitating heat and humidity of Florida. Dead-armed weakness saps all, but it hits pitchers the worst.

Trying too hard, Von fell into the habit of wrapping the ball behind his head. He lost control of his pitches. The harder he tried, the more discombobulated he became.

Von vanished from the roster two games into the 1958 season. By the time I bid farewell to the Redbird beat, so had any pennant chances.

Before I left, I offered a "lecture" to Curt Flood. After he beat Pittsburgh with a late-inning homer, 2-1, I cautioned the diminutive center-field master about swinging for the fences. "Go for average," I urged, "you are not a home run hitter."

When I checked in as sports editor, I decided to revive the daily sports column that had been missing since Ed Wray retired. I would drop all outside writing, including my weekly efforts for *The Sporting News.*

How did the staff, a few more than 60 years old and only a couple younger than my 40, accept the new boss? Pretty good, actually.

I got the kindest support from the most unlikely member of the staff. Managing Editor Raymond L. Crowley once had told friend Bill McGoogan over a couple of drinks that Mac would be the next sports editor. So 60-year-old McGoogan, whom I called "Coach," pouted when I was named.

Passing Bill as he and I were fore and aft from the rest room, I got a grunt in exchange for a cheerful greeting. Spinning, I said, softly, "You know, Coach, I didn't name *myself* sports editor."

He nodded. From then on, Bill McGoogan was just about as strong a champion as I had in the corner. I found it tough to take criticism from higher management and yet withhold it from older men I respected and admired, especially when I knew they didn't have the educational background and strong grammar base of, say, Crowley's top assistant, Art Bertelson. The stress didn't soothe the sandpaper grinding my stomach.

A lesson learned from Fred Hutchinson came to mind. I saw how this man of volatile temper could let it all hang out — punch out lights and mangle furniture — and yet keep his anger impersonal. If, I thought, I'd let off steam generally, not individually, my health would be better. So I'd fling a radio across the news room instead of resorting to personal sarcasm.

As for good ol' Hutch, the manager hadn't helped himself when, tired of face-guarding Busch to protect Tom Alston, Hutchinson gave the confused pleasant black man one more chance — a lengthy bus trip to Vero Beach, Florida, for an exhibition with the Dodgers. Tall Tom forgot to bring along his extra-long baseball knickers. So he couldn't play.

Afterward, asked again by the big boss about Alston's progress, Hutchinson snapped, "If you want a clown, Mr. Busch, why don't you get Emmett Kelly?" Alston soon burned down a church and was institutionalized.

Hutchinson was fired late in the season. Dick Meyer called me down to the brewery to talk about who might fill the job. Meyer listed the usual musical-chair managerial suspects — and Hemus.

I liked Solly as a person and a battling player. He was friendly, amusing, polite. On the field, he was an aggressive player of limited ability, a good leadoff man, and, thanks to a batting tip from Stan Musial, able to generate a little power now and then.

When Hemus was with the Cardinals a few years earlier, he had pulled off the smartest play I ever saw. The Cardinals and Dodgers were tied in the last of the ninth. The Brooks had two out and Bobby Morgan on third base when Jackie Robinson tapped a grounder to Hemus's right.

Solly quickly assessed that even with perfect fielding, he couldn't throw out Jack-Be-Quick. But out of the corner of his eye, Hemus caught Morgan dog-trotting home. Making a gloved grab across his body, the shortstop fired to the plate, where an alert Del Rice stood at the plate and made a game-saving tag.

An inning later, first up, Hemus appeared to bail out belatedly from one of big left-hander Chris Van Cuyk's pitches, and the ball nicked his blousy shirt. Next up was Stan Musial and — boom! — The Man tripled off the fence to win the game for St. Louis, 1-0.

Hemus was hired near the end of the 1958 season and benefited from an unusual post-season look at his ball club. The Cardinals went to Japan and won 16 of 18 games, greatly impressing the Japanese.

Solly Hemus (center) and Coach Harry Walker, watch from boss Busch's rooftop box.

But when box-office star Musial was asked about his interests and mentioned the restaurant, a polite Japanese reporter asked "Ah, so, Musial-san, then you are a waiter?"

I didn't make the trip after suggesting to managing editor Crowley that I had found a literary "sleeper" in the Redbird ranks, bespectacled pitcher Jim Brosnan. Jim could air-mail a piece every other day or so and wrap it up with a Sunday magazine story afterward. All this for only a few hundred dollars — I'd learned quickly about the wisdom of honoring the *Post-Dispatch* budget restraints.

Smiling, Crowley said, "You've just talked yourself out of a trip with the team." Fair enough, since I didn't believe I should leave with the football season at hand. Brosnan, scribbling with his impolite sense of humor, did well for us and inspired himself to write a couple of good baseball books.

One thing I didn't like at the end of the 1958 season was the sight of Red Schoendienst playing second base for the Milwaukee Brewers during the World Series. The haughty New York press had labeled Sudsville as "bush," i.e., meaning "bush" as in the "minor league." The Braves made the New Yorkers pay for their arrogant conceit.

Watching Schoendienst, weak and wan, rise to the occasion in the Series with three doubles and a triple, I also saw him slowly climb a spiral staircase backstage at the Broadway play, "Say Darling."

Mrs. Schoendienst, about to deliver son Kevin, had reason to be uncomfortable in her ascent, but her husband huffed more than she did. To *Post-Dispatch* baseball writer, Neal Russo, I said, "Nealie, I think you're watching a man with tuberculosis hit .300."

I'd seen Schoendienst frequently over the years. Now I recalled that when I did the national magazine piece on him several years earlier, his reasons for an early medical discharge from the Army had been hazy.

After the Braves blew the Series, I visited Schoendienst and a fellow St. Louisan, reserve catcher Del Rice, at their locker room wake. Rice held up a cup.

"I don't drink beer any more," I told him.

"This isn't beer," Rice insisted, mentioning Scotch.

Before I could react, Schoendienst held out his cup, "No," he said, "take mine." I took it and paused. Then twisting the cup around, I said to myself, "I guess I'll find out if TB really is contagious." I took a swig.

Back home in St. Louis a few days later, Red checked into a tuberculosis house for rest and treatment that led to surgery that finally excised the tubercular germ that had sapped him for years. Our shared drink caused me no ill-effects.

Red Schoendienst, after undergoing an operation to remove part of his lung to speed recovery from tuberculosis.

In 1958, as national BBWAA president, I presided over the induction ceremonies at the Hall of Fame in Cooperstown. That followed a rocky night under the flickering lights of the stately Otesaga Hotel's patio overlooking lovely Lake Otsego when I tried to match drinks, if not stories, with Frank Frisch and Ty Cobb. Silly boy.

Frisch praised Ty for hours, trying to pry stories of his spike-slashing base-running. Cobb disclaimed all legends about his savagery. Frisch taunted him softly, "Come on, Ty-rus, tell Roh-butt. . ."

Suddenly, around midnight, came a "Why, yes, Frankie, I do remember" this and that and that and this. Frisch winked at me and sat back silently.

We drank together until the bar closed—way too late. Closing in on an ulcer, I woke before dawn in misery and walked a foggy golf course, realizing that, criminy, I hadn't even sorted out what I would say at the induction ceremonies.

I saw Cobb and Frisch at breakfast. They were savoring the Otesaga's sumptuous breakfast best. I wondered if they felt as good as they looked. Why, yes.

I sighed. "Cripes, Ty, you're 70 and Uncle Frank you're 60 and I'm 40 and my damned belly feels as if it's falling on the floor."

Ty Cobb and me at Cooperstown in 1958.

34

Autumn is the season farmers finally reap rewards for their tireless toil in the soil. For me, fall has always been fascinating because of two seasons — baseball and football.

In late September of 1959, on my way to see a pennant playoff between Milwaukee and Los Angeles, I went first to Michigan to watch Mizzou battle the Wolverines.

After breakfast Saturday morning, I saw Devine at his best — or worst. Athletic director Don Faurot reported that the bus to Michigan Stadium would be late. Fussbudget Devine was outspoken in a tirade against Faurot. Typically, Faurot, impervious to criticism, was less embarrassed than I was.

Playing in the rain, Missouri led Michigan until the last 2:48. A recovered fumble permitted Michigan to kick a field goal for a 15-14 lead. Remembering Faurot's many near-misses, I ranted profanely in a first-row seat, just in front of two occupied by Faurot and Michigan's AD, Fritz Crisler.

Time was running out for the Tigers, and under limited substitution rules, defensive back Bob Haas was at quarterback. The seldom-used passer led Mizzou in a race against the clock.

With two seconds to go in the game, the Tigers capped a 78-yard drive by scoring on a third and goal from the one. Yes! Touchdown! Missouri 20, Michigan 15. Faurot leaned over and whispered, "Ye of little faith."

Wet and chilled, the Missouri players ran to their dressing room. But the doors were locked. They pounded for admission. No luck. Finally Devine roared, "Take it down."

Captain Mike Magac, a mammoth tackle from East St. Louis, executed Devine's orders — and the door — with one tremendous surge. Moments later as Devine, Faurot, and the players celebrated, Crisler stormed into the room, blustering about the smashed portal until Faurot snapped:

"Send me the bill, Fritz ... send me the damned bill. Now get the hell out of here!"

I hurried from Detroit to Chicago. There, the Dodgers' Roger Craig beat the Cubs, while at Milwaukee, the Braves kept pace when Bob Buhl defeated the last-place Phillies.

So there would be a third pennant playoff, and, like the first two, I would be an eyewitness. My only regret, then preferring the Nationals' best-of-three to the Americans' one-and-out play-off, is that I think a pennant-deciding series deserved more time for proper representation.

From Chicago, I hurried by train to Milwaukee, worked late and found myself eating dinner with the Phillies' Phi Beta Kappa manager, Eddie Sawyer. In the midst of our lengthy alcohol-fueled bull-session, Sawyer and I agreed that the National League's Manager-of-the-Year had to be Chicago's Bob Scheffing. To finish as high as fifth with Ernie Banks and an aggregate of rinky-dink associates was a remarkable feat.

Next morning as I ate breakfast late, Sawyer brushed by the table, paused and said, "Remember what we agreed last night? Scheffing as manager of the year."

"Sure."

"Forget it. Wrigley fired him this morning."

The Dodgers won that day at Milwaukee and the next in L.A. to clinch the 1959 National League pennant. They faced the Chicago White Sox in the World Series.

It was the first Series appearance for the Chisox since 1919, the year of the Black Sox scandal. Bill Veeck decked out his players in uniforms similar to the 1919 team.

At Los Angeles, where the middle three games were played, I never again saw the likes of the three successive 92,000-plus crowds sitting in the sun and the smog. The Dodgers won the '59 Series in six games.

Oh yes, one of their pitchers was a surprisingly effective young lefthander who had been frozen on the big-league roster when signed as a bonus baby four years earlier. His name was Sandy Koufax.

When the World Series ended, my attention focused on football. One Saturday, with champion Oklahoma on bowl probation, my work led me to sit in an unlikely spot, the KU press box, watching Kansas win a tight one from Iowa State.

Suddenly the press box announcer made an announcement that almost made me fall from my seat: Nebraska had upset Oklahoma, the Sooners' first conference defeat in 13 years and 73 games!

Now was Mizzou's chance to take the conference lead and go to the Orange Bowl. News about their game came soon, but it wasn't good. Gale Weidner's two fourth-quarter touchdown passes had upset the Tigers at Colorado, 21-20.

Missouri seemed over-matched the next week against unbeaten Air Force, so I opted for a pivotal mid-season Big Ten match between Wisconsin and Northwestern.

Although I missed the upset, I soon learned that Devine and his top defensive assistant, Al Onofrio, had made a defensive adjustment that reverberated through college football for years. Instead of dropping their ends into the secondary for pass defense, they used a wide-end six-man line and only one linebacker. They played an extra defensive back and gave their ends orders to meet at the quarterback.

That defiant aggressive defense, hallmark of Devine's success, rose to the occasion in the MU-KU game for the Orange Bowl bid. Missouri won a rouser, 13-9.

Morning after, expecting to interview a happy Devine, I found him grim and exhausted, with a chip on his shoulder. Why? "Because," he said, "nobody except the coaches and me had faith in this team, and I don't think we had the proper enthusiastic sendoff at Columbia."

Total involvement was mandatory for the coach. In deference to blacks, he called in campus student leaders and sought a substitute for the traditional "Dixie" and, lo, they came up with "Fight, Tiger," good and original.

In the Orange Bowl against fourth-ranked Georgia, Devine's team actually outplayed the Southeast Conference champions, but lost 13-0. Bulldog coach Wally Butts had a superlative safety named Charley Britt and a quarterback who twice avoided tacklers long enough to execute scoring passes. Fran Tarkenton became a household name.

Breathing the sweet orange scent of a fashionable Miami country club afterward, Devine told me softly and prophetically, "We lost a football game, but I think this young team is matured and ready."

Apparently over-mature and no longer ready in 1959 were two of baseball's superstars.

At Boston, Ted Williams sagged to .254. Most thought his career was over. Many felt the same way about Stan Musial, only one point higher, who seemed to have lost the snap in his swing and his power.

Teddy Ballgame told me something I am glad to pass along: Williams recommended that, daily, careful not to hit anyone, a kid or prospective player take a weighted bat and, using a normal batting stance, close eyes and swing hard at imaginary pitches.

Musial stubbornly insisted he would return for 1960, telling Bing Devine pitchers weren't throwing the ball past him. "It's my legs," said Stan. "I don't think they're in shape."

Previously, Stan had watched his weight in the off-season only by laying off desserts. Now he began a winter-long series of exercises recommended by trainer Bob Bauman's buddy, Walter C. (Doc) Eberhardt.

Doc Eberhardt now put Musial through an every other day exercise regime. Soon other players joined. Impressed, the Cardinals decided to take Eberhardt to spring training in 1960.

Ah, the sixties, happy days, the decade of the Devines, Dan and Bing. The Tigers would become the *only* major team never to lose more than three games in a season in a decade, and won four of five bowl games. Der Bingle's Cardinals won three pennants and two world championships.

And while I was at spring training in 1960, pro football returned to St. Louis. Violet Bidwill had been won over by her husband, a former St. Louisan named Walter Wolfner. She and her two adopted sons, Charles (Stormy) Bidwill Jr. and Bill, had played second fiddle too long to the Chicago czar, Papa George Halas' Bears — even after Paul Christman had helped by quarterbacking the Cardinals to a championship in 1947.

St. Louis's lure was a promise to build a new stadium. I had grumbled to my friend, congressman Mel Price, "Why build that gosh-darned croquet wicket, the Gateway Arch, instead of a riverfront stadium?" Said Price, "Why not both?"

The stadium needed Price's support and, most important, the enthusiastic backing of Gussie Busch. Equitable Life Assurance Society promised that if St. Louis could raise $20 million in private capital, Equitable would lend $33 million more. The new complex would include a stadium, four parking garages, a riverfront hotel, and later an office building. But Anheuser-Busch needed to hit an eye-opening home run up front — $5 million.

I'd have liked to sit in when Busch made his pitch to his board of directors. Bottom-liners thought they already had a ball park. Others, noting $2.5 million improvements at old Sportsman's Park, wondered if a million or two wouldn't do.

Al Fleishman told me that this argument made the Big Eagle scream. Removing a cigarette from his mouth, Busch stood and looked down over his reading specs, and roared, "No, damnit, $5 million . . . five!" It was — five!

"The Big Eagle," August A. Busch Jr.

Morton (Buster) May of Famous-Barr followed with $2.5 million and soon the capital investment drive went over the top. St. Louis baseball writers contributed $1,000. Construction would take six years. Until then both teams would play at rechristened Sportsman's Park (now Busch Stadium).

Busch might have felt good about his success with the stadium, but he wasn't smiling in 1960, even though a fit Musial looked pretty good in spring camp.

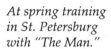

At spring training in St. Petersburg with "The Man."

The Cardinals started well but flattened in May, about the time Bing Devine traded Vinegar Bend Mizell for Julian Javier, a converted Pittsburgh shortstop, who Devine felt would make a good second baseman.

Musial, benched as Hemus began to play a medley of left fielders, finally was told to be ready for the second game of a doubleheader at Chicago. When the Cards won the first game with a righthanded-hitting lineup, Solly stupidly stuck with it in game two against right-handed Don Cardwell.

Grumbled Broeg: "I wouldn't be surprised if he pitched a three hitter." Wrong. Cardwell threw a no-hitter.

Musial, trying to play the good soldier, complained only mildly when his name wasn't in the line-up. "Solly," he said, simply and gravely, "don't kid me."

When Hemus popped off to a New York writer that Musial had been benched "indefinitely," boss Busch and Dick Meyer called Stan out to Grant's Farm and tried to break it gently that the manager sought to go with a younger club. Musial, hurt mostly because he felt he hadn't been given a fair chance, nodded and, stuttering, said a lot with a little:

"Whatever you want is all right with me, though I think I can still help the ball club . . ."

Yet he wasn't satisfied, as I realized shortly after Pittsburgh came to town and manager Danny Murtaugh, off to an early start for the Pirates' first pennant in 33 years, asked me in the ethnic slang of the dugout, "What's wrong with the Polack?"

Nothing except opportunity, I hoped and, with one word leading to another, Murtaugh said, hell, yes, if Stan were available, he'd be most interested.

Privately, I asked Musial. "I never thought I'd say this," said the Pennsylvania-born symbol of St. Louis, "but, yes."

Murtaugh told Joe L. Brown, comedian Joe E. Brown's son, who had replaced Branch Rickey as general manager of the Pirates. A couple of days later, Joe phoned and asked me to relay an off-the-record comment.

"If Stan were available, we'd grab him in a second. As Danny told you, we couldn't give up a young star for a player nearly 40, but, you know, I don't want to do this to Bing Devine. To offer too little would be unfair to Bing, because the public, I'm sure, would be behind Stan. If wouldn't be fair to Devine."

The mortification of Musial reached a new low on a night when Hemus sent up The Man to take an intentional walk, then used Carl Sawatski in the potential run-scoring situation. For the first and only time, rivals Barnes and Broeg combined to deliver a literary 1-2 punch.

I invited R. Liston, as I called Burnes, to write first. He did Saturday. I followed Sunday. When I walked into the clubhouse that day — I *always* did after a critical column — Hemus labeled me as "poison pen."

I told him I'd had it up to my Adam's apple — Burnes, presumably, too — with Hemus' contention he had 25 players and had to treat each alike. I reminded him of the playing tips Musial had given him over the years and, noting Stan's position and popularity with press and public, I suggested, "Sol, if you used Musial too much, everybody and his brother-in-law would be sympathetic to you. By jumping to what might be premature conclusions and acting too quickly, you've turned all of us against you."

Musial was down to .238 at this time. With Bob Nieman hurt, Hemus began to play Stan regularly. Musial hit so hard for the next three weeks, 20 for 41, that by the first All-Star game, he had raised his average above .300.

Gratefully, said Hemus, "Musial has delivered the most key hits the last few weeks of any player I've seen in years."

Celebrating in blistering heat of the two-game pension-aided All-Star games, Stan pinch-singled at Kansas City, then flew to New York and, pinch-hitting in Yankee Stadium, he belted one into the upper deck off White Sox relief ace and former teammate, Gerry Staley. It was his sixth All-Star game home run, still two more than any other player.

Ted Williams also rebounded remarkably at 42 in 1960 to hit .310 with 29 homers in 310 times at bat. Teddy Ballgame bowed out his last time up at Fenway Park by hitting a homer — against the wind.

Thanks to Stan the Man and reliever Lindy McDaniel, the Cardinals finished a strong third, 86-68, but not before Musial scared the Jolly Roger out of his home-town Pirates to the point, no fooling, that some old friends stopped talking to him. Stan beat the Buccos three times with home runs in a week's time in late August — Bob Friend in the ninth, 3-1; Roy Face next night in the ninth, 5-4, and then Friend again in the 14th, 3-2.

When the Cardinals couldn't win, I was glad Pittsburgh did. The 1960 World Series I regard as one of the most fascinating ever. The Yankees hit the Pirates with everything except the ring post, as they say in boxing, but the Buccos didn't buckle.

It was like a bout in which, knocked down in three different rounds, a guy got up and outpointed his foe in enough rounds to steal the decision. The Yankees hit a record World Series .338 with 91 hits, 27 for extra bases, including 10 homers. They scored 55 runs to 27 for Pittsburgh.

Although the Yanks had creamed Pittsburgh by scores of 16-3, 10-0, and 12-0, the incredible Series went down to the last batter of the last inning of the last game.

The Pirates' Bill Mazeroski hit a long shot to left field off Ralph Terry to win the game and the Series. Even before pressbox eyes could pick up the flight of the ball, it was past the scoreboard. Left fielder Yogi Berra was already lumbering off the field.

Mickey Mantle cried in frustration. Rumors began to circulate that the Yankees had decided to fire my friend Casey Stengel and "the man with the long pencil," general manager George Weiss. Those rumors turned out to be true. But the National League topped off the day's news by unofficially making it known they had made a unilateral decision to expand.

Word of the NL's imminent return to New York and an incursion into Houston annoyed the American League. A media up to its eyeballs in Mazeroski's dramatic home run now had another story to report.

Exhausted after the double dip of baseball histrionics and expansion, I wanted a relaxing Scotch, soothed down with cookies and milk. But the Hilton had no open restaurants or room service, so I trod narrow, crooked streets filled with wild celebration to reach an all-night drugstore.

En route, I stepped on a fork that almost put out my good eye. I narrowly escaped a plate of spaghetti held by a guy lurching out of a bar. Finally, I got my goodies.

When I returned to the Hilton, the outer doors were locked. Management was worried celebrants would damage their new carpets. Flashing my room key, I finally was allowed into the crowded lobby. I inched over to the elevator.

As I bellied inside the door, a drunk behind me pulled at the newspapers tucked under one arm, and then at the bag.

"Whatcha got, pal?"

"Just cookies and milk."

Slowly, floor by floor, the elevator crept up. The guy hung across me like pass interference. Suddenly, he snatched the bag and threw the package onto the floor. The cookies crumbled and . . . . I'd have to make the tedious voyage again. I snapped and knocked the surprised S.O.B. right onto his seat. As the doors opened, I backed out, scraping up my papers and packages, reaching a level only about halfway up to my floor level. Two dowagers entered the car and reproached me with grim stares as I retreated into the hallway awaiting another elevator.

Suddenly, the light flashed on. I leaped aboard and — oops! — wrong number, same car, same guy still down for the long count, and same dirty looks from the ladies.

When I got to my room, I dropped down in prayer. But all I could think was that I had to salvage my food rather than take that trip again. In the midst of seeking forgiveness, I found myself becoming indignant.

I phoned for ice and inquired as to the hotel's state. The bellman had no damage to report. Ditto at breakfast the next morning.

But I was indiscreet with a comment or two and, shortly, the item appeared in a *Washington Post* gossip column and a *Knoxville News-Sentinel*.

Cripes, what if the bastard got up and headed for a lawyer's office? I didn't think the Pulitzers would be happy to have their sports editor sued for fighting a drunk in an elevator!

35

❧

When Bing Devine signed Mizzou quarterback Mike Shannon, a physical horse at quarterback, for a whopping $65,000 bonus, Dan Devine was mighty mad. Previously, senior halfback Charley James, eager to get married, had ducked out of Missouri for $15,000. The baseball Cardinals also were making eyes at Tiger fullback Hank Kuhlmann.

I acted as peacemaker and arranged a meeting between the two Devines; the dark-haired Irish Catholic football coach and the pale Protestant baseball general manager. Der Bingle said that unless he found another club about to steal a playing prospect, he would desist.

Peace made, the Devines became great friends, and it was back to sports on the field, as usual. That's because sports were usually peaceful in those days.

Two men I greatly admire: Missouri head football coach Dan Devine (left) and Cardinals general manager Bing Devine.

The accomplishments of Dan Devine's 1960 football team have been unmatched in a century of Ol' Mizzou football. The soft-sell coach challenged his team 1) to win Mizzou's first opener since 1947, 2) to win at Norman, Oklahoma, 3) to win the conference championship, and 4) to gain MU's first bowl victory.

Missouri actually preceded Green Bay's power sweep, a devastating, streamlined, T-formation device with old-fashioned single-wingback blocking. Air Force Academy's Ben Martin described the assault as "Student body left, student body right."

The Tigers shut out SMU 20-0 to break the opening-game drought and then beat Penn State, 19-8. After a hard-fought 16-6 victory over Colorado, I began to sense this good team might be great. Now it was on to Oklahoma, where the Tigers hadn't won since 1936, Don Faurot's second season as coach.

When I flew into Norman the day before the game, I found many a recent Tiger graduate arriving. Could Devine fulfill the wild commitment he had made two years previously? After the Sooners ripped his first MU team, 39-0, the little coach had leaped onto the trainer's table and announced to his seniors:

"I promise you that two years from now when these sophomores are seniors, they'll win here and dedicate the game to you." Come now, Coach.

But they did.

A 41-19 victory brought the headiest ranking in Missouri's football history, one I thought I'd never see. With one week to go in the regular season, Ol' Mizzou was No. 1!

Although Kansas was loaded with John Hadl, Curtis McClinton, and Bert Coan — the Tigers were strong favorites. But KU's coach, Jack Mitchell, flung up what amounted to a nine-man front. The Tigers couldn't run and didn't take advantage of passing opportunities.

The 23-7 spanking gave the national title to Minnesota, though Kansas's flagrant violation of using Coan cost an asterisk in the standings and awarded the Big East title to the Tigers, who were off to the Orange Bowl against Navy.

While I was in Miami for the Orange Bowl, I went to watch St. Louis's Jesse Bowdry fight Willie Pastrano. Cassius Clay was fighting his second pro bout as part of the undercard.

Clay dispatched his foe in four rounds and soon took a ringside seat to cheer on his friend Pastrano. When he found I was from St. Louis, the gabby kid insisted Willie would belt the bejesus out of Bowdry. Betcha 10, friend, he said. Reluctantly, I agreed.Pastrano won, so I won. Cassius Clay, of course, soon became Muhammed Ali, a champion and larger-than-life legend, perhaps the most internationally popular of any American athlete ever.

A few nights later, before the New Year's Eve Orange Bowl party, Dan Devine tricked me into missing the last bus from the beach to the party. Grinning, Devine told me that the coaches were cutting out for sack time and I was on my own.

During a miffed exchange, the coach mocked that, hell, I should be studying. I didn't even know the players' numbers. For example, he'd bet a buck I didn't know reserve tackle Max Moyer's number. He would have won easily if I hadn't noticed a printed lineup speed card propped on a window sill behind his head.

Straining to get a look without tipping my hand, I said, "Max Moyer, No. 78." Surprised, Devine arched a brow and offered another buck for another obscure player. I was right again. Another one. Right. A fourth. Right. After he lost a fifth time, Devine peeled off $5 and, shaking his head in new admiration, grumbled off to bed.

I grinned my way to an early bed. The next day we all had more important things on our minds. The spectre of the school's 0-6 bowl record haunted Devine's team, especially when, climaxing a drive at the Middies' 2-yard line, Tiger quarterback Ron Taylor pitched out and Navy end Reg Mather intercepted the lateral and returned 98 yards for a shocking touchdown.

Navy followed by recovering an onside kick and drove to the Mizzou 20. Then Missouri's Norm Beal returned a leaping interception 90 yards for the game-tying touchdown.

Missouri held Heisman Trophy winner Joe Bellino to four yards and went on to a 21-14 victory. Most of us pressbox rubes spent much of our time watching on our (Navy) side of the field a white-shirted man, sleeves rolled up, munching a hot dog, sipping a beer and puffing a cigar. For president-elect John F. Kennedy these were precious days.

With Minnesota losing the Rose Bowl game, a later vote, as is done now, might have reinstated Missouri as No. 1.

After a season like that, it takes some doing to "ignite the excite." Certainly the struggling 1961 baseball Cardinals were not inspiring.

By July, when I flew west to cover the first of two All-Star games, general manager Bing Devine slipped into a seat next to me and delivered big news. He would change managers next day, and the release would be p.m., meaning for the *Post-Dispatch*.

About news releases: I'd always tried to be fair, insisting only on an even break on major stories. In other words, don't make a trade for J. Lee Donuts and give it to the *Globe-Democrat*, then announce to us that Tuesday would be Ladies Day.

Bob Burnes' executive assistant, Bill Fleishman, tried to suggest to the Cardinals that if the *Globe-Democrat* didn't get a story first, it would wind up next day hidden among the Want Ads. I made no threat, but dared the ball club to cave in to that kind of petulance. Just be fair, I said, and when we're not first, we'll be better.

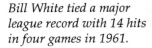

Bill White tied a major league record with 14 hits in four games in 1961.

When radio began broadcasting press conferences, I soon learned to stay mum and not give away what I wanted for publication. I became silently mute, difficult for a gabby, inquisitive guy like me, and sought afterward to find a moment or two to ask a key question privately.

Devine had decided to replace Solly Hemus with Johnny Keane, Solly's former field boss at Houston and most recently a coach. Hemus seemed to have trouble with some black players as well as his dealings with umpires.

After Bill White hit three homers in L.A., I sat with Hemus and Jack Herman at Googie's all-night restaurant near the downtown Biltmore Hotel. I knew the axe would fall.

When it did the next day, Hemus reacted poorly, suggesting disloyalty by Keane. At the Coliseum that night, where Hemus picked up his equipment and moved down the runway toward the field, I scolded him for his unfair comments about an old friend. As I did so, I was unaware that walking quietly down the ramp to the clubhouse was the owner of the Dodgers, Walter F. O'Malley.

Hemus had a sense of humor, but it wasn't funny to Bob Gibson when Solly addressed Gibby as "Bridges," confusing him with left-hander Marshall Bridges.

First time I ever saw Gibson warm up, I rushed hurriedly down from the press box to a point behind home plate occupied by the Cardinals' senior scout, Joe Mathes. "Uncle Joe," I exclaimed, "I had to get a better look. God, he's not only incredibly fast, but I've never seen a ball move like that."

Keane, taking over as manager, did three things, two of which favored black players. He told Gibby he'd start every fourth or fifth day, and assured Flood he was the regular center fielder. The manager's other immediate announcement was that Larry Jackson would get out of the bullpen and back into starting rotation. Jackson had suffered a horrible injury in spring training. The butt end of a broken bat from Duke Snider smashed his jaw.

After flying to Boston for the second All-Star game, Bob Burnes and I decided to route home through New York to attend the silver anniversary of *Sport* Magazine. We were entertained by many cover stars of the magazine at a luncheon.

Leaving New York on my own, I hopped over the Canadian border to watch Frank (Pop) Ivy's Football Cardinals team play the Toronto Argonauts under Canadian rules. I was curious to see the 12-player, wider-field, deeper end zone game, which lacks only a fourth down to be better than U.S. football. When you can't fair catch a punt and must return a kick or punt from your own (deeper) end zone, that's action, my friends.

As I stood on the field before the game, won handily by the Cardinals, a man came up to Ivy and his assistants. In the scramble of exchanging names, I think Bob Devaney thought I was a coaching jock, not a reporter. Congratulated for having coached an unbeaten Wyoming team, Devaney scoffed at the tribute. "Hell," he said, "I got kids into Wyoming I couldn't get into the Big Ten or the Big Eight."

When Nebraska hired Devaney to become head coach of the Cornhuskers, an alarm went off in my brain. Many folks, including me, wonder why'n heck so many players decide they like the wind-swept, bitter Central Plains.

I returned from Toronto in time for a weekend party at which the Cardinals brought back St. Louis and Philadelphia players from the 1931 World Series. I can recall my greeting from Neal Russo, the mad genius I had handpicked to succeed me on the baseball beat. With no attempt to throw a burr under my saddle or boobytrap my ulcer, Russo told me that when managing editor Crowley was told my time table, previously cleared with him — Los Angeles to San Francisco to Boston to New York to Toronto — he had sniffed, "Oh, on vacation *again!*"

Scheduled to emcee the dinner, I went through it in a blur that I felt all the way to the pit of my stomach, which now, indeed, did show an ulcer.

Crowley made no mention when I took him my expenses. Typically, he signed while covering the amount, showing a vote of confidence. Good. I *never* cheated.

One day when Crowley was angry in general, the M. E. said to me, "You're 90 percent reporter and only 10 percent editor." He did not include a percentage for "administrator." Or any for trying to be a luncheon or dinner speaker. Somehow, it all added up to more than 100 percent.

I liked working for the Pulitzers. I had no damned guts with my immediate superiors. Crowley, too, was chicken, as I learned belatedly.

When Crowley was a young reporter, his boss was the *Post-Dispatch*'s famed managing editor, Oliver K. Bovard. At the time Crowley pronounced his name "Krowley."

Bovard was legendary for his ruthlessness. Once when another reporter complained he needed more money on which to live, Bovard sniffed, "Not necessarily." Again, another young eager-beaver *P-D* reporter, Willie Zalken, stopped his car at Grand and Lindell to give the famed M.E. a ride downtown. Bovard listened to the chattering chipmunk all the way.

When they parted at the office, Bovard asked city editor Ben Reese if he had a reporter named Zalken? He did. "Fire him," snapped OKB. Bill Zalken went on to become business director of the famed St. Louis Symphony and Municipal Theaters, a poor man's Sol Hurok.

Bovard insisted that "Krowley" pronounce his name as spelled, like the black bird. So Raymond L. became Crowley — and he never corrected Bovard. Maybe my tormented intestinals weren't the only ones that lacked fortitude.

At heart I am a writer, not an editor. I tried to organize the *Post-Dispatch* staff so the sports section was at its best whether or not I was on the road. I'm pleased to be judged by a staff I recruited, one of which, Dave Lipman, became the *P-D*'s managing editor.

One of the reasons I liked being sports editor was my ability to pick my travel spots. Take Philadelphia, for instance. On the whole, I'd rather be at a ball game there than in my office.

With the baseball Cardinals closing their 1961 season at Connie Mack Stadium and the football Big Red playing the Eagles at Franklin Field, I opted for the football game. I'd have time later for dinner with manager Johnny Keane and traveling secretary Leo Ward.

Although the club would fly to St. Louis, the three of us could catch a train to New York for the Yankees-Cincy World Series. It would be a pleasant gathering for, under Keane, the Cardinals had improved to a solid fourth with a 41-33 record.

At O'Hare on my way to Philly, seeking out an early edition of the *Chicago Tribune*, I was reading about Missouri's tense 6-0 victory over Minnesota (last season's number 1 and number 2) when Paul Christman appeared at my shoulder. We were two proud alumni reading about our alma mater winning a defensive classic in the darndest weather Dave Lipman ever saw — September sunshine, followed by a drizzle, sleet and a freak snowstorm.

Arriving late in Philadelphia, I hurried out to the football stadium, where — I don't blame him — Joe Pollack chuckled as I hiked to the nosebleed levels of the Franklin Field press box with two canteens strapped criss-cross over my shoulders — one filled with water, the other with warm milk.

The game was close and exciting. With no time outs left, place-kicker Gerald Perry hurried off the St. Louis bench and, without pausing, toed into the ball for a game-winning, 30-27 field goal.

Game over, I ate downtown with Keane and Ward, wondering all the while what Keane felt about Musial, who would be 42 within the month.

Timidly on the train, I broached the question to Keane. Play Musial less? "No, play him more," he said, "and I've just told him so. I urged him to get into the best possible shape, because, *if* next year is his last year, let's make it a great one."

Of course, 1961 had been a great year for home runs, partly because of expansion. The New York Yankees hit a record 240 home runs, including the momentous 61 by Roger Maris. I mean no disrespect to Maris, an underrated player and consummate professional, but there were pitchers in the AL in 1961 who probably should have been in Shreveport or New Iberia.

Still, as Maris would explain later with the Cardinals, Mantle had become everyone's favorite even though he finished with "only" 54 homers.

"Suddenly, the crowds that had booed Mantle now saw him as the hero and me as the heel," Maris said. "Mick told me, 'Thank God.'"

Mickey Mantle and Roger Maris, Yankee sluggers in the 1961 home run race.

When the Series was over, I arranged a trip with Musial — "Mr. Crowley if you don't mind, I'd like to take a few days vacation" — to Donora to absorb home town material for our book, "Stan Musial: The Man's Own Story."

We stopped first at Pittsburgh to see the Big Red play Art Rooney's Steelers at Forbes Field. My main objective was *not* to see the man I'd hit in the elevator — or his lawyer.

36

ৌ

After Cincinnati won the 1961 pennant, every member of the old eight-club National League had finished first at least once during a 16-year period. Despite Yankee overall supremacy, the NL prevailed in All-Star games, the box office, and, ultimately, the World Series, because it had first incorporated black players.

Like most whites, I was blind to the unacceptable unfairness that forced Afro-American athletes in Florida to live like second-class citizens. Bill White brought the situation to light in an interview with the Associated Press' Joe Reichler.

To rectify in 1962, the Cardinals took over two contiguous motels. Executives and players — wives and kids, white and black — lived together happily and in harmony. White's wife, Mildred, ran a day school for the kids. Many of us sat in on nightly first-run films rented by Al Fleishman, founder of Fleishman-Hillard.

The Redbirds had a good spring with a raw, strong kid named Julio Gotay playing a promising shortstop. Then they opened the regular season with seven straight victories, the club's best since 1899.

But Gotay proved too awkward for shortstop, and the Cardinals sagged to sixth. The best thing about 1962 was Stan Musial's revival at nearly 43 to hit .330.

Opening day against the expansion New York Misfits . . . er, Mets, under my old friend, Casey Stengel, Musial went "3 for 3." Said Stengel, "I haf-ta say this fella hasn't changed since I left this here league."

I had written Ol' Case, closing in on 72, urging him to sit on his laurels and money in Glendale, California. I wanted Stengel to preserve the lofty managerial mark he had achieved with the Yankees. In written response, he referred to the cliché that it was nice to be wanted and, anyway, baseball was still fun.

En route home from covering the Kentucky Derby, I saw Musial, on a special day on which he tied Honus Wagner for most games played, fail to drive in the tying run in the first game of a doubleheader at Cincinnati. He popped straight up the shaft with one out and the bases loaded. Between games, I ventured into the clubhouse. Stan sat barebacked. About that time, puffing a thin cigar, manager Johnny Keane came up, slapped Musial on the back and said:

"Suit up, Stan, you're playing the second one — and you're going to win it."

In the ninth inning of that second game, Musial hit one into the distant Crosley Field bleachers for a three-run, game-winning homer.

Headed for the All-Star game in Washington, I sat in the press box for a subsequent Saturday afternoon doubleheader at the Polo Grounds. Musial, pinch-hitting, won the second game with a home run, 3-2. The next day Stan hit homers his first three times at bat. Officially, four straight round-trippers.

Afterward, grinning, The Man talked about his third home run of the day, struck off young left-hander Willard Hunter. "Here at the Polo Grounds," Stan explained, "I swing at pitches well inside, hoping to hook the ball around the close foul pole on the fair side, but this pitch was w-a-y inside when I swung and, yep, it stayed fair. I did something I never did. Taking a look at the look on Hunter's face, I laughed circling the bases."

At Washington, Musial and Stengel were escorted to see John Kennedy at the Presidential box. Musial first met Kennedy when the junior senator from Massachusetts was campaigning in Wisconsin. JFK introduced himself, "They say you're too old to play ball, Stan, and I'm too young to be president."

As they exchanged handshakes now, Musial said to Kennedy, "I think we both fooled them, Mr. President."

With Cardinals' P.R. man Jim Toomey keeping Keane abreast of the times necessary for 502 plate appearances, Musial finished behind Tommy Davis in the batting race, but he hit .330, a point below his career average. He hammered 19 homers and had 82 RBIs in 116 games. Pinch-hitting, he was extraordinary, with eight for 13, .615, reaching base 14 of 19 times.

Doubling as a columnist and beat reporter, to save the paper money, I headed west for the Cardinals' season close-out in San Francisco and Los Angeles and to see Missouri's football opener against California's Golden Bears at Berkeley.

Highly regarded Johnny Roland made his first appearance in the Mizzou backfield. Beforehand, former Marine Jerry Wallach, an offensive tackle who would become assistant attorney general for the state of Missouri, nudged me in the dressing room.

"Look," he said, "the kid's reading a sport section, calmly, and I'm nervous as hell, even though I've been through this for a couple of years. He's going to be a great one."

Like scoring three touchdowns in his first game, 21-10.

In the meantime, the Dodgers had a three-game lead with six to play. When Jack Sanford beat the Cardinals at San Francisco and Houston topped the Dodgers in La-La Land, the lead was two. Both teams won the next day, so the Dodgers were two ahead with four to go.

Giants owner Horace Stoneham invited Stan to stop by his luxury box for a drink or two. Horace admonished Musial, "Now take it easy on us tomorrow." Stan joshed back. "Last time you said that, I hit five home runs against you."

Next day, Musial got "5 for 5" for the last time in his career, and when catcher Gene Oliver hammered a three-run homer, the 7-4 blow left L.A. only one victory away from a title tie as the Cardinals flew south.

The Dodgers never got it. As loose and as amused as possible when your side is not in the title hunt, we watched in amazed amusement as 1) Larry Jackson went 10 innings to win the Friday night opener, 3-2, 2) Ernie Broglio two-hit Drysdale in a 2-0 game lost by L.A. when giant Frank Howard dropped a fly ball, and 3) Curt Simmons outdueled Johnny Podres, 1-0, when Gene Oliver homered off one of Podres' change-ups.

Because Juan Marichal had lost one game of a Saturday doubleheader for the Giants, San Francisco needed a homer by Willie Mays to beat Turk Farrell, 2-1, and set up another playoff. Once again, I was an eyewitness.

The Giants won the first game, but the Dodgers won the second and seemed an inevitable winner behind heroic Maury Wills as they led 4-2 in the ninth inning of the final.

First up for the Giants, pinch-hitter Matty Alou singled. After Dodger reliever Ed Roebuck retired Harvey Kuenn, Willie McCovey, pinch-hitting for Chuck Hiller, walked. So did Felipe Alou. Overworked, Roebuck was so tired.

Willie Mays then hit one of the damnedest line drives I ever saw, right back at Roebuck and off the reliever's right hand. One run scored on the infield smash.

I watched the Dodger bullpen. Don Drysdale got up and walked inside, away from the action. Why? Maybe so he could start the World Series?

Walter Alston beckoned for big Stan Williams. Orlando Cepeda hit a game-tying sacrifice fly. Alston had Williams pass Ed Bailey intentionally to fill the bases. A queasy feeling came over me. Sure enough, Williams walked Jim Davenport, forcing in the leading run. Another run scored when second baseman Larry Burright boxed a soft grounder by Jose Pagan.

Giants manager Dark brought in Billy Pierce to 1-2-3 the home ninth. Six to four, the Giants were champions. Personally, I wondered why'n hell Drysdale stormed around angrily. The Big Airedale could have been a St. Bernard and come to L.A.'s rescue.

The trade-wind weather was so biting at Candlestick Park for the World Series, where most visiting members had to sit outside in a makeshift press area, that I shivered for nine innings even though I had a sleeveless sweater under my sports coat under my trench coat and wore gloves, woolen socks, and a hat.

In the sunny seats below, spectators would sit shirtsleeved in the sun, and, then, as shadows lengthened and wind-chill increased, go first to sweaters, then to jackets or topcoats.

San Fran and New York split in San Francisco, and the Yankees won two of three in New York. The Series was returning to California. But I wasn't going with it.

Art Bertelson, the new managing editor, told me to forget it. A second cross-country trip was not worth the paper's money.

As ball clubs and press planes headed for the Golden Gate, I headed for Eads Bridge. I dropped off my story at the *P-D* at a decent hour and the next day returned to work. I bumped into the assistant managing editor, Evarts Graham Jr., son of the outstanding surgeon who connected cigarettes and lung cancer in the early 1950s and scared the living bejesus out of me. Young Ev, filling in for Bertelson, ordered me to use the Series open date and return to San Francisco.

Therefore, I was in an unusual situation when I arrived in the Bay area simultaneous with a three-day rainstorm. Ev Graham might have a worry, but I certainly didn't.

Because of my ulcer, I wasn't drinking. Missed it, yeah, but not as much as I feared. Instead of alcohol-driven bull sessions, I watched two theater movies a day, taking off my rain-soaked shoes and propping up my feet on the arm rests in front. Loved it!

When the rains finally stopped, Horace Stoneham spent a bundle hovering helicopters over the Point to take the sag if not the sog out of Candlestick Park sod. I shivered through another cold one as Billy Pierce beat Whitey Ford, 5-2, to force a seventh game.

New York led into the home ninth, 1-0. Matty Alou led off with a pinch-single drag bunt, but Yankee pitcher Ralph Terry struck out brother Felipe Alou and then fanned Hiller.

Two out, but here came Willie Mays. He lashed a vicious drive toward the right-field corner, where the ball skidded on the wet turf toward the wire fence. If it reached the barrier or if Maris failed to field it cleanly, Alou would score the tying run.

Maris cut the hit off before it reached the fence, wheeled, and threw perfectly to the cutoff man, Bobby Richardson. Even before Whitey Lockman, coaching third, threw up a stop sign, my opinion was that Lockman had evaluated correctly. Oh, sure, Richardson's throw to the plate was high, prompting Elston Howard to leap for the ball, but suggesting a possible run was merely a second guess. Alou still might have been out.

With the tying and winning runs in scoring position, the logical move was to intentionally pass Willie McCovey. Terry had walked none, indicating little likelihood he would force in a run. Would the right-handed pitcher do better against the left-handed McCovey or the next hitter, right-handed Orlando Cepeda?

After a brief discussion, Yankee manager Ralph Houk walked away from the mound. Terry prepared to pitch to McCovey. Why?

Why not? McCovey hit the damnedest, hottest line drive smack dab right to Richardson. Series over! If the ball had been hit an inch any which way elsewhere, including up, McCovey would have been the hero and Terry, once again, the goat.

When I returned to St. Louis, managing editor Bertelson said nothing about my second trip to the coast. Art apparently had bigger fish to fry.

Like Crowley, who had helped flower my ulcer, Bertelson didn't interfere with my hiring as suddenly as openings occurred. I'm grateful to both men. I'm sure the *P-D* is, too.

Many of my hires moved to positions of more significance than the Toy Dept., as Sports is called. I'm proud that my personnel acquisitions in the early 1960s created the backbone of a new and better sports department. Ed Wilks of the New York AP office was on my list. I knew Wilks had married a St. Louis-area woman. So I would phone — and maybe, like me, he'd want to return to St. Louis from AP duty elsewhere.

As I was picking up my phone one day, it rang. Ed was asking *me* for a job! Crowley hired Wilks, at my suggestion, but it was Bertelson who took my recommendation for golfing buff Bill Beck, a native of nearby Centralia, Illinois, who had been sports editor of the *St. Petersburg Times.*

Why would Beck want to leave St. Pete, where salaries were small, but bonuses large? Because, Stockton tipped me in a call one morning, Bill had grappled once too often with management and quit, a silly thing to do. As I preach to all malcontents, get a new job *first.*

JRS suggested I sell Beck to Bertelsen for golf, but I also knew Bill would immediately be the best-informed football man on our staff.

I brought in some fine newspaper men, i.e., Dave Lipman, Dave Dorr, John Sonderegger, Ron Powers, John Duxbury, Doug Grow, Jim Creighton, Bob McCoy, Gary Mueller, Gary Clark, Rick Hummel, Tim Renken, Jerry Stack, Jake Wieland, Tom Barnidge, Dick Kaegel, Jeff Meyers, and, of course, Wilks and Beck.

I sought raises for others and never for myself. With no children, I didn't feel inflation as acutely as others, though my purchasing power was definitely decreasing.

Urged by progressive general manager Bob Hyland of KMOX to come aboard for radio appearances, I wanted to say yes, but didn't want to offend management. Yet there was no spot for me on KSD, then Pulitzer-owned. I finally said yes to Hyland, "if you want me, you've got me."

For a time, I don't think Bertelson liked what I was doing. Newspaper versus radio rivalry for the advertising dollar was intense. I never worried about that touchiness, but I got caught between a rock and a hard place when TV sports enthusiast

Bertelson suggested we run information about televised sports. Art also beefed that we wasted a reader's time by listing only the telecast schedule rather than the actual time for the game's start.

Hyland phoned and moaned, though he never threatened. He felt we should also report that the event would be carried on KMOX radio. The explanation that everything was carried by KMOX pleased but did not mollify the intense competitor.

Art also suggested my use of an official assistant sports editor, for which Dave Lipman boldly volunteered with an unforgettable complex sentence I repeated in triumph to Bertelson. Said Dave, "I can write, but you've got better writers; but *no one* who could edit as well as I can."

So Lipman was on his way to becoming the pupil who taught the teacher, the managing editor who had rank over his old boss, even if he never pulled it.

37

The best explanation for the mental fatheadedness that overtakes players and teams was given to me by Sweden's handsome heavyweight Ingemar Johansson after his second fight with Floyd Patterson.

Ingo was the dimpled darling of his lovely live-in, Birget Lundgren. At the rematch weigh-in at the Commodore Hotel, Lundgren silhouetted herself in a ballroom window's sunlight. I joined the press crew's ogling, but was startled by a much-too-strong-to-be-friendly slap on my cheek.

Wheeling, I saw the grinning face of Howard Cosell. I also saw red and grabbed the barrister broadcaster by the throat, drew back my fist and . . . stopped. Cosell apologized and we remained friends.

When I got a private moment with Ingemar, I asked if he had been overconfident before Patterson left him twitching on the floor? Slowly, the Swede answered in broken English. "I like to think," he said, "that if I'd known I was overconfident, I would have done something about it."

In 1963, Stan Musial knew it was time to "do something about it." So over breakfast with Bing Devine one day, The Man said he would hang it up at the end of the season.

Gus Busch was unavoidably unavailable to oversee the announcement at his annual open-date team party for players, wives and children, but the secret wouldn't keep and the Big Eagle asked me to make his apologies and introduce Stan.

The day was rainy, hot, humid — and tearful — when Stan took the microphone away from me. After announcing he was leaving, he said, voice choking, "I'd like to go out with a winner. Our 1942 club was farther back."

Suddenly, we thought perhaps divinely, St. Louis started to win. A 19-of-20 surge climbed the Cardinals to within one game of first-place Los Angeles.

Musial stayed up late one night nervously awaiting a phone call announcing the birth of Jeffrey Stanton Musial. The next night Stanley Frank Musial became the first big-league grandfather to hit a home run.

Before a three-game showdown in St. Louis with the Dodgers, I drifted down to the rightfield bullpen for a visit with friend Walter Alston. Battle-scarred from two previous close-call pennant failures, Walt and the Dodgers were ready. They played magnificently.

A man I admired, Dodgers Manager Walter Alston.

Musial gave the crowd one last thrill with a game-tying home run—his 465th and last—late in the first game, but Johnny Podres hung on to win, 3-1. Sandy Koufax won the second game, 4-0, and held the Cardinals hitless until Musial singled in the seventh.

L.A. won the third game in the 13th inning and, soon after, smacked New York in the 1963 World Series. It was the only time the mighty Yankees suffered a Series sweep.

September 29, 1963, Musial's last at-bat. A hit!

Musial had finished the regular season with a flourish, getting base hits his last two times up. Then it was over. But many of us had been wrestling with an important question: How best to honor a great player and a great person? Sure, retire number "6," that's easy, but why not a bronzed memorial outside Busch Stadium, then under construction?

To make the statue less ostentatious and to please Musial, why not a twin-figured display of a young boy glancing up to Musial. The title would be "The Man and the Boy."

I posed as both for the *Post-Dispatch's* gifted sports artist, Amadee Wohlschlaeger. Dee's tremendous color blow-up led a retirement day parade at the old ball park.

We St. Louis baseball writers proposed to move up my "baby," the annual dinner, from January to October. All proceeds would go for the statue. Stan would receive the prestigious "Dr. Robert Hyland for Meritorious Service to Sports." Immediately, good ol' dynamic Bob Hyland of KMOX kicked in $5,000 and the Cardinals' board of directors $8,000.

At Musial's last game, commissioner Ford Frick delivered what I envisioned as the inscription for the statue. Frick said he hoped Musial's Hall of Fame plaque would read:

"Here stands baseball's perfect warrior. . . here stands baseball's perfect knight."

Joe Garagiola emceed the dinner and Pittsburgh broadcaster Bob Prince led off with brief breezy quips. Their standard created a program masterpiece, climaxing with a giant-screen, slow-motion, color film taken by Al Fleishman from ground level of Musial hitting a spring training home run and running around the bases, accompanied by a clever version of "Thanks for the memories."

Musial said, "What helps the self-consciousness is that you decided to put a boy with me. It's easy to keep humble when you're with kids."

The statue didn't quite work the way we envisioned. Though we raised $40,000, the city controlled the statue for income-tax purposes. Before long, we were informed we couldn't stultify the artist's creativity. Sculptor Carl Mose wanted to portray Stan alone in his unique batting stance, eliminating the boy.

Enraged and frustrated, I hurried the hell out of Mayor Raymond R. Tucker's office. I'd always regarded Tucker as "a statesman at the municipal level" but not this time.

S-o-o, the statue is a nice place to visit or to meet friends at the tree-fringed northeast corner of the attractive new ball park, but I've got only one comment: No comment! Recently I learned that Tucker and Mose were long-time bosom buddies. So much for democracy in action.

Which is exactly how I felt in November, 1963.

Over the years, I made sure I attended at least one Illinois game, but in a great Illini season, 1963, I saw two. Led by center-linebacker Dick Butkus, probably second only to Red Grange as a famed gridiron Illini, Illinois shut out Craig Morton and California, 10-0.

Hopping the *Post-Dispatch* plane at Champaign, carrying photographers, I hurried to St. Louis. Stopping, I saw most of an Oklahoma-Southern California game on television and then flew to Little Rock to watch Arkansas play Missouri.

Razorback coach Frank Broyles and Tiger mentor Dan Devine were jumping jacks on the sidelines. Devine won the gymnastics and the game, 7-6. Beating Broyles was a special thrill.

Missouri didn't have a team that year to compare with Illinois. I saw the Illini lose to Michigan, but Pete Elliott's team recovered and needed only a win over Michigan State to clinch the conference championship and a trip to the Rose Bowl.

Like everyone else I remember where I was on November 22, 1963. As I drove to Lambert Airport, bound for Lincoln and the Big Eight championship game between Nebraska and Oklahoma, I heard KMOX radio veteran Rex Davis comment: "In a speech prepared for delivery at noon today, President Kennedy said . . . "

Arriving at the airport in a hard rain, I grabbed my typewriter and small overnight bag, and ran to the entry gate. There was an inexplicable delay. When we finally boarded, the pilot announced, "The President has been shot."

I heard no more on the flight to Kansas City, but when I rushed into the old pocket-sized KayCee downtown airport, stony-faced people stumbled around, many with portable radios plastered to their ears. For a long time—too long—no one would confirm to me that the worst had happened.

I was in deep grief when my plane arrived at Lincoln. I thought it was proper the Illinois-Michigan State game had been delayed a week because of President Kennedy's death. Most other games had as well including Missouri at Kansas.

I became angry at a teenaged kid who drove me to a downtown hotel, blocking out the dramatic news in favor of rock n' roll. I grew angry again at a press party when veteran Nebraska tub-thumper John Bentley said their game, unlike most others, would be played.

OU's coach, Bud Wilkinson, who had been JFK's national director for physical fitness, was quoted as saying the President would want it that way. I learned also that an Oklahoma City theatre had been leased and sold out for a closed-circuit telecast of the game.

Tenth-ranked Nebraska knocked off sixth-ranking Oklahoma, 29-20, providing Bob Devaney his first Big Eight championship and preventing politically bound Wilkinson from going out a conference winner.

I wished I were somewhere other than behind a typewriter. This was not sports' finest hour, especially when Pete Rozelle insisted the pros play on Sunday.

Rather than watch Charley Johnson quarterback the Gridbirds to an upset over the division champion New York Giants at Yankee Stadium, 24-17, I watched with millions as Jack Ruby killed Lee Harvey Oswald.

The next week I felt like I needed sports to overcome the tragedy that I — and all of us — had experienced. I was glad to see the Illini win the Big Ten by defeating Michigan State.

Drawn by my heart, I believe, to attend the Missouri-Kansas game I would have missed had it, too, not been postponed, I saw the unbelievable, a 9-7 Mizzou victory that put the Tigers ahead of the Jayhawks for the first time in their long, long rivalry.

Ahead and two yards from a clinching touchdown, KU fullback Ken Coleman lunged into a pile at right tackle where— oops!—the ball popped out of his grasp, over the goal line, and into the hands of defensive back Vince Turner.

For a split second, Turner stood motionless. Suddenly, the senior from Chillicothe, Missouri, took off and ran 103 yards for the winning touchdown.

A lot of Missouri guys and gals desperately needed to smile. I know I did. Turner made it happen with the "Vince Turner Memorial Interception."

38

Early in 1964, I attended a two-week seminar for sports editors, offered by the American Press Institute at Columbia University's Pulitzer Building in New York. Shirley Povich was one of the teachers.

Shirley once was named one of the top 10 *women* in the United States, which was a surprise to his wife and his son, gossip yakker Maury, and daughter-in-law Connie Chung. Long-time sports editor of the *Washington Post* and a classic writer, old friend Shirley offered sage advice about covering a sports event.

Said Povich, "Don't prejudge, don't think up lead-in paragraphs. Have confidence enough to let it happen and *then* decide what to write."

Through that two-week stint in New York, I covered each session as if I were writing a report — for Bertelson, publisher Joseph Pulitzer, and my staff. That kept me busy full-time.

I broke away one weekend to watch Robert Redford and Elizabeth Ashley in "Barefoot in the Park." Two nights later, I attended an unusual Sunday night preview of an ill-fated Burt Lahr venture, "Foxy."

At intermission, I rose, turned, stretched, and looked into the blue eyes of — Robert Redford. Impulsively, I introduced myself, mentioned his show, and said, "You're going to be a great success . . ."

Redford, pleased, wondered what I did. When I told him, he arched his brows. "Then," he said, "I guess you know my high-school teammate, Don Drysdale?"

Redford told me he had played the outfield behind Drysdale when Van Nuys was a fruit-and-vegetable farm area. "I hope," said the actor, "that Drysdale makes the Hall of Fame one day."

When I later related the story to Drysdale, he assured me, "Redford was a pretty good ball player."

When I returned from the New York seminar, St. Louis was abuzz with rumors that the Football Cardinals were moving to Atlanta.

Our city wanted the Bidwills' signatures on a 30-year stadium lease, requiring them to give up their share of concessions to help finance the new structure.

Stormy and Bill held a gun to the city's head as Atlanta, feverishly building Fulton County Stadium, sought to convince the Bidwills to move there.

When I wrote a story suggesting Milwaukee might lose the baseball Braves to Atlanta, I received an angry phone call from the sports editor of the *Milwaukee Journal*, Ollie Kuechle. Teed off by my speculation, Kuechle raged, "How dare you say we might lose the Braves? Your football club probably will move to Atlanta."

Truth to tell, the St. Louis baseball outlook was almost as depressing as football. The baseball Cardinals were mediocre the first half of the season. Then, on June 15, the trading deadline, Bing Devine exchanged Ernie Broglio for Lou Brock.

I respected Devine's judgment, though I knew little about Brock. The loss of Broglio, it seemed to me, might well be what Branch Rickey labeled "an addition by subtraction."

Big "Earnshaw," as I called Broglio, was enjoying the sights, sounds, and bottle-sniffing of Gaslight Square, then a merry pocket of midtown fun.

Working a radio show on KMOX on a Saturday morning after Broglio had been jocked the night before, I was hit with a sticky-wicket question from a caller. The night before a pitching assignment, what was Broglio doing up drinking late at "Smokey Joe's?"

At the ball park I confronted Earnshaw, noting that with his duck-billed haircut and long Jay Leno jaw, he was easy to pick out. His response was that he drank because he couldn't sleep at night!

In Brock's two-plus seasons with the Cubs, Lou had hit .250. His right fielding was so-so, handicapped, as he told me, by an inability to master sunglasses for the wicked late-afternoon rays. The Cubbies hadn't run him much, but Cardinals manager Johnny Keane saw him as a fast leadoff man who might steal a lot of bases.

Brock was a cheerful, rapid-talking athlete, difficult to comprehend because of his sentence complexities at a time reporters rarely used tape recorders. I wish I had had one with Brock, Bing Devine, and Casey Stengel.

Broglio raised my ire when he joined the Cubs. "It's nice," said Earnshaw, "to join a ball club with a winning spirit." So I referred to him in a column as "Bright-Lights' Broglio, who spent more time in the arms of Bacchus than Morpheus."

When I returned to New York for the All-Star Game at new Shea Stadium, the next few weeks turned out to be among the most exciting I ever experienced.

First, there was the game itself, symbolically ended by the hottest member of the hottest team in baseball, Johnny Callison of the Philadelphia Phillies. Callison broke up a tie game with a two-out, three-run homer in the bottom of the ninth.

Thursday morning I got a reliable tip assuring me the football Cardinals definitely were going to Atlanta. Ending my role in a city-wide genuflect, I wrote that the Bidwills — "athletic carpetbaggers" — were moving to Atlanta.

That evening I watched the Cardinals end the first half of their season with a horrible loss to New York. Met pinch-hitter Frank Thomas, weakly waving a heavy bat after a bout with mononucleosis, hit a Curt Simmons change-up for a game-winning homer just inside the left-field foul pole. That left the Cardinals at 40-41.

The time had arrived to feel the players' pulse. Early at the batting cage Friday evening, I asked individual players for analysis, promising anonymity. First baseman, Bill White, agreed to speak only if I agreed to *use* his name. "*I'm* what's wrong," said White. "A year ago this time I had 70 RBIs. Now I've got only 30, but I'll get going."

Shortly after my stint at the batting cage, a drama unfolded in the privacy of the Cardinals' clubhouse. I'd have loved to know then that Keane told the players he didn't like loose talk, because it was divisive. He was ready to name names when infielder Dick Groat spoke up. Dick was an All-Star player, a gabby guy, and a clubhouse lawyer.

A few weeks earlier, after Keane withdrew Groat's automatic hit-and-run privilege, Dick whined outside the fold. Faced with his manager's ire, Groat apologized. It wouldn't happen again. Fine. The episode was over. Let's move on.

A kid just called up from the minors listened in wide-eyed silence, unusual if you know Mike Shannon. The next afternoon Shannon played right field and Brock moved to left. To old friend Jim Toomey in the press box, I said the new lineup seemed the best I'd seen that season. And on a hunch Devine called up veteran knuckleballer George (Barney) Schultz to help in the bullpen.

Devine's job was done, but, sadly, so was Der Bingle. I don't think he ever had been Gussie Busch's favorite because Devine didn't smoke, didn't drink, and didn't run around, as Branch Rickey cunningly reminded Busch, who had enjoyed all three vices at one time or another.

Worse, now Busch had the idea that Devine and Keane had been disloyal. They hadn't told him about the Groat matter, which daughter Liz related to Daddy after hearing from her future husband, Eddie Mathews, the slugging Milwaukee third baseman. When Busch pressed Devine and Keane, the GM and skipper frankly couldn't think of anything troubling them.

Gus fired Der Bingle. Aged consultant Rickey quickly nominated Bob Howsam as Devine's successor and Busch agreed. Not until Bob arrived did Gus learn that, for crizzsakes pal, he's the son-in-law of the Colorado senator, Edwin Johnston, a friend of the Colorado Coors, and a man who had publicly questioned whether ownership of a ball club by Anheuser-Busch wasn't an anti-trust violation.

With the Cardinals now nine games over .500, rather than one under, Howsam — Busch always called him *"Houseman"* — took over a unified team that had momentum, but most likely not enough time.

In the meantime, on the football front, Famous-Barr's Morton (Buster) May became a silent civic hero. He orchestrated more social acceptance for the Bill Bidwills, who resided in St. Louis. Other, more practical, means were taken to ease the straitjacket lease forcing the football and baseball teams to relinquish their share of concession profits.

That did it! The Bidwills signed the lease. The football Cardinals would stay. I didn't mind being "wrong" about their move to Atlanta. And a couple of weeks later when the College All-Star game was played in Chicago, I learned the truth at a press party the Bidwills lavishly put on at Sportsman's Park, the race track at which they were principal stockholders.

In the air-conditioned luxury lounge, I spoke to the Bidwills' wives, Billy's Nancy and Stormy's Rita. Both ignored me. Meeting Bill, I quipped that I knew it was chilly, but, cripes, Nancy and Rita were chillier.

"Because," said Bill, "of what you wrote about us." I nodded. "Yeah, calling you 'athletic carpetbaggers' wasn't nice."

"No, no, because you said we weren't 'blood brothers.'" I steamed and said, firmly, "I'll be a sonofabitch, Bill. Do you, they, or Stormy think I would have mentioned the fact that you and Stormy are not related if the whole damned thing hadn't been on Page One in the past?"

In a below-the-belt attempt by stepfather Walter Wolfner to acquire the franchise, it was disclosed that, born out of wedlock to different mothers, the adopted Bidwills were not related.

"Bill," I said, simmering, "my only reason for referring to the fact that you and Stormy weren't blood brothers is because I knew there was an area of disagreement between you and where, traditionally, backed into a corner, blood brothers fight, shoulder to shoulder, you guys might not. That's the only reason I used the word 'blood.'" Mollified, Bill Bidwill said, "I'll deny this if you ever use it, but when you wrote that we were gone, we were gone!" So, happily, the football Cardinals stayed and created a scheduling jam at old Busch Stadium, because, as Harry Caray tra-la-la-ed, "The Cardinals are coming . . . the Cardinals are coming."

The Redbirds had a long way to go with 12 games to play, trailing the Phillies by six and a half. The Reds, managed by Dick Sisler, actually had a hotter stick than the Cardinals, but both clubs continued to win, while the Phillies started to lose . . . and lose . . . and lose.

Arriving in Oklahoma City to cover a Southern California-Oklahoma football game the next day, I listened to the Cardinals sweep a Friday night doubleheader at Pittsburgh, and then take three more at Forbes Field, including a victory over big, bad Bob Veale, an overpowering left-hander. Hey, maybe this nascent miracle wasn't a mirage.

Philadelphia lost three to Cincy at home and two more to the Cardinals in St. Louis. Lo! The Cards and Reds were tied for first place!

The next night, after the Cardinals' third victory over the Phillies, players and fans and press in St. Louis gathered in their homes and in the streets around the stadium to listen to a late-inning tug o' war between the Pirates and Reds. In the 16th inning, a seldom-seen young Bucco, catcher Jerry Moore, laid down a perfect squeeze bunt that beat the Reds, 1-0, and put St. Louis in first place with three games to go!

The misfit Mets, who lost 109 of 162 games, damned near kept the Cardinals from the pennant. First, lefty Al Jackson out-dueled Gibson 1-0. Happily, the same night at Cincinnati, the Phillies rallied to snap their 10-game losing streak, 4-3.

So the Cardinals still were one up with two to play, but the next afternoon, the Mets cuffed 20-game winner Ray Sadecki 15-5. While I sat in the press box, trying to sort out the situation with the race tied and a playoff possible, my female Western Union operator decided to listen to the Missouri U. football game from Columbia.

Over the years, brought up in the typewriter clackety-clack and loud-noised disorder of earlier newsrooms, I can write or edit without distraction — unless the radio or television is broadcasting a game close to my affection. Especially, when losing, which Ol' Mizzou did that day in a 10-7 upset by Oklahoma State. "Damnit, dear," I insisted, perhaps feeling the pressure of the pennant race, "Please turn that down or off."

You see, by then, the old-fashioned, cigar-gnarled dots-and-dash male-manipulated Western Union key had been replaced by women (mostly) operating teletype machines. Personally, I didn't mind, though on hot days or nights, it no longer was possible to remove your pants and work in your underwear.

On the final day at Cincinnati, Philadelphia's Jim Bunning pitched a 10-0 shutout victory over the Reds. If the Cardinals could win their game, they would win the pennant.

Curt Simmons wasn't sharp and New York jumped to a lead, but then Curt Flood, center field defensive master, climaxed a .311 season with a home run. Bill White, fulfilling his mid-season promise, finished like a whirlwind with his 21st homer and a .303 average with 102 RBIs. Capt. Ken Boyer, whose 24 homers, 119 league-leading RBIs and defensive skill won him the Most Valuable Player award, had a couple of hits. So did the brilliant Brock.

When catcher Tim McCarver raced back near the screen for a season-ending, pennant-winning catch, Gus Busch and the crowd roared approval. So the ball club that was one game under

.500 when I felt their All-Star pulse, 40-41, wound up 24 over, winning 46 of their final 77 games, a sizzling .685 pace.

Fast, aggressive catcher Tim McCarver.

I honestly didn't know whether to laugh or cry. I'd known Bing Devine from those days we hunched over like a Quasimodo duet in the sloping public-relations cubbyhole a quarter-century earlier. Ethically, he was Sir Galahad. His wisdom had built this team and now he wasn't here to enjoy his moment of rightfully earned triumph. It wasn't fair.

Arriving late for the celebration in the manager's club-house office, I winced to see Busch, Branch Rickey, and Bob Howsam fawning over Johnny Keane, whose thin smile obviously covered his true feelings.

The 1964 World Series between the Cardinals and the New York Yankees wasn't the best I ever saw, but it was good. Games three through five were a superlative center-cut.

With Mike Shannon hitting a home run, the Cardinals won the opener at St. Louis. Mel Stottlemyre beat Gibson in the second game, 8-3.

The Series shifted to New York for Game 3. Jim Bouton dueled with Curt Simmons, who was lifted for a pinch-hitter in the Redbird ninth. Mickey Mantle was the first batter reliever Barney Schultz faced when the Yankees took their turn. Schultz threw one knuckler. Mantle hit it into the upper deck of the right-field stands for his 16th Series homer, breaking the record he shared with Babe Ruth, and winning the game for Bouton, 2-1.

Next day, the Yanks knocked out young southpaw Ray Sadecki with a three-run first inning. In the Yankee fourth, Redbird reliever Roger Craig issued bases on balls to Mantle and Elston Howard. Then Dick Groat slickered Mantle by telling Mickey how silly Shannon had looked the day before, poised at the right-field wall for a 20-foot leap into the air. While Mantle was chuckling, Groat took a perfect pickoff throw from Craig.

Still, a short Series seemed to be unfolding until the Cardinals came to bat in the sixth inning. So Ken Boyer batted with the bases loaded against lefty Al Downing and lofted a high fly just inside the left-field foul pole for a grand-slam homer. As Ken touched third base on his way around the diamond, kid brother Clete, playing third for the Yankees, winked happily to him. The four runs held up for a Series-tying St. Louis victory, 4-3.

So game No. 5 was pivotal. Gibson, who struck out 12 Yankees, helped set up a two-run fifth against Stottlemyre with a single in an inning in which Richardson again errored. In the bottom of the ninth, Mantle led off and was safe on Groat's fumble. Elston Howard struck out. Pepitone drilled a pitch right at Gibson, who, typically, had wheeled around in his follow-through into an off-balance fielding position. But as Dizzy Dean used to say, "Podnuh, show me a pitcher who's got a good-fielding position, and I'll show you a pitcher who ain't followin' through."

Pepitone's liner struck the upper right side of the pitcher's butt and squirted toward third base. Wheeling in hot pursuit, Gibson collared the ball near the third-base line. Falling away, he flipped the ball across his body to Bill White at first base. Out!

Yogi and the Yankees beefed briefly with American League umpire Al Smith, but replays showed the umpire called it right. Gibson's defensive brilliance saved the day, because Tom Tresh followed with what could have been a game-winning homer to right, but, instead, merely tied the score.

Still, victory seemed fragile after Tresh's homer, but in the Cardinals' tenth, hot-hitting McCarver lofted a fly ball to deep right-center and it kept going, going, going, until it cleared the fence for a game-winning three-run homer, 5-2.

I wrote my column and hurried with Bob Burnes to board a private plane provided by Falstaff for its executives. The Falstaffian's were headed back to St. Louis by way of Baltimore, where the football Cardinals were playing a Monday night game against the Colts. Falstaff owned 10 per cent of the Big Red then.

The game was being played in Baltimore because of the Bidwills' greed. Because of the World Series conflict, the game, originally scheduled for St. Louis, could and should have been rescheduled for the end of the season in St. Louis. But the Bidwills knew the visitors' share of a 60,000 crowd at Baltimore was worth more than the home portion of 30,000 in St. Louis. So Wally Lemm's unbeaten Gridbirds lost their home field advantage against Don Shula's unbeaten Colts, led by the great Johnny Unitas. Baltimore won 47-27. Afterward, I sat with coach Wally Lemm on the team bus to the airport for the flight home. "I wished we'd put that game at the end of the season," said Lemm. "The way the Colts are playing, they could have their division clinched and wouldn't need it then."

When the World Series returned to St. Louis for Game Six, Mantle and Maris flexed their muscles with homers off Curt Simmons, giving Bouton a second win, 8-3.

In Game 7, Boyer, White and Brock unloaded off Mel Stottlemyre and Gibson breezed into the seventh with a six-run lead. Mantle tagged the wearying right-hander with two in the seventh. Keane quietly folded his arms and, as he would put it tenderly later, made "a commitment to Gibby's heart." Struggling after homers by Clete Boyer and Phil Linz in the ninth, Gibson got Bobby Richardson on an end-all pop to second-base fill-in Dal Maxvill. The first players to grab each other were Boyer and Gibson.

That night Bill White was delayed in reaching the victory party at Stan Musial and Biggie's restaurant. Months earlier Bill had promised a group of church kids he would speak to them. He showed up and fulfilled his responsibilities before leaving for the rousing celebration.

At the party, Jack Buck, a standup guy with the skills to be a standup comedian as well as a sit-down broadcaster, risked his own future with Busch by acclaiming Bing Devine. Covering for the *Post-Dispatch*, Ed Wilks bitingly criticized the brewery because Devine was gone.

Next day, preparing for a football trip, I skipped what seemed a routine press conference at which Busch planned a new contract for Keane. But Johnny was displeased with Devine's dismissal and disgusted by Howsam's unavailability when the new general manager thought Keane was persona non grata with Busch. The manager jolted the sports nation. He said NO!

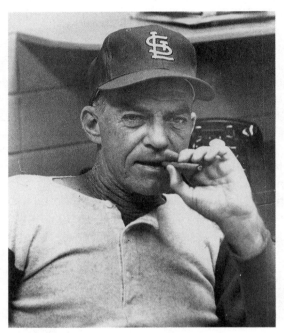

Redbirds boss Johnny Keane in '64.

Soon after the Series, President Lyndon B. Johnson came to town to name Stan Musial as national director of physical fitness. "Physical fatness," Stan the Man quipped, and then insisted, with a bow of respect for Lou Brock, "The Cardinals couldn't have won with me in left field."

On the football field, Ol' Mizzou had a "bad" year for a Devine-coached team (6-3-1). But the brothers Broeg—Freddie and I— were able to repay a debt to our social fraternity, Sigma Phi Epsilon, by replacing athletic trophies that had disappeared during World War II.

Bob and Fred Broeg—double brothers.

The Football Cardinals produced a brilliant 9-3-2 year. Even though the Big Red beat the Browns in a 28-19 game at old Busch Stadium, Cleveland finished a half-game ahead. So St. Louis settled for a 24-17 victory over Vince Lombardi's Green Bay Packers in the Playoff Bowl.

You didn't hold cheaply *any* victory over a team coached by the growling, toothy martinet, Lombardi, but, still, if it hadn't been for Bidwill's greed, there might have been two major world championships won by St. Louis teams in 1964.

39

Following the 1964 season, I wrote an article describing Mahatma Rickey as the "power behind the throne, Branch Richelieu."

Amadee Wohlschlaeger, the *Post-Dispatch*'s long-time, gifted sports illustrator, caricaturized a berobed Gussie Busch sitting in a regal chair with Rickey whispering over his shoulder. Amadee added a Rickey cartoon thought balloon depicting a miniature guillotine and a head-catching basket.

My article described B.R.'s role in Bing Devine's abrupt and unpopular dismissal. Further, aided by inside information, I detailed Rickey's August memo suggesting the Cardinals bail out of the 1964 pennant chase and build for the future by stripping their roster of players like Mike Shannon and Julian Javier.

Fortunately, for the Cardinals and their followers, Rickey's recommendations were not carried out. Unfortunately for Rickey, Busch received the blame for firing Devine.

Busch was not pleased. A few days after the *P-D* ran my story, "senior consultant" Rickey was fired and, in a separate move, Red Schoendienst was named manager. Stan Musial, listed as senior vice-president, suggested Schoendienst would last a long time.

"Like Walter Alston," said Stan the Man.

I'd always been able to talk (and joke) with Gus Busch. Like the time I quit drinking beer and there was a brief dip in A-B sales. "Jezzus, pal," rasped Busch, "I knew you drank a lot, but not *that* much."

Confident in our ability to communicate, I approached Busch when departing from the annual spring-training party at the brewery's Swiss Chalet in Tampa — a happy celebration that combined Gussie's birthday, his wedding anniversary to Trudi, and a spring pow-wow of the company's and ball club's directors.

With the head table virtually empty and many emptying out with waved or cheerful good-nights, Gus and I sat cheek to jowl.

After congratulating him again in the storybook championship, I suggested he wouldn't have fired Bing Devine if he had known that there had been no disloyalty toward the boss by either the former general manager or field manager Johnny Keane when neither mentioned the temporary showdown with Dick Groat.

Busch shook his head. Yes, he would have made the same decision. Like two school kids, we sat there. I asked a second time. Again, he said no.

Insistent, I tried once more.

Busch leaned closer and smiled, "You're right pal. I wouldn't have done it."

We shook hands.

As a newspaperman, I think I'm entitled to only one epitaph, to wit:

"He was just."

I hope I was just with Wesley Branch Rickey, a most remarkable man whose inspirational religious method did justice to John Wesley.

If Rickey had run, I'm sure he could have been elected governor during the twenties or thirties. And if he had chosen to use his law degree in the courtroom, I daresay he was sufficiently mentally nimble and oratorical to work either side of the famed Scopes monkey trial.

But the Ohio farm boy loved sports, especially baseball, reaching the majors briefly as a big leaguer after attending Ohio Wesleyan and earning his law degree at Michigan. Coaching the Michigan baseball team, Rickey uncovered his greatest athletic treasure — George Sisler.

For years, Rickey to Sisler was always "Coach," and later always "Mr. Rickey." Sisler developed into one of the greatest all-around players ever, a slick-fielding first baseman, twice author of .400-plus batting averages and the man who still had the most hits in a season — 257 in only 154 games.

The Rickey-Sisler mutual admiration society reached a climax when both men were inducted into the Missouri Sports

Hall of Fame at a dinner after the University of Missouri's football game with Oklahoma, late in November, 1965.

At Ol' Mizzou, Dan Devine had upgraded Tiger football at a propitious time. After all, pro football came to St. Louis in 1960 and Kansas City in 1963. If the Black and Gold hadn't been leaving their foes black and blue, a fair share of the sports dollar would not have found its way to Columbia.

A hard-nosed, soft-spoken devotee of rock 'em, sock 'em football and a self-styled "fussbudget" who insisted that his teams block downfield, pursue defensively, and practice with precision, Devine's "poorest" season was 6-3-1. The 1965 team was 8-2-1.

Tiger excitement in Columbia lured Branch Rickey to the ceremonies marking his induction into the state sports Hall of Fame. Honestly, many of us thought he should pass because of illness, though his absence would have greatly disappointed the few hundred people crowded into the Daniel Boone Hotel's private dining room.

The two other inductees were Sisler and the late J.G. Taylor Spink. Sisler wasn't much of a speaker, and Spink was dead. But even if Clarence Darrow and William Jennings Bryan had been scheduled to speak, Rickey would have remained the prime attraction.

Aware he was hospitalized, we had written Rickey off, but, stubbornly, he insisted on making the 125-mile trip to Columbia from St. Louis.

Because the day was colder than usual, we urged him to rest up in the hotel instead of attending the football game. A favorite Rickey philosophy — "Luck is the residue of design" — helped explain Missouri's 30-0 rout of Oklahoma for a Sugar Bowl bid. Rickey watched every minute and then, still disdaining rest, visited with friends at the hotel before the induction dinner.

As usual, I was the last man out at the press box. Groping through the dark outside Faurot Field, typewriter in one hand and knapsack in the other, I misstepped and slid sideways down an embankment.

Though I was not aware of any design, I was lucky. I landed unhurt, amused at having another gaffe to gab about.

After a hand-washing pit stop, I arrived after the dinner began. I noted Mr. Rickey at the head table, seated with Sisler and Spink's son, Johnson. When I reached Mr. Rickey, he scowled, understandably, and when I expressed concern about his having flouted medical advice by coming, he snapped, "You didn't think I wouldn't come, did you?"

When it came time for the anchor presentation, the old spellbinder rose and saluted the Missouri team and Devine, who had dropped in to shake the award winners' hands.

The "Mahatma," Branch Rickey, late in life.

Rickey rose and began to speak: "I wanted to come to be with immortals, because of George and Taylor. You can be modest and say you don't deserve it, and, frequently, people don't. But you like it, anyway."

Then B.R. hailed "the intangibles that the sports immortals have," and rhetorically asked: "What is intangible? You saw it today on the football field. Guts! Courage, they call it in literature."

Rickey defined three kinds of courage — physical, mental, and spiritual. He described the physical by telling about Jim Bottomley winning an important game by sliding on the "wrong" side and re-ripping a painful, oozing thigh "strawberry."

As he began to expound on spiritual courage, he suddenly halted, staggered back a step from the microphone and said his final words:

"I don't believe I can continue. . ."

When he collapsed, I suspect only the across-the-street proximity of the Columbia fire department and the presence of Dr. D.M. Nigro kept him from dying right there.

Weeks later, death lifted Mr. Rickey from the ensuing coma. In effect, he died as he lived, speaking inspirationally to a crowd he held in the palm of his hand.

Branch Rickey's collapse came the night my lavish review of his autobiography — Simon and Schuster's "The American Diamond" appeared in the *Post-Dispatch*.

Maybe if Mr. Rickey had seen it, he might have had a fonder last memory of the ticket-taking kid whose career he had helped launch decades earlier.

40

⁊&

I didn't like Bob Howsam for two good reasons.

The burly big guy tried to take some credit for winning the 1964 pennant, rather than suggesting, "Hey, I've got a tough act to follow, don't I?"

And Howsam fired many loyal people in the organization — including the long-time press-gate operator and a hard-working, middle-aged female cook in the press area.

For his second full season in 1966, Howsam moved rapidly, dealing off three-fourths of the championship infield — Ken Boyer, Dick Groat, and Bill White.

White's loss hurt the worst. Groat had gone over the hill, athletically, and Boyer had been bothered by a bad back.

Still, when I noted as part of the deal with New York that the Cardinals had acquired "a plumber named Charley Smith" to play third base, only inferentially questioning his ability, Managing Editor Art Bertelson thought I'd been nasty. But he joined me in a laugh when I pointed out that even if Smith didn't play third base like a plumber, he really was one — and had a union card to prove it!

White bristled at Howsam's oblique suggestions that he was older than his advertised 32. Bill helped the third-place Phillies finish three notches higher than the Cardinals. He drove in 103 runs with 22 homers, but shredded an Achilles tendon.

Bob Uecker also left St. Louis for Philadelphia in the White trade. I missed having him around, but one Uecker moment I didn't miss was probably his greatest playing-field gaffe.

The Giants were batting in a game at St. Louis, game tied in the tenth, bases loaded, one out. The Cardinals had positioned their infield halfway, hopeful for a sharply-hit infield grounder that might be turned into a double play, yet able to go to the plate if the twin killing seemed unlikely.

Alvin Dark grounded sharply to Julian Javier. The masterful second baseman had a double-play in sight, but juggled the ball long enough to make him question whether he could get two. So Hoolie fired home.

Trouble was, Uecker had left the plate and was racing down toward first base, hustling to back up a potential play.   Ball, runner, and — umpire — met at home plate.   The winning run scored.

When I groaned aloud that I'd never seen that play in 40 years of watching baseball, Giants super-scout Tom Sheehan cracked, "And how many times have you seen a catcher whose name began with 'U'"?

A sense of humor would have helped one of Howsam's acquisitions, Alex Johnson. He was the most indolent outfielder I ever saw but was as fast as Rogers Hornsby, Ken Boyer, or Mickey Mantle going from the batter's box to first base.

After writing a spring-training piece critical of Johnson from St. Petersburg, I received the paper a couple of days later and put the clipping in Alex's locker. He amazed me with a response I seldom received from players. He shrugged, said, "you wrote it, I read it" and walked away.

Once Bob Gibson stumbled over Johnson's foot on a bus ride and apologized. Johnson pointed to his foot and said, "You don't have to apologize to me, 'cause that's who gonna kick yo' ass."   If there had been a fight between Johnson and Gibson, I gladly would have paid to see it.

Howsam had to be prodded hard into making two meaningful deals, acquiring Roger Maris to play right field after Mike Shannon proved he could play third base, and Orlando Cepeda to play first.

At San Fran, "Orlanda," as Willie Mays called him in a high-pitched voice, was a devastating right-handed hitter, a fast runner, and a good fielder. But Willie McCovey was also a Giants first baseman and Cepeda had become expendable after falling into manager Herman Franks' doghouse.

With Dick Meyer and Gus Busch prodding him, Howsam hemmed and hawed, trying to milk something extra from the Giants. Meanwhile, our grapevine indicated at least one other team was closing in on a deal for Cepeda.

Herman Franks was amenable to helping old friend Leo Durocher, now managing the Cubs. But Leo, like Howsam, wanted to get a little extra to sweeten the pot. Horace Stoneham resisted and so did his astute nephew Chub Feeney.

Here, I pulled a dirty trick. Bing Devine was in town, serving now as George Weiss's right-hand man, preparatory to taking over the Mets presidency. I asked him if he'd make a Ray Sadecki-for-Cepeda deal.

"Sure," he said, "off the record."

Off-the-record, my elbow. I felt that a quote from Devine might tip the scales for the deal. So I wrote it that way.

That same day, prior to the final game played at Sportsman's Park, with the Giants clobbering the Cardinals, Redbird team surgeon Dr. I.C. Middleman checked out Cepeda's damaged knee as OK.

Howsam pulled the trigger and the deal was done. Cepeda, fleet though limping, hit.303 with 17 homers, despite the larger park.

With Gibson winning 21 games, the only strange thing in the second subpar season was that a big young left-hander named Larry Jasters had a remarkable five straight *shutouts* over pennant-winning Los Angeles.

Jaster's ways and means were duly noted by the American League pennant winners, the Baltimore Orioles, and their energetic super-scout, Jim Russo.

For the Dodgers' second straight pennant, though they had pretty good pitching overall, L.A. owed it all to the guy who put the capital "K" in strikeout — Sandy Koufax.

Koufax was absolutely incredible in 1965, 26-8 with a 2.04 earned-run average and in 1966, Sandy went 27-9 with a spectacular 1.73 ERA.

Just think: 53-17 those last two years despite a pinching circulatory problem in his left hand and elbow arthritis so bad he was forced to bend far to his left to shave.

I was more than sorrowful when Sandy had to pitch the last day of the season to help the Dodgers win the pennant. As a result, he was tired and the Dodgers were too, when they ran up against the youthful, strong-armed Orioles.

The 1966 World Series was awful and one-sided. The weary Dodgers, fed fast balls by scout Russo's interpretation of Jaster's success, scored only two runs in four games.

For Hank Bauer's O's, the Robinsons, Frank and Brooks, were aces in the pennant surge of the old St. Louis Browns. Brooksie drove in 100 runs, giving evidence of the best-ever defensively at third base, and F. Robby, acquired from Cincinnati, was even more spectacular. He won the Triple Crown — .316, 49, 122.

Two Hall of Famers, pitchers Sandy Koufax (left) and Jim Palmer.

After the Series sweep, hard-losing Warren Giles, National League president, grumped that he didn't want to see any more sales of superstars to the American League.

For the Orioles, I was most impressed by handsome young Jim Palmer's potential, a Hall of Famer, and was delighted that Moe Drabowsky had one of the outstanding relief efforts in World Series play. Taking over from staggering Dave McNally in the third inning of the opener at L.A., with the Orioles ahead, 4-2, the big right-hander worked six and a third innings, allowing only one hit, walking two and, incredibly, striking out 11.

When I think of Drabowsky, I think of his fellow Pole Stan Musial, which, in this instance, reminds me of a dramatic phone call from Al Fleishman.

"Are you seated?" Al asked, and then went on to tell me that Bob Howsam had left the Cardinals for Cincinnati. Fleishman also had one more bit of news that can wait for four paragraphs.

I wrote a smart-alecky column that began: "Bob Howsam, an old bee-keeper from Colorado, is the kind of guy who could fall into an apiary and come out, unstung, clutching a jar of honey.

"Close to being fired, Howsam had left insecurity and $33,000 a year for a three-year contract at $50,000 per and, if reports are true, a piece of the action at Cincinnati."

I did salute Bob for the "Straight-A" program he began with the *Post-Dispatch*, honoring topflight students with free tickets, a reward for scholarship the Redbirds and newspaper still embrace.

What was Fleishman's second news flash?

Simply this: Howsam's successor as general manager was Stan Musial.

I swore in anger. You can't do that to Stan the Man or the ball club. Musial hasn't been trained in the technicalities of front office operation.

Oh, Fleishman understood, but Big Eagle Busch and right-bower Dick Meyer had solved that. They had named Bob Stewart as Stan's assistant.

Bob Stewart! I doubled my profanity. Why, the former St. Louis University athletic director might know the intricacies of the NCAA, but not the administrative ways and means of major league baseball.

I shouldn't have worried. With intelligent public-relations man Jim Toomey nosey enough to know the rule book, and the unselfish assistance of Bing Devine, a phone call away in New York, Musial was well-armed.

41

ও

By now, I should have known not to underestimate Stan
Musial. Though far from the stereotype of a successful general
manager, Musial used his strengths wisely in 1967. The players
enjoyed having him around. His greatness was a constant
inspiration. His back-slapping, hands-on leadership worked.

And, of course, Musial had to make only one roster change,
grabbing Jack Lamabe as an extra man for the bullpen after Bob
Gibson was injured.

Gibson and the Giants' Juan Marichal had replaced retired
Sandy Koufax as the National League's best pitchers.

Or should I say Gibson.

With the Cardinals winning their first six games, Rapid
Robert twice beat Marichal. Thereafter the Giants saw to it that
there were no more confrontations. Too bad. It could have been
like Dean-Hubbell, Feller-Newhouser, Spahn-Roberts.

With no regard for grammar, coach Joe Schultz, who had
managed in Caribbean winter leagues, hung the nickname "El
Birdos" on the 1967 Cardinals. Orlando Cepeda popularized the
phrase and became the team's emotional anchor.

1967 National League MVP,
Orlando Cepeda.

Orlando did more than cheerlead. He won the National League Most Valuable Player award, hitting .325 with 25 homers and a league-leading 111 RBIs.

Watching him hit long line drives to right-center and left-center in the large ball park, I wondered what might have happened if Herman Franks had been able to deliver him to friend Leo Durocher. "At Chicago," said Cepeda, smiling, "I think I hit *feefty* home runs." I agreed.

Maturing stars — Gibson, Lou Brock, Curt Flood, and Tim McCarver — made "El Birdos" a winning team that made few mistakes.

With 101 victories, El Birdos had five pitchers with win totals in double figures, including Ray Washburn, who might have become one of the best pitchers ever, if not for injury.

The Cardinals brought Steve Carlton up from the minors to pitch the exhibition Hall of Fame game at Cooperstown, New York. I had the opportunity beforehand to watch the induction there of my old friend, Casey Stengel, and the superstar who would become a good friend, Ted Williams.

Williams outclassed even Casey with the best acceptance speech I've ever heard at Cooperstown. His insightful comments about the barrier that kept Afro-Americans like Satchel Paige, Josh Gibson, and others out of the Hall of Fame did the most to eliminate the color line for the athletic ancient.

Though I had always respected Ted's desire to be left alone, after his speech I sought him out. It turned out that Williams enjoyed sparking bull-sessions in which he would ask direct questions, such as, "Who was the better pitcher, Dizzy Dean or Bob Gibson?"

My answer? Gibson. He was certainly the toughest.

En route with my wife to Anaheim for a look-see at Disneyland before the 1967 All-Star game, I missed a playing-field rarity, a real fight, not the typical dainty diamond schoolgirl hair-tugging.

After Cincinnati's Don Nottebart threw at Lou Brock, Gibson retaliated the next time the Reds came to bat by buzzing a pitch past Tony Perez's head. The Reds' young slugging first baseman flied out on Gibson's next offering and, peeling off near the mound, made an ugly comment.

Gibson, and this is redundant, didn't back down.

Cepeda charged over from first base to be a peacemaker. Putting two and two together and getting five, a giant Redleg reliever nicknamed "Man Mountain" — Bob Lee — charged in from the bullpen, shouting that he was going to punch the "fuck" out of Cepeda.

Cepeda cold-cocked Man Mountain with a one-punch knockout. Afterward . . . well, Gibson went to work against young Pete Rose and Tommy Helms and Perez.

Broadcaster Jack Buck reminisced: "There was Gibson in the Reds' dugout visibly manhandling about three Reds and tossing them bodily out of the dugout onto the field. That was just a sample of something you saw from Gibson every time he went out there. He was the toughest athlete mentally I ever saw, and the greatest competitor."

In Ken Burns' blockbuster *Baseball* book, an oblique reference was made that Frank Robinson was the fiercest competitor. Hell, I can remember when Frank slid too vigorously into the Braves' Eddie Mathews. Eddie knocked F. Robby onto his southern exposure.

En route back to St. Louis after watching Perez hit a homer in the 15th to give the National League a 2-1 All-Star victory, Dorothy and I stopped off for a couple of nights in the Las Vegas' show-business strip.

I'm a damned hard loser to spend too much gambling and too dumb to understand the odds. Dorth set a record, though. She found a dime, put it in a Vegas slot machine and won $1.40.

We stayed at Caesar's Palace, where friend Jimmy Snyder was P.R. man. The Greek arranged tickets for shows we wanted to see. After an early dinner performance, I entered the main lobby of the Stardust and glanced at the giant blackboard featuring odds on the pennant races.

Under the name of St. Louis's starting pitcher that day, Bob Gibson, a chalkmaker added an underlined word: "H-u-r-t."

At that moment, another man walked over to a list of printed odds and changed the figures, lowering the chances of the Cardinals' retaining their league lead.

Two shows and several hours later, after a post-midnight snack in the Palace's 'round-the-clock coffee shop, we reached the elevators and met a familiar face and friend.

"I see your club has just lost your Big Guy," said Joe DiMaggio.

Struck savagely on the right shin by a line drive off the bat of Roberto Clemente, Gibson got up, walked one batter, retired the next on a pop fly and then, reaching back for something extra on a full-count pitch, simply collapsed. The fibula bone, already broken, snapped above the ankle.

Slick-fielding Dal Maxvill called Gibson's "pitching to three hitters with a broken leg" the most extraordinary thing he ever saw.

For the Cardinals, happily, a chunky, guitar-playing young right-hander, Nelson Kelley "Nellie" Briles, rose to the occasion. A 4-15 pitcher in 1966, Briles went 14-5 in 1967 with *nine* in a row when Gibson was hors d' combat.

"But not," said Briles, "before Gibson chewed me out about trying to strike out too many hitters, which prompted me to groove the ball too often to the guys who don't strike out — the good hitters!"

Gibson came back in early September, pitched five innings in one game, seven in another and when he went all the way in the pennant-clinching game against Philadelphia, giving the Redbirds a 10-game pennant-winning cakewalk margin and a World Series rendezvous with the Boston Red Sox, Red Schoendienst's Series pitching pattern was set.

Boston had won the AL title despite being 100-to-1 underdogs. Carl Yastrzemski had a career season, and pitcher Jim Lonborg was outstanding, winning 22. The Great Yaz won a Triple Crown with .326, 44 homers, and 131 RBIs.

Happy for owner Tom Yawkey and manager Dick Williams, I celebrated my return to Boston uniquely. Thumbing the papers that final Sunday, I saw that Gig Young, a comedic leading man like Charles Grodin now, was playing at the Colonial, the downtown legitimate theatre. Could I get a ticket?

I could, yeah, and enjoyed the show. Awash with sentiment with my love-hate relationship for my 13 months in what really amounted to the AP's penal colony, I decided on a late night walk from Boylston and Tremont, the southeast corner of the famed Boston Common.

I walked up to the Parker House, angled down narrow, winding Washington Street, site of the old *Boston Globe* building in which I'd worked. It was gone.

Then to Scollay Square to see the burlesque house and famous Joe and Nemo's hot dog stand. Gone, gone.

I trudged up Joy Street to Beacon Hill. Then, with a fond look at Louisburg Square, the historic high-rent district close by my old housing horror, the Beacon Chambers, I slanted past Massachusetts' sturdy State House and angled through the Common to the Park Street subway station, where I grabbed a subway back out to Kenmore Square.

Next night at the hospitality gathering of the media and other free-loaders, I mentioned my midnight meandering to Boston sports writers. They thought I was nuts to walk at night in their city. But memory lane is always a happy stroll for me.

The Bosox were handicapped by not having a rested Lonborg to start the Series. Williams almost got away with one because Jose Santiago, moved up in the rotation, pitched effectively and hit a home run off the great Gibson. But Gibby allowed only five other hits, struck out 10, and Brock was "4 for 4" with two stolen bases.

Yet it was the professional craftsmanship of the former Yankee slugger Maris that enabled the Cardinals to win Game One. A weak wrist kept Rog from frequently hitting the long ball, but he knew what to do with a runner on third and the infield back. Twice, he pulled grounders to his right. His RBIs won the game, 2-1.

Lonborg allowed only one hit in Game Two, a double by Julian Javier. Yastrzemski hit two home runs, and Boston walked over El Birdos, 5-0.

Back in St. Louis for the third game, the Cardinals faced a crisis of another sort. Generous general manager Stan Musial had sold more tickets than Busch Stadium had seats.

Only the quick wit of a young assistant ticket manager, Mike Bertami, saved the day. Mike and top management convinced the St. Louis fire marshal that the Busch Stadium aisles were wide enough to provide room in each for a single folding chair. So the 54,575 overflow crowd was safely shoehorned into the ballpark.

They saw Briles come through in Game Three as he had when Gibson was hurt in July. Brock led off against Gary Bell with a triple to set up one run and beat out a bunt and drew a two-base wild pickoff throw for another and the Cardinals prevailed, 5-2.

Gibby put the Cardinals one game away from the title with

a 6-0 six-hit shutout over Santiago. Jose was victimized by Brock, per usual, and by Maris, who smacked a two-run double.

Lonborg's artistry and lanky lefty Carlton's inability to handle a ball hit back through the pitcher's box permitted the Sox to prevail in a 3-1 game that sent the Series back to Fenway Park. After two outings and 18 innings, the Cardinals had only three hits off Lonborg, one of which was a ninth-inning homer by Maris that prevented a second shutout.

When the scene shifted back to Boston, the Sox outslugged the Cardinals, 8-4. Rico Petrocelli hit two home runs, Yaz added one, and rookie Reggie Smith another. Brock hit one for the Cardinals.

The Series was tied three games to three, and that meant one more night in a motel because the Somerset Hotel, within walking distance of Fenway, wasn't available to the Cardinals.

The motel was in Quincy — pronounced "Quinzy" in New England. Boston is balkanized with mini-municipalities even more than St. Louis. Obviously, the motel folks there had never had so many mouths to feed at once.

Because of my ulcer, I had become a finicky eater. Daily I drank carrot juice because of a tummy-soothing breakfast tip from Jolly Cholly Grimm.

I ate early and simply, squirreling cookies into my ball park knapsack because press box hot dogs and fried hamburgers were a no-no. But my service was slow, and the later-arriving ballplayers faced their own troubles.

As the bus to Fenway Park was about to pull out, Gibson steamed aboard, angry and hungry. He had been pointedly bypassed in the dining room. Belatedly, he had been brought burnt toast. He stomped out empty and growling.

I fretted. Although he would work Game Seven with one day more rest than Lonborg — three compared with two — how far could he go on an empty tank?

As the bus approached Fenway, I spotted an oasis with a Hayes-Bickford cafeteria and ordered the driver to stop. Typewriter and knapsack in hand, I jumped off, rushed in and ordered two ham-and-egg sandwiches to go. Then I hailed a cab for the short haul to Jersey Street. When I got to the park, I went to the closed clubhouse and gave the sandwiches to Butch Yatkeman to relay to Gibson.

To the annoyance of Gibson and everyone else in the clubhouse, Dick Williams had been headlined in the tabloid *Boston Record-American* as saying about Game Seven, "LONBORG AND CHAMPAGNE."

Poor Jim never tasted the bubbly. He gave up two runs in the third, an inning light-hitting Dal Maxvill led off with a triple, and served up a homer to Gibson before Javier added the clincher with a three-run shot in the seventh.

Watching Gibson hang on to a six-run lead, I crowed to *Post-Dispatch* colleagues in the press box that Gibby got 'em for seven and my eggs got 'em in the eighth and my ham in the ninth.

By the time Gibson rared back and fanned George Scott, who had publicly jived that "Gibson would go in five," the great pitcher had fanned a record 26 in 27 World Series innings, allowing just 14 hits and three runs.

Sport Magazine, then giving away a sports car annually to the Series Most Valuable Player, handed the keys to Gibson. Brock, having hit .414, with four extra-base hits among 12 and a Series-tying seven stolen bases, wasn't even offered a free ride. That is, until Bob Hyland, KMOX's civic-minded, baseball-buff boss, told True-Blue Lou to pick out a car, too.

Brock chose a Cadillac El Dorado. If Hyland was secretly hoping Lou would opt for a used VW Bug, he never mentioned it.

I'd taken some "credit" for Gibson's success, but upon entering the clubhouse, I saw him washing down one of my ham-and-egg sandwiches with champagne. Grinning, he said one pre-game sandwich had been sufficient.

I've written about athletes' pre-game eating habits often. Back in my undergraduate days, Paul Christman couldn't eat at all before a game. John Kadlec upchucked after eating sauerkraut and spareribs before his first game as a freshman at St. Louis U.

Another time involved Gibson himself. Though reporters weren't supposed to disturb Bob on a day he was pitching, I approached him anyway and asked how he'd prepared to pitch in the unusual May heat.

Oh, he said, he'd run a little bit before the game the night before — didn't like to run — and had gone to his hotel, relaxed over a glass of wine and a Caesar salad. And for breakfast, Gib? Oh, prune juice and a pot of coffee and —.

"Hey, when did you last *really* eat?"

Gibson looked at the clock. "Oh, about this time yesterday afternoon I had a sandwich."

I arched a brow. "So for 24 hours you've really had only a Caesar salad and prune juice?" He nodded.

I watched with extra interest as Gibson then struck out 15 Cincinnati players. I wrote a column about his pre-game routine.

When I saw him two nights' later he stormed up to me in mock anger and shouted, "You misquoted me."

I bristled. "I don't *misquote* people!"

Slowly, Gibson spelled out, "I told you that Sunday morning I had prune juice, a pot of coffee" and, grinning, "a good . . ."

The word he used rhymed with what Bob Gibson rarely allowed — a hit.

Cardinals pitcher Bob Gibson celebrates after winning the '67 World Series.

42

If my Pop had the wealth to go with his kind nature, I like to think he would have bought me a personal "toy," as Sidney Salomon Jr. did for his son, Sid the Third.

I would have wanted a big league baseball club even—ugh, the lowly Browns— but Sonny Salomon wanted a hockey team.

Sid Jr., plays happy follow-the-leader to son Sid III in golf, too.

Thus St. Louis gave birth to the Blues on blades.

The '67 Cardinals and St. Louis press corps returned home from Game Seven in Boston too late for the Blues' opening game, attended by a crowd of 11,339, including U.S. Senator Stuart C. Symington, radio legend Arthur Godfrey, singer Ann Maria Alberghetti, and Guy Lombardo and his Royal Canadians. The Blues battled to a 2-2 tie with the Minnesota North Stars.

The game was played in The Arena because the Salomons were willing to spend the money — and time — to turn the old pig sty into a pink palace. It was The Arena, after all, which, more than anything else, brought the Blues to St. Louis.

The National Hockey League, a tight six-city circuit since the Depression Thirties, decided in 1965 to double in size. Twenty-four groups representing 12 cities bid to pay $2 million each to join Montreal, Toronto, New York, Boston, Detroit, and Chicago.

Within a year's time, five cities were admitted — Los Angeles, Minneapolis-St. Paul, Pittsburgh, Philadelphia, and Oakland. St. Louis, Vancouver, Buffalo, Baltimore, and others were competing for the sixth franchise.

The consensus was to bet all your crabcakes on Baltimore, which was building a downtown Civic Center where hockey would fit better than a goalie's glove.

But, wait, Blackhawks owner Arthur Wirtz had a St. Louis "barn" to unload.

I always referred to The Arena as "an old dirigible hangar," unaware for a time that a German architect who built Zeppelin sky ships had designed the building. The Arena was not finished when Depression economics forced out its financial backers.

Times were so bad, the multi-million dollar building was available for $250,000. St. Louis University was offered it as a gift, but passed because the institution figured it couldn't handle the upkeep.

Gradually, over the years, fewer and fewer events were held in the decaying building. Wirtz and his Detroit neighbor, Jim Norris, acted as if The Arena's operational losses could offset profits from their Chicago Stadium and Detroit Olympia. Their representative in St. Louis, Emory Jones, came across to me as a wily Scrooge who seemed to protect his bosses' interests by keeping events out of their building, and, therefore, out of St. Louis.

A classic case occurred when St. Louis U. athletic director Bob Stewart actively sought to host the Final Four. When NCAA officials walked through the building and saw cats and mice playing tag on mounds of dirt and lumber under the stands, they quickly declined to show any further interest.

This dusty, dying building, rocked by a 1959 tornado that tore off one of its twin spires suddenly was offered (ahem!) to Salomon for $4 million plus $2 million if he and St. Louis wanted the sixth NHL franchise.

Salomon, Chicago born, was a long-time sportsminded St. Louis citizen, a crackerjack insurance salesman, and a prominent Democratic politician. He had enjoyed brief stock ventures with the baseball Cardinals and Browns. Now he purchased The Arena and, with it, the sixth franchise.

The city didn't know whether to be impressed more by what he did to put together a winning hockey club or his refurbishing of The Arena.

The Arena was given a general sprucing. More seats were added, raising the capacity to 18,000. Escalators brought premium-paying spectators to an attractive private club where the cats and rats used to play. Everything the Salomons did had the purpose of building a winning hockey team. They overpaid players and indulged them with gifts and expensive trips, including an annual familial team vacation at the Sids' Florida resort. Their Blues were given every schedule priority, unlike most cities where the team often takes a hike so other profitable events can be booked.

I never pretended to be a hockey "expert," but I did know enough to salute Sid Salomon Jr. for picking a name from the signature song written by largely unappreciated W. C. Handy.

Heck, the couple of times I was on skates, I took more pratfalls than when I tiptoed onto the frozen Grand Lagoon beneath Forest Park's Art Hill for the 1931 Silver Skates. Yep, ice thick enough to handle thousands and to permit the newly christened Flyers, using railroad ties as side boards, to play a short intra-squad scrimmage.

Over the years as a kid, I saw the Flyers now and then, but not until I was an adult did I get acquainted with witty Shrimp McPherson at brother Freddie Broeg's Chevrolet agency, and also the lean, noble, quiet captain of those early championship minor league years, Leo Carbol.

I remember fondly the golden beginning of the Blues because of the Salomons' efforts, the early roster efforts of Lynn Patrick, and the coaching of Scotty Bowman, a talent and friend I still respect.

The Salomons were willing to pay older players like Glenn Hall, Jacques Plante, Dickie Moore, and Doug Harvey to play a little longer and, at the same time, help motivate younger talent. If it hadn't been for expansion, the likes of Al Arbour, Barclay Plager, Bob Plager, Noel Picard, and others wouldn't have had their big league chance. That would have been a frozen-faced shame.

Patrick steered the early player choices, leading off with "Mr. Goalie," Hall, the Black Hawks' venerable veteran, and set a winning tone. By his own choice, Patrick soon turned over the coaching toga to a young assistant he had brought along, Scotty Bowman.

That first year, the Blues waffled in the new cities division until a late January rally from three goals down earned them a victory over the New York Rangers, 4-3.

A large crowd watched that game. Their emotional response was contagious. Soon a Blues' game was almost an "in" thing socially, prompting women, particularly, to come out dressed as if for a night on the town.

The Blues finished the regular season third behind expansion champion Philadelphia and drew Philly in the first round. The seventh-game clincher stands out because it reminded me of a pro basketball game 20 years earlier—also at Philadelphia—when coach Ken Loeffler slowed down the ball to upset the Warriors.

The day before the game, Bowman told me, "I hope Kansas City loses. I'd like to have Harvey in the lineup."

Doug Harvey had been one of the game's best defensemen at Montreal. Now, he was player/coaching the Blues' KayCee farm club, and, as Bowman suggested with a wistful smile, a Kansas City play-off defeat Saturday night could make Harvey available.

Kansas City lost, and Harvey caught a plane to Philadelphia. The chunky veteran took charge of the game. As a hockey green pea, I was flabbergasted at his domination. Harvey skated slowly and authoritatively, stick handling with skill.

St. Louis held a one-goal lead into the final minute. Philadelphia pulled its goalie and had a six-player-to-five edge at a midcourt face-off.

For the Blues, Gordon (Red) Berenson won the face-off and slid the puck half the length of the rink for a bull's-eye biscuit in the basket. Final: St. Louis, 3, Philadelphia, 1.

That set up a western final with Minnesota. Blues goalie Glenn Hall was at his best. I always marveled at the difference between the chunky, flopping Hall and another gifted guardian of the goal, Jacques Plante, who played a standup, roving game exciting to a crowd unaccustomed to that style or Monsieur Jacques' other innovation, the face mask.

Hall was a witty, quiet, low-keyed man, who had to endure a series of dry heaves shortly before every game. I never heard

Mr. Goalie's retching, but I learned about it from teammates speaking with sober compassion, not amusement.

Minnesota's Cesare Maniago was magnifico in goal, dueling Hall in a seven-game shootout decided in a tense double overtime finale ended on a goal by St. Louis's Ron Shock.

I regard the celebratory hullabaloo in the Blues' dressing room one of the most spontaneous and heartfelt I ever encountered. Yeah, the first was the best in many ways.

We were all overjoyed that the Blues, a first-year expansion team, had made the Stanley Cup finals. Before I get too carried away, I guess it is important (and just) to note that every team in their division was a first-year expansion team. One had to make the finals.

I can still see the joy in Lynn Patrick's bulging eyes and grinning red face that the "one" was St. Louis.

Sure, the Bluenotes lost their Stanley Cup opportunity to heavily favored Montreal by a goal a game. Two of their losses were in overtime. But Hall was so brilliant that the Connie Smythe Trophy as the finals' Most Valuable Player went to him, even though he was the losing goalie!

43

ও

Biggie Garagnani had a fatal heart attack in 1968, and restaurant partner Stan Musial thought he ought to spend more time with the business. So the Cardinals needed another general manager.

Musial left the Redbirds' front office with an impeccable record — one world championship in one year. Who should replace him? Gosh, I wished Bing Devine were available.

Would Der Bingle want to come back? At New York, he had maneuvered successfully to sign Tom Seaver, acquired a defensive master and leader, catcher Jerry Grote, and adroitly arranged for the return of Brooklyn favorite Gil Hodges as manager.

Stan Musial at the statue dedication in 1968.

The Mets were A-1 to their new president Devine, whose wife, Mary, balked at taking their three daughters out of school in St. Louis. The club put up Devine at the Hilton Hotel on Sixth Avenue and paid for his frequent plane trips back to St. Louis.

When Dick Meyer tried to persuade Bing to return to St. Louis, the Mets countered by offering Devine more money and a piece of the action. Bing didn't even ask for the details because the team he'd enjoyed as a Knothole Gang kid — and first worked for in 1939 — wanted him back.

He said yes to the Cardinals and headed home. The man who had constructed the team headed to its third pennant in five years finally got to enjoy one.

Nineteen sixty-eight was the Year of the Pitcher, topped by Denny McLain's spectacular 31-game season at Detroit and Gibson's remarkable 1.12 earned-run average, lowest ever for a pitcher working 300 or more innings.

Gibby, starting slowly, hit an incredible stride that earned him 15 consecutive victories. Except for a delivery labeled a wild pitch rather than a passed ball, he would have broken Don Drysdale's record for consecutive scoreless innings.

And Drysdale had been aided by a weird call when umpire Harry Wendelstedt ruled that the Giants' Dick Dietz didn't try to get away from an inside pitch that hit him and would have forced in a run.

Year of the pitcher, indeed. At San Francisco's Candlestick Park, the Giants' Gaylord Perry and Cardinals' Ray Washburn pitched no-hit games on *successive* days.

Old friend Bill Jackowski worked home plate for the Perry no-hitter. A few days later, Bill and I had lunch. He told me a story about their four-umpire team. Rookie ump Harry Wendelstedt, by tradition, was responsible for making travel arrangements. He had scheduled the group inconveniently from Cincinnati by way of Houston to San Francisco.

Eagle-eyed Frank Secory, sauntering through Houston's airport lobby, spotted another flight that would get them to the Coast earlier. So Jackowski's crew switched planes. The one scheduled by Wendelstedt crashed and killed all 85 people aboard.

Gibson was a killer of another kind in 1968. In 305 innings he allowed 198 hits, walked 62, and struck out 268. Thirteen of his 22 victories were shutouts—Gibby couldn't lose if the other guys didn't even score — and as he took the mound for the last time prior to the World Series, I pep-talked him about lowering his ERA below the record held by Walter Johnson. He nodded and goose-egged Houston to get the 1.12 ERA.

His remarkable year didn't give him the national attention achieved by McLain. A bon vivant and nightclub organist, Mac was a good-time guy.

Before the opening game of the 1968 World Series, broadcaster Sandy Koufax told David Lipman privately, "I know how much Gibson hurts physically—his arthritis might not be as bad as mine, but it's tough on his elbow and painful—but you'd never know it. I don't know who'll win the Series, but I'll tell you one thing— Gibson is going to eat McLain alive."

In Game One, big number "45" threw strikes that must have looked as they came out of a .45. Allowing five hits and one walk, Gibson compiled strikeout after strikeout. By the ninth inning, with the Cardinals leading, the scoreboard in center field kept track of his k's.

When Gibson struck out Kaline for the third time, the board signaled that he had tied Koufax's Series record of 15. From behind the plate, McCarver popped out toward the mound, motioning toward the printed message.

Bob Gibson

Gibson stuck out his glove for the ball and his jaw defiantly. "Gimme the damned ball and get back there," Gibson snarled.

He then fanned Norm Cash, breaking the record, and made it 17 with a game-ending wicked slider outside corner called third strike past Willie Horton. Although I've seen more significant games, I still regard Robert (Hoot) Gibson's 17 strikeout, 4-0 World Series performance as the most meaningful I ever saw.

But when folks say the Cardinals probably would have won the 1968 World Series if Lou Brock had slid in the fifth inning of the fifth game, it angers me. Brock's World Series performance needs no defending. He had his second successive sensational Series, as did Gibson.

More important, I'm certain Brock was safe, not out.

I recognize that veteran National League umpire Doug Harvey was almost as good as he thought he was, which was considerable. I believe many umpires might have pre-judged the critical play and automatically called Brock safe, unaware that Tigers' left fielder Willie Horton would uncork the throw of his career.

As Brock and Horton's throw raced for the plate, the umpire nicknamed "God" waited along with catcher Bill Freehan.

Brock faced a dilemma. Big Freehan stood in front of the plate with his foot pointed down the third base line. "I've seen that so often, " said Brock. "As you slide left or right, the catcher moves his foot with you, hooks you off the plate, reaches down and tags you out. I thought I could stride onto the plate and, if necessary, into him."

Brock, standing up rather than sliding, was tagged by catcher Bill Freehan as he *stepped on* home plate, not *before* he reached the hard rubber haven.

Harvey threw up an out signal and with the Tigers down by only one run, not two, the second guessers suggest the Detroit manager let Lolich hit for himself in the seventh with one out.

Maybe, though I felt that as the Series ERA of other Tiger pitchers were in double figures, Mayo would have let Lolich bat regardless.

Brock was mocked and maligned. Sportswriters are often quick to jump to conclusions. There can be a herd mentality in the press box, especially from those who fear competition, which frequently allows the superficial observation to dominate.

Brock's speaking style befuddles the less than careful listener, but he is an intelligent and articulate man. The media gave him short thrift. He shrugged it off, but the criticism of his "failure" to slide bothered me.

So after the Series, I retreated to the air-cooled security vaults at Cooperstown and ran the video of that play again and again, rocking it back and forth, meticulously examining it frame by frame. So help me, because Horton's throw didn't arrive in time for Freehan to extend his arms, the runner and catcher collided in a tag *on home plate*.

The episode reaffirmed my belief that because home plate is almost sunken, not raised like a base, too many times a catcher peels off a runner or blocks the plate before he has possession of the ball. My solution? Give the runner what the real-estate folks call "air rights," the privilege to slide high enough across the plate to avoid the catcher's foot without the necessity of trying to scrape the shoe across the plate.

Hall of Famer Cool "Papa" Bell presents the record-setting base to Lou Brock after Brock set a new stolen base record in 1974.

I make more out of this than Brock does, largely because the Redbird leadoff man once again had a remarkable World Series. The hot blood of competitive enthusiasm must pump adrenalin through him. He reached base 18 times in 33 tries, tied the Series record of 13 hits including three doubles, a triple and two homers. He also tied the Series record for stolen bases he'd set in 1967.

If Gibson's buddy, the brilliant-fielding Curt Flood, hadn't misjudged a fly ball and slipped in the seventh inning of the seventh game, the Cardinals might have won despite Harvey's mistaken call.

Ifs and ands are sinking sands. The real winners were the Tigers and Mickey Lolich, who won three games with a dandy 1.67 earned-run average and richly deserved the Most Valuable Player trophy and sports car.

I also warmly appreciated Al Kaline's participation in the Series. After meeting him in spring training when he was 20 and closely following his career, I thought Detroit's No. "6" was most worthy of the number made famous by my friend Stan Musial.

This was Kaline's only Series opportunity. Though injured in 1968 and able to generate only 98 of his 3,007 regular season hits, manager Mayo Smith brazenly moved center fielder Mickey Stanley to a pivotal position, shortstop and Jim Northrup to center, so Kaline could play right, where his considerable defensive skills were paramount. Stanley made only two harmless errors at short. Kaline had a .379 Series average, including a key hit in the decisive fifth game. The Tigers won Game Six to tie the Series at 3-3.

I had a funny feeling before the seventh game and expressed it on KSD-TV's noonday show. Aware that seven times the Cardinals had found Game Seven lucky in Series play, I wondered about pushing things too far. I wondered about Gibby, too, though the other two-game winner, jelly-bellied Lolich, had less rest.

Still, the Cardinals had the best early chance and lost it, partly out of arrogance. Brock led off the home sixth with a single, ventured wide into the most outrageous lead I ever saw anyone take and, sure enough, Lolich picked him off. Then Curt Flood singled, also took an oversized lead, and also was picked off. The Cardinals wouldn't score until Mike Shannon homered with two out in the ninth.

It seemed as if Gibson would have a smooth seventh. With two out, Cash singled to right and Horton singled to left. Gibby faced left-handed hitting Jim Northrup, who had been no problem. Jim lined the ball sharply to center field.

Seated smack center in the pressbox, I wanted the ball to stay up, not dip for a run-scoring single that would break the scoreless tie. When the ball did carry, I barely had time to sigh for relief when Flood took a step in, realized his mistake and, pivoting, dug up a divot like a goofed-up golfer. The slip swung him farther to his right. By the time he straightened out and darted back toward the centerfield fence he was too late. The ball cleared his head and bounced off the centerfield wall for a two-run triple.

In the clubhouse after the loss, I was miffed when Curt Flood disclaimed any gosh-I'm-sorry-Gibby remorse over playing a putout into a triple. Gibson humanized it. Although he knew exactly what had happened behind him and could be a master needler, he was gentle with a friend and gracious in defeat. "Flood," said Gibson, " has saved too many runs for me to criticize him now."

The Redbird locker room was generally quiet, as you might expect. Yet there was an undeniable air of unusual excitement despite the loss. The players and their wives were departing directly from the stadium on a baseball junket to Japan. And, with Maris retiring as previously planned, it was authoritatively rumored that the Cardinals had obtained Vada Pinson from Cincinnati for two fledgling Redbirds, outfielder Bobby Tolan and pitcher Wayne Granger. The consensus among Series reporters was that, egad, the Cardinals had just clinched a third straight division title. Personally, I wasn't so overjoyed. For one, I felt Pinson was no longer the same quality player, either offensively or defensively that he had been in his early seasons. Second, as I mentioned to Schoendienst when I strolled into Red's office when the others had gone, swift young lefty Tolan had shown me something by hanging in tough against southpaw pitchers. Red nodded in agreement, but I don't think he opposed Devine's deal.

When all was done that day, I remember walking with a sinking feeling the many blocks to the *Post-Dispatch* in the fading, quiet, October afternoon. The game crowd was gone and so, too the downtown traffic. I hated having to write my now-we-know-how-the-other-guy-feels funeral piece. But write it I did. That's the nature of my job.

The cycle of sports competition always presents an observer with another season, another team, another reason to pay interested attention. The 1968 Missouri University football team went 8-2 and was picked to play Bear Bryant's Alabama team in the Gator Bowl. Rain fell all day until the famed, crusty old coach with the houndstooth hat ambled onto the field. Then the sun broke through the clouds and began to shine on the field. Someone in the press box cracked wise, "It figures cause the Bear walks on water."

Missouri passed just twice— both into Tide hands —and dumped 'Bama's Scott Hunter for 75 yards lost to Tiger sacks when he tried to pass. Dan Devine's lads ground out the most yardage ever yielded by a Bryant team and won 35-10. Said the Bear, "They ran through us like we were a barber's college. They out-thinged us in everything."

At the dinner shared by the two teams afterward, Bryant grilled Devine about his recruiting and handling of black players. Devine confided, "I told him, honestly, that I had less trouble with black players than white."

Smiling, Dan confided, "I knew that from then on, the Bear and 'Bama would be color blind."

44

శు

After the 1968 baseball season, Curt Flood demanded a pay raise from $72,000 to $100,000. I winced because Curt crowed, "And I don't mean $99,999.99."

Gus Busch wasn't pleased, to say the least. The Big Eagle liked Flood and had helped the highly skilled outfielder escape from more than one personal scrape.

When Flood, using a photograph as a model, painted a color portrait of Busch, Gus lauded the work and accepted the gift eagerly. He commissioned Curt to portray wife Trudi and his many children.

But with his seemingly non-negotiable public posturing, Flood had irritated the wrong Dutchman. Ultimately, Curt signed for $90,000, but the damage had been done. Gus felt a friend for whom he had gone to bat had turned on him. It was unlikely Busch would go out of his way to help Curt again.

Curt Flood, frustrated star.

On one unforgettable day in spring training, a younger Flood brother engaged in a running shoot out with police in downtown St. Louis after a jewelry theft.

That same day, long-time Redbird traveling secretary Leo Ward suffered a stroke, and Bing Devine began to dismantle the championship ball club. Ward, who nearly a quarter century earlier had clanked the pass gate in my face, had become my dear friend during our years of traveling together. His stroke came while my wife and I were about to treat Bing and Mary Devine and their three young daughters to dinner and a movie. When Leo was stricken, Bing and Mary headed for the hospital and we took their children to a movie.

I was paged to the box office and was told that when we dropped off the girls at Devine's spring apartment, to make certain I talked with Bing. When I did, I learned he had dealt Orlando Cepeda to the Atlanta Braves for Joe Torre.

Cepeda, a cohesive rah-rah guy in the clubhouse, had sagged at bat, but, worse, both the player and the ball club had been bothered by his creditors. The Cardinals became alarmed when money collectors invaded the runway behind the dugout to badger Cepeda between innings.

Torre had been a good-hitting catcher and handyman with the Braves at Milwaukee and Atlanta, but had fallen into contractual troubles with taciturn Paul Richards, the club's general manager.

In 1969, baseball introduced the concept of two divisions per league and, alarmed at pitching domination, lowered the pitching mound from 15 inches to 10 and narrowed the strike zone.

Back in 1963, when rule makers heightened the strike zone to cut down bases on balls and shorten games, my thought was that in making the strike zone larger, baseball had increased an action-killing factor—strike outs!

In '69, when the width was decreased by officials, umpires took it on themselves to lower the zone further. Most pitches above the belly button became a ball. Gibson shrieked loudly about the injustice.

"Blame yourself, Gib," I said. "It's harder to score runs now than goals in hockey." All Gibby did was to go out and win 20 again with a 2.17 earned-run average. Steve Carlton had a 2.70 ERA and 17 victories.

The lowering of the mound began to take its toll on shorter pitchers. When Nelson Briles, for example, tried to get on top of his curve ball, he didn't have sufficient trajectory. His breaking ball often flattened out.

After the pennants of '67 and '68 and high expectations with the new "wonder" outfield of Brock, Flood, and Tolan, the disappointment of a mediocre Cardinals season was hard to take.

But the amazin' success of the lowly Mets marked 1969 as a remarkable baseball year. New manager Gill Hodges' team caught Leo Durocher's surprising Chicago Cubs in August and soon left the Cubbies and all others behind.

New York was so darlinged by destiny that on a raw September Monday night in St. Louis, Steve Carlton struck out a record 19 batters, and the Mets still won, 4-3. Ron Swoboda hit a pair of two-run homers.

I blundered by skipping that game to watch a private screening of a new football film— "No. 1"—starring my friend Charlton Heston. Another friend, actor Pat O'Brien, sat in my pressbox seat that chilly night. He really ribbed me.

Even though the Mets won the National League East going away with 100 victories and demolished Atlanta in the premiere League Championship Series, the AL's Baltimore Orioles were a heavy Series favorite.

The O's Mike Cuellar bested Seaver in a 4-1 opener at Baltimore and the expected seemed to be happening. Many figured Jerry Koosman's second game 2-1 victory, aided by Don Clendenon's homer, merely delayed the inevitable.

When the competition moved to Shea Stadium, the crowd roared almost as loudly as the overhead flights from nearby La Guardia. Center fielder Tommy Agee gave the home fans reason to cheer with the best two fielding plays I ever saw one player make in a World Series.

Agee made a spectacular snowcone catch of Elrod Hendricks' bid for a two-run triple in the fourth. Three innings later, Paul Blair's bases-loaded line shot to right center seemed to have found the alley for extra bases. But Agee raced over, dived to his left, snared the ball, saved the shutout and maybe the Series.

Seaver pitched Game Four, and the Mets led by one in the ninth. The Orioles filled the bases with only one out, and Brooks Robinson hit a soft liner to shallow right center. Big lumbering

"Saboda," as Stengel always called Ron Swoboda, raced in and over, flung himself to the grass and —lo!— caught the ball. So Baltimore merely got a sacrifice fly tying run on the play.

In the tenth, Jerry Grote blooped a double. Normally light-hitting Al Weis, hitting .455 in the Series, was given an intentional pass. Left-handed swinger J. C. Martin pinch-hit for Seaver and the Orioles manager countered with lefty Pete Richert.

Martin bunted softly toward first, drawing Richert in and over to make the play. Pete's throw down the line struck Martin's left wrist and kicked off into right field for a sacrifice and game-deciding error.

Afterward I was offered a ride back into town by commissioner Ford Frick and baseball secretary Charley Segar in their limousine. I suggested that there would be hell to pay because neither Crawford, working the plate, nor the American League's Lou DiMuro at first base had called interference. I was wrong. The film was inconclusive, and the incident passed into baseball lore.

In the fifth game, Dave McNally led Koosman early by three runs. But a McNally pitch to Cleon Jones, which had been ruled a ball, was shown to have shoe polish on it. Jones was awarded first base. Don Clendennon followed with his third homer of the Series. New York tied it in the seventh on a homer by Weiss. And in the eighth doubles by Jones and Swoboda produced two runs and a 5-3 New York victory.

Hallelujah, the meek had inherited the Earth. The expansion Mets, deemed laughable as "Mutts" a few short years ago, were world champions!

I'll never forget the pockmarked post-game playing field. A huge crowd had surged onto the diamond and pocketed patches of grass. Shea Stadium looked like a crater of the Moon.

Later, as I rode the subway to Manhattan, a neat, well-dressed young man sat in the same car. He suddenly opened his attache case and, grinning, pulled out a hunk of Shea Stadium grass. Gadzooks! A constant reminder of a happy memory!

The 1969 Missouri football team became one of my happiest memories. That squad was the best I've ever seen at Mizzou, even though Roger Wehrli had graduated.

The best St. Louis player not yet named to the pro football Hall of Fame, Wehrli was so good as a professional for the

Gridbirds that he earned constant All-Pro honors even though the opposition would not throw into his territory.

Ol' Mizzou in '69 was devastating, handing Rose Bowl-bound Michigan its only home defeat in Bo Schembechler's first ten seasons. Dan Devine's Orange Bowl team was a great coach's best — Mizzou's, too.

Nineteen sixty-nine was a year for the Devines. Much of the credit for the '69 Mets' success goes to Bing. Once again a team of his design won a championship and, once again, he was not around to witness the action. But since Bing's departure had been voluntary, there were no hard feelings and, from a distance, I'm sure he savored the championship. As long, that is, as his first —and true —love wasn't able to win.

The Cardinals hadn't had the look or feel of a winner in 1969, and Devine set out to remedy the situation. When it came to reconstructing the Cardinals, Bing sought firepower. "Perhaps," he told me, "I over-reacted to the team's popgun attack."

One slugger who was available was Philadelphia's tempestuous Richie Allen, regarded as entirely undisciplined, but undoubtedly one of the best hitters around and certainly one of the most powerful. Maybe the most powerful.

Devine could acquire him for St. Louis, but the price was substantial, including Tim McCarver and Curt Flood. The personable and aggressive McCarver, fast for a catcher, once led the league in triples and was a certified World Series hero.

Tim took the shocking trade from his boyhood favorite team in professional stride. Flood? No!

Seven times in his last nine seasons, Curt had hit .300 or better, and he ranked with Willie Mays and Richie Ashburn as an excellent defensive center fielder. Late in the 1969 season, in which he batted .285, I scolded him gently, noting he had been burning the candles at both ends and spending considerable time painting.

He told me he painted only as a leisurely hobby. I knew that was horseshit and said so, "You have to take better care of your baseball skills. You're only a couple or three .300 seasons away from Hall of Fame stature. Harry Walker (managing Houston) has bunched the defense up the middle for you and other clubs have copied him. But St. Louis is going to have artificial turf here next year and more of your ground balls will move quickly through the gaps."

When Flood was phoned by Jim Toomey with the news that he had been traded, Curt's first words were: "Oh, not to the Phillies!" Flood asked commissioner Bowie Kuhn to be released from the slave-aspect of the player renewal clause, the one providing a ball club a right to a player's services the next season. Kuhn, as expected, turned him down. Philadelphia general manager John Quinn offered Flood a chance to become baseball's first $100,000 singles' hitter. Curt declined.

When Flood wouldn't report, Kuhn didn't endear himself to Busch, the Cardinals or the brewery by requiring St. Louis to give Philly outfielder Willie Montanez and pitcher Jim Browning. Backed by the Major League Player's Association and Marvin Miller, Flood sued Major League Baseball for $4.1 million in damages and his release from the reserve clause. Former Supreme Court Justice Arthur Goldberg represented him, and Flood was also supported by men of prestige including Jackie Robinson, Hank Greenberg and Bill Veeck.

Back in 1943 when Bill was in the Marines and the Phillies became available, Veeck tried to buy the mediocre team, which he would have stocked with black talent. Commissioner Judge Landis, painfully bigoted, made sure the Phils fell into "safer" white hands.

As part of Flood's legal argument, Veeck urged a several season reserve system limit, similar to a Hollywood talent contract. But Judge Irving Ben Cooper of the U. S. District Court in New York turned thumbs down. Flood fled to Denmark to paint in 1970, honestly believing he would be blackballed in baseball. But, no, Washington's Bob Short was willing to talk big — $110,000 —and to give up three minor league players for Flood. Kuhn would permit it only if Curt recognized the "sanctity" of the reserve clause. Reluctantly, he did.

Thirteen assorted games into the 1971 season, playing poorly, Curtis Charles Flood chucked it. Washington's team doctor said the man who had missed the 1970 season had the "oldest" 33-year-old body the Doc had ever seen.

45

⁊⋆

Time flies faster as age increases and death insists on being taken seriously. More attention is focused on milestones and passages. Perhaps this best explains the parade of memories from the later decades of my life.

• Because I remember Rich Allen, Abraham Lincoln comes to mind, the great president who watched U. S. Grant prevail where so many other Union commanders had failed. Responding to criticisms of Grant's drinking, Lincoln suggested that all other generals should be issued Grant's preferred brand.

Allen received an astounding 90-second reverberating standing ovation on opening night in St. Louis in 1970. The Cardinals faithful extended a warm welcome, and the former Philly slugger became the best power hitter ever to call Busch Stadium home.

Allen was a superb player even, as on occasion, when drunk. His presence bothered manager Red Schoendienst, who hadn't wanted him in the first place.

So after Rich sat out the final month of the season rather than take the physical therapy urged to rehabilitate an injured hamstring, he was dealt to Los Angeles for Ted Sizemore, a peppery little second baseman who took a lot of pitches to allow Lou Brock to steal a lot of bases.

• I remember Paul Christman dying of a heart attack in 1970, at age 51, right after having been selected by ABC to work on Monday Night Football. After his death, the network's next choice was Don Meredith. "Dandy," I suggested to the former SMU and Dallas star, "if Paul Christman hadn't died, you'd be selling neckties in Texas."

• I remember a generation of Big Red players leaving without having won a championship. Gone or soon to be gone were Jimmy Hill, Bill Koman and Dale Meinert, big Luke Owens and Ken Gray, John David Crow, Bobby Joe Conrad, Sonny Randle, and Pat Fischer. Free safety Larry Wilson, tackle Ernie McMillan, and quarterback Charley Johnson were still around, soon to be joined by Jackie Smith, Roger Wehrli, Dan Dierdorf, Jim Bakken, Mel Gray, Terry Metcalf, and Jim Hart.

My man was Charley Johnson, smart, talented, educated, and gracious, with the guts of a street fighter, an exemplary scholar-athlete model, like basketball's Bill Bradley.

At one point in the 1970 Football Cardinals season, coach Charley Winner, a favorite of co-owner Bill Bidwill, had the team breezing at 8-2. Then the Big Red were held to a tie at Kansas City, won at Philadelphia and lost at Detroit.

Now they had to beat the New York Giants in St. Louis. I gulped as I saw the home side limber up, so tight I could hear them squeak. They lost to Alex (Red) Webster's Giants, 34-17, putting New York in the division lead.

A week later the usually reliable Bakken missed a late field goal at Washington, and the one-point loss, 28-27, killed the team's chance to take the championship because the Giants had been upset. At the Super Bowl, I bumped into Webster and asked him about the Giants' surprising final game loss. Red grimaced. "With the title at stake, my team looked and played as tight as yours did the week before."

The near miss by the close-call Cards cost Winner his job. Older brother Charles, living up to his "Stormy" nickname, wanted a new coach and lined up a leadership survey team to find the right man. The anointed one was Bob Holway, long an assistant to Bud Grant at Minnesota.

• I remember a January, 1971, phone call from Dan Devine to my hotel in Miami, where I was covering the Super Bowl game. Forty-eight hours earlier, with Mom, Dorth, and her aunt along, I had been held up outside a pancake house by a slick young pro whose shiny gun looked as big as a bazooka. He got me for $300.

Devine was not being robbed at gunpoint. The Green Bay Packers had offered him $75,000 yearly and lucrative fringe benefits to leave Mizzou and bring back the Pack.

Aware I knew he once had turned down an offer to coach Notre Dame, Dan'l explained his current predicament from a Kansas City motel hideaway. He had been a boyhood admirer of the Packers in the same way young Bing Devine had followed the Cardinals.

I knew Dan to be a private person who had to force himself to observe some university-related work necessities. If he accepted the Green Bay offer, he could have more time for football and more fun on the field.

Naturally I hoped Dan would stay at Mizzou, but if he expected me to make a strong appeal, I disappointed him. As Shakespeare said, to thine ownself be true, or, as Mike Gonzalez put it, only you can die for you.

Devine hung up after telling me he would recite his rosary in a prayer for guidance. I felt he was gone. And he was. Missouri football has never been the same.

• Tact is the ability to give the other fellow a shot in the arm without letting him feel the needle. Scotty Bowman, the shining knight who brought hockey's Camelot its finest hours, was a master of tactics, but his impatience led him to be completely tactless.

Bowman led the Blues to two division championships and three Stanley Cup finals in four seasons before "resigning" in 1971.

It's unbelievable the Salomons would have let Bowman leave unless father and/or son hadn't felt completely fed up by Scotty's attitude toward them and their team.

What began as fun and excitement for the son —and what father doesn't get a vicarious thrill when junior is happiest? — lost zest when Bowman excluded both men from discussions and decisions.

Scotty should have been able to stay here until his bright, shoe-button eyes were wrinkled and bifocaled, but he didn't consult sufficiently with his superiors.

Scotty Bowman

• I remember Joe Torre winning the NL MVP award in 1971. Torre, reacting to brother Frank's teasing about his weight, slimmed down. Like Hornsby and Medwick before him, Joe had the ability as a right-handed batter to stroke line drives to right center. He hit 24 home runs and led the league in hitting, base hits and runs batted in—.363, 230, and 137.

1971 NL MVP Joe Torre hit .363.

Joe made a pressbox gaffer glow when he credited me for having helped his career year. "You stayed on me, when we were eliminated by Pittsburgh the last few days, to bear down and stay over .360. You were right — .360 sounds a lot better than .359."

Torre played third base exclusively that season because a rare kidney disease threatened Mike Shannon's life and forced his retirement. The Cardinals' Bing Devine and KMOX's Bob Hyland combined to give Moon Man another way to earn a living—with his mouth.

Gus Busch threw an irrational fit over Steve Carlton's brief holdout and made a classic boo-boo. The subpar fourth-place Redbirds traded Lefty, who promptly won 27 games for last place Philadelphia.

• After a slow recovery from his first stroke two years earlier, Leo Ward eventually retired, angry at Bing Devine for taking him off the road. On St. Patrick's day, 1972, I was watching a beautiful sunset with Jack Buck at his St. Pete beach digs when KMOX tipped us that the sun had set for my buddy back home.

• Despite Stormy Bidwill's leadership selection process, Bob Holway demonstrated the efficacy of the Peter Principle. He had been promoted to a job for which he was not competent. Holway suffered two straight 4-9-1- seasons and was pink slipped by Bill Bidwill.

The clash over coaches was the final straw between the non-blood brothers. Stormy assumed he could afford to buy out Bill and Bill couldn't afford to do the same to him. So he issued an either-or proposal. With wife Nancy's help, Bill Bidwill won the round and the ball club.

Bidwill hired Don Coryell as his new coach. I'll never forget my first meeting with the wasp-waisted former University of Washington halfback and one-time light heavyweight boxer. Although at times he could sputter with a school girl's lisp, Coryell was a man's man, a survivor of a snow patrol unit virtually wiped out under an idiot officer in mountainous military training.

At a private one-on-one session, the kind I favored over the years, seeking better to understand a new manager, coach, or player, I stuck my nose into Coryell's business, not always the wisest move. "Coach, I don't know how many films you've seen, if any, but you've got one guy who really can throw the ball."

Jim Hart! He won the starting job but for the third straight year the Big Red were Pale Pink —4-9-1.

• The descent at Mizzou after Devine departed was dramatic and depressing. Al Onofrio had a horrible 1-10 first season.

Dan Devine (right) and head coaching successor Al Onofrio discuss a call with the official.

• In August, 1972, my old boss and constant mentor, J. Roy Stockton died at 79 in St. Petersburg, shortly after I told him that he had been voted to receive a Hall of Fame writing award at Cooperstown.

Dear J. Roy did me a last great favor. His recommendation convinced the Hall of Fame to ask me to join its Veterans' Committee. Secretly, I had hoped that when I became an old man around 65 or so, Cooperstown might want me in retirement. But — joy! —they asked when I was only 54. Two years later they asked me to become a member of their board of directors.

• Roberto Clemente died in a dramatic plane crash while on a mission of mercy on New Year's Eve, 1972. I'd become close to the great Pittsburgh superstar from Puerto Rico, whom I'd always felt was underrated. Sensitive to suggestions that he was a hypochondriac, he appreciated my encouragement. Some of the best, most durable, hustling players moaned the most, i.e., Frisch, Enos Slaughter, and the Chicago White Sox's Luke Appling.

I learned a couple of years before Clemente's death that he was a frequent patient at Logan College of Chiropractics in St. Louis. They showed me the x-rays of an old automobile accident and its effect on his arthritic spine. Their concern: "Roberto doesn't help his cervical condition with his habit of jerking his neck in the batter's box."

Willie Mays welcomes Roberto Clemente to the 3,000-hit club in 1972.

I was most happy that the 38-year-old reached the mythical 3,000 total with his final major league hit in the last game he played before his death.

• I remember with great pain the 1973 death of Frank Frisch, my boyhood idol, whom I had come to call Uncle Frank. We were scheduled to spend frequent dinner hours together in the spring training camp of the "Cawd'nals," but he blew a tire near Wilmington, Delaware, lingered with injuries caused by the subsequent accident, and then suffered a fatal heart attack. Back in '33, a palm reader had zeroed his death at — bull's eye — 75.

• Death also claimed, at age 92, my old high school coach and friend, Bert Fenenga. Until near the end, the Coach and his wife, Ruth, worked as substitute teachers in Seal Beach, California. Every time I traveled west, I would take him or them to a meal and a ball game.

Coach Fenenga ranked with my father and J. Roy Stockton as men who did the most for me. When Fenenga would come to St. Louis, my friends would ask him what kind of athlete I had been, and the old Coach would answer with great diplomacy — a "good competitor."

• After waiting for years to see Missouri play Notre Dame at South Bend, I was glad I had the World Series to schedule myself as an excuse to avoid Rockne Stadium (My designation for the Irish stadium.)

Missouri, not much better in 1972 than they had been in 1971, had lost to Nebraska, 62-0. Frankly, I didn't want to watch the slaughter. I opted for the West Coast middle games of an Oakland-Cincinnati World Series, then figured myself to drop in at Boulder en route home, to cover a meaningful Oklahoma-Colorado game.

Memories are the true richness of a newspaper life. For instance, the late afternoon flight to San Francisco and, the helicopter lift over the Bay bridges, and the string of lighted pearls from The City to Oakland.

Uh-huh, and banana splits with Monte Irvin, and breakfast with Buck Canal, the Graham McNamee of the Caribbean, the Spanish language newspaper/radio man.

The sole distasteful note was provided by Oakland owner Charley Finley, who paraded into the press hospitality suite with his high-hinied Missouri mule, who jutted his rear end over my dinner plate.

Nice-guy Gene Tenace, then an obscure catcher-first baseman for Oakland, hit four homers and gathered nine RBIs to lead the Athletics to the franchise's first world championship since they won with Philadelphia's colors over the 1930 Cardinals.

• At Boulder, I expected a thriller between favored Oklahoma and Colorado and was in the midst of getting it when an early first quarter score came over the pressbox squawk-box, "Missouri 7, Notre Dame 0." I laughed and said, "Well, at least this week they won't be shut out." Other wise guys tittered.

At halftime, while I was using the restroom, a man burst in. Bob Meyers, a young Missouri assistant scouting Colorado, shouted:

"Final score: Mi-z-z-o-r-a-h 30, Notre Dame 26!"

I turned quickly, without thinking. Well, I hope Bob felt the victory was worth the drenching.

Nebraska's Devaney wrote Al Onofrio, "that your preparation —mentally, physically and technically—was the best job done by any coach in the history of football." As the saying goes, it couldn't have happened to a nicer guy.

• Of course, I remember Air Coryell. The Big Red won so many close games, they were hailed as the Cardiac Cardinals. Over three smashing seasons, by far the team's best ever in an undernourished 28-year stay in St. Louis, 19 of 31 regular season victories were gained by a touchdown or less.

The combination of an overpowering offensive line, the speed of Mel Gray, elusiveness of Terry Metcalf, quarterbacking of Jim Hart, and battering of back Jim Otis finally, if briefly, brought fans pleasant rooting experiences.

The Cardiacs finished first in 1974 and won again in 1975. The only flaw was the playoffs, both times away, a 30-14 spanking by Minnesota in 1974 and 35-23 by Los Angeles in 1975. St. Louis never hosted a postseason game.

• I remember catcher Ted (Simba) Simmons played with the defiance that gave him the confidence to become the first major league player to compete without a signed contract.

Simmons let his bat do his talking, and Dick Meyers arranged an eventual multiple-year contract that didn't offend the Big Eagle and gave Simba the lion's share.

• I remember the "Mad Hungarian" coming in from the bullpen, wicked-looking Al Hrabosky with his Fu Manchu mustache, and his back to the plate pep talks. More than once, he walked the bases loaded and then struck out the side with his bristling fast ball.

Perhaps nothing sums up Hrabosky better than the time he allowed a home run and then, just to show he wasn't daunted, brushed back the next hitter, who got back up and homered on the next pitch.

What did Al do when the next hitter stepped into the batter's box? Threw at him, of course.

• During the pennant stretch of 1974, Dorth and I returned from a pleasant two-week trip to Germany with Monsignor Louis F. Meyer and a Catholic Youth Council plane of soccer buffs who had attended the World Cup tournament in Frankfurt and Munich.

My wife and I bivouacked primarily in a beautiful Bavarian mountain village, Reit Im Winkl —"right in the corner" between Germany, Austria, and Switzerland.

Our first day back home, Dorth noticed a little lump at her left clavicle. Later, at a routine medical examination, a biopsy was performed.

Lung cancer, metastasized, life expectancy three to six months. Dorth fought the disease longer, using radiation and chemotherapy to check it in the lungs. But the treatment weakened her.

We made a last trip together to St. Petersburg. Agonizingly, the Cardinals' minor league hitting instructor, Joe Medwick, happy over hip surgery that had restored his golf swing, unexpectedly died virtually next door to our rooms.

Joe Garagiola dropped in to see Dorth, who whipped off her wig that covered the chemo-caused baldness, stuck her shiny head next to Garagiola's and, grinning, said, "Take our picture, George."

Then one day the cancer spread to her liver, and she went into the hospital for the third and last time.

She was — and remains — the best editor I've ever had. Her last editing job was my University of Missouri football history book. She urged me to follow through with my scheduled book signings at Columbia and to serve as Grand Marshal for the Homecoming Parade. I went because of her request. After that, I was with her daily except when fulfilling only the requirements of my job.

On a Friday night, I left her room and when I returned Saturday morning, she was in a coma. The chemotherapist gravely told me she would only live another 48 hours or so. I spent the entire day talking to her and holding her hand but received no response.

Using virtually no television volume, I watched that afternoon as Nebraska beat Missouri in football. I'm sure if she could have talked, she would have said, "That figures, George."

From the first bad news to the last, 14 months later, the noble woman never let me see her cry. That night — November 1, 1975 — I left the hospital about 10:30 p.m. and was barely back in my apartment when the phone rang.

When Dorth began cancer treatment in late 1974, nephew David Carr came from Montana with a wolf puppy.

46

Shortly after Dorth died, I pulled into my downtown parking spot one night and popped open my car hood to check a worrisome knock.

As I peered at the engine, a young man approached, pointed a gun right at me, and demanded my money. I fished into my pant's pocket and pulled out two $20 bills. The robber took them and ordered me to give him my jewelry and put my head under the hood.

On my left ring finger was a treasured gift from my wife. "George" had bought me a scarab in Egypt and had it made into a ring. I wasn't about to give that up.

Turning toward the gunman, I said: "No! You've got 40 bucks. You've done all right."

Time seemed to stop as we stood eyeball to eyeball. Finally the thief turned and ran up the driveway to Pine Street, yelling, "Don't follow me!"

Slamming down the hood fiercely, I shouted, "FUCK YOU."

I mentioned the incident to my mother, omitting my angry curse. "Oh, Robert," Mom said shrilly, alarmed, "he could have shot you." Possibly, but like so many times in my life, something protected me. Maybe my pure desire to keep Dorothy's gift.

Whatever its nature, my guardian remained busy. A friend, knowing about my sweet tooth, gave me a handsome menu from a small restaurant that featured exquisite desserts. Its name, Louis IX, meant nothing to me.

One Sunday late in Dorth's life, I was driving her and my Mom when we saw a squat gray one-story building in Webster Groves, billboarded with the name, Louis IX.

Only two persons were seated when we entered. One was Steve Mizerany, St. Louis's colorful, wise-cracking, roller-skating comic made locally famous by his appliance family's television commercials.

Steve rushed over to say hello and introduced proprietor Pat Freasier, who became my good friend. Freasier's menu was good and versatile, especially his mouth-watering desserts. After a few more Sunday stops, Dorth was hospitalized the last time.

Months later, early in 1976, on a Sunday he knew I would be eating at Louis IX, Freasier played Cupid and coaxed a friend of his to join him for an early dinner. When Mom and I arrived, Pat was sitting with a singularly attractive, olive-skinned young woman graced with glistening black hair. Her name was Lynette Anton Emmenegger.

They joined us, and I began to know Lynne. Soon I had met her children, handsome son Greg, and stunningly beautiful daughter Lisa, in the process of earning her Ph.D. in psychology.

After Dorth's death, I had figured I would live out the rest of my life as a single man in my city apartment near the *Post-Dispatch*. But now, unexpectedly and wondrously, I found myself in love.

Our courtship lasted more than a year. We were married on July 23, 1977. Lynette Anton Broeg owned an immaculate and comfortable home in the western suburbs. She wanted to live there. No more was I an urban cliff-dwelling codger.

Shortly after we married, my job at the *Post-Dispatch* took an abrupt and unexpected turn. Ten years earlier, publisher Joseph Pulitzer had asked me to become assistant to the publisher. I declined with gratitude. But now, a decade later, JP Jr. politely asked me to reconsider. It didn't seem wise to decline again.

So I physically moved out of the sports department, though for a time I retained the title of sports editor. My new job offered disappointingly little direct contact with Joseph Pulitzer Jr., a shy man and a gifted speaker who didn't like to speak.

My assignment was to communicate with prominent people whose feathers had been ruffled by the paper. I made sure I listened to everything they had to say. My sports column responsibilities were reduced from five to two a week.

As a sports editor, I rest my case with the people I recruited, many now in responsible positions at the paper. They set a standard for excellent reporting and writing. Equally important, they were a smoothly functioning team. I prided myself on studying background and temperament of the people I hired.

The compatibility of a working newspaper staff is as valuable as that of an athletic team.

About the time I took on my new responsibilities, my life was saved by my love. Lynne had been trained as a registered nurse. In 1978, her early detection of a stroke proved crucial to my survival and gave us many more happy years together.

My lovely wife Lynne.

However, Missouri's declining football fortunes made many fall Saturdays of those years miserable. The teams of Faurot, Dan Devine and Al Onofrio had spoiled me and many others. Then athletic director Sparky Stalcup summed it up well in 1971 when he said, "I reached the point where I thought 6-and-4 was a bad year and a 60,000 crowd only average."

With long-time Missouri coach Don Faurot when the field was named for him in 1972.

Stalcup died in 1972 and was followed by Mel Sheehan who was forced out in 1978 and replaced by Missouri Chancellor Barbara Uehling's choice, Dave Hart. Uehling came to Missouri suspicious of athletics because her experience at Oklahoma had convinced her it was a "football factory."

Al Onofrio was fired in 1977. Although his teams lost three games more than they won in his seven seasons, oh, those giant-killing upsets. He beat Nebraska,13-10; smacked the Huskers again, 21-10; overwhelmed Bear Bryant's 'Bama at Birmingham, 20-7; spoiled John Robinson's first game as USC coach, 46-35; used a last-minute two-point extra point to heartbreak Ohio State, 22-21; and surprised Nebraska a third time, 34-24.

Uncle Al also handed Frank Kush's Sun Devils their first shut out defeat in 10 years, 9-0. Kush grumbled that Missouri had removed its grass tarpaulin too soon, and the field had been too wet to allow a fair game. The next time Mizzouri again shut out ASU on the bone dry field at Tempe. Post-game at mid-field, Onofrio said to old friend Kush, "This time, Frank, the field wasn't wet."

Dave Hart hired Warren Powers to replace Al. Warren might have been too distant or too busy to spend enough time recruiting high school players or acquiring the goodwill of the guys who coached them during their prep years.

After seven seasons, with average attendance down to 47,000 and falling fast, the 43-year-old coach was canned, though Powers' record of 46-33-3 might have merited more time.

Missouri's long-time sports information director and my good friend Bill Callahan told me, "I wonder if we didn't fire our last two coaches (Onofrio and Powers) prematurely."

Woody Widenhofer replaced Powers, inheriting talent not nearly so capable as Warren had inherited from Onofrio. Yeah, and a phony carpet field that unfrocked lack of team speed. Woody began with a 1-10 season, and the long slide down gained momentum. So that's the end of my Missouri memories — at least as far as this book is concerned. Live your own nightmares.

I'd also give similar short shrift to the football Cardinals except for a phone call I received one spring night in 1978. Jim Toomey had me paged in a movie theater in St. Petersburg. Kevin Byrnes, his football p.r. counterpart, was desperately trying to reach me. Would I please phone St. Louis as soon as possible?

Kev had surprising news. Bud Wilkinson had been named the Big Red's head coach. Wilkinson, the graying Galahad of the gridiron, had dominated college football with national championships, conference titles, and bowl victories. His teams had earned 31 straight victories, then 47, and had played 73 conference games over a 13-year period.

But after 16 years out of coaching, could he succeed in the NFL? He was a football genius, so perhaps he might. But Wilkinson was promised much by Bidwill and given little.

I had a unique perspective on Wilkinson's travails with Butthead Bidwill. Our home — Lynne's house — suffered a horrible fire on July 3, 1978. Lynne exhibited great composure and leadership as she took command to make the best of a bad situation.

She, Lisa, Greg, and I spent the next 13 months living in a cathedral suite at the Chase Park Plaza as State Farm's guests, just down the hall from where Bud and Donna Wilkinson lived while awaiting construction of a nearby townhouse. So the coach I'd known from afar became a friendly neighbor.

Greg Emmenegger and Lisa Emmenegger.

Bud had developed the interesting offensive strategy of moving his tight end into the offensive backfield and requiring the defense to commit. But his team didn't have a tight end with sufficient talent to make the scheme work.

Jackie Smith had been urged to retire, and J.V. Cain had suffered a torn Achilles tendon. Wilkinson suggested bringing back Smith, but Bidwill declined.

Though he lost his first eight games in 1978, Wilkinson was obviously learning. He won six of the last eight and had high hopes for 1979.

That year, Lou Brock retired from baseball after having joined the 3,000 hit club and becoming the National League's premier base stealer, both for a single season with 118, and a career with 893.

Brock's steal attempts were carefully choreographed by the thoughtful man. It took him 13 strides to get from first to second. His characteristic pop up, feet-first slide propelled him immediately to his feet.

Brock told me, "With plastic cleats and no steel spikes, it's now much easier and safer for a second baseman or shortstop, bending for a low throw, to block you illegally off the bag. More than once, obviously aware of the unfairness of the block, I've had umpires call me safe, when I actually didn't reach the bag."

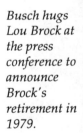

Busch hugs Lou Brock at the press conference to announce Brock's retirement in 1979.

Worried his quick slide impeded the umpire's backside view, Brock quietly urged National League president Chub Feeney to move NL umps out of the infield and station them behind the bases. He thought that would give the arbitrators a better sight-line.

I agree with Brock and add a reason of my own. One of these days an important game will be decided because an umpire will be struck with a ball that might have been an out, maybe even a certain double play.

Under the rules, the play will be dead. But when an umpire is struck in a position behind the infielders, the ball is in play.

Meanwhile, back with the Big (Little) Red (Pink), Bidwill seemed to be doing everything he could to keep Bud Wilkinson from putting a good team in play. Bud needed more players with talent but none were forthcoming either through the draft or trades.

Then J.V. Cain dropped dead from an undetected heart disorder in training camp. High command made no effort to fill the team's critical vacancy at tight end.

And as if trying to haze Wilkinson, Bidwill and his front-office lackeys nit-picked Bud ad nauseam, once not even *selling* four tickets to the coach for a close friend. Day in and day out the harassment continued, fueled, perhaps, by Bidwill's resenting Wilkinson's popularity. He feared that the St. Louis community wished that he would go away and Bud would stay.

Finally, after Bud made an offer to buy the franchise, Bidwill fired the legendary coach. Wilkinson stepped out without a murmur, though he had a myriad of reasons to bad-mouth Bidwill and *millions* of eager listeners.

Class is class, even when unfairly treated by no class.

In my opinion, Bud Wilkinson might easily have become President of the United States. Richard Nixon admired — and to a great extent idolized — Wilkinson. If Bud had won his 1964 Senate bid, I think Nixon would have balanced his 1968 ticket by choosing Wilkinson of Oklahoma rather than Agnew of Maryland. When Nixon was forced to resign because of Watergate, Bud could have succeeded him as President.

Bud closely espoused presidential candidate Barry Goldwater at a time Lyndon Johnson was benefiting from the country's passion for the fallen JFK. Oklahoma ticket splitters favorable to Bud gave him 100,000 votes more than they gave Goldwater in the Democratic landslide. But Fred Harris received the majority of the vote.

Unexpectedly, I won an election of my own in 1980. It involved Baseball's Hall of Fame.

If, as is often suggested, practice makes perfect, hell, I'd have been what I wanted to be — a Hall of Fame ballplayer — rather than a Hall of Fame baseball writer.

Despite the pleasant billing, I'm not a Hall of Fame writer either. The annual award to a writer, named for *The Sporting News'* colorful old editor-publisher, J.G. Taylor Spink, is presented at Cooperstown, but does not carry Hall of Fame stature.

Personally, I'd prefer to see the Hall reserved entirely for players, excluding managers, umpires, and executives, and, of course, writers and broadcasters.

After receiving the honor, I was eating lunch with Lynette at the patio dining area of the beautiful Cooperstown lakeside hotel, the Ot-e-sa-ga. Passing, Detroit writer Joe Falls mischievously stage-whispered to his companion, Ted Williams, "I wouldn't have voted for Broeg."

Wheeling, Ted stopped, shook my hand and said, "I would — even if he *is* a Musial man."

I passed along the comment to Hall of Fame chairman Joe Cronin, retired American League president who had been Ted's first big-league boss as playing manager at Boston.

Cronin chuckled, "With Ted, you always know where you stand."

Accepting the Hall of Fame baseball writing award in 1980 at Cooperstown.

47

ஐ

Lawyer Lou Susman wormed his way into Gussie Busch's confidence and tightened the access circle around the Big Eagle.

After the team's 1979 third-place finish in Brock's final season, Susman seemed to have a strong hand in the firing of general manager Bing Devine, who had given up the presidency of the Mets — and a potential piece of the action. Subsequently, the lawyer twice nixed Devine's return as a consultant. Why? Susman never gave a reason. In matters of baseball or ethics, I don't think Susman could carry Devine's jock strap.

Devine's hand-picked manager, Ken Boyer, had some able talent with which to work, notably catcher Ted Simmons and first-baseman Keith Hernandez, whose superior fielding kept shortstop Garry Templeton's throwing errors to a minimum.

Templeton became the first switch-hitter to gain 100 hits from each side of the plate in a single season. He also was the first player since Detroit's Sam Crawford to lead the league in triples three straight years. Garry was the best young talent I had ever seen, and I was confident he would end up in the Hall of Fame.

Although miffed about what happened to Bing, I tried to help new general manager John Claiborne, one of Devine's front-office pups. I knew the Chicago Cubs' Bruce Sutter had angered Cubbie management by winning arbitration.

Arbitration is a bone in baseball's throat, because it isn't mediation. The arbitrator has to pick one number or the other. For instance, if Sutter was making $150,000, and the Cubs offered $350,000 and he asked for the moon — $700,000 — and got it, management became damned indignant.

I took Cubs manager Preston Gomez to dinner at Louis IX. Preston was willing to trade Sutter, but it had to be a good deal. Oh, maybe a promising young catcher, Terry Kennedy, first baseman Leon (Bull) Durham and maybe a pitcher like John Fulgham or an infielder, meaning a Ken Oberkfell or Tommy

Herr. Stiff, yes, but not if it turns the Cardinals into a winner, I reported to Claiborne. John froze and didn't make the deal.

So Boyer was fired. The new manager was Dorrel Norman Elvert Herzog, from nearby New Athens, Illinois. The White Rat was fearless and funny, aggressive and smart — v-e-r-y smart. Best manager I ever saw.

Herzog was the leader for whom Busch long had waited. "Chief," Whitey told Gus, "You ain't won the damned thing the last 12 years. Let me do it my way."

New manager Whitey Herzog's cockiness delighted Busch.

Whitey took over personnel duties in addition to his field responsibility. He didn't like the 9 to 5 shtick, preferring to cogitate player moves while resting in a boat. I wonder if his fishing was as good as his thinking.

In the history of the Cardinals and perhaps of baseball, no one wheeled and dealed as well as Herzog did after witnessing the 1980 season. His blueprint called for speed and defense, topped by good pitching, especially in relief.

Unimpressed by Ted Simmons's defense, Herzog signed Kansas City's Darrell Porter, who had stopped drinking and drugging, simultaneously morphing himself, in the words of an American League scout, "into a marshmallow."

Herzog then traded for Rollie Fingers and, finally, Bruce Sutter. He made a better deal than the one I had brought to Claiborne. Then Whitey boldly swapped Simmons, Fingers, and Pete Vuckovich to Milwaukee for outfielder Sixto Lezcano, pitchers Larry Sorensen and Dave LaPoint, and a promising kid outfielder, Dave Green.

Aided by Bing Devine's last trade, which brought the club Silent George Hendrick, Herzog had the best overall won-and-lost record in the 1981 season shortened to 102 games by a player strike. Unfortunately, the team did not finish first during either half of the bastardized split season.

Herzog then convinced Busch to let him bring in his man as general manager. Joe McDonald became GM, but Whitey called all the shots, including dumping Templeton, whose personal problems led to a nasty obscene gesture to the fans.

The night before Tempy had acted like he was on drugs. Articulating with difficulty he taunted me drowsily, "We don't want to hear about F-r-a-n-k F-r-i-s-c-h and G-e-o-r-g-e S-i-s-l-e-r."

Herzog quickly traded Templeton for Ozzie Smith. The backflipping Wizard of Oz not only would prove to be the finest-fielding shortstop I ever saw — even better than fabulous Marty Marion — but year by year, he progressed as a hitter to the point I think he will be selected to the Hall of Fame his first eligible year.

Whitey waited until the Phils swapped Lonnie Smith to Cleveland and then dealt pitchers Silvio Martinez and Ted Sorensen to the Indians for Smith. "Skates," as they called the swift outfielder, proved one of the club's best hitters in 1982.

Yes, that's the year the pennant drought ended in St. Louis. The Cardinals played "Whitey Ball" — bunt, stolen base, hitting behind the runner, squeeze play and plenty of doubles and triples up the outfield slots. They won one game when a lumbering third-string catcher Glenn Brummer, playing with both Porter and Tenace hurt, stole home with the winning run with two out and two strikes on the batter!

Suddenly it was September and somber. At Philadelphia, Sutter strode in from the visitors' bullpen at Veterans' Stadium to face slugger Mike Schmidt with the bases loaded and the Cardinals clinging precariously to a 2-0 lead.

Ah, hah, fooled by that dipping split-fingered fast ball, a lopsided forkball, the home-run slugger tapped the ball back to Sutter for a home-to-first double play. First place was regained.

The pennant was won when road-running newcomer Willie McGee hit a three-run homer at Montreal. When you're six up with five to play, you can't lose.

The Cardinals swept Atlanta in the LCS (their first) and faced Milwaukee in the 1982 World Series. The Brewers were managed by Harvey Kuenn and had ex-Redbirds Simmons and Vuckovich in starring roles. Simba would unload two homers and Vuckovich would pitch tenaciously. In addition, the 1-2 hitters in the Brewers' lineup were likely Hall of Famers Paul Molitor and Robin Yount, who led Milwaukee to a 10-0 victory in Game One.

In the sixth inning of Game Two, the Brewers led 4-2, when the left-handed-hitting Porter, who had a mediocre year but was the Cardinals' MVP in the LCS, doubled into the left-field corner to tie the score. The Cardinals scored in the eighth to take the lead.

Molitor took off on a hit-and-run play in the ninth. Yount swung and missed. Porter gunned out the runner and nailed down the victory, earning a snarling aside from Herzog. "They can boo him all they want," snapped the White Rat, "but he's always been a money player."

Game Three belonged to Willie McGee.

1. To begin, he leaped high at the 402-mark to take an extra-base hit away from leadoff man Molitor.

2. With the game scoreless in the sixth inning, McGee tagged Vuckovich for a three-run homer.

3. Vuckovich knocked McGee down in the seventh. Willie got up, dusted himself off, and hit another homer.

4. In the ninth, McGee raced to the fence in deep left-center, leaped gracefully and took an extra-base hit away from Gorman Thomas.

Herzog carefully assessed the situation, "Nobody ever played a better World Series game than Willie McGee tonight."

The Series progressed to a seventh game in St. Louis. Herzog directed his foghorn-voiced pitching coach, Hub Kittle, to make certain Joaquin Andujar was able to pitch. The self-styled "One Tough Dominican" had been felled in the seventh inning of McGee's game by a savage line drive off Ted Simmons's bat.

Warming up slowly, then throwing harder and harder, Andujar finally told Kittle he *was* ready. Despite Joaquin pitching well, the Brewers led 3-1 in the bottom of the eighth.

With one out, Ozzie Smith singled to left and Lonnie Smith doubled him to third. Brewer manager Harvey Kuenn replaced starter Pete Vuckovich with lefty Bob McClure, who walked Gene Tenace, filling the bases.

A culminating confrontation had arrived, a moment of truth, the epiphany of sports. Do or die, win or lose, put up or shut up.

Left-handed-hitting Hernandez valiantly fought lefty McClure's breaking ball before arching a long single to right-center, scoring the Smiths with the tying runs and sending Ramsey to third.

Hendrick poked a run-scoring single to right. The Cardinals led by one and would get two more in the eighth. With the crowd roaring "B-r-u-c-e," Sutter relieved in the ninth and finished with a flourish, striking out Thomas. The emotion was summed up best by Porter in his Ozarkian twang, "Hoo-ee, I been to two county fairs and a goat roast — and I ain't never seen nuthin' like this!"

In May of 1985, I saw something I'd seen before. Wife Lynne saved my life again. This gifted lady has the ability to step into any situation and turn a negative into a positive. Once she saved a publishing house from going under and, in the process, rescued my royalties. And, though her favorite profession is real estate, she called on her nurse's training when, unbeknownst to me, I faced an unseen danger.

I felt a slight left arm tingle three straight days while jogging up downtown post office steps and shrugged it off. I happened to tell her in a lazy husband-wife late evening conversation. She took my report seriously and insisted I have a checkup. Right away!

Even after a sobering CAT scan, the first cardiologist suggested I take heavy doses of medication. But Lynne had seen clogged artery patients go that route and she didn't like my chances. She sought a second opinion and, using her considerable problem-solving skills, soon brought me into the offices of Dr. John P. Connors.

Lynne's research had confirmed her opinion that Dr. Connors, formerly a Holy Cross basketball star, was the best heart surgeon in town and as good as the best anywhere else.

Thanks to my wife's persistence and my doctor's skill, the

six-valve bypass surgery I had in 1985 earned me an additional healthy decade . . . and counting.

Lovely Lynne and her lucky husband.

As for the Cardinals, 1985 was a heck of a year. Keith Hernandez was gone. While with the Cardinals he indulged in drugs, though he denied it until plea-bargaining to save his own skin in a multiple-player mess. Then he sang like a bird.

I didn't like that the new Mets matinee idol twice walked blithely away from his wife Sue, both times while she was pregnant.

Bruce Sutter left the team for bigger bucks at Atlanta and, as a result, many "experts" picked St. Louis to finish last in the National League's East Division.

But Whitey and new general manager Dal Maxvill acquired Jack Clark from San Francisco to provide power and left-handed John Tudor from Pittsburgh to bolster the pitching staff. After the trades, Herzog's confidence in the team increased, "Like most everybody else, I said we could finish anywhere from first to last. Now, I say — *not* last!"

A fun kid named Vince Coleman, brought up temporarily from Louisville became the catalyst of Whitey's speedo ball club. Vince stole 110 bases.

Coleman and the modest McGee, who led the NL with a .353 average, pulled off a beaut in a game at Chicago. Ever hear of two guys getting *four* steals on the same play?

Coming from second, Vince overslid third and, trapped, ran for home rather than retreat. He scored, and McGee, running from first, wound up at third base. Two stolen bases each.

Joaquin Andujar won 21 games, Danny Cox 18, and Tudor truly had a great season after a slow start — 21-8 with 10 shutouts and a 1.93 earned-run average. Other keys were Tommy Herr and the bullpen by committee. That is, Jeff Lahti, lefty Ken Dayley, and flame-throwing right-handed rookie Todd Worrell.

Acquired for pennant insurance, Cesar Cedeno was red hot in September. At New York, he homered off Jesse Oresco to give Tudor a 1-0 10-inning win over Doc Gooden.

A weekend every-game-come-from-behind sweep over Montreal turned second place into first. First, a single by McGee, and triples by Cedeno and newcomer Terry Pendleton turned the tide in a 7-5 game. Next day the Cards were five down and won on Jack Clark's two-run homer, 7-6. On Sunday, Herzog's heroes triumphed on a ninth-inning two-run shot by Herr, 6-5.

In a crucial end-of-the-season series against the closely pursuing Mets, Hernandez went "5 for 5" despite a harrowing divorce court trial that same afternoon. But the 4-3 pennant-clinching Redbird victory was assured when Andy Van Slyke, playing right field, nonchalantly one-handed a game-ending fly ball.

The 1985 season had extra meaning for me. After my surgery, the Cardinals' success was a daily booster. Late in the season, glad to be alive and feeling friskier, I posted a thank-you-note on the clubhouse bulletin board.

Western champion Los Angeles was favored in the League Championship Series and won the first two games in L.A., Fernando Valenzuela over Tudor, 4-1, and then Orel Hershiser, 8-2, over Andujar, who had won only one game since late August.

When the LCS came to St. Louis, Coleman's speed opened up the offense in a 4-2 victory over Bob Welch, with Danny Cox pitching well and Ken Dayley beginning the most overpowering combined playoff and World Series pitching I ever saw.

Before the fourth game, Coleman was "caught" by the playing-field tarpaulin — the tortoise overtaking the hare, if you will — in just about the damnedest fluke accident I ever saw. With rain interrupting practice, the mechanical tarp crept up and grabbed Vince by one of his legs, benching the upfront go-go guy.

For one night, the mishap didn't hurt, because Tito Landrum, expected to warm the bench, doubled back from a late autograph session at Carbondale, Illinois, to find himself in the starting lineup. Tito got four hits, and Tudor won 12-2.

Game Five was tied 2-2 into the home ninth when Ozzie Smith faced big Dodger right-hander, Tom Niedenfuer. The little left-handed batter, though much improved, was a Punch-and-Judy hitter. So when he swung unusually hard at one pitch, fouling it off, I grunted in disgust. When he again swung with velocity and a hitting arc, fouling off another pitch, I growled to the press box observer next to me: "Who 'n hell does he think he is, Babe Ruth?"

I guess so, because on the next pitch, Ozzie cuffed a high fly to right field, deep. Suddenly it hit a girder above the yellow home-run stripe on the wall. The ball bounced back onto the playing surface, but it *was* a home run, Smith's first *left-handed* in the switch-hitter's nine professional seasons.

But the Dodgers bounced back in Game Six and had a 5-4 lead with the Cardinals batting in their ninth. McGee was on third base, and Ozzie on second. Jack Clark came to bat.

Niedenfuer pitched. Jack ripped. Niedenfuer moaned, "As soon as the ball left his bat, I knew the only way to keep it in the park was if the damned thing hit the Goodyear blimp."

Clark lurched to his right and looked into the visitors' third-base dugout. He explained, "I looked over at them. I wanted them to know it was for them. They'd carried me when I was hurt."

The 1985 World Series was sub-titled the I-70 Series because of the highway ribbon that runs across Missouri and bonds St. Louis and Kansas City. With Pendleton making a tremendous over-the-shoulder catch on a long foul fly and throwing out a runner at the plate, Tudor and Worrell won the opener, 3-1. Next night, down a run, Pendleton's ninth-inning opposite-field double scored three runs and the Cards won, 4-2. KayCee's Bret Saberhagen beat a floundering Andujar, 6-2, before the cunning Tudor, aided with homers by McGee and Landrum, put the Cardinals one-game away from the championship with an 8-0 shutout. But Kansas City hammered old pro Bob Forsch, 8-1, so that the Series would have to go back up the highway.

The Cardinals took a 1-0 lead late in Game Six. Aware the Redbirds had scored a total of only 13 runs with a .185 batting average, I muttered, "My God, the Cardinals have *stolen* the World Series."

Ken Dayley overpoweringly retired the Royals in their eighth and the clincher seemed likely. But Herzog replaced Dayley with Worrell in the home ninth.

Left-handed-hitting Jose Orta batted for Darryl Motely and topped a slow roller to Clark's right at first base. Clark got over, made the stop and fed an underhanded flip. Worrell gloved the throw and stepped onto the bag, a firm step ahead of Orta, who tripped over the pitcher's foot and tumbled onto the turf behind first. Only then did American League umpire Don Denkinger give a signal — a delayed, vigorous, sideward hands' down signal. Safe!

Even before instant replay made the umpire's mistake more glaring than the initial view, Worrell and Clark stormed Denkinger, and Herzog huffed out of the visitors' dugout.

Denkinger first blustered at Herzog and then admitted to Whitey that he had missed the call. The outraged Herzog considered telling baseball commissioner Peter Ueberroth (watching from the stands) that the Cardinals would not continue play unless the error was rectified, but decided against such drastic action.

With one on, none out, Clark was forced to hold the runner on base. As a result, when Steve Balboni lifted a high foul near the first-base dugout, Clark had to stride directly and awkwardly to his left, rather than in and over from his deeper normal fielding position.

The Ripper didn't make an extremely catchable catch. Reprieved, Balboni grounded a single to left. With two on, Jim Sundberg tried a sacrifice bunt, but forced Orta at third.

Darrell Porter bollixed a pitch into a passed ball, moving both runners into scoring position. Now the guy Herzog had worried about, Hal McRae, came up a pinch-hitter. Naturally, Whitey walked him to fill the bases.

With pitcher Dan Quiesenberry scheduled to bat, manager Dick Howser beckoned for ex-Redbird Dane Iorg, a good hitter. Iorg lifted a base hit to right field.

Strong-armed Andy Van Slyke cut loose a powerful throw that might have prevented a second run, the game-winner, but catcher Porter left too much of the plate uncovered. Just like that, a Series-winning 1-0 victory became a heartbreaking 2-1 loss.

I feared the worst — and it was worse than I feared. The Cardinals folded hysterically. Herzog was thrown out of Game Seven by a defensive Denkinger, who then booted pouting pitcher Andujar, who reacted foully. Even before the yakking Caribbean character left the field, I *knew* he was gone from the club. Gussie wouldn't put up with on-the-field temper tantrums.

Denkinger's bad call ranks as one of the all-time most incompetent sporting decisions. I'm basically a forgiving guy, sympathetic and friendly with umpires, but this officiating error — and Denkinger's unprofessional emotional immaturity that day and the next — were too flagrant.

Two years later, in 1987, the Cardinals had a narrow division lead when Montreal came to town for a makeup double-header the final week. If the Expos won the double dip and the Mets won their game, St. Louis's lead would be only one game over New York with Montreal a mere half game further back.

I mention this day because it turned into one of the biggest sporting thrills. Lynne sat with me in choice seats provided by Jim Toomey as 52,864 crowded into Busch Stadium, part of the Cardinals' first 3 million-plus attendance.

As the crowd twirled those T-shirts, prompting later victory towels in St. Louis and Homer Hankies at Minneapolis in the World Series, an impressed geezer watched lefties Greg Mathews and Joe Magrane throw shutouts and figured he'd seen something even more historically significant than the 1934 twinbill at Brooklyn when Paul and Dizzy Dean pitched a no-hitter and three-hitter against the Dodgers. After all, back then, Me n' Paul didn't have first place to defend.

The Cardinals defeated the favored San Francisco Giants in the LCS and took on muscular Minnesota in the 1987 World Series. The Twins won the first two games in their Decibel Dome, and the Cardinals won the next three in Busch Stadium.

Before Game Six, watching the broad-beamed Twins tee off against the cozy seats of their roofed stadium, I realized that when they turned up the air-conditioning, the ball would fly. They did and it did, and the Twins roughed up the Redbirds in the final two games, 11-5 and then 4-2. For only the second time in history, the Cardinals lost two successive World Series in which they appeared. The previous unpleasantry happened in 1928 and 1930.

The '80s were an excellent time for the Cardinals, even considering their World Series record. Gussie Busch savored the decade's success, even though drinking buddy Herzog was stonewalled away.

But time waits for no man, not even a Busch. In September, 1989, just as Dal Maxvill's Cardinals were coming up short in Herzog's last full season as manager, August Adolpus Busch Jr. died at his home at 90 years of age. KMOX phoned me shortly after learning he was dead. Would I say a few words about the Big Eagle? As Gus would put it, you can bet your sweet life. When? How about now?

After a short on-the-air commentary, I hung up. The phone rang again. This time the nursing home was calling. My dear mother had just died at 95. Within moments, I'd lost both a good friend and my best friend.

Our Mom with, as she always put it, "her biggest valentine," my brother Freddie, born February 14, 1923.

48

੧ਖ

When Ronald Reagan was president, he told a group of
Hall of Fame baseball writers (including me) and broadcasters at
a lunch in the White House, "It is a pleasure to take a pause and
talk baseball with people my own age."

At the same dinner, I gave the President one of my books,
which included a picture of a grinning Reagan and Grover
Cleveland Alexander's widow, Aimee, a technical adviser for the
president's 1952 "Winning Team" film about Alexander.

Nostalgically, I left in the book a note about my own
theatrical aspirations, including a press clipping about my play
"The Babe and Mrs. Custer," a fantasy of a chance meeting in
1933 between Babe Ruth, 38, and Mrs. George Armstrong Custer,
92. I recalled that Reagan once had played Custer.

A few days later, back home in St. Louis, I received a letter
from the President. He'd read my note. In part, he wrote: "It was
great seeing you and all our friends. The Cabinet Room has never
seen anything like it. Thanks for the book and the press clipping
on 'The Babe and Mrs. Custer.' It suddenly struck me how short
our history is that two people's lives who seem to be from
different eras could actually overlap. You are right about me
playing Custer. It was in 'Santa Fe Trail.' Errol Flynn played Jeb
Stuart, the Confederate cavalry hero. My very best to your wife."

Thank you, Mr. President.

Reflecting now, I wonder if Reagan would agree with the
All-Half-Century team I picked in 1950 to win a contest in which
writers sought to match a secret panel led by Connie Mack.

My winning roster included George Sisler, 1B; Rogers
Hornsby, 2B (The panel named Eddie Collins); Honus Wagner,
SS; Pie Traynor, 3B; Babe Ruth, LF; Tris Speaker, CF; Ty Cobb, RF;
Mickey Cochrane and Bill Dickey, C; and Cy Young, Walter
Johnson, Christy Mathewson, Grover Alexander, Lefty Grove,
and Carl Hubbell, pitchers.

As a reserve outfielder and utility infielder were required,

I listed Joe DiMaggio and Frankie Frisch. You didn't think I was going to leave the Flash off my own team, did you?

Having watched nearly 50 additional years of baseball since winning that contest, I'd honestly make only one change. Mike Schmidt would be my new third baseman.

But jeepers creepers, how to leave off Warren Spahn and Steve Carlton, lefthanders who won more than Grove or Hubbell, or the short-order superstar of southpaws, Sandy Koufax?

Or those great war-straddling outfielders Stan Musial and Ted Williams? Or Henry Aaron, Willie Mays, and Roberto Clemente? And at catcher, how to leave off Gabby Hartnett, or Yogi Berra, Roy Campanella, or Johnny Bench? And what about utility infielders Jackie Robinson and Pete Rose?

No, I am unable to select an All-Century team. There are simply too many truly *great* players to choose one over the other. I'd have to watch them play against each other, every one at his peak.

Say, Uncle Frank, save me a good seat for the Celestial League World Series, won't you? And while you're at it, why don't you run a few of my rule change suggestions past the Powers That Be?

I'd let the visiting ball club bat last. And I'd permit no game to be cancelled by weather. If rain fell after the first pitch or with two out in the bottom of the ninth, I'd have the game finished later. Also: when a pitcher is replaced and strategy calls for an intentional walk, why not charge the base on balls to the relieved, not the reliever?

Yeah, yeah, Flash, you've got your own ideas. We'll talk later.

At the White House with President Ronald Reagan, presenting him with one of my books.

49

Sportswriting has gone from prosy paeans to obsessive locker-room coverage, and what athletes *say* has replaced what athletes *do*.

Oh, somewhere in this promised land is a compromise.

We don't need over-written flowery pieces preceded by rhymes or limericks. Nor do we need to be told again and again that this batter was said by that pitcher to have hit a hanging curve or that the offensive line in front of the bull-necked ball carrier opened gates big enough for the entire student body.

In the past, sportswriters dropped the word "courage" into stories as if they were writing medal inscriptions. The truth is, World War II cooled off that kind of label for athletic endeavors. Now, by contrast, there's a tendency to adopt a smart-aleck approach.

Athletes now are quoted too often. Obviously, from the retreat of so many into silence, they don't like it.

As a writer, I don't like it when a player or coach or manager won't answer a short, direct question, intended to straighten me out and clarify for the reader's benefit.

I also don't like it when a writer won't analyze for me what he has seen or felt, but, instead, lazily relies on the self-serving platitudes of players, coaches, and managers.

A good old-fashioned narrative helps make a key situation come alive for the reader. Yeah, even one who might have seen or heard the game or watched it on the tube.

A writer who has looked and listened day after day should be able to review a sport with the confidence of a drama or movie critic. Why not use quotes only when they expand or explain what happened?

Obviously, in the need to compete, editors encourage the controversial to the point that some reporters make literary wild pitches. These *do* infuriate athletes, believe me.